Expanding Energy

The Global Story of Christianity Series
History, Context, and Communities

Seven One-Volume Books

SERIES EDITORS
Emma Wild-Wood & Mark A. Lamport

SERIES ASSISTANT EDITOR
Gina A. Zurlo

SERIES INTRODUCTION
Dana L. Robert

BOOK EDITORS
Mitri Raheb *(Middle East)* | Amos Yong *(Asia)* | Wanjiru Gitau *(Africa)*
Alex Ryrie *(Europe)* | Raimundo Barreto *(Latin America)*
Upolu Lumā Vaai *(Oceania)* | Christopher Evans *(North America)*

SERIES EDITORIAL ADVISORY BOARD
Edwin Aponte *(Louisville Institute)*
Elias Bongmba *(Rice University)*
Arun Jones *(Candler School of Theology/Emory University)*
Brett Knowles *(University of Otago)*
David Maxwell *(University of Cambridge, UK)*
Elizabeth Monier *(University of Cambridge, UK)*
Dana L. Robert *(Center for Global Christianity and Mission/Boston University)*
Nelly van Doorn-Harder *(Wake Forest University)*
Stephanie Wong *(Valparaiso University)*

SENIOR EDITORIAL CONSULTANT
Joshua Erb

Expanding Energy

The Dynamic Story of Christianity in North America

EDITED BY
Christopher H. Evans
AND
Mark A. Lamport

Introductions by Dana L. Robert and Anne Blue Wills

CASCADE *Books* • Eugene, Oregon

EXPANDING ENERGY
The Dynamic Story of Christianity in North America

The Global Story of Christianity Series, vol. 7

Copyright © 2024 Wipf and Stock Publishers. All rights reserved. Except for brief quotations in critical publications or reviews, no part of this book may be reproduced in any manner without prior written permission from the publisher. Write: Permissions, Wipf and Stock Publishers, 199 W. 8th Ave., Suite 3, Eugene, OR 97401.

Cascade Books
An Imprint of Wipf and Stock Publishers
199 W. 8th Ave., Suite 3
Eugene, OR 97401

www.wipfandstock.com

PAPERBACK ISBN: 978-1-6667-3123-1
HARDCOVER ISBN: 978-1-6667-2350-2
EBOOK ISBN: 978-1-6667-2353-3

Cataloguing-in-Publication data:

Names: Evans, Christopher H. [editor]. | Lamport, Mark A. [editor]

Title: Expanding energy : the dynamic story of Christianity in North America / edited by Christopher H. Evans and Mark A. Lamport.

Description: Eugene, OR: Cascade Books, 2024 | Series: The Global Story of Christianity Series, vol. 7 | Includes bibliographical references and index.

Identifiers: ISBN 978-1-6667-3123-1 (paperback) | ISBN 978-1-6667-2350-2 (hardcover) | ISBN 978-1-6667-2353-3 (ebook)

Subjects: LCSH: United States—Church history. | Canada—Church history. | Church history.

Classification: BR515 E93 2024 (paperback) | BR515 (ebook)

VERSION NUMBER 02/01/24

The editors gratefully acknowledge permission to have drawn portions of "Indigenous Christianity in North America" from "First Nations Canada," by Terry LeBlanc, in *Christianity in North America*, edited by Kenneth Ross et al. (Edinburgh: Edinburgh University Press, 2023; Edinburgh Companions to Global Christianity), 25–39.

Scripture quotations marked KJV are from the King James or Authorized Version.

Scripture quotations marked NIV are taken from the Holy Bible, New International Version®, NIV®. Copyright © 1973, 1978, 1984, 2011 by Biblica, Inc.® Used by permission of Zondervan. All rights reserved worldwide.

For *Chris*—To my students

For *Mark*—To *William Brewster* (first minister in America and my Mayflower ancestor, 1566–1644), *Roger Williams* (Baptist minister, missionary, and founder of Providence Plantations [i.e., Rhode Island], 1603–83), *Jonathan Edwards* (Congregational revivalist, 1703–58), *Francis Asbury* (English Methodist bishop to the United States, 1745–1816), *Martin E. Marty* (Lutheran historian on religion in the United States, 1928–present), *Daniel J. Baker* (1981–present), and the prolific American parachurch and mission societies movements

Contents

Series Introduction—DANA L. ROBERT | ix
Editors and Introducers | xix
Preface—GINA A. ZURLO AND MARK A. LAMPORT | xxi
Abbreviations | xxvii
Acknowledgments | xxix
Contributors | xxxi
Book Introduction—ANNE BLUE WILLS | xxxv

Section One

The Story of Christianity Narrated in Historical Context: Versions of Dominance and Diversity

1. Indigenous Christianity in North America: Good Intentions?—TERRY LEBLANC | 3
2. Chosen Nations: Christianity and the Founding Legends of Canada and the United States—JOHN G. STACKHOUSE JR. | 21
3. Heavenly Retreat: The Haven of Slave Religion—VINCE BANTU | 35
4. North American Catholicism—CHARLES T. STRAUSS | 51

Section Two

The Story of Christianity Expressed in a Grand Church Family Mosaic: An Evolutionary Tale of Evangelicalism

5. Revivalism, Restorationism, and Reform in Antebellum America—BRANTLEY W. GASAWAY | 71

6. Called to Arouse, Warn, and Save: The American Fascination with Premillennial Dispensationalism—CHRISTOPHER H. EVANS | 87

7. North American Pentecostalisms—ALLISON KACH-YAWNGHWE | 103

8. Before Modern Feminism: Protestant Women in the Twentieth Century—PRISCILLA POPE-LEVISON | 120

9 Between Faith and Doubt: The American Protestant Intellectual Mind—DAVID MISLIN | 136

10. The Social Gospel in Canada—GORDON L. HEATH | 152

Section Three

The Story of Christianity Encounters Twenty-First-Century Issues: Immigration and the Future of North American Christianity

11. North American Christianities: A West Coast Perspective—PATRICIA O'CONNELL KILLEN | 169

12. God to Texas: A Selective Tale of Christianity from the South—JEREMY HEGI | 187

13. Unintended Consequences: Refugee Resettlement in the United States—CINDY M. WU | 204

14. Evangelicals and Systems of Domination: A Call for Reformation—JAMES K. WELLMAN JR. | 220

Time Line: North America—BRETT KNOWLES | 236

Index of Names and Subjects | 249

Series Introduction

The Global Story of Christianity

History, Contexts, and Communities

DANA L. ROBERT

WHAT DOES IT MEAN *to tell the story* of global Christianity? Storytelling is important for personal identity, for community life, and for shared humanity. When people tell their own stories, both individually and as communities of faith, they share who they are and who they hope to become. When people make friends, they swap stories. They introduce themselves. They discuss their work, or where they went to school. They might talk about the sports teams they support, or what activities they enjoy. As people get to know each other better, they exchange stories about their families, or politics, or other important issues. Friends do things together—and the being together creates memories that launch new stories they recall when they see each other again. In listening to each other, people's stories merge and create a common basis for relationships—even across boundaries or divisions.

Global Christianity is the story of a huge extended family. Christians are rooted in a common ancestor, Jesus Christ. For two thousand years, the followers of Jesus of Nazareth have traced their spiritual lineage through him to the God of ancient Israel, as spoken through the prophets and written in the Bible and celebrated in worship and outreach. Christianity is now the world's largest religion, encompassing one-third of the world's peoples. During the twentieth century, the family of faith burst out of European frameworks and began growing rapidly in Africa, Asia, and Latin America. By 2018, Africa had become the continent with the largest number of Christians, followed by Latin America, and Europe, with Asia soon to become second in numbers.[1] Christianity as a global story reminds me of the chatter at a giant family reunion, where the relatives get together and reminisce about their distant family history, and the departed saints that

---

1. Zurlo, "Who Owns Global Christianity?"

they remember—and the old family arguments that never seem to end. For better or worse, whether or not they know each other personally, the people who call themselves Christians are spiritual brothers, sisters, and long-lost cousins. Shared family history connects them.

And yet, nobody has only *one* story. This book series on the global story of Christianity embodies many stories that have unfolded across two thousand years of time, and which inhabit wide-ranging geographic and cultural spaces. The sheer size and complexity of the global Christian family means that a shared history is composed of multiple memories, from thousands of contexts. Being part of a community means organizing the stories into a convincing whole and claiming a common identity through them. Communities can be direct sets of relationships, such as families, neighborhoods, sports clubs, therapy groups, and local churches. They can also be "imagined" and thus composed of people who may never meet in person, but whose groups—including ethnicities, cities, political parties, and even nations—share common interpretations of experiences. For Christians, both personal and imagined faith communities use shared narratives to organize their spiritual realities. And yet, the meaning and identity of faith communities also changes over time, depending on the context. Depending on one's purpose or needs, different parts of one's story become more important than others. I am reminded of a friend who was the new pastor of a small church. Each week, no matter how hard he tried to get the old-timers to move, nobody would sit in the front section of the church. Finally, in frustration he asked one old man why he wouldn't move toward the front of the church. "I've been sitting in this pew for forty years," he replied. "It is not my fault that the people who used to sit in front of me have died or moved away." In his mind, the old man was still sitting in his imagined community made up of previous generations of friends and neighbors who had composed his church. But the new minister, looking out every week, saw nothing but empty front pews, waiting to be filled with new faces and new stories. Because the context had changed, the church community had changed; and because the community had changed, the context had changed—even though the old man had not moved anywhere at all. And yet, until the old man shared his story, the history of his community, the new minister couldn't understand the old man's resistance to his request.

History, contexts, and communities—all these pieces are important frameworks for organizing the many stories that together paint a global picture of Christianity. The connection among history, contexts, and communities was beautifully expressed by the late Andrew Walls, Scottish historian and expert on African Christianity, and a founder of the field of "world

Christianity."[2] Walls asked his readers to imagine a visitor from outer space, a professor of comparative religions, who visits Earth for fieldwork every few centuries, to observe the practices and beliefs of representative Christians. First the space man visits the original Christians in Jerusalem, a few years after the death of Jesus. He finds that they are Jewish and follow Jewish customs, including offering animal sacrifices, worshiping on the seventh day, and reading old scrolls in Hebrew. They identify the Messiah, Son of Man and Suffering Servant, with their teacher who just died, Jesus of Nazareth. They live in close-knit families and eat meals together in each other's homes. When the visitor from space next returns to earth, he observes a big church meeting of church leaders around 325 CE, in Nicaea (now in Turkey). Hardly any are Jewish and most are unmarried. To them, sacrifice means a ritual meal of bread and wine and they worship God on the first day of the week, not the seventh. They talk about Jesus, but they are debating whether the Greek words *homoousios* or *homoiousios* better characterize his nature. They argue a lot about theology.

Walls goes on to describe the space visitor's next field visit, Ireland in the 600s. There monks are gathered on a rocky coastline reciting the psalms. Some are going into a small boat with a box of beautiful manuscripts heading toward nearby islands to ask the inhabitants to give up worship of multiple nature divinities. Other monks sit alone in caves, denying themselves food. Upon examining the manuscripts, he finds they are the same writings he saw on his last visit, and he hears the monks recite the same basic statement of belief or creed he heard at Nicaea in 325. Yet these monks seem much more interested in being holy than in debating theology.

Next the space visitor returns to earth in 1840s London. He finds a convention of mostly White Christians hearing speeches about the desirability of promoting Christianity and trade in Africa. To eliminate the slave trade, they are planning to send missionaries, lobby the government, and promote the education of Black Africans. He sees many people carrying printed Bibles and finds out they accept the creed of Nicaea. They talk about holiness but would be shocked at the thought of praying alone in a cave. Rather, they are well fed and committed to political activism.

Finally, the space visitor returns in the 1980s to Lagos, Nigeria, in time to see a white-robed procession of people dancing and chanting through the streets. They are inviting people to come with them and

---

2. Walls preferred the term *world Christianity* to what this book series is calling *global Christianity*. On the use of the terms *world* versus *global*, see Robert, "World Christianity," 17–18; Sanneh and McClymond, introduction to *The Wiley Blackwell Companion to World Christianity*, 4–6; Johnson and Kim, "Describing the Worldwide Christian Phenomenon," 80–84.

experience the power of God. They talk about healing and driving out evil spirits. They say they accept the creed of Nicaea, but they are not really interested in theological creeds or in political activism. They do care passionately about personal empowerment through prayer, preaching, and healing. Back on his own planet, the professor must figure out what it all means. He notes that the location of the Christian heartland has shifted each time he has visited. How does he conclude what it means to be a Christian? Is there any coherence across time? What do Christians around the world have in common, despite the visible differences in culture, race, locations, ethnicities, and practices that he observed?

Andrew Walls's fantasy about the space visitor illustrates the complexities of telling the global story of Christianity. What each era had in common was its historical connection. Like links in a chain, history connected the different communities to each other. Jews from Jerusalem preached to Greeks and led to the events of Nicaea in 325. Emissaries from the Mediterranean planted the seeds that became Irish Christianity. Celtic missionaries launched what became the religion of London in the 1840s, and the British evangelical lobby sent the messengers who energized churches in Africa. To bring the story up to the present, today Nigerian churches send missionaries around the world, including to London. In fact, some of the largest churches in Europe have African pastors. Other historical connections involve a "continuity of consciousness" across time.[3] In each group's story, Jesus Christ "has ultimate significance." They use the "same sacred writings," though in different formats and languages. Writes Walls, "Each group thinks of itself as having some community with the others," continuous with ancient Israel, even though they are no longer Jews.[4] These elements of continuity, however, are embedded in very different contexts, ranging from the Middle East to West Asia, to Europe, Africa, and beyond. In each context, the space visitor found worshipping communities, ranging in form from house churches to bishops' gatherings, from monasteries to conferences and popular processions. The shape of the Christian communities and what they do differs according to their local cultures, politics, and historical period. And yet, taken together, the many stories echo the shared memory of Jesus Christ, passed down through the ages.

---

3. Walls, "Gospel as Prisoner," 6.
4. Walls, "Gospel as Prisoner," 6–7.

About This Book Series

To tell the global story of Christianity, each book in this series is organized into a common format. If we think about what goes into telling our stories, the elements are common to the books in the series. The *first* thing to notice is that the books each cover a different *geographic region*. In other words, they are organized by "neighborhood." This organization allows the editors, who come from each region, to explore the "historical context" and to answer the questions: Where are we from and how did we get here? Who are the people who brought Christianity? How did the Christian story change in each part of the globe, and what difference did it make? How are the followers of Jesus in that region anchored in his heritage? What is the testimony of the people of each region about their Christian identity, and how did they become part of the global story of Christianity? There are a range of answers to questions like "Where are we from and how did we get here?," including stories of migration and mission, slavery and coercion, violence and resistance, joy and struggle. Analyzing where they have come from also allows the editors to build toward where they think their region might be going.

The *second* section of each book in the series talks about the kind of *faith communities* found in each geographic region, and the issues they face. Communities reflect group identities shaped by such factors as theology, ethnicity, language, or persecution. In the case of the volume on Asia, a vast continent with thousands of different ethnic groups, the communities described are organized by subregion. The North America volume discusses some of the fundamental theological and organizational issues behind different groups of North American Christians. In Christian parlance, faith communities shaped by shared theologies and histories are often called "denominations," organized groups of Christians that recognize each other as brothers and sisters but have different stories to tell about how they got to be where they are today. Some faith communities are rather like private clubs, with high membership fees and strict rules as to who can belong. Others are more like groups of sports fans, open to anyone who feels like supporting the team and participating in its activities. In all cases, the discussion of different communities shows how their identity reflects both its local context and its participation in the global story of Christianity. Communities each have their own special saints, prophets, and leaders—people who have guided them and symbolize their identity to the world. They have their own favorite religious practices. Conversations internal to each community spill into the outside world, and sometimes attract others to join them. Contexts shape communities, and communities shape contexts.

Faith communities are where the global story of Christianity forms church families and creates spaces in which they build a home.

The *third* section of each volume discusses *global issues* that are important to each region today. This is where the urgency behind each volume becomes clear. What are the passions that drive the communities in context? What problems do they face? What political and social issues are vital to their well-being? Some of the volumes explicitly discuss what churches call "ecumenism," churches cooperating and joining together to pursue shared ideals and common goals. Important twenty-first-century issues such as climate change, racism, interfaith relations, war and peace, gender, church-state relations, and religious persecution are global issues that affect people on every continent. It is often these pressing issues that connect Christians in solidarity with others across geographic boundaries.

Elements of a Global Story

Although each book in the series stands alone, putting them into dialogue with each other paints a bigger picture of what is called "global (or world) Christianity." As already mentioned, Christianity in the twenty-first century has become a multicultural religion practiced by one third of the world. The fact that it exists nearly everywhere means that to tell the story of Christianity in one region affects the story of Christianity in another region. To think of Christianity as a global story requires seeing each region as connected. In scholarly terms, this idea is called "entanglement," an important concept in global history. The idea of historical entanglement means that each region is shaped by its relationship to the others. To think of Christianity as a global story means looking for ways in which the local and the global are entangled—all mixed up together, influencing each other, and not easily separated. As people in each region embrace what they see as the universal story of Jesus Christ, the way they practice their faith affects the nature of the religion as a whole. To be "global" means that regional stories are linked, with and through their Christian faiths.

Looking for interconnections among the regions is a way to trace how the assumption of entanglement creates a global story out of what are usually thought of as separate stories. As you read the different books in this series, also zoom out and look for common themes that bind the regions together to create a global story, though from different perspectives and angles. What follows are three major themes that intersect all the volumes—movement, translation, and public theologies:

- *Movement* is central to the global story of Christianity. Without new people entering old spaces, or people on the move, Christianity could not spread from one place to another. The New Testament journeys of Paul throughout the Mediterranean modeled how Christians moved from place to place in spreading their faith. Migration and "global diaspora" are features of the global Christian story, especially today when more people are on the move than ever before. When people deliberately cross boundaries to spread their faith, they are often called missionaries. During the era of colonialism, Europeans sent missionaries around the world. Today missionaries go from everywhere to everywhere, including especially from Korea, Brazil, Nigeria, and North America.[5] Sometimes movement to new areas causes migrants to embrace Christianity as a new way of life. Although migrants typically seek economic security over religious change, sometimes the act of moving to a new place can inspire them to launch missions of their own: Central Americans moving to North American cities, and Africans moving to Eastern Europe, have started numerous churches. Forced migration can also spread Christianity. In a monstrous crime against humanity, over ten million Africans were sent to the Americas as slaves. Many of their descendants became Christians and reshaped the faith into a vehicle of resistance. Migrating people—whether forced or by choice—bind together their places of origin with their destinations and change both places in the process.[6]

- *Translation* is another theme that makes Christianity a global story. In literal terms, translation of the Bible into thousands of languages has been the foundation of Protestant missions for centuries, and the basis for faith-sharing across linguistic and cultural boundaries. Once people have the Bible in their own language, they interpret it according to their own cultural norms and needs.[7] During the twentieth century, many Indigenous prophets—equipped with the Bible in their own language and inspired by dreams and visions—launched new Christian movements in Africa, Asia, and Latin America. Studies of conversion show how new Christians translate the Christian faith into their own personal contexts, or use it to revitalize their surroundings.[8] At a more theoretical level, translation can refer to cultural processes

---

5. Robert, *Christian Mission.*

6. See Frederiks and Nagy, *Religion, Migration, and Identity*; see also Hanciles, *Migration and the Making*, and Hanciles, *Beyond Christendom.*

7. Sanneh, *Translating the Message.*

8. Kling, *History of Christian Conversion.*

of hybridization, of adopting the Christian message and reframing it to fit new contexts and to energize Christian communities.[9] Since all communication comes packaged in particular cultural forms, the process of translation is necessary for sharing the Christian faith across all kinds of ethnic, cultural, and geographic barriers. As Christians encounter other cultures and live alongside persons of other religions, their faith is often stimulated into renewed life. The translation process, both on personal and social levels, is an endlessly rich source of innovation that feeds into the global story of Christianity.

- *Public theologies* also shape the global story of Christianity. In the modern West, people often think of faith as a private matter, separate from politics or social life. But the idea that religion is a matter of personal choice, irrelevant to community life, is a fairly recent cultural innovation that itself assumes a public theology of secularism.[10] In most of the world, in most periods of history, religion carries practical implications for how people live in community. Christianity shapes people's attitudes toward authority, power, nature, gender relations, and human rights. Such ideas as "the doctrine of discovery," or the "priesthood of all believers," or "one nation under God" express the relationship of Christianity to peoples, politics, and land. The global story of Christianity consists of theological flows that spread around the world through migration and social media.[11] Public theologies require analyzing flows of power, including the supernatural and spiritual power embedded in Christian belief itself, the unequal political and economic power of Christians who use faith to justify control of others, and the tenacious power of resilience by Christians who are suffering or persecuted. By the late 1900s, evangelicalism, liberation theologies, and Pentecostal practices were all vehicles for political power, especially in Africa and the Americas. Christian charitable outreach through nongovernmental organizations remains a major social factor throughout the world, especially in poor communities. Half of all Christians are Roman Catholics, a worldwide faith network with a central teaching authority lodged in the pope and the Vatican. Public theologies—the globalization of religious ideas, institutions, power, and practices—are a key feature of Christianity as a world religion.

---

9. For a postcolonial analysis and typology of historical religious encounters, including syncretism and selection, see Lindenfeld, *World Christianity and Indigenous Experience*, 1–30. See also Jones, *Christian Interculture*, and Gruber, *Intercultural Theology*.

10. Casanova, *Public Religions in the Modern World*.

11. Schreiter, *New Catholicity*.

Conclusion: From Local Stories to Global Story and Back Again

To tell the global story of Christianity requires reconstructing the entangled histories of communities down through the ages, in different regions. It requires retracing their historical contexts and learning how communities respond to the urgent issues of the day. As this series shows, only as different Christian communities tell their own stories—and listen to the stories of others—can the global story of Christianity be glimpsed in all its fullness.

For Further Reading

Casanova, José. *Public Religions in the Modern World*. Chicago: University of Chicago Press, 2011.

Frederiks, Martha, and Dorottya Nagy, eds. *Religion, Migration, and Identity: Methodological and Theological Explorations*. Theology and Mission in World Christianity 2. Leiden: Brill, 2016.

Gruber, Judith. *Intercultural Theology: Exploring World Christianity after the Cultural Turn*. Göttingen: Vandenhoeck & Ruprecht, 2018.

Hanciles, Jehu J. *Beyond Christendom: Globalization, African Migration, and the Transformation of the West*. Maryknoll, NY: Orbis, 2008.

———. *Migration and the Making of Global Christianity*. Grand Rapids: Eerdmans, 2021.

Johnson, Todd M., and Sandra S. Kim. "Describing the Worldwide Christian Phenomenon." *International Bulletin of Missionary Research* 29 (2005) 80–84.

Johnson, Todd M., and Gina A. Zurlo. *World Christian Encyclopedia*. 3rd ed. Edinburgh: Edinburgh University Press, 2019.

Jones, Arun, ed. *Christian Interculture: Texts and Voices from Colonial and Postcolonial Worlds*. University Park: Penn State University Press, 2021.

Kling, David. *A History of Christian Conversion*. New York: Oxford University Press, 2020.

Lindenfeld, David. *World Christianity and Indigenous Experience: A Global History, 1500–2000*. Cambridge: Cambridge University Press, 2021.

Robert, Dana L. *Christian Mission: How Christianity Became a World Religion*. Hoboken, NJ: Wiley-Blackwell, 2009.

———. "World Christianity as a Revitalization Movement." In *World Christianity: History, Methodologies, Horizons*, edited by Jehu Hanciles, 17–18. Maryknoll, NY: Orbis, 2021.

Sanneh, Lamin, and Michael J. McClymond. Introduction to *The Wiley Blackwell Companion to World Christianity*, edited by Lamin Sanneh and Michael McClymond, 1–18. Malden, MA: Wiley-Blackwell, 2016.

Sanneh, Lamin O. *Translating the Message: The Missionary Impact on Culture*. Maryknoll, NY: Orbis, 2009.

Schreiter, Robert J. *The New Catholicity: Theology between the Global and the Local*. Maryknoll, NY: Orbis, 2004.

Walls, Andrew. "The Gospel as Prisoner and Liberator of Culture." In *The Missionary Movement in Christian History Studies in the Transmission of Faith*, 3–15. Maryknoll, NY: Orbis, 1996.

Zurlo, Gina A. "Who Owns Global Christianity?" https://www.gordonconwell.edu/blog/who-owns-global-christianity/.

Editors and Introducers

Series Editors

Mark A. Lamport (PhD, Michigan State University) has been a professor for forty years at graduate theological schools in the United States and Europe. He is author of *Nurturing Faith: A Practical Theology for Educating Christians* (2021) and editor of *Emerging Theologies from the Global South* (2022); *Christianity in the Middle East* (2 vols., 2020); *Encyclopedia of Christianity in the Global South* (2 vols., 2018); *Encyclopedia of Martin Luther and the Reformation* (2 vols., 2017); *Encyclopedia of Christianity in the United States* (5 vols., 2016); *Encyclopedia of Christian Education* (3 vols., 2015).

Emma Wild-Wood (PhD, University of Edinburgh) is Director of the Centre for the Study of World Christianity, University of Edinburgh School of Divinity, and Senior Lecturer of African Christianity and African Indigenous Religions. She is the former Director of the Cambridge Centre for Christianity Worldwide and Lecturer in World Christianities in the Faculty of Divinity of the University of Cambridge. Wild-Wood is the editor of *Studies in World Christianity* journal and a fellow of the Royal Historical Society.

Gina Zurlo (PhD, Boston University) is Codirector of the Center for the Study of Global Christianity at Gordon-Conwell Theological Seminary (South Hamilton, Massachusetts). She is coauthor of the *World Christian Encyclopedia* (3rd ed.) and coeditor of the *World Christian Database*.

Book Editors

Christopher H. Evans (PhD, Northwestern University) is Professor of History of Christianity and Methodist Studies at Boston University's School of Theology. He is the author of several books, including *The Faith of Fifty*

Million: Baseball, Religion, and American Culture* (coedited with William R. Herzog II); *The Kingdom Is Always but Coming: A Life of Walter Rauschenbusch*, which received an Award of Merit for the best work in history/biography from *Christianity Today*; *Liberalism without Illusions: Renewing an American Christian Tradition*; *Histories of American Christianity: An Introduction*; *The Social Gospel in American Religion*; and a biography on the nineteenth-century women's rights reformer Frances Willard (2023).

Mark A. Lamport—see above

Series Introduction

Dana L. Robert (PhD, Yale University) is Truman Collins Professor of World Christianity and History of Mission, and Director of the Center for Global Christianity and Mission at Boston University School of Theology. She is a member of the American Academy of Arts and Sciences and in 2017, she received the Lifetime Achievement Award from the American Society of Missiology. Recent books include *Faithful Friendships: Embracing Diversity in Christian Community* (2019) and *African Christian Biography: Stories, Lives, and Challenges* (2018). An active lay United Methodist, in 2019 Roberts spoke at the 150th anniversary of the United Methodist Women.

Book Introduction

Anne Blue Wills (PhD, Duke University) chairs the Religious Studies Department at Davidson College, North Carolina. She published *An Odd Cross to Bear: A Biography of Ruth Bell Graham* (2022) and coedited *Billy Graham: American Pilgrim* (2017) with Andrew Finstuen and Grant Wacker.

Preface

North America

GINA A. ZURLO AND MARK A. LAMPORT

NORTH AMERICA CONSISTS OF two very large countries, the United States and Canada, and three smaller nations: Bermuda, Greenland, and Saint Pierre and Miquelon. From a demographic perspective, trends in the United States (245 million Christians) and Canada (24 million Christians) dictate the regional analysis presented here. Christianity continues its demographic shift from the Global North (Europe and North America) to the Global South (Asia, Africa, Latin America, and Oceania). However, North America still has a tremendously important place in world Christianity studies, as well as in overall trends in global Christianity. The United States is the country with the most Christians in the world (the next largest is Brazil with 193 million Christians). As a result, the USA has a major role in missionary sending, theological education, Christian finance, and the production of theology and other Christian scholarship, much of which impacts Christianity around the world. The United States is also home to the most Evangelicals globally (69 million; Nigeria is second with 46 million), although generally the debates and concerns of American Evangelicals are not those of Evangelicals elsewhere in the world.

The statistics presented in this demographic overview reflect membership and affiliation trends, not beliefs, practices, or attitudes. Canada and the United States are experiencing their own unique secularization trends. However, Christian affiliation remains relatively high in the region, even if church attendance, for example, might be declining rapidly. One of the major markers of North American society is diversity—linguistic, ethnic, religious, gender, socioeconomic, and more. Such demographic characteristics most certainly impact Christian trends in the region. For example, substantial differences exist in Christian faith and practice by race, ethnicity, and sex, where communities of Color and women tend to report higher levels of religiosity than White communities and men.

Figure 1. North/South Distribution of Christianity, 33–2050 CE

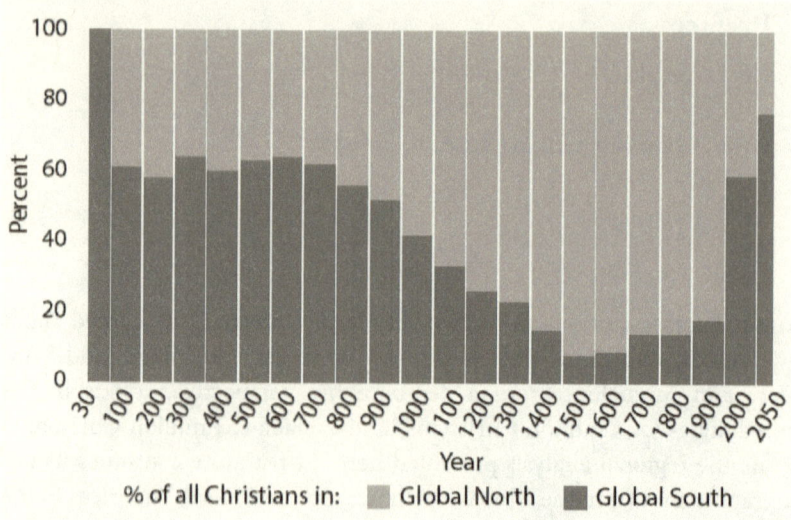

Source: Todd M. Johnson and Gina A. Zurlo, *World Christian Encyclopedia*, 3rd ed. (Edinburgh: Edinburgh University Press, 2019), 4. Used by permission of the authors.

Table 1 shows trends in religion and nonreligion in North America from 1900 to 2020, with projections to 2050. In 1900, North America was nearly entirely religious (99 percent), mostly Christians, but also a small population of Jews (1 percent). By the turn of the twenty-first century, religious affiliation in North America had dropped to just under 88 percent, with an increase of atheists and agnostics from 1 percent to nearly 13 percent. This trend has continued, with the nonreligious representing 80 percent of the population in 2020 and an anticipated 74 percent by 2050. While the increased presence and influence of nonreligion is a major part of North American trends in the twentieth and twenty-first centuries, so is the substantial increase of followers of other religions. In 1900, there were only very small populations of Muslims and Buddhists. But by 2020, Muslims represented 1.5 percent of the continent's population (nearly 6 million), and Buddhists were 1.3 percent (5 million). Jewish communities have remained somewhat steady (roughly 1 percent), though Jews experienced substantial growth from 1 million in 1900 to nearly 6 million in 2020. Each of these religious traditions has grown by immigration, along with Hindus, Sikhs,

Jains, and followers of other major world religions (each less than 1 percent in 2020). The Christian share of North America's population has decreased substantially, from 97 percent in 1900 to 73 percent in 2020. This trend is likely to continue, with Christians representing 65 percent by 2050. The nonreligious are expected to make the most gains, to perhaps 26 percent of North America's population in 2050.

Table 1. Religions over 1 Percent in North America, 1900–2050

Year	1900		2000		1900–2000 % p.a.	2020		2000–2020 % p.a.	2050	
Religious	80,614,000	98.8	273,507,000	87.5	1.23	294,128,000	79.7	0.36	312,843,000	73.6
Christians	79,254,000	97.1	253,547,000	81.2	1.17	269,524,000	73.1	0.31	276,078,000	64.9
Catholics	13,011,000	15.9	76,433,000	24.5	1.79	88,015,000	23.9	0.71	95,213,000	22.4
Independents	6,672,000	8.2	57,957,000	18.6	2.19	65,115,000	17.7	0.58	74,510,000	17.5
Protestants	39,914,000	48.9	63,273,000	20.3	0.46	57,575,000	15.6	-0.47	63,359,000	14.9
Orthodox	415,000	0.5	6,764,000	2.2	2.83	8,370,000	2.3	1.07	10,100,000	2.4
Unaffiliated Christians	19,242,000	23.6	49,357,000	15.8	0.95	50,592,000	13.7	0.12	33,093,000	7.8
Jews	1,074,000	1.3	5,659,000	1.8	1.68	5,940,000	1.6	0.24	5,390,000	1.3
Muslims	10,100	0.0	4,107,000	1.3	6.20	5,671,000	1.5	1.63	12,551,000	3.0
Buddhists	40,400	0.0	3,970,000	1.3	4.69	4,953,000	1.3	1.11	7,951,000	1.9
Nonreligious	1,012,000	1.2	38,920,000	12.5	3.72	74,741,000	20.3	3.32	112,357,000	26.4
Agnostics	1,010,000	1.2	33,758,000	10.8	3.57	64,155,000	17.4	3.26	91,007,000	21.4
Atheists	2,000	0.0	5,162,000	1.7	8.17	10,587,000	2.9	3.66	21,351,000	5.0
Total population	81,626,000	100.0	312,427,000	100.0	1.35	368,870,000	100.0	0.83	425,200,000	100.0

Data source: Gina A. Zurlo and Todd M. Johnson, eds., *World Religion Database* (Leiden/Boston: Brill, accessed May 2023).

North American religion has always been very diverse. First Nations and Native Americans long inhabited Turtle Island until the arrival of European colonists amid terror and destruction of people and land. The sixteenth century marked the arrival of, for example, French Catholics in Canada, Dutch Reformed in New York, Germans in Pennsylvania, and Spanish Catholics in the American Southwest. In 1619, the first enslaved men and women arrived with their own religious traditions from West Africa. By 1900, Protestants made up half of all Christians, followed by Catholics (16 percent of all Christians), independents (8 percent), and Orthodox (<1 percent). Most independents were members of the Church of Jesus Christ of Latter-day Saints, founded in upstate New York in 1830 (which now has more than 17 million members worldwide).

Catholics increased their share of all Christians from 16 percent in 1900 to 34 percent in 2020. Catholics experienced intense discrimination amid waves of immigration in the nineteenth and early twentieth centuries, where millions of Italians, Irish, and Poles arrived (as well as Jews). Independent Christianity has both grown (from 8 percent in 1900 to 24 percent in 2020) and diversified. In this analysis, historically Black denominations are considered independents because these churches explicitly formed in reaction to, or by splitting from, White-led churches that either supported or participated in the slave trade or otherwise discriminated against Black people. Some of the largest denominations today are majority Black, such as the National Baptist Convention USA, the Church of God in Christ, and the National Baptist Convention of America. The independent category also includes third-wave or neo-Pentecostal churches that emerged during the charismatic movement in the 1960s. Examples include Vineyard churches, the International Revival Fellowship (the Toronto Blessing), and Calvary Chapels (from the Jesus Movement). The Pentecostal/charismatic movement has also dovetailed with the arrival of newer churches from the Global South, such as the Redeemed Christian Church of God (Nigeria) and the Universal Church of the Kingdom of God (Brazil).

Table 2. Christianity in North America by Country, 1900–2050

Country	Pop. 1900	% Christian 1900	Pop. 2020	% Christian 2020	Pop. 2050	% Christian 2050
Bermuda	20,300	100.0	55,200	88.7	44,600	83.6
Canada	5,504,000	98.4	23,952,000	63.5	24,602,000	53.9
Greenland	10,500	90.0	54,400	95.9	49,800	93.5
Saint Pierre and Miquelon	6,500	100.0	5,500	94.4	4,700	89.0
United States	73,712,000	97.0	245,457,000	74.2	251,376,000	66.3
Northern America	79,254,000	97.1	269,524,000	73.1	276,078,000	64.9

Data source: Todd M. Johnson and Gina A. Zurlo, eds. *World Christian Database* (Leiden/Boston: Brill, accessed May 2023).

Christians' share of the US population declined from 97 percent in 1900 to 74 percent in 2020, with a continued decline expected to 65 percent by 2050. Many Americans are affiliated with or members of churches, networks, and denominations even if they do not regularly attend services, pray frequently, or believe in God as traditionally understood in Western Christianity. In Western secularization processes, it is generally observed that individuals drop belief and church attendance first, although remain self-identified Christians for much longer. Canada's Christian population dropped more rapidly that the US's, from 98 percent in 1900 to 64 percent in 2020, likely continuing to 54 percent by 2050.

Figure 2. Christianity in North America

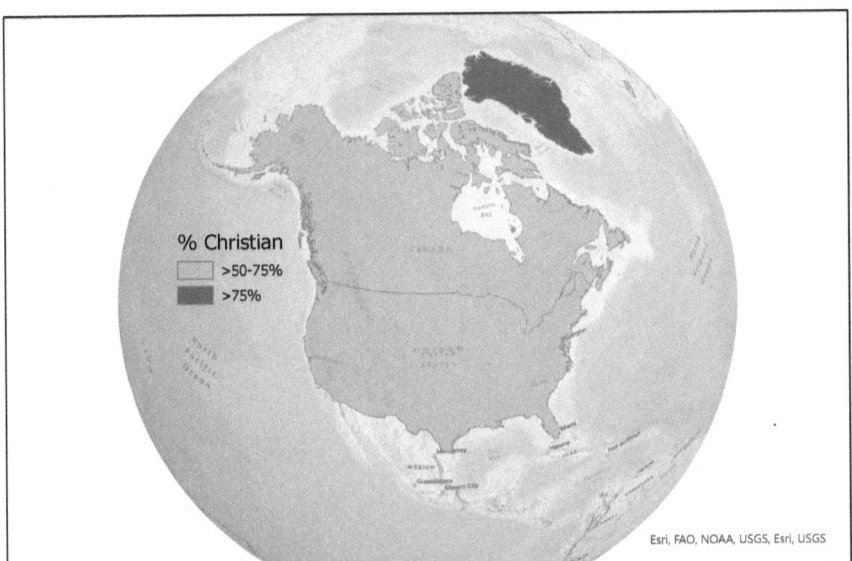

Data source: Todd M. Johnson and Gina A. Zurlo, eds. *World Christian Database* (Leiden/Boston: Brill, accessed May 2023).

It is difficult to predict future trends related to Christianity in North America. Yet, it can be relatively safely assumed that migration, disaffiliation, the decline of institutional Christianity, and increased racial, ethnic, and linguistic diversity will all have an impact on faith and practice in the region. In the United States, Christianity is tightly intertwined with the political realm, with implications for health, education, finances, and all other aspects of society. Yet, in Canada, in stark contrast to its neighbor, religion is becoming increasingly less relevant in these societal spheres.

Abbreviations

AAWP	American Association of Women Preachers
ACS	American Colonization Society
AG	Assemblies of God
AME	African Methodist Episcopal
AMEZ	African Methodist Episcopal Zion
CCF	Co-operative Commonwealth Federation
CH	*Church History*
CIC	Commission on Interracial Cooperation
CMA	Christian and Missionary Alliance
CRC	Christian Reformed Church
ExpTim	*Expository Times*
JAAR	*Journal of the American Academy of Religion*
JSSR	*Journal for the Scientific Study of Religion*
MEC	Methodist Episcopal Church
NACW	National Association for Colored Women
NAWSA	National American Woman Suffrage Association
NCNW	National Council of Negro Women
OIMC	Oklahoma Indian Missionary Conference
NCWC	National Catholic War Council; later, National Catholic Welfare Conference
PAOC	Pentecostal Assemblies of Canada
Pneuma	*Pneuma: Journal for the Society of Pentecostal Studies*
R&T	*Religion and Theology*
RelSRev	*Religious Studies Review*
RevScRel	*Revue des sciences religieuses*

SA	Salvation Army
UCC	United Church of Canada
UMC	United Methodist Church
UNHCR	United Nations High Commissioner for Refugees
WCTU	Woman's Christian Temperance Union
WUNT	Wissenschaftliche Untersuchungen zum Neuen Testament

Acknowledgments

THE GERM OF AN idea pollinated into a book-length treatment of the history, plight, and experiences of the multifaceted expressions of global Christianity celebrated in the church, and in this sixth book in our seven-volume series, North America. A more detailed treatment of this topic has been published in the five-volume *Encyclopedia of Christianity in the United States* (2015).

The series editors, Emma, Gina, and I, have been more than a little assisted by the comments, guidance, and perspective of sensational scholars Elias Bongmba (Rice University), Arun Jones (Candler School of Theology/Emory University), Brett Knowles (University of Otago), David Maxwell (University of Cambridge, UK), Elizabeth Monier (University of Cambridge, UK), Dana L. Robert (Center for Global Christianity and Mission/Boston University), Nelly van Doorn-Harder (Wake Forest University), and Stephanie Wong (Valparaiso University). Thanks one and all for your friendship and collegiality in the spirit of collaboration.

Conceptualizing on the angle for the book titles and their intended appealing splash came from the fertile minds of Rachel Baker, Jean Van Horn, Gary Camlin, Bill Engvall, Alayna Baker, Aaron Lamport, Jay Ellis, Amy Grubbs, Zachary Grubbs, and Michelle Lamport.

The following were instrumental in shepherding the contents of the book into production-worthy copy—Joshua Erb (senior editorial consultant) and Philip Bustrum and Mel Wilhoit for tremendous skill and detail in indexing the contents.

Further, we are beholden to Michael Thomson, acquisitions and development director for Wipf & Stock Publishers. He tracked Mark down in the produce aisle of a large grocery chain in Grand Rapids and proposed the first book in the series to him! Alec Ryrie filled out the team nicely. Soon thereafter Mark came back to Michael and pitched *this* book to fill out this seven-book series: to tell the global story of Christianity. Michael is at once analytical and spontaneous, perceptive and intelligent, exacting and gracious. We are pleased that an additional large international edited book is also in process under Michael's guidance describing *Emerging Theologies from the Global South* (Cascade, 2022), as well as *Post-Conservative Theological Interpretation* (Cascade, forthcoming). Thank you for cheering on our vision.

Finally, we feel great respect for Christians in North America and wish to tell their historic, unique, and inspiring stories of Christianity.

Contributors

Vince Bantu (PhD, Catholic University of America) is Assistant Professor of Church History and Black Church Studies at Fuller Seminary. His recent publications include *Gospel Haymanot: A Constructive Theology and Critical Reflection on African and Diasporic Christianity* (2020) and *A Multitude of All Peoples: Engaging Ancient Christianity's Global Identity* (2020).

Brantley W. Gasaway (PhD, University of North Carolina at Chapel Hill) is Associate Professor of Religious Studies at Bucknell University. His recent publications have analyzed topics ranging from debates about religious freedom to conflicting attitudes toward environmentalism among evangelicals and fundamentalists. He is the author of *Progressive Evangelicals and the Pursuit of Social Justice* (2014).

Gordon L. Heath (PhD, St. Michael's College), FRHistS, is Professor of Christian History and Centenary Chair in World Christianity at McMaster Divinity College. His most recent book is entitled *Christians, the State, and War: An Ancient Tradition for the Modern World* (2022).

Jeremy Hegi (PhD, Boston University) is Assistant Professor of the History of Christianity at Lubbock Christian University. His recent publications include contributions to the *World Christian Encyclopedia* (3rd ed.) and *Edinburgh Companions to Global Christianity* (vol. 7, *Christianity in North America*).

Allison Kach-Yawnghwe is a PhD candidate at the Boston University School of Theology. She is coeditor of *Creative Collaborations: Case Studies of North American Missional Practices* (2023).

Patricia O'Connell Killen (PhD, Stanford University) is Professor of Religion Emerita at Pacific Lutheran University. She is coeditor of *Selected Letters of A. M. A. Blanchet, Bishop of Walla Walla and Nesqualy, 1846–1879*

(2013) and coeditor of *Religion at the Edge: Nature, Spirituality, and Secularity in the Pacific Northwest* (2022).

Brett Knowles (PhD, University of Otago) recently retired as Associate Professor of Church History at Sydney College of Divinity, Australia, and Teaching Fellow in Church History at the University of Otago, Dunedin, New Zealand. His most recent publication is *A Timeline of Global Christianity* (2020).

Terry LeBlanc (PhD, Asbury Theological Seminary) is the Founding Chair and Director of NAIITS: An Indigenous Learning Community. He has accrued over forty-two years as an educator and community practitioner in global Indigenous contexts.

David Mislin (PhD, Boston University) is Associate Professor in the Intellectual Heritage Program at Temple University. He is the author of *Saving Faith: Making Religious Pluralism an American Value at the Dawn of the Secular Age* (2015) and *Washington Gladden's Church: The Minister Who Made Modern American Protestantism* (2019).

Richard W. Pointer (PhD, Johns Hopkins University) is Professor Emeritus of History at Westmont College in Santa Barbara, California. His most recent book is *Pacifist Prophet: Papunhank and the Quest for Peace in Early America* (2020).

Priscilla Pope-Levison (PhD, University of St. Andrews) is Research Professor of Practical Theology at Southern Methodist University. Her published areas of research—seven books and more than thirty articles, dictionary entries, and chapters—include women's religious history, contextual theology, missiology, evangelism, and ecumenism.

John G. Stackhouse Jr. (PhD, University of Chicago) is the Samuel J. Mikolaski Professor of Religious Studies at Crandall University in Moncton, Canada. His most recent book is *Evangelicalism: A Very Short Introduction* (2022).

Ulrike Stockhausen (PhD, University of Münster) is the author of *The Strangers in Our Midst: American Evangelicals and Immigration from the Cold War to the Twenty-First Century* (2021). She is the Digital Science Communication Officer at the Max Weber Stiftung in Bonn, Germany.

Charles T. Strauss (PhD, University of Notre Dame) is Associate Professor of History at Mount St. Mary's University, Maryland. His recent publications include articles in *U.S. Catholic Historian* and *American Catholic Studies*. He is also Executive Director of the American Catholic Historical Association.

James K. Wellman Jr. (PhD, University of Chicago) is Professor and Chair of Comparative Religion and Director of the Initiative for Global Christian Studies at the Jackson School of International Studies, University of Washington. His most recent project is a chapter with Katie Corcoran on *Evangelicals and Liberal Protestants* for *The Land of Tomorrow: Religion, Spirituality and Secularity in the Pacific Northwest*. Wellman is coauthor of *High on God: How the Megachurch Conquered America* (2020).

Cindy M. Wu (MA, Gordon-Conwell Theological Seminary) is an author, mobilizer, and ordained minister. She is Codirector of Mosaic Formation and is the author of books on global Christianity and the refugee crisis.

Book Introduction

The Church in North America
What Was, What Is, What Next?

ANNE BLUE WILLS

ATTENDING TO THE STORY of the church in the whole of North America, as this volume does, pays dividends as one recognizes the fruitful contrasts and important commonalities among Canada, the US, and Mexico. In this introduction, I will very briefly trace historical milestones that seem significant for describing important details in the character of church in each country. Then I will explore some contemporary trends in each country that are currently reshaping churches. Finally, I want to ponder how we might expect churches in North America to change in the twenty-first century. Will churches' character persist but shift, as each country engages the foreseen and unforeseen challenges of the future?

What Was

Mexico

Historians trace the coming of the church to Spanish explorer Hernán Cortés's arrival in 1519 on the Yucatan Peninsula. Accompanied by two Catholic priests, Cortés's party eventually made their way to the center of the Nahuatl-speaking Aztec empire, Tenochtitlan. The stunning city, built on a lake in the center of the Mesoamerican isthmus, boasted a population of almost half a million people. Within two years of his arrival, Cortés and his small force had destroyed the city and visited torture, rape, and death on its inhabitants.[1] Five years later, a small group of Franciscan missionaries

---

1. See Hartch, *Understanding World Christianity*, ch. 1: "Chronological: A Brief History of Christianity in Mexico"; Restall, *When Montezuma Met Cortés*.

initiated a tide of Catholic missionaries coming to continue the Spanish goal of Christianizing and "civilizing" the conquered Aztecs.

Precontact religious practice of the Aztecs involved human sacrifice of conquered peoples or honored volunteers. Their blood fed the pantheon of gods the Aztecs depended on for security and stability.[2] Their culture revered a code of warrior fitness and revered their political leader, Montezuma, as a consummate warrior—a near-god himself. The Catholic missionaries demanded exclusive commitment to their God and their understanding of how to worship him. They baptized the Indigenous people in Tenochtitlan and elsewhere on a massive scale. Many of these baptisms were perfunctory, accompanied by little, if any, instruction and often accepted under duress. Yet with the establishment of missions led by cadres of priests who celebrated Mass, established and oversaw codes of moral conduct, and otherwise shepherded native communities, Catholicism rooted and grew and even took on some qualities of its environment. Where Indigenous traditions emphasized practices that balanced natural forces, sought healing of land and body, and allowed for local variety, colonial Catholicism also often incorporated these practices.

As political and military struggles played out in Europe in the early nineteenth century, the priest Miguel Hidalgo in 1810 appealed to the Virgin of Guadalupe and roused a popular uprising of Indigenous and *mestizo* people, aimed at Mexico's independence. The movement caught on in a limited way around Mexico City (the former Tenochtitlan). Although Hidalgo was executed in 1811, Mexico did achieve independence from Spain in 1821, thanks in large part to the many priests who followed Hidalgo's lead and inspired laypeople to join the struggle.[3] The Catholic Church remained an important presence in many localities, although not necessarily an orthodox presence.

The tension that broke into the open during Mexico's struggle for independence shows that local parishes were often at odds with the political powers. During the later long revolutionary struggle (1910–20), the pro-revolutionaries' antagonism of the Catholic Church resulted in enduring suspicions between their new government and the churches. In spite of this fraught relationship—or perhaps precisely because church membership and activity built solidarity and strength for resistance—the nation's population continues to identify overwhelmingly as Catholic and as "actively religious."[4]

2. Hartch, *Understanding World Christianity*, loc. 247.
3. Hartch, *Understanding World Christianity*, loc. 419–34.
4. Pew Research Center, "Religion's Relationship to Happiness," esp. the graphic titled "In Many Countries, a Minority of the Population Is Actively Religious." Pew Research Center, "Key Findings," based its information on the 2010–2014 World Values

As of 2020, Mexico's population was more than 94 percent Christian and, of all three North American countries, had the lowest percentage of people unaffiliated with a religious group (under 6 percent).[5] Catholicism is not the official religion of Mexico. Indeed, in the early 1990s, the national government granted more liberties for religious pluralism and practice.[6] And yet the Catholic Church suffuses Mexican culture.

Canada

The beginnings of the church in what would become Canada arrived, as it had in Mexico, alongside the project of colonization of lands and people and exploration for resources. But the source of colonizing energies was France rather than Spain. French political and religious control—the latter through missions to Indigenous communities—focused on and endured in Quebec, even after the mid-eighteenth-century defeat of French forces by the British.[7] Those British victors brought their own Christian tradition of Anglicanism with them, and began a westward expansion. During the later revolution in the British colonies to the south, many who remained loyal to the British monarch fled north to settle in eastern Canada, bringing their Anglican religious commitments with them.

Canada's situation vis-à-vis a national church is unique. Quebec continues to be overwhelmingly Roman Catholic, reflecting its founding and history. The Anglican Church's continued presence speaks of the nation's long connection to Great Britain; their relationship changed somewhat in 1867 with confederation, but the church remained.[8] A nationwide 1925 agreement among the broad Protestant traditions created the United Church of Canada.[9] The population of Canada's Maritime provinces (New

---

Surveys and the International Social Survey Programme's 2011 Health and Health Care module; according to Pew, this reports that 18 percent of Mexico's population identifies as "unaffiliated" with any religious group, 24 percent say they are "inactive" in the religious tradition with which they identify, and 58 percent describe themselves as "active" participants in their religious tradition, attending services at least once monthly. As we shall see, this percentage of "actives" exceeds that in the US by almost twenty percentage points.

5. Pew Research Center, "Religious Composition by Country."

6. Hartch, *Understanding World Christianity*, loc. 685.

7. Noll, *History of Christianity*, 17.

8. Noll, *History of Christianity*, 248–49. Quebec, Ontario, Nova Scotia, and New Brunswick gained some autonomy from England while also retaining the mother country's protection against an expansionist US.

9. Noll, *History of Christianity*, 281–84.

Brunswick, Nova Scotia, and Prince Edward Island) continues to be majority Protestant. Canada's church landscape reflects a kind of historical mosaic, with concentrations of Catholics, Protestants, and Anglicans dotted across its map.

Canada differs from Mexico in that its population, as of 2020, was only a little more than 66 percent Christian. Unlike Mexico, too, Canada has noticeable percentages of non-Christian religious people (Muslims, Hindus, Buddhists, Jews, and Indigenous).[10] Moreover, Canada has a quite sizable percentage of citizens—almost one-quarter of the population—who do not affiliate with any religious tradition.[11] Indeed, this percentage is the highest in North America. Canada's history has created a unique landscape featuring long-standing Christian traditions, regional particularities, and a noncompetitive pluralism.

United States

The beginnings of the church in what would become the United States in some ways look quite similar to those of its southern and northern neighbors. Again, as a function of colonialist exploits in the mid-sixteenth century, Spanish explorers, accompanied by Catholic religious, moved through the continent's southern tier and up the West Coast. They built mission stations that placed Indigenous Americans into rigorously organized communities of work and worship.[12] In this setting especially did Indigenous populations incorporate Catholic theology and saints into their existing worldviews, perhaps as a strategy to mollify missionaries' sometimes aggressive tactics and also because the sacramentalism of the Catholic tradition lent itself to this kind of adaptation.

As for the non-Catholic incursion into this part of North America, separating Puritans (or Pilgrims) coming to the Atlantic coast established Plymouth in 1620; ten years later, a different group of non-separating Puritans began settling the Massachusetts Bay Colony, which eventually became Boston. This latter group aimed to establish a community in which the church and civil government, while distinct, would reinforce each other's authority.[13] This early religious establishment caused some, including Roger Williams, to decamp for Rhode Island in the later 1630s. There, Williams intended to allow freedom of conscience and noncoercion in matters of

---

10. Pew Research Center, "Religious Composition by Country."
11. Pew Research Center, "Religious Composition by Country."
12. Noll, *History of Christianity*, 14–17.
13. Noll, *History of Christianity*, 42.

religious belief. In other colonial settlements to the south—Virginia and South Carolina particularly—relatively weak Anglican establishments took hold, although populations were more dispersed, religious officials were scarce, and the commercial motivations outweighed missionary interests.[14]

The distinctive US formula of nonestablishment and voluntarism, influenced by the series of prerevolutionary revivals now known as the First Great Awakening, was encoded into law through negotiations that happened after the ratification of the US Constitution. As part of the Bill of Rights, the First Amendment, alongside protections for the press and for speaking, petitioning, and assembling, guards against the establishment or official support for any religious tradition and allows for the "free exercise" of religious practices by citizens.

Many, if not all, of the men who crafted the Constitution were church members (all but one, Protestant). Some of them, influenced by Enlightenment skepticism about supernaturalism, held theistic or deistic beliefs. They worried that a national religious establishment (such as existed in England) would infringe upon the individual liberties of the new nation's free, White citizens. At the same time, they felt that religious faith (specifically, something that resembled Protestant Christianity without the supernatural elements) encouraged good morality. They did not want to discourage individuals from (Christian) faith or practice.[15]

This combination of solicitude for and wariness about "religion" created space for a simmering undercurrent of Protestant revivalism, which bubbled up periodically and more intensely during the early nineteenth century and then periodically again midcentury. These revival waves not only brought new members to existing Protestant traditions, but also helped create new Christian traditions such as the restorationist Stone-Campbell movement, the Church of Jesus Christ of Latter-day Saints (Mormons), and the Seventh-Day Adventists.[16] The absence of an established national church encouraged a spirit of experimentation, creating a profusion of churches, old and new, in the nineteenth century. Some of the founders thought that churches would fade away without government support. Instead, churches

---

14. Noll, *History of Christianity*, 51–53.

15. For example, Thomas Jefferson, who did not believe that Jesus of Nazareth was actually a supernatural being embodying God, credited him with sound moral teaching. He created his own version of the New Testament that excluded most of the supernatural elements of the four Gospels and emphasized Jesus's ethical teachings. Many contemporary editions of this text exist, including Jefferson, *Jefferson Bible*, which features an introduction by Forrest Church and an afterword by church historian Jaroslav Pelikan, as well as some images of Jefferson's actual cut-and-paste handiwork.

16. See Noll, *History of Christianity*, ch. 8, "Outsiders."

in ever greater variety have been central to US self-understanding and identity over the past two and a half centuries.

What May Be

Given the vibrant, devotionally inflected Catholicism in Mexico; pluralistic, regionally rooted churches in Canada; and "pervasive" yet "invisible" religion in the US,[17] what is the state of churches in the national communities today? The Pew Research Center reports that Christianity is and will continue to be the dominant religious tradition in North America. But because of slower population growth among Christians, churches will cede some of their dominance to two groups. By 2050, numbers of unaffiliated people are projected to double as people leave churches. In addition, the Muslim population is projected to triple by 2050.[18]

Only the US and Brazil have larger Christian populations than Mexico.[19] According to the Pew Research Center's Pew-Templeton Global Religious Futures Project, in Mexico, where around 78 percent of the population identifies itself as Catholic,[20] the percentage of people who say that "religion is very important in their lives" is 45 percent.[21] Mexican people surveyed in 2018 also were about evenly divided when asked whether religion is more, less, or equally important as it was twenty years ago.[22] The strength of Mexican Christianity in the contemporary world is especially noteworthy in light of both the 1910 revolution's hostility toward the Catholic Church and the enduring presence of Indigenous traditions.[23] But as Hartch observes, the Catholic Church has been a stabilizing fixture on Mexican soil longer that "any national government or political tradition."[24] Pew researchers project that by 2050 the number of Christians in Mexico will increase, and do so

17. Brekus and Gilpin, *American Christianities*, 1.
18. Pew Research Center, "Future of World Religions," subsect. "Regional and Country-Level Projections," para 6.
19. Hartch, *Understanding World Christianity*, loc. 184.
20. Office of International Religious Freedom, *2022 Report [Mexico]*, "Section I: Religious Demography."
21. Pew Research Center, "Key Findings," graphic "Religion Is Very Important to People in Africa, the Middle East, South Asia, Latin America."
22. Pew Research Center, "Key Findings," subsect. "Is Religion Gaining or Losing Influence?," graphic "People in North America, Europe and Australia Say Religion Plays a Less Important Role Today."
23. See Hartch, *Understanding World Christianity*, ch. 2, "Denominational Resilience and Innovation in Mexican Catholicism and Protestantism."
24. Hartch, *Understanding World Christianity*, loc. 840.

primarily through population growth, by perhaps twelve million people. That increase would represent the largest increase among all religious groups in Mexico.[25]

Canada stands out from both of its North American neighbors in that only 27 percent of people claimed that religion had significant importance to them.[26] Indeed, when asked if religion was more, less, or as important as it was two decades ago, an overwhelming percentage responded that it was less important.[27] Quebec, with its enduring ties to the Catholic Church, may remain an exception in this regard, given that in 2011, the Canadian census showed that almost 75 percent of Quebecois were Catholic, compared to under 30 percent nationwide.[28] Moreover, only 12 percent of Quebec residents said that they were "religiously unaffiliated"; that percentage is much higher in most other parts of Canada.[29] The only other region with higher church membership and participation is the Maritimes, which continue to be majority Protestant.[30]

Quebec has been an outlier more recently in other ways as well in attempting to legislate the appropriateness of public religious display. In 2019, its legislature passed a law that forbade many different types of public employees from wearing religious symbols at their jobs.[31] Although supporters insisted that the law aimed to protect public religious neutrality, critics worried about the law's potential to land unevenly on Muslim women who cover their hair.[32]

Viewed in national perspective, Canada's population is becoming less "churched"—less active and/or less tightly affiliated in church communities—even more quickly than is the US population. Quebec, with its deep and abiding Catholic heritage, has so far not followed that trend.

---

25. Pew Research Center, "Religious Composition by Country."

26. "Religion is very important to people."

27. Pew Research Center, "Key Findings," subsect. "Is Religion Gaining or Losing Influence?," graphic "People in North America, Europe and Australia Say Religion Plays a Less Important Role Today."

28. *CBC News*, "All French Canadians," para. 7; Office of International Religious Freedom, *2022 Report [Canada]*, "Section I: Religious Demography."

29. Pew Research Center, "Canada's Changing Religious Landscape," subsect. "Differences with the United States."

30. Noll, *History of Christianity*, 265.

31. Bilefsky, "Quebec Bans Religious Symbols."

32. Lipka, "5 Facts about Religion"; Bilefsky, "Quebec's Ban," which reports that English-minority schools and those elected to the province's legislature were exempted from the law.

The US leads its North American neighbors in the percentage of respondents identifying "religion [as] very important in their lives," with 53 percent.[33] As in Canada, however, a large percentage of US respondents said that religion was less important than it was twenty years ago.[34] Almost a third of US adults now report that they have "no religion," an identification that has been rising since at least 2007. At the same time, the percentage of those identifying themselves as Christian has been declining, from more than three-quarters of respondents to a little more than two-thirds identifying as Christians.[35] Identification as well as observance are declining.

In tracking trends in membership and participation, Pew predicts that Christianity will be less dominant in the US by 2050.[36] While in 2010 the number of people who said they were "unaffiliated" with any religious tradition comprised about one-eighth of the total US population, Pew projects that perhaps more than a quarter of the population will so identify by 2050.[37]

What Next?

What do these current conditions portend for the future of the church in North America? As a scholar trained to look carefully at the past, I find the future an unaccustomed territory. If, as Pew's researchers contend, "people who are active in religious congregations tend to be happier and more civically engaged"[38] than unaffiliated people or than those who are affiliated but inactive, how might a larger number of unaffiliated people affect civil society in Canada and the US? Will citizens in Ontario or Kansas successfully locate other, nonreligious communities where they can feel belonging, seek counsel, and experience joy? To what extent will citizens in Alberta or Ohio withdraw from their everyday engagements in civil society—activities

33. Pew Research Center, "Key Findings," graphic "Religion Is Very Important to People in Africa, the Middle East, South Asia, Latin America."

34. Pew Research Center, "Key Findings," subsect. "Is Religion Gaining or Losing Influence?," graphic "People in North America, Europe and Australia Say Religion Plays a Less Important Role Today."

35. Pew Research Center, "Key Findings," subsect. "People Are Becoming Less Religious in the U.S. and Many Other Countries," graphic "In U.S., Roughly Three-in-Ten Adults Now Religiously Unaffiliated."

36. Pew Research Center, "Future of World Religions," ch. 2, subsect. "Christians: Change in Countries with Largest Christian Populations," table "Projected Population Change in Countries with Largest Christian Populations in 2010."

37. Pew Research Center, "Future of World Religions," ch. 2, subsect. "Religiously Unaffiliated: Change in Countries with Largest Unaffiliated Populations," table "Projected Population Change in Countries with Largest Unaffiliated Populations in 2010."

38. Pew Research Center, "Religion's Relationship to Happiness," para. 1.

such as helping neighbors, volunteering at nonprofit organizations, voting, or running for office? How might a potentially smaller church leverage its remaining influence as North America faces alarming challenges? Will churches have the resources to address in meaningful ways the intensifying climate crisis or the constant ethical challenges posed by technological developments like artificial intelligence and biomedical innovation?

Scholar Philip Jenkins has taken account of Christianity's continuing and accelerating movements to new places around the world. The church, he explains, is experiencing "dramatic" growth in the Global South.[39] Just as in the early modern period when it accompanied and often justified exploration, settler colonialism, and imperialism, Christianity will continue to evolve in this new century. So far, according to Jenkins, Christianity's greatest growth has been among "traditionalist and fideistic" Roman Catholicism and Protestant groups. These groups typically are not politically "radical" in the style of late twentieth-century liberation theology; rather, their radicality shows itself in commitment to deeply conservative theological approaches. Such Christians in the Global South take seriously both sin (rather than injustice) in the world and the resources of spiritual power to combat sin.[40] What will be the effects in North America as Christians in Canada, Mexico, and the US engage with these different ways of doing church? Once again, we may see transformations in keeping with the rich histories and spiritual resources of the church in North America.

Bibliography

Bilefsky, Dan. "Quebec Bans Religious Symbols in Some Public Sector Jobs." *New York Times*, June 17, 2019. https://www.nytimes.com/2019/06/17/world/canada/quebec-religious-symbols-secularism-bill.html.

———. "Quebec's Ban on Public Religious Symbols Largely Upheld." *New York Times*, Apr. 20, 2021. https://www.nytimes.com/2021/04/20/world/canada/quebec-religious-symbols-ruling.html.

Brekus, Catherine A., ed. *The Religious History of American Women: Reimagining the Past*. Chapel Hill: University of North Carolina Press, 2007.

———, and W. Clark Gilpin. *American Christianities: A History of Dominance & Diversity*. Chapel Hill: University of North Carolina Press, 2011.

CBC News. "'All French Canadians' Are Catholic, Quebec Premier Tells Governor of California." *CBC News*, Dec. 11, 2019. https://www.cbc.ca/news/canada/montreal/catholic-quebec-california-fran%C3%A7ois-legault-gavin-newsom-1.5393170.

Hartch, Todd. *Understanding World Christianity: Mexico*. Understanding World Christianity 3. Minneapolis: Fortress, 2015. Kindle.

---

39. Jenkins, *Next Christendom*, 21–22.
40. Jenkins, *Next Christendom*, 22.

Jefferson, Thomas. *The Jefferson Bible: The Life and Morals of Jesus of Nazareth*. Boston: Beacon, 1989.

Jenkins, Philip. *The Next Christendom: The Coming of Global Christianity*. 3rd ed. New York: Oxford University Press, 2011.

Lipka, Michael. "5 Facts about Religion in Canada." Pew Research Center, July 1, 2019. https://www.pewresearch.org/short-reads/2019/07/01/5-facts-about-religion-in-canada/.

Noll, Mark A. *A History of Christianity in the United States and Canada*. Grand Rapids: Eerdmans, 1992.

Office of International Religious Freedom. *2022 Report on International Religious Freedom: Canada*. U.S. Department of State, 2022. https://www.state.gov/reports/2022-report-on-international-religious-freedom/canada/.

———. *2022 Report on International Religious Freedom: Mexico*. U.S. Department of State, 2022. https://www.state.gov/reports/ 2022-report-on-international-religious-freedom/mexico/.

Pew Research Center. "Canada's Changing Religious Landscape." Pew Research Center, June 27, 2013. https://www.pewresearch.org/religion/2013/06/27/canadas-changing-religious-landscape/#regional-differences.

———. "The Future of World Religions: Population Growth Projections, 2010–2050." Pew Research Center, Apr. 2, 2015. https://www.pewresearch.org/religion/2015/04/02/religious-projections-2010-2050/.

———. "Key Findings from the Global Religious Futures Project." Pew Research Center, Dec. 21, 2022. https://www.pewresearch.org/religion/2022/12/21/key-findings-from-the-global-religious-futures-project/.

———. "Religion's Relationship to Happiness, Civic Engagement and Health around the World." Pew Research Center, Jan. 31, 2019. https://www.pewresearch.org/religion/2019/01/31/religions-relationship-to-happiness-civic-engagement-and-health-around-the-world/.

———. "Religious Composition by Country, 2010–2050." Pew Research Center, Dec. 21, 2022. https://www.pewresearch.org/religion/interactives/religious-composition-by-country-2010-2050/.

Restall, Matthew. *When Montezuma Met Cortés: The True Story of the Meeting That Changed History*. New York: Ecco, 2018.

Tweed, Thomas A., ed. *Retelling U.S. Religious History*. Berkeley: University of California Press, 1997.

Section One

The Story of Christianity Narrated in Historical Context:
Versions of Dominance and Diversity

Chapter 1

Indigenous Christianity in North America

Good Intentions?

TERRY LeBLANC

The newcomers looked out on the land with disdain. How was it possible that such vast and fertile lands—lands cluttered with bounty—could lie untouched? Sights and sounds of abundance were everywhere. "Why," they asked themselves, "were these savages allowed by God to inhabit such prosperous holdings—holdings rich with resources they were so ill-equipped to utilize?" It seemed inconsistent with all they knew and understood about the use of lands and goods. It must be that God had prepared this bounty, keeping it in trust just for them. Prosperity waited.

THIS CHAPTER IS WRITTEN not as an indictment of mission or the church, but rather out of a clear hope that what was once considered to be Indigenous mission and Christianity is no longer; further, that the self-directed, self-governing Indigenous church, irrespective of its denominational affiliations, will not suffer colonially-driven mission again.

Acts 15 records what appears to be the first clash of cultures in the life of the early church. Believers from the sect of the Pharisees demanded that gentiles turning to Jesus first become Jews so that they might then become Christ followers. But it wasn't a one-off clash. It was a scenario that repeats itself throughout the church's history, albeit with new casts of players.[1]

---

1. See, for example, Fletcher, *Barbarian Conversion*, 11–21.

Was said mission based in good intentions? In the case of the Acts 15 encounter of Jew and gentile, the Jerusalem Council said no. In fact, they were quite adamant that there were minimal cultural expectations for the gentiles who were turning to Jesus. "If you do these things, you will do well," they noted. Unfortunately, their response was not repeated with any regularity down through the centuries. In fact, within a hundred years or so of the council's decision, the gentile church required the repudiation of Jewishness to be Christ followers. Just over a century following the resolution of gentile membership requirements, the tables had turned. The church embraced a deepening posture of anti-Semitism,[2] and a centuries-old anti-cultural stance followed.

By the thirteenth century, while the "attitude toward Jews seemed to hover between severity and tolerance," praxis was not even remotely charitable.[3] The Jews' 1497 forced conversion in Portugal would not be the last effort at expunging Jews from the world religiously and/or physically.[4] Nor would they be the only ethnic, cultural, or "racial" group targeted for such treatment. As the fifteenth century ended, the "press-gang" approach to Christian mission among Jews had now expanded to include most everyone who was "other." The doctrine of discovery, *terra nullius,* and the sociopolitically ethnocentric notion of manifest destiny now philosophically drove this "othering."

From the days of the Hebrew cry "Give us a king," organized followers of God have struggled to differentiate the kingdom of God, from the kingdom of their monarch. Too often, the kingdom of God and the kingdoms of this world have been conflated, in both form and function. Arguably, from Acts 15 onward, the church has witnessed one group of believers and/or people seeking dominion over another, empire becoming the principal mechanism of this undertaking. This is what lay at the heart of Christian mission to Indigenous people.

Dvornik, in his study of the early ecumenical councils, describes the conflation of church/state leadership thus:

> We can be certain that such gatherings of bishops gradually modelled themselves on the rules under which the sessions of the Roman Senate were held. The presiding bishop assumed the role of the Emperor or of his representative in the Senate. He

---

2. For more, see Dunn, *Jews and Christians.*
3. Webster, "Achievement and Technique," 175.
4. Barrett, *World Christian Encyclopedia,* 26.

used the same words for the convocation of the Council as were used in the imperial summons for the meeting of the Senate.[5]

Reflecting further on what he terms the church's Constantinian roots, Dvornik describes a syncretic consolidation whereby Roman ecclesial and temporal authority is increasingly woven together with the church's celestial spirituality. He observes,

> Of course, he [Constantine] knew only one political system, that of the autocratic monarchy into which the Roman Republic had been transformed under the influence of the Hellenistic political philosophy. This philosophy had deified the ruler and had given him absolute power over the material and spiritual interests of his subjects. The first Christian political philosophers ... adapted this political system to Christian teaching. The Emperor was thus deprived of his divine character but made to be the representative of God on earth, who had been given by God supreme power in things material and spiritual.[6]

Following this line of reasoning then, it could be said that it was under the pretext of pursuing and obtaining unity of thought, doctrine, and ecclesial action, were this even possible, that the councils were convened. To obtain this unity required a degree of standardization that many continued to militate against, for it necessitated that Christian unity mean homogeneity. Heterodoxy was not welcome; orthodoxy and orthopraxy were the order of the day.[7] Erasure of difference became normative.

By the turn of the fourth century with the convening of the ecumenical councils, church and state had begun to be all but indistinguishable, one from the other.[8] Arguably then, by the time of Chalcedon, the pattern had become firmly set. The sword of state wielding steel, not the sword of the supplicant Spirit, would now increasingly characterize the "conversion" experience.[9] In many ways the church's justification for mission, as well

---

5. Dvornik, *Ecumenical Councils*, 10.

6. Dvornik, *Ecumenical Councils*, 11.

7. The very exclusion of oppositional positions by the councils and their representatives through censure and/or execution for heresy ensured this would continue to be the chosen means for dealing with diversity of opinion and theology throughout history, further ensuring that the trajectory of mission would inevitably be that which Indigenous peoples of the globe experienced—assimilation and/or social, cultural, or physical eradication.

8. For a reasoned discussion of the formation of this amalgam, see Fanning, "Dark Age Church Period," 10–11.

9. See Fletcher's discussion, *Barbarian*, 36–87.

as many of its operational and missional settings, would be supplied to the church by empire through newly forged ties with empire.

Fanning pushes us to understand that conversion here involved more than simply reciting a creed or saying the sinner's prayer. He argues that "the evolving Roman-Germanic culture became inseparable to the culture of the Church. To become a Christian, you had to become a Roman citizen culturally. Thus, the Christianizing of a nation became the civilizing of a people."[10] What's more, as the empire continued to be conflated with the church and vice versa, people's "authentic Christian conversion" was now almost always experienced alongside their concomitant conquest and allegiance to the state. The resultant faith was not simply anemic; it became a seedbed for the furthering, even intensification, of this pattern. Fanning's question then, is entirely apropos:

> Did these methods generate true "belief" or merely nominal faith? Nominalism will result from "conversions" based on false premises (intimidation, peer pressure, coercion, or an emotional experience), rather than an understanding of the truth of the gospel and a commitment to trust that biblical truth. However, in a day when everyone was obligated to hold to a faith that was the faith of your nobleman or prince, then nominal followers were inevitable.[11]

Not only did this collusion in mission produce questionable outcomes in terms of authentic conversion, but it also led to a greater likelihood that "state converts" would uphold the continued purpose and function of the state as agent of conversion. By the time we arrive at the more recent colonial eras, we see this phenomenon reflected in legislative doctrines and joint ventures of church and state.[12] In Canada, the Gradual Civilizations Act and the Indian Act are examples of this thinking, as are the residential and boarding school policies of Canada and the US, respectively. Each of these was clearly situated in an assimilative mentality; each was fully supported by church leadership; and albeit in modified ways, each continues today.

---

10. Fanning, "Dark Age Church Period," 2.

11. Fanning, "Dark Age Church Period," 22.

12. The establishment of the United Church in Canada is a clear case in point. See United Church of Canada/L'Église Unie du Canada, *Manual*, 9.

Toward Intent

Of the various responses that one could muster to answer the question of intent, two of the more common ones include "They were people of their times" and its corollary, "We cannot impose contemporary understandings on historic circumstance."

While Gregory Boer's focus is not mission framed, his observations are nonetheless germane since the essence of his reflection pertains fully to Christian mission. He notes,

> We lose history through what has come to be known as biased historical knowledge. An example of this bias is . . . a general written history of Western civilization that has excluded significant contributions of people of color. Again, we find memory the faulty mechanism in the keeping of historical evidence.[13]

Since the version of Christianity engaged by Christian mission in North America, forged in the developmental fires of Western civilization, was the regularizing foundation of missional thought until recently, only those ideas and interpretive frameworks set in place by its progressive Western thought-framed scholarship have been considered historically normative.[14] It is this steamroller progression of Western civilization cum mission, repeating the same errors, that demands the decolonizing and colorizing of the evaluation of missional intent in North America.

Indigenous theologians, missiologists, and biblical scholars, many of whose thinking was initially framed within the Western monolith, are now offering alternative ways of engaging and understanding mission from within Indigenous epistemologies, ontologies, hermeneutical frameworks, and histories.

A Necessary Retrospective

Clearly incensed by the thought that anything good might have come from churches engaged in North American colonial mission, my friend wondered why I was a Jesus follower. The question and the attitude that appeared to underlie it caught me up. I wasn't ignoring the experience of colonization—it was always salient in my thinking and experience. It's simply that I had somehow been able to separate following Jesus, the clear focus

---

13. Boer, "Images of Depression," 41–42.

14. Note the lack of significant input by the Majority World in Edinburgh 1910 and even in Edinburgh 1910's centenary.

of Christian faith, from the work of mission and the actions of "Christian" colonial nation-states.

Christian mission did a very good job of dividing Indigenous peoples into neat packages to be parceled out and missioned by the large denominational traditions within what became the Canadian and American nation-states. Equity of opportunity, boundaries, policies, and guarantees that "our" version of Christianity would be present in the land split sociocultural groups. It was not uncommon to find an Indigenous extended family divided up into two and perhaps more denominational traditions, existing in two different and newly formed nation-states or territories—in the case of the two largest initial missions in Canada and the US, also being made either Catholic or Anglican.

Of course, the reader can imagine the potential, never mind real, conflicts this created among an otherwise highly communal, relational, and ceremonial people whose identities as Ray Aldred, Cree theologian, notes are narrated, communal identities, inclusive of land.[15]

We might have imagined this Christian mission disposition to have been positively impacted by the Edinburgh 1910 mission conference. Yet, that would not be at all accurate. In fact, following the centenary Edinburgh conference, in a response titled "A Majority Report," the Indigenous and Global Southern participants noted the following:

> An examination of the policies and practices that emerged from or, were otherwise sanctioned by the 1910 gathering—either directly or, through inaction, indirectly—would show that the intent of missionary efforts from that point forward was an intensification of the on-going process of Christianizing and civilizing those peoples in the global southern and Indigenous communities. The inescapable reality, had this been completely successful, is that we would have become "Europeanized" and therefore completely comfortable in a Euro-centric setting. Our cultures and languages would have been absorbed into the body politic of the church and its surrounding society—at best tactically assimilated, becoming "window dressing" to the historic and more "authentic" culture(s) of the church; at worst our uniquenesses in the Creator's economy would have been eradicated entirely. Sadly, for some of the peoples we represent, the latter became their current reality.[16]

---

15. Aldred, "Alternative Starting Place," 287.
16. LeBlanc et al., "Majority Report," 347.

It had become evident by this time that Augustine's understanding of sin, distilled in the structures, allegiances, and successive ecumenical councils inaugurated under Constantine, did not provide the kind of theological framework necessary for culturally diverse expressions of Christianity. When applied in mission to the Indigenous community, in fact, it became toxic.

For many Indigenous Christians, detoxification meant embracing what might be described as the triple restorative mandates of: right relationship with God and other spiritual powers, right relationship with one another in the human community, and right relationship with and relatedness to the rest of creation of which humanity is but a part. To put it in more classic theological jargon, these three relational spheres when breached, dysfunctional, or altogether absent describe the nature of sin. Amelioration for sin is then made possible not by becoming culturally, legally, or morally compliant with the Eurocentric church, but through the relationally restorative work of Jesus Christ.

Considering the prevailing philosophies of the times, it is all but inevitable that the missional duo of civilize and Christianize continued to undergird, almost entirely, mission to Indigenous people. What's more, this was true irrespective of the denominational or missional tradition.[17]

Colonial administrators in North America, as elsewhere, believed Christianizing and civilizing went together, the Bible and the plow considered mutually supportive. Over time, this took on a social and material betterment focus. Mark Francis notes that this era "relied solely on the simplest and most basic idea of 'civilization' in the Victorian period—material culture."[18] The development of Christianity among Indigenous peoples, therefore, was significantly framed by the effort to convert a people lacking material wealth and goods, to those acquiring and then becoming dependent upon them. They were prime targets since they were not in possession of a great deal of individual or communal material wealth as measured in European terms. Nor, it would seem, did they possess an appropriate social or political structure or spirituality within which to receive mission efforts differently.[19]

---

17. See the work of Adas, *Dominance by Design*, 135.

18. Francis, "'Civilizing' of Indigenous People," 51.

19. Pierre LeJeune, for example, notes, "As they have neither political organization, nor offices, nor dignities, nor any authority, for they only obey their Chief through good will toward him, therefore they never kill each other to acquire these honors. Also, as they are contented with a mere living, not one of them gives himself to the Devil to acquire wealth" (Thwaites, *Jesuit Relations*, 6:66).

Further to missional intent, then, it was not that European missionaries observed Indigenous peoples to be wholly reprobate, thus justifying the methods employed. In fact, observations made across the years of mission by ship captains, missionaries, and even lawyers suggest something else. The words of Marc Lescarbot for example, are biting and condemnatory:

> And, in this respect, I consider all these poor savages, whom we commiserate, to be very happy; for pale Envy doth not emaciate them, neither do they feel the inhumanity of those who serve God hypocritically, harassing their fellow-creatures under this mask: nor are they subject to the artifices of those who, lacking virtue and goodness wrap themselves up in a mantle of false piety to nourish their ambition. If they do not know God, at least they do not blaspheme him, as the greater number of Christians do. Nor do they understand the art of poisoning, or of corrupting chastity by devilish artifice.[20]

Expectations of Indigenous Jesus followers, in some cases even into the twenty-first century, owe much to the continued rejection by Western Christianity of Indigenous cultural forms within anything "Christian." Many people have noted that were you to be blindfolded on your entry to a service of worship, you would be hard pressed to find any difference between an Indigenous church and one that was mainstream Euro North American, except perhaps the slower cadence of familiar hymns and songs.[21]

While there were some "bright spots," such as the resistance to the Indian Removal Act of the US government by the American Board of Commissioners for Foreign Missions during Jeremiah Evarts's tenure,[22] even here a civilizing trajectory clearly described the arc of its mission irrespective of the colonial or missional context in which it took place.

One could be forgiven at this point for echoing the words of Jesus to the Pharisees upon reading the chronicles of North American mission:

> Woe to you, teachers of the law and Pharisees, you hypocrites! You travel over land and sea to win a single convert, and when you have succeeded, you make them twice as much a child of hell as you are. (Matt 23:13 NIV)

---

20. Thwaites, *Jesuit Relations*, 1:28.
21. Twiss, *One Church*, 14.
22. See Evarts, *Cherokee Removal*, 31.

The North American Indigenous Church

The Indigenous church in North America[23] exhibits a plethora of cultural practices and a significant diversity of belief. What's more, it comes into existence under differing missional and colonial experiences, including some good, some clearly bad, and some outright ugly.

Those traditions that have or are beginning to make a difference are those engaging the words of the Jerusalem Council with integrity. They are seeking to engage Indigenous ways of knowing, being, and doing in decolonial and/or contextualized ways in their ministries. In some cases, there is also an increase of visible and active Indigenous leadership; in others, it is a result of risk-taking on the part of non-Indigenous denominational leadership; in still others the denominational presence is because of a cooperative approach of Indigenous and non-Indigenous peoples to address the impacts of colonization.

Space limits the ability to describe the Indigenous church in North America in any detail. So, what follows is an "aerial view" consisting of Catholic, mainline Protestant (Anglican/Episcopalian, United Church, and United Methodist), two evangelical traditions, and "some of the rest" that find significant representation in North America. This is not to say that other or smaller representations of Christian faith and life are not to be found, or that they do not have Indigenous participation, even leadership, but rather that in the space available, these few effectively capture the broad landscape of Indigenous Christianity in North America.

Catholicism

Not surprisingly, the oldest organized church tradition among Indigenous people in Canada and the United States is Roman Catholicism. Franciscan mission, in what is now California, began in roughly 1565, where "reductions" began to be established. "Reductions" were used to herd Indigenous peoples into manageable communities for the purpose of evangelization and assimilation. Stern notes that "the reduction of the Indians was intended to break down ethnic and kinship ties and detribalize the residents to create a generic, pan-Indian population, disregarding their numerous tribes and different cultures."[24]

23. While geography makes clear that Mexico is part of North America, this chapter focuses on Indigenous mission experience of the church in Canada and the United States only, since the allotted space would not allow for a proper treatment of the Mexican Indigenous church.

24. Stern, *Peru's Indian Peoples*, 80.

Other Catholic orders also used this strategy of gathering Indigenous peoples to a specific "settled" location to be Christianized and civilized. Jesuit enclaves at Tadoussac, Trois Rivieres, and Sillery are notable in eastern Canada. According to George Stanley, these could be considered the first "reserves" in Canada. Not improbably, they could also have provided a model for the residential and boarding schools in the US and Canada in the nineteenth and twentieth centuries.[25]

While there are differing views of Catholic Christianity's early seventeenth-century birth among the Mi'kmaq, a strong oral tradition exists to suggest that the baptisms of Saqamaw Membertou and his family on June 24, 1610, were of a dual significance: conversion to Christ and allegiance to France. Which one is to be understood as being of greater priority, or even authenticity, depends on who tells, and who interprets, the story. Catholicism might simply have been viewed by some as a kind of continuity with preexisting lifeways, spirituality, and sovereignty.[26]

One of the most well-known Indigenous Catholic figures in the US is Nicholas Black Elk, currently a "servant of God" on his way to sainthood in the Catholic tradition. Black Elk's vision and his lived experience are, perhaps, the most noteworthy examples of an Indigenous person seeking to contextualize Catholic Christian faith. A survivor of Wounded Knee Creek, Black Elk and his life and faith are still the subject of animated discussion.

St. Kateri of the Kahnawake Mohawk community was similarly recognized in her efforts to engage Mohawk tradition alongside Catholic teachings and liturgies. When she and her Mohawk sisters in Christ were told that could not form a religious order, they did so anyway out of their love for Jesus.

Like all church traditions, Indigenous Catholicism is not static. There are many questions about the nature of leadership and the relationship to a complicated past. Yet Indigenous Catholics continue to lead in charting their own way, drawing on the examples of those who went before them.

Mainline Protestantism

Protestantism and its branches[27] have varying degrees of representation in Indigenous North America. What follows is an admittedly truncated picture.

---

25. G. Stanley, "Indian Reserves."

26. See LeBlanc, "Mi'kmaq and French/Jesuit Understandings," 201.

27. Protestantism's branches include but are not limited to: Adventist, Anglican (Episcopalian in the US), Baptist, Calvinist, Lutheran, Methodist, Pentecostal, Brethren, Quaker, and various non-denominationalists, grouped here as Evangelicalism.

While the Church of England made its first appearance on the North American continent in 1578 as part of Martin Frobisher's Arctic expedition, it was not until the eighteenth century, as Anglicans spread out across what is now called Canada, that the first Anglican missionary arrived among the Mi'kmaq in Eastern Canada. The year was 1752 and coincided with Mi'kmaw *sachem* Jean Baptiste Cope signing the Treaty for Peace and Friendship in that same year.

Almost three quarters of a century later, in 1822, a Norway House Cree man named Sakacewescam was baptized with the English name Henry Budd. Budd was ordained deacon and priest, becoming the first ordained Indigenous Anglican. He worked with diligence among his own and other Indigenous people, realizing significant fruit for his labors, yet the English missionaries who followed him complained of lack of evangelistic opportunity. It seemed clear in what followed that non-Eurocentricity equated to lack of mission opportunity.

Today, under the auspices of the culturally framed leadership of the Anglican Council of Indigenous People, the Indigenous church has thrived. Church structures are framed in Indigenous ideologies, epistemologies, ontological frameworks, liturgical interpretations, and missional applications. In short, Indigenous. In the late 2000s under the leadership of its first National Indigenous archbishop, the Most Rev. Mark MacDonald, it became increasingly autonomous.

Established in Jamestown, Virginia, in 1607, the American expression of the worldwide Anglican Communion, the Episcopal Church, was organized in 1789 as the successor to the Church of England in the American colonies.

The Episcopal Church appears to describe itself less in terms of its autonomy within the Anglican Communion than a division within. For instance, an Indigenous archbishop leads the Indigenous Anglican Church, whereas the Episcopal leader is designated as the "missioner for Indigenous ministries."

By the late twentieth century, it was clear that the Anglican/Episcopal Church had been most fruitful and durable when led by Indigenous peoples themselves. That being said, there is this curious expectation that Indigenous ecclesial realities reflect those of their European kin, a point of frustration for more than a few. At an Episcopalian gathering of clergy some years ago, when asked why they put up with what was obviously very colonial and frustrating, the response was simply, "We like the liturgy."[28]

---

28. Ginny Doctor, personal conversation with author, San Diego, 2009.

The United Church/United Methodism

When the United Church of Canada (UCC) was formed in Canada, Indigenous peoples and/or churches were absent any mention in the Articles of the Basis of Union. In 2012 Indigenous churches were added to the document and the UCC crest was changed to include the four colors of the Indigenous medicine wheel and the Mohawk phrase *Akwe Nia'Tetewá:neren* (All my relations) was added.

In the mid 1960s, Indigenous leaders evolved a system of training that included learning circles and on-the-job placements in Indigenous communities. Today, candidates are prepared at Sandy-Saulteaux Spiritual Centre for ordination, commissioning as diaconal ministers, and recognition as designated lay leaders. The Indigenous UCC presently includes seventy-one communities of faith.

In the United Methodist Church (UMC) Indigenous ministry is represented at its strongest in the Oklahoma Indian Missionary Conference (OIMC). Originally founded in 1818, the OIMC has been active in local church and fellowship settings across the US since approximately 1820. Today there are active ministries in scores of small Indigenous communities and in many urban centers. While these ministries do not always present as a classically described church body, culturally framed worship, pastoral care, and sacramental ministry are nonetheless provided.

Viewed with suspicion by some because their cultural engagement was thought to be theologically liberal and religiously syncretistic, in several significant ways the UCC and UMC each provide working examples of how one might reengage culture alongside an authentic Christian faith.

The Evangelicals

Attitudes toward culture and faith vary across the wide array of evangelical traditions in each of the countries, so also within the traditions themselves. The Christian and Missionary Alliance (CMA) is a good example with which to begin.

Rooted in the more conservative values of mainstream US Evangelicalism, the Native American District of the CMA shunned anything of an Indigenous cultural nature almost entirely in their congregations and ministries. In a clear statement to this effect in the mid-1990s Craig Smith, director for the Native American District, stated,

> Recently, there has been introduced in the Native evangelical church community the concept that drums, rattles, and other

sacred paraphanelia [sic] formerly used in animistic worship can be redeemed for use in Christian worship. This position does not enjoy consensus among Native evangelical church leaders.[29]

He further noted that "this report serves to provide the theological and cultural bookends within which the member churches and official workers of the Native American District of the C&MA would operate."[30] Was this effective? Based on a report in 2018 by the US church covering the period 1997 to 2017, probably not. That report noted, "The past twenty-two years are not twenty-two years of operating under indigenous principles. They are twenty-two years of operating under mainly a mission mentality."[31]

Though the Canadian entity had formally separated from the US in 1980, its approach to Indigenous ministry still utilized this same US-framed missiology. But it took only a short time following Smith's statement above for it to become clear that the US and Canadian Indigenous work had diverged, and that the different methods used were at least in part rooted in their approach to culture and faith.

It was finally under the leadership of Ray Aldred, Cree pastor and first Indigenous director of the First Nations Alliance churches in Canada, that a more obvious shift could be seen. Eschewing US cultural conservatism, Aldred sought to create an approach that was not "one size fits all," where decisions about such things were vested instead in local congregations.

Perhaps the most geographically widespread evangelical ministry among Indigenous peoples in Canada and the US is the work of the Pentecostal Assemblies of Canada (PAOC) and its sister, the Assemblies of God (AG).

While churches like the Vancouver Native Pentecostal church have sought to engage the culture and faith conversation in legitimate ways, and new young leaders are emerging who understand the culture and faith conversation very differently, there is still much work to be done. The question of whether a person can be fully Indigenous and fully Christian continues to create real and tangible difficulties.

In describing hurdles to an authentic experience of Christian faith for Indigenous peoples, both denominations lay some of the blame on mainstream North American values. They believe social issues such as suicide, substance abuse, past hurts, and hopelessness are a product of these values. It is difficult to ascertain if the PAOC or AG place any responsibility for the

---

29. Smith, "Boundary Lines," 101.
30. Smith, "Boundary Lines," 102.
31. Haskins, "Journey to Indigenous Church," para. 32.

origins or current expression of these social problems on the church's theology and/or mission praxis.

While there is a small Baptist presence, most Indigenous people aligned with Baptist traditions attend churches that are not specifically Indigenous. Danny Zacharias, Cree New Testament scholar at Acadia Divinity College, notes that there are no specific Indigenous Baptist congregations in the Atlantic region with which he is familiar. Others with whom I have spoken in the preparation of this chapter have affirmed the same. Indigenous Baptist congregations appear scarce.

Where regular meetings for worship exist, they tend to be small gatherings of related family members simply holding to Baptist forms and theology. These assemblies, if pastored at all, are frequently served by missionaries associated with US-based Baptist groups. Many mission organizations, some nearly a century old, are aligned with Baptist theology. In more than a few of these settings, Christianizing and civilizing continues apace, and particularly in northern areas, deep criticism of Indigenous cultures and lifeways persists.

Until relatively recently, one might have assumed the Salvation Army (SA) was ignorant of the connections between colonization and overrepresentation of Indigenous people in society's harsh statistics. We might overlook this were it not that poverty and addiction were and are their stock-in-trade. But, by the latter decades of the twentieth century, indicators of the impact of colonial history were manifold. However, many SA ministries continued to simply enfold Indigenous people into their regular ministry routines, oblivious to the very specific circumstance of Indigenous people and their history.

Within SA worshipping communities, assimilationism was not uncommon. The overriding culture of the SA required conformity: "give up" cultural expressions and forms of any sort, and comport strictly with SA expectations. Indigenous and other peoples were simply absorbed into the SA ethos without thought for their unique cultures. And, whereas Indigenous people in many contexts will now integrate culture and traditions more, some non-Indigenous ministry leaders are still not at all receptive.

In 2017, together with Indigenous Pathways, a wholly Indigenous-led Christian NGO, the Salvation Army struck out on a new path for its ministry with Indigenous people in Canada called Celebration of Culture. Now in its sixth year, the event gathers Indigenous and non-Indigenous people together on a journey of culture and faith that is transformative.

Though it affirms itself as binational, there is no single strategy for Indigenous ministry within the North American Christian Reformed Church (CRC). Its presence among Indigenous people is therefore spotty, its total

Indigenous membership small; much of that in Canada, the result of either the 60's scoop,[32] being schooled in a CRC setting, or through intermarriage. According to some CRC sources, a best guesstimate of the presence of Indigenous people in Canada is likely limited to approximately three hundred persons.

Sources within the CRC note that there appeared to be an intentional decision in later years, particularly in Canada, to avoid the mission approach used in the Southwest US among Navajo and Zuni communities—viz. the Rehoboth Christian School. In the opinion of these sources, such an approach shared similarities in philosophy and methodology with the residential and boarding schools.

At the present time in Canada the CRC operates three urban ministries, two of which are Indigenous led. These Urban Indigenous Ministries are in Winnipeg, Regina, and Edmonton. These ministries appear strong and exhibit good leadership, providing excellent community-based ministry, community development initiatives, and community-based pastoral care. They also provide strong cultural programs and contextualized worship and prayer practices, employing the expertise and knowledge base of traditional Indigenous elders and community leadership. While their founding aspirations to be Indigenous led, self-governing, and self-sustaining are not fully realized, all have majority Indigenous staff, and all are self-governing.

Nondenominationalism

Nondenominational gatherings of the Indigenous church are often small, at times consisting only of related family members. They are generally of two types: charismatic, including fringe groups such as the apostolic and prophetic movements, and Baptists. At times each exhibits a "remnant" theological disposition expressed in withdrawal from or resistance to "the world," including their own people.

It is not at all surprising that members of each of these groups have been heavily influenced by US theological teachings and political attitudes. Many of the iconic figures of American populist, nationalist Christianity figure prominently among the highly esteemed teachers of such groups. A closer examination suggests these are more like movements or conference-focused gatherings than they are regular meetings.

32. Indigenous people were swept up by child welfare systems in large numbers and placed in mostly non-Indigenous homes beginning in the late 1950s and ending somewhere in the late 80s; some suggest it continues today but has simply become more sophisticated.

Conclusion: The Intent of It All?

It seems quite clear that while one cannot truly know what was in someone's thinking a few hundred or even ten years ago, mission to Indigenous peoples in North America, and the Christianity that resulted, was heavily influenced by what the Edinburgh Mission Conference of 1910 formalized as the dynamic duo of civilize and Christianize. To think otherwise is to miss the many markers of assimilationist theology and its attendant missiology in North American Indigenous Christian ministry.

Whatever the Indigenous church should look like today in North America, it should at least be authentically Indigenous as well as authentically Christian. If it is not, it is a pale imitation of something else. What's more, it is far less than an obedient response to the words of the Jerusalem Council in its admonition to each missioner to "place upon you no greater burden." This means it should reflect the context of Indigenous peoples culturally, linguistically, and organizationally—with limited, if any, exceptions. It should not have to comport with or reflect in even a small way the illusory ideals that the church of the West itself was unable to maintain or keep. As Peter noted in Acts 15:10,

> Now then, why do you try to test God by putting on the necks of Gentiles a yoke that neither we nor our ancestors have been able to bear?

When the world's largest energy company of the day, Enron, collapsed, people spoke of greed, corruption, embezzlement, and mismanagement. Given the fact that Ken Lay, CEO and chairman of the board of Enron was also chair of the board of his Methodist church, one would have expected some comment from the Christian church—if only his. The only written word that emerged, however, was a book titled *The Tao of Enron* coauthored by a Christian person.[33] No one in the church appeared willing to named it for what it was—idolatry: specifically, the worship of mammon.

To the casual observer it might appear that when Indigenous Christianity is in discussion, the Western church was, and perhaps still is, more concerned with sweat lodges, prayer ceremonies using smoke, and social dances at powwows than it is with graft, greed, corruption, embezzlement, and, in short, the worship of mammon. It seems then, that the Jerusalem Council's decision two millennia ago is still far from reflecting Peter's words and the church's praxis.

---

33. Seay and Bryan, *Tao of Enron*, 37.

Bibliography

Adas, Michael. *Dominance by Design: Technological Imperatives and America's Civilizing Mission.* Cambridge, MA: Belknap, 2006.

Aldred, Ray. "An Alternative Starting Place for a Cree Theology." ThD diss., University of Toronto, 2019.

Anderson, William H. U., and Charles Muskego, eds. *Indigenous People and the Christian Faith: A New Way Forward.* Series in Philosophy of Religion. Wilmington: Vernon, 2019.

Barrett, David, ed. *World Christian Encyclopedia.* Oxford: Oxford University Press, 1982.

Boer, Gregory. "Images of Depression: A Theoretical Study of Depression and Melancholia as Expressions of an Absence of Imagining and an Unrequited Unconscious Need for Transformation." PhD diss., Pacifica Graduate Institute, 2008.

Brett, Mark G., and H. Daniel Zacharias. "To Serve Her and Conform to Her: An Intercultural Reading of Gen 2:15." In *A Pact of Love with Criticism, A Pact of Blood with the World: Towards Geopolitical Biblical Criticism; Essays in Honor of Fernando F. Segovia*, edited by Amy Lindeman Allen et al., x–xx. Atlanta: SBL, forthcoming.

Davis, Wade. "The Unraveling of America." *Rolling Stone*, Aug. 6, 2020. https://www.rollingstone.com/politics/political-commentary/covid-19-end-of-american-era-wade-davis-1038206/.

Dickason, Olive Patricia, and William Newbigging. *Indigenous Peoples within Canada: A Concise History.* 4th ed. Toronto: Oxford University Press, 2019.

Dunn, James D. G., ed. *Jews and Christians: The Parting of the Ways, A.D. 70 to 135; The Second Durham-Tübingen Research Symposium on Earliest Christianity and Judaism (Durham, September, 1989).* WUNT 66. Tübingen: Mohr Siebeck, 1992.

Dvornik, Francis. *The Ecumenical Councils.* Vol. 82 of *The Twentieth Century Encyclopedia of Catholicism.* N.p.: Hawthorn, 1961. https://books.google.ca/books?id=oz4DxwEACAAJ.

Evarts, Jeremiah. *Cherokee Removal: The William Penn Essays and Other Writings.* Edited by and Francis Paul Prucha. Knoxville: University of Tennessee Press, 1981.

Fanning, Don. "The Dark Age Church Period of Barbarian Invasions." Liberty University, 2009. From History and Survey of Missions course. http://digitalcommons.liberty.edu/cgm_hist/3.

Fletcher, R. A. *The Barbarian Conversion: From Paganism to Christianity.* New York: Holt, 1998.

Francis, Mark. "The 'Civilizing' of Indigenous People in Nineteenth Century Canada." *Journal of World History* 9 (1998) 51–87. https://www.jstor.org/stable/20078713.

Haskins, Doug. "The Journey to an Indigenous Church: The History of the Christian and Missionary Alliance Work with Native Americans." AWF, May 28, 2018. https://awf.world/repository/the-journey-to-an-indigenous-church-the-history-of-the-alliance-work-with-native-americans/.

LeBlanc, Terry. "Mi'kmaq and French/Jesuit Understandings of the Spiritual and Spirituality: Implications for Faith." PhD diss., Asbury Theological Seminary, 2012.

LeBlanc, Terry, et al. "A Majority Report." In *Edinburgh 2010: Mission Today and Tomorrow*, edited by Kirsteen Kim and Andrew Anderson, 345–50. Regnum Edinburgh Centenary. Oxford: Regnum, 2011.

Le Clercq, Chrestien, and William F. Ganong. *New Relation of Gaspesia: With the Customs and Religion of the Gaspesian Indians*. Publications of the Champlain Society. Toronto: Champlain Society, 1910.

Seay, Chris, with Chris Bryan. *The Tao of Enron: Spiritual Lessons from a Fortune 500 Fallout*. Colorado Springs: NavPress, 2002.

Smith, Craig S. "Boundary Lines: Christ, Indigenous Worship, and Native American Culture." *Journal of the North American Institute for Indigenous Theological Studies* 1 (2003) 101–39.

Stanley, Brian. *The World Missionary Conference, Edinburgh 1910*. Studies in the History of Christian Missions. Grand Rapids: Eerdmans, 2009.

Stanley, George F. G. "The First Indian 'Reserves' in Canada." *Revue d'histoire de l'Amerique Francaise* 4 (1950) 178–210.

Stern, Steve J. *Peru's Indian Peoples and the Challenge of Spanish Conquest: Huamanga to 1640*. Madison: University of Wisconsin Press, 1993.

Thwaites, Reuben Gold, ed. *The Jesuit Relations and Allied Documents: Travels and Explorations of the Jesuit Missionaries in New France, 1610–1791; The Original French, Latin, and Italian Texts, with English Translations and Notes; Illustrated by Portraits, Maps, and Facsimiles*. 73 vols. Cleveland: Burrows, 1896.

Twiss, Richard. *One Church, Many Tribes: Following Jesus the Way God Made You*. Ventura, CA: Regal, 2000.

United Church of Canada/L'Église Unie du Canada. *The Manual, 2023*. Toronto: United Church, 2023.

Webster, D. "The Achievement and the Technique of Missions in the Middle Ages." Mission. *Churchman* 59 (1945) 170–79. https://biblicalstudies.org.uk/pdf/churchman/059-04_170.pdf.

Woodley, Randy. "Early Dialogue in the Community of Creation." In *Buffalo Shout, Salmon Cry: Conversations on Creation, Land Justice, and Life Together*, edited by Steve Heinrichs, 92–108. Harrisonburg, VA: Herald, 2013.

———. *Shalom and the Community of Creation: An Indigenous Vision*. Prophetic Christianity. Grand Rapids: Eerdmans, 2012.

Chapter 2

Chosen Nations

Christianity and the Founding Legends of Canada and the United States

JOHN G. STACKHOUSE JR.

THE FOURTH OF JULY is a party. A big party. Every year. Independence Day, as it is officially known, commemorates the Declaration of Independence. The declaration was ratified by the Second Continental Congress on July 4, 1776, and established the United States of America as a new nation separate from Great Britain—and, perforce, the other British colonies in North America, some of which became Canada a century later. Americans—as individuals, as families, as communities, even as (sometimes especially as) churches—celebrate the Fourth of July with patriotic fervor and festivities great and small.

Three days earlier in the calendar, on July 1, Canada Day is celebrated also with a party. Every year. Just not a *big* party. Canada Day commemorates the founding of Canada as a country independent of Great Britain constituted by the four original colonies—east to west: Nova Scotia, New Brunswick, Quebec, and Ontario—by an act of the British Parliament on July 1, 1867. Nowadays, yes, there is generally a public concert held in the square before the Parliament Buildings in Ottawa, attended by thousands wearing red and white and waving red-and-white flags. Other municipalities might host a small parade and later shoot off some fireworks over the ocean, lake, or river—as most Canadian towns of any size are on an ocean, lake, or river. And families generally gather for a picnic or a backyard barbecue (what those in the southern United States will recognize as actually *grilling*).

So on Canada Day there is a party too. But not a big party. This chapter explains the difference in the celebration of the two holidays—and why it matters every day, not just once a year, in terms of the very different experiences of nationalism, diversity, church-state relations, and even foreign policy between the two countries. It also explores how Christianity is, and isn't, bound up with these countries' nativity stories.

America: A City on a Hill

It was early 1961. In less than a fortnight, John F. Kennedy would leave his office as senator from the state of Massachusetts and become the thirty-fifth president of the United States of America.

In a speech to the Joint Convention of the General Court of the Commonwealth of Massachusetts, in the Boston statehouse, Kennedy made clear that while he was going to Washington, DC, he would not be leaving his home state of Massachusetts:

> And so it is that I carry with me from this state to that high and lonely office to which I now succeed more than fond memories of firm friendships. The enduring qualities of Massachusetts—the common threads woven by the Pilgrim and the Puritan, the fisherman and the farmer, the Yankee and the immigrant—will not be and could not be forgotten in this nation's executive mansion.
>
> They are an indelible part of my life, my convictions, my view of the past, and my hopes for the future.

Kennedy then drew explicitly on his state's Puritan heritage as he referred to a sermon now widely identified as germinal to American identity, John Winthrop's address to the colonists about to found the Massachusetts Bay Colony in 1630. Known as the "Model of Christian Charity" sermon, it has become better known for its evocation of a key gospel metaphor as the "City on a Hill" sermon. And Kennedy took it for his own:

> I have been guided by the standard John Winthrop set before his shipmates on the flagship *Arbella* three hundred and thirty-one years ago, as they, too, faced the task of building a new government on a perilous frontier.
>
> "We must always consider," he said, "that we shall be as a city upon a hill—the eyes of all people are upon us."
>
> Today the eyes of all people are truly upon us—and our governments, in every branch, at every level, national, state and local, must be as a city upon a hill—constructed and inhabited by men aware of their great trust and their great responsibilities.[1]

---

1. Kennedy, "City upon a Hill," paras. 9–10. The "city on a hill" motif has become so commonplace in American culture that it has shown in an impressive survey of American urban architecture (Krieger, *City on a Hill*) to a TV series and a set of dystopian novels.

As was often the case in his short presidential career, Kennedy spoke on behalf of all Americans. For all Americans, not just native New Englanders, inherited the burden placed upon the shoulders of Massachusetts Bay those several centuries ago. Also like Kennedy, however, all Americans have chosen to select some parts of his sermon for faithful observance while letting others lie ignored in the deeps of American history.

Winthrop's sermon, especially when read in abridged form (as it usually is), sounds much more Deuteronomic than it does evangelical. Despite the reference to the Sermon on the Mount's "city on a hill" image, Winthrop sounds far more like Moses than like Jesus. Indeed, he concludes his exhortation with explicit reference to Deut 30: "Beloved, there is now set before us life and death, good and evil." The covenant of God will either be honored to our blessing or disobeyed to our destruction. Thus this new American colony—and eventually America itself—was viewed to be the new Israel taking possession of a new land under the providence of God for the welfare of all.[2]

This new venture, furthermore, would shine like a model of charity to the globe, and especially (implicitly) to the Old World, a paragon of true righteousness as a body politic. "He shall make us a praise and glory that men shall say of succeeding plantations, 'May the Lord make it like that of New England.'"[3]

Thus America's mission was given by God to be the Great Alternative, the Instructive Exception, the Best Nation in the World. And the Founding Fathers carried this messianic vision forward a century later into the constitutive documents of the new country, from the Declaration of Independence to, indeed, the Constitution of the United States.

The original vision, to be sure, was refracted greatly through the ideological lens of Enlightenment Deism and the pressing political need for unity among the disparate thirteen colonies, many of which would not resonate with Puritan pieties. Furthermore, despite some of the myths about the Founding Fathers as uniformly pious churchmen, while some of them were indeed observant, orthodox believers, many were not, including George

---

2. Winthrop, "Model of Christian Charity," 306. An excellent resource on this speech is Washington University in St. Louis's City on a Hill Archive, accessible at https://sites.wustl.edu/americanexceptionalism/. It should be noted that missionary work among the "heathen" as a motive for colonization featured from time to time in charters and other documents relevant to the American colonies, just as it did in Canada, and among both French and English ventures—such as the founding of Montreal itself as a mission station in 1639. Evangelism of Native peoples so quickly became embroiled, however, in political matters of survival, expansion, and defense that missionary work was undertaken only fitfully and often in modes of deep moral ambiguity, if not actual disaster, as in the Canadian residential schools of the nineteenth and twentieth centuries.

3. Winthrop, "Model of Christian Charity," 307.

Washington and Thomas Jefferson. So the rhetoric of the revolution was far more positively aspirational and more humanistically confident than was Winthrop's sermon. For Winthrop dwelt more heavily on the warning rather than the promise, the fear of disobedience and the withdrawal of God's favor rather than the delight in whatever good might come of the adventure.

Americans would have to wait a long time for a president to address the country this way: Abraham Lincoln's second inaugural address comes darkly to mind.[4] And when a much later American president spoke to the country in similar accents, although with precious little explicit religious content, Jimmy Carter was soon soundly defeated by the much sunnier Ronald Reagan.[5] The Constitution itself begins with high aspirations indeed: "We the People of the United States, in Order to form a more perfect Union, establish Justice, insure domestic Tranquility, provide for the common defence, promote the general Welfare, and secure the Blessings of Liberty to ourselves and our Posterity, do ordain and establish this Constitution for the United States of America."[6]

---

4. Fully half of Lincoln's famously short speech is in this mode: "Both [North and South] read the same Bible and pray to the same God and each invokes His aid against the other. It may seem strange that any men should dare to ask a just God's assistance in wringing their bread from the sweat of other men's faces but let us judge not that we be not judged. The prayers of both could not be answered—that of neither has been answered fully. The Almighty has His own purposes. 'Woe unto the world because of offenses for it must needs be that offenses come but woe to that man by whom the offense cometh.' If we shall suppose that American slavery is one of those offenses which in the providence of God must needs come but which having continued through His appointed time He now wills to remove and that He gives to both North and South this terrible war as the woe due to those by whom the offense came shall we discern therein any departure from those divine attributes which the believers in a living God always ascribe to Him. Fondly do we hope—fervently do we pray—that this mighty scourge of war may speedily pass away. Yet, if God wills that it continue until all the wealth piled by the bondsman's two hundred and fifty years of unrequited toil shall be sunk and until every drop of blood drawn with the lash shall be paid by another drawn with the sword as was said three thousand years ago so still it must be said 'the judgments of the Lord are true and righteous altogether.' . . . With malice toward none with charity for all with firmness in the right as God gives us to see the right let us strive on to finish the work we are in to bind up the nation's wounds, to care for him who shall have borne the battle and for his widow and his orphan—to do all which may achieve and cherish a just and lasting peace among ourselves and with all nations" (Lincoln, "Lincoln's Second Inaugural Address").

5. I have in mind Carter's infamous "malaise" speech of July 15, 1979 (Carter, "Crisis of Confidence").

6. The text is from a transcription of the Constitution as it was inscribed by Jacob Shallus on parchment (the document on display in the Rotunda at the National Archives Museum). The spelling and punctuation reflect the original: https://www.archives.gov/founding-docs/constitution-transcript.

The secularization of Winthrop's prophetic vision proceeded apace so that by the nineteenth century God's commission to New Englanders to set up a model society had become a vaguely but definitely divine charge to Americans to take over the entire continent. It was now America's manifest destiny to drive the British and Spanish, the remnants of the Old World, off North America once and for all, leaving Americans alone in charge of the New World.

A second key assumption of Winthrop's was also abandoned in the new republic. Winthrop makes very clear that God Almighty has ordained that some be rich and the rest be poor, "some high and eminent in power and dignity; others mean and in subjection."[7] American society has not yet opened up fully to just any enterprising person. The powerful continue to preserve their prerogatives, and prejudice continues to constrain anyone who is not White, male, and propertied, as it did at the founding of the country. But the principle of social mobility and the expectation of "doing better" than one's parents became an integral part of the American dream in the nineteenth century—"Anyone can be president." The actual freedom to do so has indeed extended further and further to this day. Not for some time have Americans echoed Winthrop's sense of economic vocations assigned by God for social stability and mutual benefit. They tend instead to invoke the principle that "God helps those who help themselves," a saying often attributed to Scripture but traceable in fact back through Benjamin Franklin and Algernon Sidney to Greek proverbs as old as Aesop's tales.

Finally, and related to this "self-made man" motif, another of Winthrop's key concerns was largely dropped. Lawyer and Puritan as Winthrop was, his sermon frequently reads like a contract—he uses the biblical word *covenant*—with multiple numbered points outlining in detail exactly what Winthrop believed God was saying and demanding of his people. What God was particularly demanding, Winthrop made almost exhaustively clear, was that these Christians love each other deeply, strongly, and practically. Winthrop can sound positively socialist, even Communist, at times in his references to the self-giving and mutual support of New Testament churches.

"We must be willing to abridge ourselves of our superfluities, for the supply of others' necessities."[8] (Marx himself popularized the slogan "From each according to his ability, to each according to his needs." Marx had gone to Sunday school until his teens and evidently learned a few things.) In great detail Winthrop sets out a biblical apologia for spiritual unity that would be shine out in the practical sharing of financial as well as spiritual resources.

7. Winthrop, "Model of Christian Charity," 306.
8. Winthrop, "Model of Christian Charity," 304.

> We must delight in each other; make others' conditions our own; rejoice together, mourn together, labor and suffer together, always having before our eyes our commission and community in the work, as members of the same body.[9]

It hardly needs to be said that American culture has largely chosen a different political, economic, and social path—one more consonant with Milton Friedman's values than John Winthrop's—as the United States notoriously provides a smaller and weaker social safety net than virtually any other developed country. The declaration's individualistic accent upon "life, liberty, and the pursuit of happiness" unmoored from biblical texts and norms, and the later "rugged individualism" so typical of American popular culture, are flatly contradictory to the Christian communitarianism of Winthrop's address.

Thus America's origins were decisively stamped in 1630.[10] But then they were crucially restamped in 1776, so that only some of the Puritan ethos remained. By the time John F. Kennedy was drawing on that heritage, it had become something that John F. Kennedy—nobody's idea of a Puritan—could cheerfully adopt as a symbol of his presidency. Later, of course, his widow would confirm that the "city on a hill" was not so much a Christian community as . . . the kingdom of Camelot, a romantic, resplendent vision more in keeping with a Washingtonian or Jeffersonian vision of American life than the sober and pious realism of John Winthrop and his band.

Canada: A Quietly Astonishing Arrangement

Canadians don't get worked up over Canada Day. The French are stirred whenever "La Marseillaise" is played. The Brits stand up anytime they hear "God Save the King." Nobody outdoes the Americans for red-white-and-blue extravagance on the Fourth of July. And Aussies get excited every time someone opens a fridge. But Canadians?

They typically throw on a red-and-white T-shirt, and grill some food, and remember hockey gold medals, and maybe see what's on TV from Parliament Hill. No big deal, though. Nice to have a summer day off.

Canadians could, however, celebrate confederation as a political miracle.

In 1867, two communities decided to form a country together. Yes, they had each mistreated Native peoples, and 150 years later, Canadians

---

9. Winthrop, "Model of Christian Charity," 306.
10. McKenzie, *First Thanksgiving*, critically explores another of America's myths of origin.

generally agree that they have a lot left to do on that account. Yes, Canadians would be hard on immigrants from countries other than Britain and France, generally isolating them on vast prairies or in urban enclaves. And, yes, they would mistrust and insult each other, almost to the breaking point. After a century and a half, however, Canada remains. And that is, historically speaking, amazing.

Why? By 1867, the year of the confederation of four eastern British colonies that would soon to be joined by provinces "from sea to sea," English people and French people had spent a thousand years trying to conquer or exterminate each other. And the defeat of the insatiable French emperor Napoleon at Waterloo by the duke of Wellington and his Prussian allies was within the living memory of many Canadians at the time of confederation.

Yet here was John A. Macdonald, the Scottish immigrant from Ontario joining hands and fortunes with Quebecer George-Étienne Cartier (definitely not a Scottish immigrant) to work with the leaders of Nova Scotia and New Brunswick—provinces with their own troubled histories of French-English relations (not least the British expulsion of Francophone Acadians in the mid-eighteenth century)—to form a new country.

More astounding still was the fact that confederation also brought together Protestant and Catholic Christians who for half a millennium had been trying to convert or excommunicate each other all over Europe and out into the New World. The rupture of the sixteenth-century Reformation had provoked inquisitions, burnings, and wars for decades afterward.

Yet on July 1, 1867, a new country was born that not only happened to include English and French, and Protestants and Catholics, but whose constitution explicitly allowed for the cultural differences between them at the time. In fact, the British North America Act, Canada's constitution until a new, Canadian-made one was adopted in 1982, made breathtaking accommodations in the crucial zone of education. Imagine granting liberty to your neighbors to school their children in ideas you are convinced are not only entirely wrong, but also harmful to the eternal welfare of those children. That's what the Fathers of Confederation were willing to grant each other.

It's not as if Canada has been a multicultural and interreligious Happy Valley since then. One recalls the strange religious views of Louis Riel that prompted him to prophethood—and martyrdom—in Manitoba rebellions; the conscientious objection to wartime conscription of the Doukhobors on the prairies that resulted in harsh punishments of these eccentric Orthodox believers; and the intemperance of Jehovah's Witnesses on the radio in the 1930s that prompted the Canadian Radio and Television Commission to clamp down on religious broadcasting for half a century. For decades after confederation, Roman Catholic priests worked with local jurists and police officers to persecute Protestant missionaries in towns throughout Quebec with jail and sometimes worse, while Protestant Orangemen held loud and sometimes violent parades in Ontario and the Maritimes to proclaim the supremacy of their version of Christianity.

It's certainly not as if religion didn't matter back at the time of confederation. It mattered a great deal. Indeed, it was an integral part of English-French cultural conflict, and it was the political genius of Macdonald, Cartier, and the other Fathers of Confederation to sense their common need for union and to somehow pull it off.

"Getting along," one must admit, is not the stuff of legend. It doesn't prompt the fevered composition of patriotic poetry or jingoistic jingles. But for English and French, Protestant and Catholic, to even think about getting along together in the 1860s, and to manage to keep doing so for another century and a half, deserves more admiration than Canadians themselves typically afford it. And, in these fractious times when everyone seems determined to force his or her views on everything from climate change to sex to taxation to race down everyone else's throat, confederation is all the more worth understanding and, indeed, celebrating.

Why, however, did these Canadians form a new country in 1867? Was there some sort of religious revival that charitably blurred the lines between Catholics and Protestants? Some sort of overarching political ideology that appealed to the hearts of English and French alike? Not exactly.

The birth of the Canadian state was, in crude terms, basically a business deal. At best, it was a kind of social compact. Canada was not conceived as a sacred project, a light to the nations. There was no cry of "Liberté! Egalité! Fraternité!" Nor was there any sense of divine vocation to demonstrate righteousness to the rest of the world, nor to take a stand for liberty against an ostensible tyrant "appealing to the Supreme Judge of the world for the rectitude of our intentions."[11] Instead, some sensible people took a few meetings to form a country that could accomplish three pressing tasks:

1. To let Britain off the colonial hook. Running a colony is expensive, and with fish and furs no longer paying the bills, especially as the long-standing fashion in warm hats had changed in Europe to the ruin of the fur trade, Britain was glad to be rid of its huge North American colonial investment.

2. To keep out the predatory and unruly Americans. Americans had invaded Canada twice within the previous century: in 1775—in an attack on Quebec under, of all people, Benedict Arnold—and in 1812,

---

11. Declaration of Independence. See https://www.archives.gov/founding-docs/declaration-transcript.

during which Canadians took out a little vengeance on their American cousins, burning down the White House. Then the Americans turned their considerable energies to invading each other, catastrophically, in a Civil War (1861–65) for which Canadians had a front-row seat. And shortly thereafter, in the very year of confederation, Senator Charles Sumner was defending the purchase of Alaska from the Russians—for the huge sum of $7.2 million the Americans were getting rock and ice and trees, since no one yet knew about gold or salmon—as part of a pincer movement prompted by America's manifest destiny to drive the British into the Atlantic once and for all.[12]

(Canadians' traditional anti-Americanism, it thus should be noted, is not an artifact of the United States' global power since World War II, but goes back to the very founding of the country. It isn't paranoia if they really are out to get you.)

3. To endure another winter—and ultimately to find a way to make a living in a vast, resource-full, cold, and forbidding land. The Fathers of Confederation aimed higher than Margaret Atwood's famous summary of Canadian literary culture as *Survival*, but not a lot higher. Canada was formed simply to help Canadians live as best they could.

It must be noted, to be sure, that the motto of the country, *A mari usque ad mare*, came from Ps 72 ("He shall have dominion from sea to sea"). And in a country as well churched as Canada was—with the vast majority attending church regularly, as Canadians would for about another century—Christianity was the accepted outlook for all that was said and done in Canada. One common term for Canada was, indeed, "His Dominion."[13] But what was said and done in the British North America Act (1867) was entirely secular. God isn't mentioned, nor is the Bible. Christian doctrine, clergy, or institutions don't figure in it at all. The formation of the new country of Canada was about getting about the business of life as safely and prosperously as possible.

Such basic concerns, of course, were entirely in keeping with Christianity, so Christians—who, again, made up the vast majority of Canadians at the time—could cheerfully endorse them. So could, of course, many other people of many other convictions, hence the attractiveness of Canada as an immigration destination for people from around the world.

---

12. The manifest destiny to rid the continent of the British monarchy is mentioned in Library of Congress, "Alaska Purchase."
13. Clifford, "His Dominion."

The point here, especially in comparison with the United States, is that Canada from its origin has had no holy vocation, no messianic purpose, no obligation to defend the faith or to make the world safe for any particular ideology or religion.[14] Canada, in sum, has been a secular enterprise. As such, religious people of many sorts can participate in it, as can people of nonreligious outlooks as well. And everybody, one might suggest, should be open to a little wonder each July 1 that Canada is still here.

Flags, Fervor, and Faithfulness

What, then, about the lasting implications of these origin legends? How is Christianity involved when national identity, let alone patriotism, is at issue?

Flags in churches. Let's start there.

Growing up as I did in a northern Ontario assembly of the small Anglo-Irish group known as the Christian (or Plymouth) Brethren, I saw no flags in my church. In fact, I saw no images or symbols of any kind. "Let the LORD be magnified" (Ps 35:27) was emblazoned on the back wall of the stage in blond wood letters against medium-brown wood paneling (it was the mid-1960s and the church was new). That was the entire graphic package to focus the eyes and hearts of believers in our Bible-centered congregation.

Visiting American relatives, I occasionally noticed a white flag with a navy upper-left quadrant featuring a red Latin cross. I asked about it and was told that it was "the Christian flag." That puzzled me. *We* were Christians too. Why didn't *we* have that flag? Why didn't *every* church?

I also noticed, however, that the American churches featured American flags, usually opposite the Christian one. As I had time to ponder symbols during boring sermons, I wondered whether this meant that the congregation had a dual allegiance, even a competing allegiance, to God and country. Or did the Christian flag trump the American flag, the way a national flag might trump a provincial one? Did my American cousins see a union between the two such that allegiance to God or allegiance to America simply implied allegiance to the other?

Recent worship with an Anglican congregation here in Maritime Canada has presented an array of flags in a lovely Gothic church: Canada, New Brunswick, the Anglican Church of Canada—and several regimental

---

14. One might note here that Quebec is the exception to this rule. It has traditionally viewed itself as the redoubt of French culture in an English North American sea, a culture so deeply shaped by Roman Catholicism that even the more recent highly secular governments of Quebec have defended maintaining a crucifix in the very National Assembly as a symbol of Québécois identity. Taking Canada itself as an enterprise, however, Quebecers would see things largely as do other Canadians.

flags, which reinforce the stained glass and brass-plate memorials to war dead. Princess Anne was in our church two weeks ago to commemorate an anniversary of a local military unit of which she is patron. Rigorous separation of church and state? Not exactly.

Given even this brief account of national origins, one will appreciate why the younger me was confused about those flags. One will also appreciate why the confusion has lingered. What, precisely, is the relationship between the kingdom of God and Canada or the United States of America? What ought it to be?

This isn't the place for a full-orbed philosophy of Christian citizenship. But we can make a start at outlining some basic principles that might help Christians in conducting ourselves during an election, or in making the right demands regarding the public education of our children, or in protecting the speech of Christians that may be unwelcome to some.

The following discussion will not make any important distinction between *patriotism* and *nationalism*. Both words mean more than one thing, and their semantic fields overlap considerably. So for now we will mean by either term simply *a strong loyalty to one's country*.

Put that way, the Bible has no problem with identifying with and advancing the interests of one's nation. Paul says that "in Christ there is neither Jew nor Greek" (Gal 5:28), of course, but that has to do with our unity in the church universal, the glorious fact that the economy of salvation is open to all regardless of ethnicity. The Revelation given to John sings us a counterpoint to that theme, echoing Old Testament apocalyptic, as it depicts the world's various peoples streaming in to the joint worship of the Lamb *without turning into generic, indistinguishable humans*. Quite the contrary: their representatives (their "kings") bring the best they have in praise to the God of all peoples (Rev 21:24).

The implications of God's love of diversity deserve careful tracing out in our time and place: for immigration policy; for diversity, equity, and inclusion practices; and for the tension between the benefits, even the requirements, of social unity and the desiderata of multicultural distinctiveness. In sum, however, the Bible valorizes *both* ethnic identity *and* cooperative diversity.

Another guideline comes from Jewish exile in Babylon. In a shocking paradox, the Jews are told by God to seek the welfare of the city to which God has sent them: Babylon the Great (Jer 29:7). For as their (immediate) living was inextricably connected with the Babylonians', mutual interest should be pursued. One of the Bible's great spiritual heroes, Daniel himself, served as a high governmental advisor to advance Babylonian interests. And this is the city that will live on symbolically to the end of the Bible as the great enemy of the people of God! In short, if the people of God can abide in Babylon, they can certainly abide even in Toronto or in New York, in Ottawa or in Washington, DC.

One must note, however, that Jeremiah's prophecy is time limited. Just a few verses later he says that in just a few decades Judah will be restored to their promised land. It's not as if the people of God are to be fully and forever allied and aligned with Babylon. Certainly not. And the same applies to Christians in North America.

In our modern North American situation, therefore (and in similar situations in the Anglosphere and beyond), we can and should identify *temporarily*, *penultimately*, and *secondarily* with our nations—whether political states or ethnic groups. As Augustine warned us through *The City of God*, however, we must be careful always to subordinate the patriotism we might feel toward our particular *polis* or *ethnē* to our *permanent, ultimate, and primary* identity as Christians, citizens of the kingdom of God.

Church and state relations? Nothing in the Bible says much in detail about how they are to get along optimally in any particular culture. Christians therefore have plausibly differed as to how secular and spiritual authorities should cooperate or separate. And the history of Christianity indicates, I suggest, that no one model is justified as inherently superior, in all times and places, to all the others. Americans typically maintain a formal separation of church and state, even as (since the 1950s, at least) they have characterized themselves as "under God" (so the Pledge of Allegiance) and are a people who declare "in God we trust." Canadian society since the 1960s has rapidly secularized in most respects, even as Canadians have also in latter days added a bit of theistic language to their official statements ("God" appears in the preamble of the constitution of 1982 and the recent phrase "God keep our land" adds theistic petition to the English version of the national anthem, whose French version has always mentioned God). Paradoxes and outright inconsistencies thus continue in both countries when it comes to the narrower questions of church and state and the larger interactions of religion and society.

What the Bible makes clear, however, is that *the church is not the nation nor the state*; that *neither the nation nor the state is the church*; and that *the prior allegiance for the Christian must be to the church—above nation or state or even family*. "Jesus is Lord" cuts away any other rival for sovereignty for the Christian. "We must obey God rather than humans" (Acts 5:29 author's translation) is an early Christian declaration, and faithful Christians need to hear it afresh in every generation, particularly in those situations in which divine and human interests seem temptingly aligned.

Indeed, Christians must be most on our guard when the world seems to be gladly on the side of the gospel. In any given circumstance we may encounter a temporary alliance that can advance God's purposes, as the Jews briefly found in Babylon. But the Bible hammers home again and again the brutal fact that the world typically and constantly is disordered and disrespectful toward God's values, no matter how benign it may look and sound. Christians therefore should be looking for trouble so as not to be surprised or co-opted by it.

Christians in Canada would do well, therefore, to affirm the key virtues of Canadian Confederation:

- Realism and pragmatism
- Tolerance and accommodation
- Compromise and cooperation

These virtues are under heavy pressure in Canada today. But they are true to Canada's original identity and purpose, and they deserve championing by Christians, along with all other Canadians, in perpetuity.

As for American messianism, that certainly is another question. Those Canadian Confederation virtues can, after all, be applied directly to any other country. What makes Canada unusual relative to America—and to other countries whose national holidays seem more spirited than Canada Day—is that Canadians have *no superior values* that trump these.

What, then, about the American dream? What about the American way? What about that divine call to exemplary sanctity, and that more expansive destiny to make the world safe for democracy, freedom, and other good things?

It is easy, even reflexive, for a Canadian to snort at what can so easily appear to be hubris. Certainly the American record of self-righteous self-seeking should humble any but the most impervious booster.

Still, the historical record shows America performing great good in the world, sometimes right alongside self-serving machinations and the outright oppression of weaker countries—not to mention America's domestic stains of usurping Native peoples' patrimony and despising African Americans' freedom and dignity. Yes, the Trail of Tears and Jim Crow and Japanese internment camps and so much more count damningly against any American jingoism—or should, and especially in the teeth of any delusional nostalgia about returning America to some former golden age. Still, still, still: the Marshall Plan. American foreign missions. Interventions in Korea, Rwanda, the Balkans, and other places in which the tolls of misery and death would otherwise have been so much higher.

It is not for a mere historian, let alone a foreigner, to pronounce upon the divine call of America. We might conclude, therefore, by observing that the call of God on almost everyone in Scripture—from Adam and Eve to Noah and his wife, from Abraham and Sarah to Moses, Aaron, and Miriam, from Daniel to Jeremiah, and from Mary and Jesus to Peter and Paul—was to obedience and self-sacrifice in the cause of the greater good. These individuals were to seek first the kingdom of God even at the cost of a cross.

Any call other than that is *not* from God, for nations as for individuals. And Americans must therefore be wary of any call other than that, especially in an election year. (And every second year is, indeed, an election year.) But if the United States of America will carry on a special mission on *those* terms, however fitfully they can, then, yes: God bless America.

Bibliography

Atwood, Margaret. *Survival: A Thematic Guide to Canadian Literature*. Toronto: Anansi, 1972.

Carter, Jimmy. "Crisis of Confidence." *PBS*, July 15, 1979. https://www.pbs.org/wgbh/americanexperience/features/carter-crisis/.

Clifford, N. K. "His Dominion: A Vision in Crisis." *RevScRel* 2 (Spring 1973) 315–26. https://doi.org/10.1177/000842987300200404.

Creighton, Donald. *The Road to Confederation: The Emergence of Canada, 1863–1867*. Oxford: Oxford University Press, 1964.

Kennedy, John F. "The City upon a Hill Speech." JFK Library, Jan. 9, 1961. https://www.jfklibrary.org/learn/about-jfk/historic-speeches/the-city-upon-a-hill-speech.

Krieger, Alex. *City on a Hill: Urban Idealism in America from the Puritans to the Present*. Cambridge, MA: Harvard University Press, 2019.

Library of Congress. "The Alaska Purchase." Library of Congress, 2000. https://www.loc.gov/collections/meeting-of-frontiers/articles-and-essays/alaska/the-alaska-purchase/.

Lincoln, Abraham. "Lincoln's Second Inaugural Address." NPS, Mar. 4, 1865. https://www.nps.gov/linc/learn/historyculture/lincoln-second-inaugural.htm.

McKenzie, Robert Tracy. *The First Thanksgiving: What the Real Story Tells Us about Loving God and Learning from History*. Downers Grove, IL: IVP Academic, 2013.

Moore, Christopher. *1867: How the Fathers Made a Deal*. Toronto: McLelland & Stewart, 1997.

Noll, Mark A., et al. *The Search for Christian America*. Rev. ed. Colorado Springs: Helmers & Howard, 1989.

Rogers, Daniel T. *As a City on a Hill: The Story of America's Most Famous Lay Sermon*. Princeton, NJ: Princeton University Press, 2018.

Van Engen, Abram C. *City on a Hill: A History of American Exceptionalism*. New Haven, CT: Yale University Press, 2020.

Winthrop, John. "A Model of Christian Charity." *Early Colonial Literature, 1607–1675*, edited by Edmund Clarence Stedman and Ellen Mackay Hutchinson, 304–7. Vol. 1 of *A Library of American Literature*. New York: Webster, 1892.

Chapter 3

Heavenly Retreat

The Haven of Slave Religion

VINCE BANTU

Black Customs as Liturgies of Resistance

AFRICANS WHO WERE BROUGHT to the Western Hemisphere in slavery developed a liturgical traditional that served as a mechanism of worship, liberation, and identity formation. The Negro spirituals are the foundation of every modern form of music that has emerged in the US and, through globalization, spread throughout the world. The Negro spirituals were musical compositions that drew upon African traditions—including repetitive lyrics, percussive accompaniment, natural imagery, and call-and-response—expressed through a Christian worldview. Enslaved Africans would sing spirituals while working fields and during worship on Sunday morning. These songs were powerful expressions of hope and a call to justice. The spirituals themselves were a haven for Africans undergoing slavery. Despite the Christian identity of slave masters, Christianity and the person of Jesus were a source of hope for enslaved Africans:

> Oh, you got Jesus, hold him fast
> One more river to cross
> Oh, better love was never told
> One more river to cross
> 'Tis sweeter than honeycomb
> One more river to cross
> One more river to cross
> I pray, good Lord, shall I be one?
> One more river to cross

Africans in America would admonish one another to "hold fast" to Jesus. Jesus represented hope and identity for enslaved Africans. Spirituals also served as prophetic voices of radicalism, calling for an end to the system of slavery:

> No more auction block for me
> No more, no more
> No more auction block for me
> Many thousand gone

Indeed, spirituals often served as organizing mechanisms for enslaved Africans to plan escapes from slavery.

Black Christianity and Rebellion

A poignant example of early African American Christianity serving as a source of empowerment was the Stono Rebellion of 1739. The largest slave revolt in the Southern colonies, a group of around sixty enslaved Africans killed over twenty White captors in attempt to reach Spanish-controlled Florida. The freedom fighters were defeated by local White militia. One of the most fascinating aspects of this rebellion was that it was initiated by African Christians from the kingdom of Kongo (Angola):

> Amongst the Negroe Slaves there are a people brought from the Kingdom of Angola in Africa, many of these speak Portugueze (which Language is as near Spanish as Scotch is to English), by reason that the Portugueze have considerable Settlement, and the Jesuits have a Mission and School in that Kingdom and many Thousands of the Negroes there profess the Roman Catholic Religion.[1]

Founded in the late fourteenth century, the kingdom of the Kongo freely adopted Christianity as its imperial religion in 1491. Portuguese missionaries and slave traders made contact with Kongolese leaders, and the two empires established trade relations, including slavery. However, the Portuguese began exceeding the agreed-upon method and quantity of slaves:

> Each day the traders are kidnapping our people—children of this country, sons of our nobles and vassals, even people of our own family.... This corruption and depravity are so widespread that our land is entirely depopulated.... We need in this kingdom only priests and schoolteachers, and no merchandise,

---

1. M. Smith, *Stono*, 14.

unless it is wine and flour for Mass . . . [it] is our wish that this kingdom not be a place for the trade or transport of slaves.²

Nzinga Mbemba learned Portuguese and wrote several letters, providing an importance witness to early Kongolese Christianity from an emic perspective. Equally noteworthy with the king's protesting against the excessive slave-trading by the Portuguese is his statement that the Kongolese desire only ecclesiastical and theological resources for the building of the church. Nzinga Mbemba's comments indicate a Kongolese Church that greatly valued the Christian tradition. It follows then, that those Kongolese Christians who were stolen in slavery and revolted in the Stono Rebellion also viewed the Christian faith as a source of empowerment and liberation. Many of the enslaved Africans in North American, South America, and the Caribbean were from the Christian Kongo kingdom, and many of these people brought their unique traditions with them through the Middle Passage and adapted them to new, creolized identities. For example, the Kongolese Christian communal warrior dance—called the *sangamento*—appeared throughout the eighteenth and nineteenth centuries in Brazil, the Caribbean, and New Orleans.³ It is likely that the freedom fighters in the Stono Rebellion were engaging in *sangamento* practices during their musical parading. The Black church is not entirely the result of contact with European American Christian traditions; there were some Africans who were already Christian and whose Christian tradition continued to serve as a source of empowerment and spiritual vitality.

Black Christianity in Earliest America

Ottobah Cugoano composed what is perhaps the most extensive refutation of slavery from a Christian perspective. Cugoano composed a biographical narrative much like those of his contemporaries and successors. However, unlike many other slave narratives, Cugoano extensively engages the Bible and provides an apologetic argument against the reigning view in the White world that supported slavery from the Scriptures. For Cugoano, the Bible was his primary source of consolation and truth:

> I am highly indebted to many of the good people of England for learning and principles unknown to the people of my native country. But, above all, what have I obtained from the Lord God of Hosts, the God of the Christians! In that divine revelation

2. Lushombo, *Christian and African Ethic*, 23.
3. Fromont, *Afro-Catholic Festivals*, 26.

of the only true God, and the Saviour of men, what a treasure of wisdom and blessings are involved? How wonderful is the divine goodness displayed in those invaluable books the Old and New Testaments, that inestimable compilation of books, the Bible? And, O what a treasure to have, and one of the greatest advantages to be able to read therein, and a divine blessing to understand![4]

For Cugoano, the Bible represented freedom. The proslavery arguments utilizing biblical texts were aberrations of true Christian practice: "I can find nothing imported thereby, in the least degree, to warrant the modern practice of slavery. But on the contrary, and what was principally intended thereby, and in the most particular manner, as respecting Christians, that it (Torah) contains the strongest prohibition against it."[5] Cugoano by no means endorsed slavery or interpreted his conversion experience as an end that justified the means of the Middle Passage. Slavery is "that torrent of robbery and wickedness" and "horrid and brutal."[6] He interprets his experience through the lens of biblical Joseph, who was also sold into slavery by his brothers whom he eventually saved from starvation: "In some manner, I may say with Joseph, as he did with respect to the evil intention of his brethren, when they sold him to Egypt, that whatever evil intentions and bad motives those insidious robbers had in carrying me away from my native country and friends, I trust, was what the Lord intended for my good."

Phillis Wheatley was born in the early 1750s in West Africa, stolen in slavery when she was a little girl, and brought to Massachusetts. After learning to read and write, she became a renowned poet and one of the earliest-known African Americans to publish a book. Phillis Wheatley became a Christian and celebrated her conversion from traditional African religion:

> 'Twas mercy brought me from my Pagan land,
> Taught my benighted soul to understand
> That there's a God, that there's a Saviour too:
> Once I redemption neither sought nor knew.
> Some view our sable race with scornful eye,
> "Their colour is a diabolic die."
> Remember, Christians, Negros, black as Cain,
> May be refin'd, and join th' angelic train.[7]

---

4. Cugoano, *Thoughts on the Sentiments*, 18.
5. Cugoano, *Thoughts on the Sentiments*, 44.
6. Cugoano, *Thoughts on the Sentiments*, 17.
7. "On Being Brought from Africa to America," in Wheatley, *Poems on Various Subjects*, 17.

While Wheatley referred to Africa as "Pagan," she still embraced much of her traditional African religious practices, especially the veneration of the sun.[8] In fact, another early African American poet—Jupiter Hammon—criticized Wheatley for her sun imagery.[9] Therefore, Wheatley did not completely reject traditional African culture. At the same time, she gives praise to God for his salvation even in the midst of slavery. Like Cugoano, Wheatley's gratefulness for the gospel did not entail an embrace of slavery. In fact, one of her poems publicly denounced the peculiar institution:

> No more, America, in mournful strain
> Of wrongs, and grievance uredress'd complain
> No longer shall thou dread the iron chain,
> Which wanton Tyranny with lawless hand
> Had made, and with it meant t'enslave the land.
> Should you, my lord, while you peruse my song,
> Wonder from whence my love of Freedom sprung,
> Whence flow these wishes for the common good,
> By feelings hearts alone best understood,
> I, young in life, by seeming cruel fate
> Was snatch'd from Afric's fancy'd happy feat:
> What pangs excruciating must molest,
> What sorrows labour in my parent's breast?
> Steel'd was that soul and by no misery mov'd
> That from a father seiz'd his babe belov'd:
> Such, such my case. And can I then but pray
> Others may never feel tyrannic sway?[10]

Phillis used her poetry as a mechanism for fighting the evils of slavery. And yet, Christianity was a haven for the eighteenth-century poet.

Olaudah Equiano was born in southern Nigeria in the 1740s and was stolen into slavery in the Caribbean, and then taken by an English naval officer to the UK. Equiano joined the Sons of Africa along with Cugoano and others, fighting against slavery. Equiano also wrote an autobiography in which he recounts the events of his life. Equiano described the Indigenous religious practices in his native Benin kingdom, indicating that his people had no knowledge of Christianity, though some of their religious practices were similar to Judeo-Christian principles. Equiano embraced Christianity and was baptized in Westminster in 1759. He stated the following concerning his faith in Jesus Christ:

---

8. Jennings, "African Sun Imagery."
9. "An Address to Miss Phillis Wheatley," in Hammon, *Collected Works*, 11.
10. "To the Right Honourable William," in Wheatley, *Poems on Various Subjects*, 67.

> I began to think I had lived a moral life, and that I had a proper ground to believe I had an interest in the divine favour; but still meditating on the subject, not knowing whether salvation was to be had partly for our own good deeds, or solely as the sovereign gift of God; in this deep consternation the Lord was pleased to break in upon my soul with his bright beams of heavenly light; and in an instant as it were, removing the veil, and letting light into a dark place, I saw clearly with the eye of faith the crucified Saviour bleeding on the cross on mount Calvary: the scriptures became an unsealed book, I saw myself a condemned criminal under the law, which came with its full force to my conscience, and "when the commandment came sin revived, and I died," I saw the Lord Jesus Christ in his humiliation, loaded and bearing my reproach, sin, and shame.[11]

While Equiano was stolen again to the Caribbean and US after his conversion, he eventually attained his freedom in 1766. Equiano returned to England, where he published his autobiography and continued to work for the cause of abolitionism on both sides of the Atlantic. Christianity served as a haven and agent of liberation for Equiano. His autobiography was supported financially by Selina Hastings, an English Methodist missionary and evangelist. Equiano also worked with Quaker and Anglican communities in England and the US in their efforts to end slavery in both empires. Equiano represented an emerging African Christian voice calling for freedom rooted in faith in Jesus Christ.

A colleague of Equiano and Cugoano in the abolitionist movement was Ignatius Sancho. Sancho was born on a slave ship bound for the Caribbean and was taken to England after his parents died. Sancho escaped slavery and became literate as well as a shopkeeper. Being a property owner, Sancho was able to become one of the first documented British citizens of African descent to vote. In one of his letters to an anonymous young man, Sancho exhorted the recipient to follow the example of a Mr. Garrick. According to Sancho, Mr. Garrick was a model to the recipient for how Black people should be treated and empowered. As is the case with all of his letters, Sancho's comments were filled with references to God:

> May the God of all Mercy give you grace to follow his friendly dictates! I shall ever truly rejoice to hear from you—and your well doing will be a comfort to me ever; it is not in your own power and option to command riches—wisdom and health are immediately the gift of God—but it is in your own breast to be

---

11. Equiano, *Life of Olaudah Equiano*, 189–90.

good—therefore, my dear child, make the only right election—be good, and trust the rest to God; and remember he is about your bed, and about your paths, spieth out all your ways.[12]

Sancho's faith in the Christian God formed the foundation of all his letters, which were replete with exhortations regarding Christian conduct. When writing to a friend about their child's illness as well as his own wife's ailment, Sancho exhorted his friend by calling to memory the goodness of God: "Trust in the Almighty—his providence is your shield—'tis his love, 'tis his mercy, which has hitherto supported and kept you up. See, see cries Hope! Look where Religion, with Faith on her right, and Charity on her left, and a numerous train of blessings in her rear, come to thy support."[13] Sancho celebrated the reading and proclamation of the Bible and claimed that "true Christian charities" included feeding the hungry and clothing the naked.[14] Sancho also criticized the British practices of slavery and colonialism: "I am sorry to observe that the practice of your country (which as a resident I love—and for its freedom—and for the many blessings I enjoy in it—shall ever have my warmest wishes—prayers—and blessings): I say it is with reluctance, that I must observe your country's conduct has been uniformly wicked in the East-West-Indies—and even on the coast of Guinea."[15]

Black Christianity Institutionalized

The Black Methodists

As Black congregations continued to thrive throughout the US, eventually independent Black denominations began to form at the outset of the nineteenth century. One of the first, and most well-known, Black denominations was initiated by Richard Allen. Allen was born in slavery in Delaware in 1760 and worked for his freedom when he was twenty years old. Allen had been an active minister since his teen years, and he eventually moved to Philadelphia where he would later meet his wife, Sarah. Allen took a position as a minister at St. George's Episcopal Church in 1786, where he ministered to the Black portion of the church, who worshipped in segregated seating on Sunday mornings. The biography of Richard Allen describes the dramatic final straw that led to the exodus of the marginalized Black community of St. George's:

12. Sancho, *Letters*, 40–41.
13. Sancho, *Letters*, 78.
14. Sancho, *Letters*, 115.
15. Gregg, *Empire and Identity*, 226.

When the colored people began to get numerous in attending the church, they moved us from the seats we usually sat on, and placed us around the wall, and on Sabbath morning we went to church and the sexton stood at the door, and told us to go in the gallery. He told us to go, and we would see where to sit. We expected to take seats over the ones we formerly occupied below, not knowing any better. We took those seats. Meeting had begun, and they were nearly done singing, and just as we got to the seats, the elder said, "Let us pray." We had not been long upon our knees before I heard considerable scuffling and low talking. I raised my head up and saw one of the trustees, H—M—, having hold of the Rev. Absalom Jones, pulling him up off of his knees, and saying, "You must get up—you must not kneel here." Mr. Jones replied, "Wait until prayer is over." Mr. H—M—said, "No, you must get up now, or I will call for aid and force you away." Mr. Jones said, "Wait until prayer is over, and I will get up and trouble you no more." With that he beckoned to one of the other trustees, Mr. L—S— to come to his assistance. He came, and went to William White to pull him up. By this time prayer was over, and we all went out of the church in a body, and they were no more plagued with us in the church. This raised a great excitement and inquiry among the citizens, in so much that I believe they were ashamed of their conduct. But my dear Lord was with us, and we were filled with fresh vigor to get a house erected to worship God in.[16]

Rev. Allen, Rev. Jones, and others formed Mother Bethel African Methodist Episcopal Church in 1787 after purchasing the parcel of land the church still stands on today. The role of the Black church as a haven is exemplified in that the land on which Mother Bethel still stands is the oldest piece of real estate continuously owned by African Americans in the entire United States. This is a powerful symbol of agency. In a nation where African Americans continue to suffer the consequences of federal and local policies preventing Blacks from property ownership well into the late twentieth century, it is significant that the oldest property that Blacks have been able to hold onto is a church! Mother Bethel personifies the divine favor and social empowerment that the Black church has had from its beginnings. Only a few years after its founding, Mother Bethel served as the primary source of care during a yellow fever epidemic in 1783. While George Washington hid in his country estate and the broader White community even blamed the Black community for this epidemic—while positing the

---

16. Allen, *Life Experiences*, 14–15.

ludicrous claim that Blacks were immune to yellow fever—Allen and the community of Mother Bethel were on the front lines of providing aid to people of all races in the Philadelphia area. Despite critique from the White community and even contracting the disease himself, Allen led his church community in providing healing to the entire city. Allen and his community petitioned Congress to repeal the Fugitive Slave Act, which gave captors rights to recapture formerly enslaved persons in the North. Allen and others established the first Black publication and lobbied for compensation for Black workers during the yellow fever epidemic.

During Bishop Allen's tenure at Mother Bethel, the ministry of the first Black woman preacher and author began. Jarena Lee was born in a free Black family in 1783 and became a Christian in 1804. While working as a domestic servant for Whites in Philadelphia, Lee converted through the preaching of Richard Allen and joined Mother Bethel. Lee felt a call to preach despite the fact that women were not allowed to do so in the beginning years of Mother Bethel: "If the man may preach, because the Saviour died for him, why not the woman? Seeing he died for her also. Is he not a whole Saviour, instead of a half one? As those who hold it wrong for a woman to preach, would seem to make it appear."[17] Lee approached Bishop Allen to obtain permission to preach publicly, which the bishop denied. Later one Sunday, a certain Rev. Richard Williams took the pulpit to preach. However, the audience noticed that Rev. Williams had "lost the spirit," which prompted Lee to take over preaching the biblical text. "During the exhortation, God made manifest his power in a manner sufficient to show the world that I was called to labour according to my ability, and the grace given unto me, in the vineyard of the good husbandman."[18] Because the power of the Spirit upon Lee was evident to all of Mother Bethel, Allen publicly endorsed her to preach. Lee began to preach throughout the US. However, after getting married and not being supported to preach by her husband, Lee spent many years struggling with depression for not being empowered to preach. After the passing of her husband, Lee continued her ministry and preached throughout the US.

A younger contemporary of Lee who also was a Methodist living in Philadelphia was Zilpha Elaw. Elaw was born in Pennsylvania to a free mother and later moved to South New Jersey after getting married. Elaw had powerful visions, which led her to become a Christian:

> I never experienced that terrific dread of hell by which some Christians appear to have been exercised; but I felt an oddly sorrow for sin in having grieved my God by a course of

17. Lee, *Religious Experiences and Journal*, 15.
18. Lee, *Religious Experiences and Journal*, 24.

disobedience to His commands.... One evening, whilst singing one of the songs of Zion, I distinctly saw the Lord Jesus approach me with open arms, and a most divine and heavenly smile upon his countenance. As He advanced towards me, I felt that his very looks spoke, and said, "Thy prayer is accepted, I own thy name."[19]

Elaw later traveled throughout the US and to England preaching the gospel.

A younger contemporary Methodist who traveled to England was Amanda Berry Smith. Smith was born to an enslaved family in 1837 near Baltimore. She eventually traveled as a missionary to India, Africa, and England. Her ministry and preaching later influenced C. H. Mason, the founding bishop of the Church of God in Christ. Smith was raised in a Christian household that aided enslaved persons in the Underground Railroad: "At one time (the family landlord) was Magistrate, and of course did not hunt down poor slaves, and would support the law whenever things were brought before him in a proper way, but my father and mother were level headed and had good broad common sense, so they never brought him into any trouble. Our house was one of the main stations of the Under Ground Railroad."[20] The ministry of figures such as Allen, Lee, Elaw, and Smith demonstrates the centrality of Black Methodism in the earliest years of the haven of the Black church.

Despite continuing lack of support from White churches, Mother Bethel and several other Mid-Atlantic congregations came together in 1816 to form the African Methodist Episcopal (AME) Church, the oldest Black denomination in the United States. The AME pioneered the way for other Black denominations. In New York City, Black Methodists led by William Hamilton left racist White churches in 1800 and formed independent congregations. These congregations came together in 1821 to form the African Methodist Episcopal Zion (AMEZ) Church. The Christian Methodist Episcopal Church was founded in Jackson, Tennessee, in 1870.

One of the most well-known AMEZ missionaries was Julia Foote. Foote was born to formerly enslaved parents in Schenectady, New York, in 1823. Foote originally was a part of the AME church, but she moved to the AMEZ denomination as she found the opportunity there to preach. Foote became the first ordained woman deacon and second elder in this denomination. In her autobiography, Foote strongly critiqued the marginalization of women in the church:

---

19. Elaw, *Memoirs of the Life*, 5.
20. A. Smith, *Autobiography*, 31.

> We are sometimes told that if a woman pretends to a Divine call, and thereon grounds the right to plead the cause of a crucified Redeemer in public, she will be believed when she shows credentials from heaven; that is, when she works a miracle. If it be necessary to prove one's right to preach the Gospel, I ask of my brethren to show me their credentials, or I can not believe in the propriety of their ministry.[21]

The Black Baptists

While the Black Methodists were the first to organize a denomination, there were also many independent Baptist denominations that formed in the nineteenth and twentieth centuries. These congregations were built upon the earlier ministry work of Black Baptist missionaries and preachers.

One of the most foundational Black Baptist figures was the pastor and missionary George Liele. Liele was born in the early 1750s into slavery. Raised in a Georgia plantation, Liele described his conversion thusly:

> I was brought to perceive that my life hung by a slender thread, and if it was the will of God to cut me off at that time, I was sure I should be found in hell, as sure as God was in Heaven. I saw my condemnation in my own heart, and I found no way wherein I could escape the damnation of hell, only through the merits of my dying Lord and Saviour Jesus Christ; which caused me to make intercession with Christ, for the salvation of my poor immortal soul; and I full well recollect, I requested of my Lord and Master to give me a work, I did not care how mean it was, only to try and see how good I would do it.[22]

Liele became the first Black preacher licensed by the Baptists in 1773, and he was freed in 1777. He immediately began to preach among Black Baptists in Savannah and converted David George and Andrew Bryan, who would go on to pastor the Silver Bluff Baptist Church in Aiken, South Carolina, and Bryan Street African Baptist Church, respectively. The congregation that Liele began forming in 1773 officially incorporated as the First African Baptist Church in 1788. These congregations are among the oldest Black churches in North America. After the US insurrection of 1777, Liele fled Georgia with many other Blacks and White loyalists. Many of these citizens fled to Nova Scotia, which formed the foundation of Afro-Canadian

---

21. Foote, *Brand Plucked from Fire*, 78–79.
22. Sernett, *African American Religious History*, 45.

community. Liele, however, went to Jamaica where he served as a missionary and formed the Ethiopian Baptist Church of Jamaica. Liele lived the rest of his life in Jamaica, where he created Jamaican church covenants and where he was imprisoned for his empowerment of enslaved Blacks. One of the distinguishing marks of Liele's ministry is that he is the first documented missionary from the US.

Another prominent Black Baptist missionary and younger contemporary of Liele was Lott Cary. Cary was born in 1780 in Virginia into slavery. Cary was baptized in a White Baptist church in Richmond in 1807 and he purchased his freedom in 1813. Cary became successful in the tobacco industry—a major crop in Virginia during this time—and he even became a landowner. However, in 1816, the American Colonization Society (ACS) was formed with the goal of "repatriating" Blacks to Africa. The ACS was supported by White abolitionists who felt that Blacks would fare better in Africa away from American discrimination, and by supporters of slavery who did not want the presence of free Blacks to undermine the slavery industry. Lott Cary desired to join the ranks of Blacks moving to Africa. Although he was free and a landowner, Cary expressed a desire to surrender the material comforts of life in the US in order to do ministry in the land of his ancestors:

> He was willing to leave all, and to venture all for Christ, and for the sake of those who were perishing for lack of vision, in a far distant land. When a ministering brother inquired, why he could determine to quit a station of so much comfort and usefulness, to encounter the dangers of an African climate, and hazard every thing to plant a colony on a distant heathen shore;—his reply was to this effect: "I am an African, and in this country, however meritorious my conduct, and respectable my character, I cannot receive the credit due to either. I wish to go to a country where I shall be estimated by my merits, not by my complexion; and I feel bound to labor for my suffering race." He seemed to have imbibed the sentiment of Paul, and to have great heaviness and continual sorrow in his heart, for his brethren, his kinsmen according to the flesh.[23]

Cary and his family became part of the migration of African Americans who formed the initial colony of Liberia in 1819. Cary lived the last decade of his life engaged in ministry in Liberia, as he founded the Providence Baptist Church in Monrovia. Cary's ministry exemplifies the theological

---

23. Taylor, *Elder Lott Cary*, 16.

and political influence of many Black Christian leaders during the era of US slavery.

Black Baptist missionaries, such as Nancy Prince, also traveled to Europe. Prince was a free woman born in 1799 in Newburyport, Massachusetts. Prince worked as a servant to Whites and eventually married a Russian named Nero Prince. The Princes moved to Russia where Nancy described many interesting encounters with Russian culture. Nancy survived the flood of 1824 and met with many Russian dignitaries. After the death of her husband, Prince returned to the US and described her feelings about religion and abolitionism thusly:

> The weight of prejudice has again oppressed me, and were it not for the promises of God, one's heart would fail, for He made man in his own image, in the image of God, created he him, male and female, that they should have dominion over the fish of the sea, the fowl of the air, and the beast of the field, &c. This power did God give man, that thus far should he go and no farther but man has disobeyed his Maker, and become vain in his imagination, and their foolish hearts are darkened. We gather from this, that God has in all ages of the world punished every nation and people for their sins. The sins of my beloved country are not hid from his notice; his all seeing eye sees and knows the secrets of all hearts; the angels that kept not their first estate but left their own habitations, he hath reserved in everlasting chains unto the great day.[24]

Prince then lived in Jamaica for a number of years as a missionary, working with returned Maroons from Sierra Leone and helping to run a school for girls. Prince lived the last years of her life in Boston, where she worked alongside abolitionists like William Lloyd Garrison against the Fugitive Slave Act.

Black Christianity and Racial Uplift

In his autobiography, Booker T. Washington articulated the providence of God working within the Black community through the experience of slavery. While Washington condemned slavery and the Jim Crow segregation and terror lynchings of his day, he still viewed the Christian faith as the ultimate truth:

---

24. Prince, *Narrative of the Life*, 43–44.

> Negroes in this country, who themselves or whose forefathers went through the school of slavery, are constantly returning to Africa as missionaries to enlighten those who remained in the fatherland. This I say, not to justify slavery—on the other hand, I condemn it as an institution, as we all know that in America it was established for selfish and financial reasons, and not from a missionary motive—but to call attention to a fact, and to show how Providence so often uses men and instructions to accomplish a purpose. When persons ask me in these days how, in the midst of what sometimes seem hopelessly discouraging conditions, I can have such faith in the future of my race in this country, I remind them of the wilderness through which and out of which a good Providence has already led us.[25]

Washington viewed African Americans as uniquely poised to use the experience of slavery and removal from Africa to be Christian missionaries in their ancestral homeland. Born into slavery in 1856, Washington was educated in seminary and used an African Methodist Episcopal church as the first meeting place for the Tuskegee Institute. Washington espoused a more gradualist approach to justice for African Americans, arguing that segregation was inevitable and that Blacks could best advance by excelling through education and business in Black institutions. This approach caused controversy and critique from other Black leaders, notably W. E. B. Du Bois. What is clear, however, is that Washington—like many African Americans during this period—viewed Christianity as a source of empowerment and vitality.

Perhaps the most poignant statement regarding the haven of Christianity for African Americans in bondage came in the autobiography of Frederick Douglass. In the appendix of his autobiography, Douglass desired to clarify that his criticism of US slavery and the ways in which Christianity were abused in support of slavery were not an attack on "Christianity proper." Douglass unequivocally denounced slaveholding Christianity, but he did not consider this the same as true Christianity:

> What I have said respecting and against religion, I mean strictly to apply to the slaveholding religion of this land, and with no possible reference to Christianity proper; for, between the Christianity of this land, and the Christianity of Christ, I recognize the widest possible difference—so wide, that to receive the one as good, pure, and holy, is of necessity to reject the other as bad, corrupt, and wicked. To be the friend of the one, is of necessity to be the enemy of the other. I love the pure, peaceable,

25. Washington, *Up from Slavery*, 16.

and impartial Christianity of Christ: I therefore hate the corrupt, slaveholding, women-whipping, cradle-plundering, partial and hypocritical Christianity of this land. Indeed, I can see no reason, but the most deceitful one, for calling the religion of this land Christianity.[26]

In addition to working as an abolitionist and participant on the Underground Railroad, Douglass was a licensed preacher in the African Methodist Episcopal Zion Church. Douglass preached at numerous churches and supervised Sunday schools. The AMEZ denomination was more agreeable to Douglass than White Methodist churches, because of the White churches' segregation practices. Faith and involvement in the church and fighting for freedom from slavery were inseparable dynamics for Douglass. Indeed, Douglass was known for esteeming the Bible most highly and abolitionist periodicals secondly.

Bibliography

Allen, Richard. *The Life Experiences, and Gospel Labors of the Rt. Rev. Richard Allen, to Which Is Annexed the Rise and Progress of the African Methodist Episcopal Church in the United States of America*. Philadelphia: Ford and Riply, 1880.

Cugoano, Quobna Ottobah. *Thoughts on the Sentiments on the Evil of Slavery and Other Writings*. Edited by Vincent Carretta. Penguin Classics. New York: Penguin, 1999.

Douglass, Frederick. *Narrative of the Life of Frederick Douglass: An American Slave*. Cambridge, MA: Belknap, 2009.

Elaw, Zilpha. *Memoirs of the Life, Religious Experience, Ministerial Travels and Labours, of Mrs. Zilpha Elaw, an American Female of Colour*. London: self-published, 1846.

Equiano, Olaudah. *The Interesting Narrative of the Life of Olaudah Equiano*. Penguin Classics. New York: Penguin, 1995.

Foote, Julia A. J. *A Brand Plucked from the Fire: An Autobiographical Sketch*. Cleveland: Schneider, 1879.

Fromont, Cécile. *Afro-Catholic Festivals in the Americas: Performance, Representation, and the Making of Black Atlantic Tradition*. Africana Religions. University Park: Pennsylvania State University Press, 2019.

Gregg, Stephen H. *Empire and Identity: An Eighteenth-Century Sourcebook*. New York: Bloomsbury, 2005.

Hammon, Jupiter. *The Collected Works of Jupiter Hammon: Poems and Essays*. Knoxville: University of Tennessee Press, 2017.

Jennings, Regina. "African Sun Imagery in the Poetry of Phillis Wheatley." *Pennsylvania English* 22 (2000) 68–76.

Lee, Jarena. *Religious Experiences and Journal of Mrs. Jarena Lee: Giving an Account of Her Call to Preach the Gospel*. Philadelphia: n.p., 1836.

---

26. Douglass, *Narrative of the Life*, 115.

Lushombo, Léocadie W. *A Christian and African Ethic of Women's Political Participation: Living as Risen Beings*. Postcolonial and Decolonial Studies in Religion and Theology. London: Lexington, 2023.

Prince, Nancy. *A Narrative of the Life and Travels of Mrs. Nancy Prince*. 2nd ed. Boston: Hall, 1853.

Sancho, Ignatius. *Letters of the Late Ignatius Sancho, an African*. London: Nichols & Dilly, 1783.

Sernett, Milton C. *African American Religious History: A Documentary Witness*. 2nd ed. C. Eric Lincoln Series on the Black Experience. Durham, NC: Duke University Press, 2000.

Smith, Amanda Berry. *An Autobiography: The Story of the Lord's Dealings with Mrs. Amanda Smith the Colored Evangelist; Containing an Account of Her Life Work of Faith, and Her Travels in America, England, Ireland, Scotland, India, and Africa, as an Independent Missionary*. Chicago: Meyer, 1893.

Smith, Mark K. *Stono: Documenting and Interpreting a Southern Slave Revolt*. Columbia: University of South Carolina, 2005.

Taylor, J. B. *Biography of Elder Lott Cary, Late Missionary to Africa*. Baltimore: Armstrong & Berry, 1837.

Washington, Booker T. *Up from Slavery: An Autobiography*. New York: Doubleday, 1901.

Wheatley, Phillis. *Poems on Various Subjects, Religious and Moral*. Denver: Lawrence, 1887.

Chapter 4

North American Catholicism

CHARLES T. STRAUSS

IN HIS 1895 ENCYCLICAL *Longinqua Oceani* (Wide expansion of the ocean), Pope Leo XIII (1810–1903) celebrated the history of Catholicism in the United States:

> That your Republic is progressing and developing by giant strides is patent to all; and this holds good in religious matters also. For even as your cities, in the course of one century, have made a marvelous increase in wealth and power, so do we behold the Church, from scant and slender beginnings, grown with rapidity to be great and exceedingly flourishing.[1]

From its first arrival on the North American continent in the early sixteenth century, Catholicism has both mirrored the multifaceted cultural realities of its time, and actively shaped the moral, political, and social structures of specific regions and the larger United States. This chapter explores the diverse ideas and identities, political dynamics, and cultural shifts that defined Catholicism's presence in North America over the course of five centuries.

During the period of European colonization of North America from the early sixteenth to the late eighteenth centuries, Catholicism was deeply entwined with the ambitions of European empires. Catholics participated in the imperial rivalries of Spain, France, and England and also engaged with multiple Indigenous cultures, resulting in episodes of violent conflict and also times of cultural adaptation and even syncretism. As English colonists came to dominate the Eastern Seaboard of North America and successfully declared independence from England in the late eighteenth century, English Catholics in North America grappled with the complexities of an emerging republic. Catholics in North America balanced their religious convictions with the broader cultural shifts of a nation taking shape; they faced periodic

---

1. Leo XIII, "*Longinqua*," para. 5.

skepticism, marginalization, and instances of persecution and violence. These challenges, along with influxes of European immigrants from Europe and Mexico by the mid-nineteenth century, birthed a tenacious immigrant subculture that profoundly shaped United States and Catholic histories. By the mid-twentieth century, and specifically after American Catholic participation in two world wars, Catholicism's influence burgeoned, touching multiple segments of American society. The reforms of the Second Vatican Council (1962–65), where bishops convened in Rome to revive, renew, and reform Catholic teaching, liturgical practices, governance, and outreach to the world for a new, modern time were also crucial to United States Catholics' growing confidence and influence in American society. However, the latter half of the century, especially from the late 1960s onwards, brought its set of challenges, including waning participation in church practices such as the Sunday Mass, decline in the number of Catholics choosing to enter religious life as priests and sisters, and increased skepticism about Catholic Church authority. These realities were heightened by the revelations of the abuse of children by clergy and mismanagement by church leadership beginning in the late 1990s, which cast a shadow over the Catholic Church's broader public role in American society. Despite these hurdles, the Catholic Church remained a potent political force in the twenty-first century, taking significant stances on issues, including the pro-life movement, the stockpiling of nuclear weapons, and immigration reform. Additionally, Catholic universities expanded their role in higher education, Catholics took multiple seats on the United States Supreme Court, and the elections and actions of a series of Catholic popes reverberated in American culture.

This chapter, then, traces the Catholic Church's trajectory from its frontier origins to its contemporary significance.

Catholics on the North American Frontiers of European Empires, 1513–1789

Europeans first arrived in North America during an age of empire-building and religious competition that brought conquistadors, colonists, and clergy to new shores. This historical context meant that the first Catholic experiences in what would later become the United States and Canada were defined by asymmetrical power relations between Indigenous peoples who had inhabited the land for approximately thirteen thousand years and agents of Spain, France, and England who sought to dominate new frontiers. The missionary activity, mercantilism, and violence of these imperial projects had lasting implications for Catholic life in North America from the early sixteenth to the late eighteenth centuries. Rivalries between Protestants and Catholics were also consequential to the contours of Catholicism during this period. The Protestant Reformation that swept through Europe in the 1500s made its way to the New World through the expansionism of the Catholic empire of Spain, the trading and missionary enterprises of Catholic France, and the contestations over authority and religious expression within the predominantly Protestant English colonies of North America's Eastern Seaboard. Thus, the first Catholics on the North American frontiers of three European empires were a diverse set of actors operating on local and international registers over three volatile centuries.

The Spanish established the first European empire in the Americas. Spanish exploration of the Florida peninsula by Juan Ponce de León (1474–1521) in 1513 eventually produced the city of Saint Augustine, the first European settlement in the land later known as the United States, in 1565. At that time, there were at least seven million Indigenous people living in North America. The Spanish were motivated by a desire for labor as many Indigenous people had died while being forced into brutal work in mining and agriculture on Spanish-occupied land in the Caribbean. Conquest crushed Indigenous civilizations from South America and Mexico north into present-day Florida, the American South and Southwest, and California into the eighteenth century. Catholic priests, drawn largely from the Franciscan, Dominican, and Jesuit orders in Spain, accompanied the conquistadors and emphasized the conversion of Indigenous peoples as they established mission stations.[2] The enduring legacy of the Spanish Catholic missionary enterprise is a story of severe tactics, including physical punishments by priests such as Fr. Junípero Serra (1713–84), a Franciscan missionary from Mallorca, Spain, who worked in California, and whom Pope Benedict XVI (1927–2021) canonized a saint not without controversy in 2015.[3] It also includes the popular devotion to the Virgin of Guadalupe, who appeared as a compassionate, Indigenous woman to a peasant man in Mexico City in 1531 and who remains the patroness of the Americas.[4] Out of conquest and conversion, a new identity was born in the Americas: it was defined by the Spanish language and the practice of Catholicism, as well as by a lower socioeconomic position relative to the Spanish colonizers.

The French did not share the aspirations of the Spanish to expand their empire by conquest and colonization, nor did they seek to force Indigenous

2. Weber, *Spanish Frontier*.
3. Hackel, *Junípero Serra*, 139–236.
4. William B. Taylor, "Mexico's Virgin of Guadalupe in the Seventeenth Century: Hagiography and Beyond," in Greer and Bilinkoff, *Colonial Saints*, 277–98.

peoples into labor. Catholic settlements in New France began in service of the French fur trade during the seventeenth century, beginning with the establishment of the city of Quebec in 1608. French imperial agents attempted to foster good relations with Indigenous peoples who served the fur trade as well as the intelligence efforts that were crucial to Catholic France's ongoing wars with Protestant England.[5] Soldiers and civilians were not necessary for these projects, and the French must have concluded that a large presence of either group would have risked alienating the Indigenous peoples. French Franciscan and Jesuit missionaries established mission stations in Canada and Maine via the Saint Lawrence Seaway to the Great Lakes Region and south on the Mississippi River to New Orleans. The Jesuits were well suited to living among and within Indigenous communities as they practiced a kind of openness to Indigenous language and cultural practices. The mission of "inculturation," as it is frequently described, served the Jesuit motive for conversion, and it also fit neatly with French imperial interests in commercial trade and military intelligence. The relationship was not without conflict as the French priests would not accommodate Indigenous customs related to sex outside marriage or any deviation from monogamy. The *Jesuit Relations*, a collection of reports detailing Jesuit missionary activity in New France, includes graphic accounts of the martyrdom of French Jesuits who battled Indigenous customs that they found abhorrent. These stories fed French Catholicism's Counter-Reformation spirituality, which circled the themes of self-abnegation, extreme acts of penance, and even mysticism.[6] Although France ultimately surrendered its holdings in North America in 1763 with the practice of inculturation failing to produce a new Catholic identity in the Americas, as was the case in New Spain, French Catholic religious congregations, including the Jesuits, the Ursuline Sisters (a Catholic female religious order founded in Italy in 1535, dedicated to the education of girls and care of the sick), and other religious orders of women, successfully established settlements and schools from Canada and Maine westward well into the nineteenth century.[7]

The English were the last group of Catholics to arrive on the New World frontier. Unlike the Spanish and French, they did not set out to evangelize Indigenous peoples nor accompany imperial armies. English Catholics, a minority in the Protestant English world, sailed first to the colony of Maryland as planters and laborers to escape religious persecution at home

---

5. Taylor, *American Colonies*, 91–116, 363–95.

6. Moore, *Indian and Jesuit*; Greer, *Mohawk Saint*.

7. Clark, *Masterless Mistresses*; Pasquier, *Fathers on the Frontier*; Leavelle, *Catholic Calumet*.

and avoid Protestant colonies in North America. In 1634, the Calvert family, a prominent Catholic family in England, received a royal charter from King Charles I (1600–1649) to establish Maryland as a haven for English Catholics. In 1649, Maryland's colonial assembly passed the Act of Religious Toleration, a piece of legislation granting religious freedom to all Christians in the colony. However, as a result of the Protestant victory in the English Civil War (1642–51) and because Catholics were always a minority population in the colony of Maryland, English Puritans assumed authority over the colony and outlawed Catholicism in 1654. Subsequent colonial assemblies further restricted Catholic political rights within Maryland, leaving Catholic families to maintain secret chapels in their homes where itinerant priests could celebrate Mass. The American Revolution restored religious tolerance and rights for Catholics in Maryland. Charles Carroll (1737–1832), a wealthy Catholic planter, was a delegate to the Continental Congress and the sole Catholic to sign the Declaration of Independence. His cousin, Jesuit priest John Carroll (1735–1815), became the chief administrator of the Catholic Church in the United States in 1784. Five years later and just several weeks after George Washington (1732–99) was inaugurated as president, Pope Pius VI (1717–99) confirmed the election of John Carroll by the American clergy as the nation's first bishop. The year was 1789, which also marked the founding of Georgetown College (later University) by the Jesuits as the first Catholic university in the United States.[8]

English Catholicism survived the century of religious and political suppression under Protestant control in Maryland and in other Catholic settlements on the Eastern Seaboard largely by seeking to avoid attention and by accommodating the language, customs, and even church architecture of their compatriots. Historians have described the style of Catholicism practiced in the colony of Maryland and during the first years of the fledgling nation as "republican Catholicism," which endured in the United States until the middle of the nineteenth century.[9]

Republican Catholicism to Immigrant Subculture, 1789–1908

John Carroll (1735–1815) was responsible for shepherding thirty thousand Catholics in the United States during his tenure as bishop of Baltimore (1790–1815). As he navigated the nation's Protestant establishment with a history of anti-Catholicism, Carroll adopted a "republican style" by adapting Catholic practices to the American landscape. He supported the practice of

8. Curran, *Papist Devils*.
9. O'Brien, *Public Catholicism*, 9–33.

the clergy electing their bishops rather than the Vatican appointing them. He consented, albeit reluctantly, to a practice whereby lay Catholic trustees elected their own pastoral leadership and held the titles to parish properties and the responsibility to manage them. In 1784 Carroll joined Protestants in Maryland in protesting a state tax to support churches, and thus, in his own way, advocated for a separation of church and state. This meant that lay trustees and religious orders were tasked with raising their own funds, and some religious communities of men and women drew revenue from their practice of the institution of slavery.[10]

Carroll also favored the English language over Latin in specific liturgical circumstances, and neoclassical over Gothic architecture. Carroll's "republican style" helped to cement Catholicism in a territory often hostile to a church that Protestants deemed foreign. Carroll's agenda was shaped by an urgent need to train local, English-speaking clergy to minister to families of Catholic planters known since the colonial period for their independence from church authority, as well as to educate their children.[11] One of Carroll's first moves as bishop was to invite the French priests of the Society of Saint Sulpice, or Sulpicians, to establish Saint Mary's Seminary in Baltimore for the local training of clergy in 1791. Until that time, Carroll relied on priests that he recruited from Germany or Ireland, but the number was never sufficient to serve an expanding Catholic population. Carroll also welcomed congregations of women religious to open convents and schools, including the Carmelite community of Port Tobacco, Maryland, and the Poor Claires of Georgetown. Both were vital religious communities dedicated to contemplation and service.[12]

Carroll's greatest challenge, shared by his successors who served as bishops of Catholic dioceses in the nineteenth century United States, was navigating consistent and significant waves of Catholic immigration from Europe. By 1908, the year the Vatican officially decreed that the United States was no longer a Catholic "mission territory," there were fourteen million Catholics in the country. They were or had descended from immigrants from Ireland, Germany, and across Eastern Europe and Mexico. This ethnic diversity came with European devotional practices and manifested itself in the construction of a Catholic immigrant subculture, all of which was anathema to Carroll's "republican style." This transformation in Catholic life in the United States occurred simultaneously with and was connected to the centralization of Catholic authority at the Vatican. This result was effectively

---

10. McGuinness, *Called to Serve*, 23–25.
11. Dolan, *American Catholic Experience*, 101–26.
12. Kauffman, *Tradition and Transformation*; and McGuinness, *Called to Serve*.

a pause on the "republican style" of Catholicism in the United States as new leaders of an immigrant church were named by Rome.[13]

Unlike the affluent planters of Maryland who traced their arrivals to the sixteenth century, the nineteenth-century Catholic immigrants arrived in North America with limited resources and without a familiarity with Enlightenment-era thinking on republicanism. Arriving during the devastating potato famine of the 1840s, Irish Catholic immigrants leveraged their English proficiency, educational institutions, and significant numbers to establish themselves as the new dominant force in the United States by the end of the nineteenth century. Their roles in professions such as city police and Catholic clergy aided their integration.[14] Meanwhile, Germans, who arrived with more education and economic resources, migrated to the Midwest, particularly to areas such as Cincinnati, Saint Louis, and Milwaukee. German Catholics established themselves in these places through economic enterprise rather than through the institutions of the police and clergy. They fiercely protected their language and customs, establishing parishes and schools based on nationality.[15] From 1880 to World War I, Italian Catholics established family-centric urban neighborhoods that integrated their faith with their family and community cultures, whereas Polish Catholics emulated the German approach, supporting national parishes and schools in cities such as Chicago and Milwaukee.[16] Catholicism in the United States during this period was organized as distinct ethnic subcultures, which provided access, even if limited, to status and places of power in American life. By contrast, African American Catholics in the South had fewer opportunities to shape their identity. There were notable exceptions, such as Henriette DeLille (1813–62) who founded religious orders in the mid-nineteenth century, seeking to address the spiritual and social needs of the African American community.[17]

Catholic influence grew in the United States during this period, marked by four traits that distinguished American Catholics from earlier communities of English Catholics and America's Protestant establishment. Historian Jay Dolan labeled "authority, sin, ritual, and the miraculous" as the defining markers of Catholic life during the period of immigrant subcultures.[18] The subsequent construction of Catholic institutions signaled significant

13. Dolan, *American Catholic Experience*, 127–348.
14. McCaffrey, *Irish Catholic Diaspora*, 63–78.
15. Dolan, *American Catholic Experience*, 130–31, 137–39, 145–47.
16. Orsi, *Madonna of 115th Street*; O'Toole, *Faithful*, 94–144.
17. Clark, *Masterless Mistresses*, 192, 257.
18. Dolan, *American Catholic Experience*, 221–40.

Catholic growth. Concurrently, Pope Pius IX (1792–1878) during the late nineteenth century emphasized the church's authority through various doctrines and councils, leading to a stronger assertion of papal power. American Catholics ardently supported him, and the spirit of the time was marked by revivals of efforts for churches around the world to fund the papacy and obey authoritative church councils located in Rome.[19]

American Catholics faced opposition to growth at the boundaries of their subculture. Notable incidents included the burning of a convent in 1834 and the proliferation of anti-Catholic organizations and publications. Responding to this adversity, conservative Catholic leaders such as Bishop Michael A. Corrigan (1839–1902) of New York advocated self-isolation, emphasizing the establishment of a protective network of parochial schools. The Knights of Columbus, founded in 1882, aimed to support Catholic men and their families while countering negative stereotypes. Conversely, figures such as Cardinal James Gibbons (1834–1921) encouraged more integrative Catholicism that embraced "American values," such as democratic governance and religious freedom. This group of church leaders advocated for labor rights, founded educational institutions, and supported the idea of a nation without a state church. The Vatican's 1899 papal letter *Testem Benevolentiae Nostrae* ultimately critiqued the "Americanism" perceived in the church's practices. The conservative-liberal divide would persist throughout the twentieth century.[20]

The rapid growth of American Catholicism and the issues Catholics faced as a result required effective church leadership and a resilient community. While the challenges were numerous, Catholics established institutions, communities, and social frameworks during the nineteenth century that have since become foundational to Catholic life in the United States.

Catholics in "The American Century," 1908–68[21]

At the outset of the twentieth century, the office of the Propagation of the Faith or *Propaganda Fide*, the Vatican office responsible for Catholic missions, revised its perspective on the United States, no longer viewing it as

---

19. Chinnici and Dries, *Prayer and Practice*.
20. Morris, *American Catholic*, 3–140.
21. In 1941, newspaper publisher Henry R. Luce (1898–1967) encouraged the United States to take on the responsibility of leading the globe through what he prophesied as "The American Century" in *Life* magazine (Feb. 1941; see Luce, "American Century"). Appleby and Cummings, *Catholics in American Century*, explored the crucial role played by Catholics during this period.

a mission territory for the Catholic Church. This recognition signaled that the Catholic Church in the United States had matured over time, and was prepared to engage more directly with the domestic and international issues facing the nation and the world.

One of the first areas of this engagement involved economics, and specifically the implications of nineteenth-century industrialization and urbanization on Catholic immigrant labor. Pope Leo XIII's *Rerum Novarum*, an encyclical addressing workers' rights, committed the Catholic Church to confronting the social and economic issues of the time. Father John A. Ryan (1869–1945) manifested this teaching in his advocacy for a minimum wage and affordable housing policies.[22] A Catholic tradition in organized labor emerged as a result and had moments where it captured the attention of the entire labor movement, such as with the Xavier Labor School, run by Jesuits in New York City in the 1930s.[23]

Labor activism was the first but not the only political or social outreach initiated by the American Catholic Church in the early twentieth century. The United States Catholic bishops founded the National Catholic War Council (NCWC) in 1917 to offer Catholic support for soldiers, their families, and all Americans seeking economic relief during World War I. The NCWC transitioned to the National Catholic Welfare Conference in 1923, which continued the Catholic Church's work in social services. Alfred E. Smith (1873–1944) ran as the first Catholic nominee for the United States presidency from a major political party in 1928. Though he did not secure victory, Smith's campaign highlighted the strengthening ties between Catholics and the Democratic Party in the 1920s.[24]

The passage of immigration restrictions by the United States Congress in 1921, which became even more stringent by 1924, combined with the devastating economic impact of the Great Depression, restricted Catholic immigration by the 1930s. Moreover, a nationwide dip in birth rates, which also affected Catholic families, threatened the potency of Catholic subculture.[25] Despite these challenges, religious devotion among Catholics surged during this period, with a notable emphasis on Marian practices. Organizations such as the Catholic Students' Mission Crusade, established in 1918, championed missionary efforts in Asia. Eucharistic congresses, the Holy Rosary movement, and lay spiritual retreats gained momentum. Finally, Dorothy Day (1897–1980) founded the Catholic Worker Movement

22. McShane, *Sufficiently Radical*.
23. Fisher, *On the Irish Waterfront*, 67–170.
24. Halsey, *Survival of American Innocence*.
25. Tentler, *American Catholics*, 167–68.

in Lower Manhattan to address issues of poverty, war, and spiritual despair through a newspaper and houses of hospitality.[26]

The aftermath of World War II witnessed a boom in the national birth rate, peaking in 1957 before experiencing a gradual decline through the mid-1960s and a steeper drop thereafter. However, Catholics continued to have a birth rate approximately 20 percent higher than the national average.[27] The steady demographic evolution supported the assimilation of European-descended Catholics into mainstream American life in emerging suburbs in the Northeast and Midwest, which led to the closing or merging of ethnic churches and the establishment of new nonethnic parishes.[28] At the same time, Catholic immigrant communities from Mexico and Puerto Rico increased during the mid-twentieth century, resulting in sizable new Catholic communities in Texas and southern California.[29]

The mid-twentieth century also marked a significant moment for Catholic representation in popular culture. The golden age of film featured prominent American actors such as Bing Crosby portraying likable Catholic priests; films about Catholic devotionalism, such as *The Song of Bernadette*, reached mainstream American audiences. The images of Catholic clergy and liturgical practices on film demonstrated the normalization if not the championing of Catholic culture within wider American culture as the United States entered the Cold War era.[30]

The Cold War also saw the rise of formidable Catholic figures who championed American anti-Communism, such as Bishop Fulton J. Sheen (1895–1979), who became famous for his preaching on television and radio, and Clare Booth Luce (1903–87), who became a public and influential conservative in domestic politics and foreign affairs. Their influence on mainstream American culture, after decades of anti-Catholicism, signaled that Catholic participation in World War II and anti-Communist efforts in the early years of the Cold War had solidified a bond between American Catholic identity and United States nationalism. This bond strengthened as the Cold War focus turned to Asia, specifically China, Korea, and Vietnam, where Catholic missionaries had built a significant presence since the early twentieth century.[31] Finally, the Second Vatican Council (1962–65) was a watershed moment in modern Catholic history, as well as in United

26. O'Toole, *Faithful*, 145–98; Halsey, *Survival of American Innocence*.
27. Tentler, *American Catholics*, 217–20.
28. Kelly, *Transformation of American Catholicism*.
29. Matovina, *Latino Catholicism*.
30. Smith, *Look of Catholics*; McDannell, *Catholics in the Movies*.
31. Dries, *Missionary Movement*, 108–48.

States history. The reforms encouraged Catholic laity to embrace "a call to holiness," which would manifest in new lay leadership roles in Catholic parishes and in offices focused on peace and social justice. Catholic universities embraced new standards for academic freedom in order to improve faculty scholarship and to graduate students who could apply Catholic theology in their professions. Fiery Catholic anti-Communism of the 1950s was inflected with a more idealistic, confident, and hopeful tone by the mid-1960s, which had been established to some degree by the Second Vatican Council.[32]

Reform and Realignment, 1968–2023

The years after the Second Vatican Council witnessed increasing numbers of Catholics thinking and making decisions about their politics and their management over their families and individual lives independent of Catholic Church teaching or authority. By the late 1960s, Catholic identity reflected a general American way of suburban living, with Catholic families having moved from blue-collar occupations in American cities to high-skilled positions and new homes in America's growing suburbs. More Catholic children were attending public rather than parochial schools by this period. America's pressing domestic and international challenges, such as the Vietnam War, became focal points for Catholic discourse by the late 1960s, as were the pressing moral issues, including birth control.

In 1968 Pope Paul VI released the encyclical *Humanae Vitae*, which reaffirmed the Catholic Church's traditional stance against artificial contraception. For many American Catholics, the encyclical clashed with their modern understanding of sexuality, personal conscience, and individual rights. Its release came at a time when the birth control pill was becoming widely accepted, not just as a contraceptive method, but also as a symbol of women's liberation and autonomy. Many American Catholics expected the church to relax its position on contraception and were disillusioned when Paul VI upheld the prohibition.[33] *Humanae Vitae* also had an unintended consequence: it galvanized discussions about individual conscience and the role of the laity in the Catholic Church's decision-making. Numerous theologians, priests, and even bishops expressed their reservations and disagreements with the papal encyclical. One of the most notable responses was the

---

32. McGreevy, *Catholicism and American Freedom*, 189–215; McDannell, *Spirit of Vatican II*; Massa, *American Catholic Revolution*.

33. Tentler, *Catholics and Contraception*; McGreevy, *Catholicism and American Freedom*, 216–81.

"Statement of Dissent" signed by eighty-seven theologians, which argued that Catholics could, in good conscience, choose to use artificial contraception.[34] The deep divisions over *Humanae Vitae* foreshadowed subsequent debates on topics like abortion, same-sex marriage, and the role of women in the church. The rippling effects of the tumultuous 1960s set the stage for several subsequent transformative decades for the Catholic Church.

In the decade following the Second Vatican Council, there was an air of anticipation and uncertainty about how the church's teachings and decisions would be translated into the realities of everyday life. Sponsored by the United States bishops, the 1976 Call to Action conference in Detroit sought to apply the teachings of the Second Vatican Council to the American context by exploring new approaches to issues ranging from liturgical practices to social justice organizing. Progressive voices called for a greater role for the laity, women's ordination, and a more open dialogue on contentious issues such as sexuality and celibacy. On the other hand, conservative participants defended the traditional teachings of the church, expressing concerns about the pace and direction of change.[35] The decade also saw a flourishing of lay movements and engagement, such as the Catholic charismatic renewal. Emphasizing a personal experience of the Holy Spirit and charismatic prayer meetings, the movement at its peak attracted millions and revitalized Catholic parishes and schools.[36] Thus, the 1970s marked a time of both tumult and transformation for American Catholicism.

As the Catholic Church entered the 1980s, marked by the pontificate of John Paul II, there was a noticeable shift toward a more conservative stance on moral, political, and liturgical issues. Throughout the 1970s, American Catholics had actively engaged, debated, and at times, contested Catholic teachings and rituals. John Paul II can be seen as attempting to reign in the period of vitality and volatility that followed the Second Vatican Council. In his visits to the United States in 1979, 1987, and 1995, for example, John Paul II demonstrated his ability to attract massive crowds, speaking directly to the youth and emphasizing issues including the sanctity of life, family values, and the importance of religious freedom.

Despite the enduring popularity of John Paul II through the 1980s and 1990s, American Catholics remained divided over moral issues as well as the pope's positions on Cold War geopolitics, which some believed were too closely intertwined with President Ronald Reagan's foreign policy.[37] Al-

---

34. Massa, *American Catholic Revolution*, 29–74.
35. Bonner et al., *Empowering the People of God*.
36. McCartin, *Prayers of the Faithful*, 13.
37. Keeley, *Reagan's Gun-Toting Nuns*.

though a large number of Catholics voted for Ronald Reagan in 1980 and 1984, signaling a shift away from the Catholic alliance with the Democratic Party and toward the conservative wing of the Republican Party, the United States Catholic bishops effectively criticized Reagan policies in two pastoral letters. *The Challenge of Peace* (1983) promoted nuclear disarmament and questioned the morality of nuclear deterrence, which put the bishops at odds with the Reagan administration's defense policies.[38] By observing the excesses of American capitalism and advocating for the rights of the poor and workers, *Economic Justice for All* (1986) challenged the idea of Reagan's trickle-down economics.[39] There was indeed no single Catholic position on many of the national and global issues of the 1980s. Moreover, as a result of rapid immigration from Latin America, Asia, and Africa after the immigration reforms of the 1960s, parishes across the United States became more ethnically diverse. This brought about liturgical adaptations and a greater emphasis on inclusivity, but also challenges to integrating diverse traditions and practices. Volatility persisted in the history of American Catholic politics and culture well beyond the 1970s.

During this 1990s the Catholic Church grappled with its role in an increasingly diverse and pluralistic society. Signaling a move toward ecumenism, Catholic leaders more regularly engaged in dialogues with other Christian denominations and faiths. At the same time, the 1994 *Catechism of the Catholic Church*, the first adult catechism of its kind in over four centuries, aimed at providing clear doctrinal statements in the face of societal change. By the twenty-first century, the Catholic Church faced arguably its gravest crisis in modern times: the revelations of widespread clerical abuse. This exposed not just the sins of individual priests but institutional failures that deeply wounded the credibility of Catholic leaders. The changing political landscape of the 2000s and 2010s also significantly impacted American Catholics. The church found itself navigating an intricate maze of issues, including religious freedom, abortion, euthanasia, and immigration. The Affordable Care Act, implemented during Barack Obama's presidency, brought the Catholic Church into direct conflict with the government over contraception mandates, leading to legal battles that highlighted the tension between religious liberties and government policies.

The election of Pope Francis in 2013 marked another pivotal moment for the global Catholic Church, and its ripples were keenly felt in the United States. Pope Francis's emphasis on social justice, care for the environment, and a pastoral approach to divisive issues resonated with many, especially

38. National Conference of Catholic Bishops, *Challenge of Peace*.
39. United States Catholic Bishops, *Economic Justice for All*.

the younger generation. At the same time that Pope Francis excited progressive impulses in American Catholicism, the increasing representation of Catholics on the Supreme Court demonstrated Catholics' enduring contribution to American conservatism. From facing discrimination in earlier centuries to having a formidable presence in foundational American institutions, the journey of American Catholicism in these decades mirrored the broader story of a community continually seeking to reconcile its faith with the demands of an ever-changing world.

Conclusion

Catholicism in North America, which Pope Leo XIII celebrated for its resilience in 1895, is a story of transitions from being one among many diverse religious expressions to take up root in North America to becoming, as Charles Morris put it, "America's Most Powerful Church."[40] During the early days of European colonization, Catholicism engaged Indigenous cultures and participated in European's imperial rivalries. As the American republic established its governing structures and a cultural identity that was largely influenced by England, the Catholic Church faced challenges in positioning, often balancing its religious tenets against the prevailing sentiments of the English-styled democratic republic. However, by the twentieth century, a confluence of internal church reforms and external societal shifts had positioned Catholicism as a crucial component within life in the United States and as an institution that Americans exported abroad. The second half of the twentieth century and the first decades of the twenty-first century demonstrate that Catholics' participation in the neuralgic issues of United States culture and politics has grown only stronger even if a single and distinctive Catholic position or view has become less clear.

Bibliography

Appleby, R. Scott, and Kathleen Sprows Cummings, eds. *Catholics in the American Century: Recasting Narratives of U.S. History*. Ithaca, NY: Cornell University Press, 2012.

Bonner, Jeremy, et al. *Empowering the People of God: Catholic Action before and after Vatican II*. Catholic Practice in North America. New York: Fordham University Press, 2014.

Cajka, Peter. *Follow Your Conscience: The Catholic Church and the Spirit of the Sixties*. Chicago: University of Chicago Press, 2021.

---

40. Morris, *American Catholic*, vii.

Chinnici, Joseph P., and Angelyn Dries, eds. *Prayer and Practice in the American Catholic Community*. American Catholic Identities: A Documentary History. Maryknoll, NY: Orbis, 2000.

Clark, Emily. *Masterless Mistresses: The New Orleans Ursulines and the Development of a New World Society, 1724–1834*. Chapel Hill: University of North Carolina Press, 2007.

Cressler, Matthew J. *Authentically Black and Truly Catholic: The Rise of Black Catholicism in the Great Migration*. New York: New York University Press, 2017.

Curran, Robert Emmett. *Papist Devils: Catholics in British America, 1754–1783*. Washington, DC: Catholic University of America Press, 2014.

D'Agostino, Peter R. *Rome in America: Transnational Catholic Ideology from the Risorgimento to Fascism*. Chapel Hill: University of North Carolina Press, 2004.

Davis, Cyprian. *The History of Black Catholics in the United States*. New York: Crossroad, 1990.

Dolan, Jay P. *The American Catholic Experience*. Garden City, NY: Doubleday, 1985.

Dries, Angelyn. *The Missionary Movement in American Catholic History*. Maryknoll, NY: Orbis, 1998.

Farrelly, Maura Jane. *Papist Patriots: The Making of an American Catholic Identity*. New York: Oxford University Press, 2012.

Fisher, James T. *On the Irish Waterfront: The Crusader, the Movie, and the Soul of the Port of New York*. Cushwa Center Studies of Catholicism in Twentieth-Century America. Ithaca, NY: Cornell University Press, 2009.

Gleason, Philip. *Contending with Modernity: Catholic Higher Education in the Twentieth Century*. New York: Oxford University Press, 1995.

Greer, Allan. *Mohawk Saint: Catherine Tekakwitha and the Jesuits*. New York: Oxford University Press, 2005.

Greer, Allan, and Jodi Bilinkoff, eds. *Colonial Saints: Discovering the Holy in the Americas, 1500–1800*. New York: Routledge, 2003.

Guttiérrez, Ramón A. *When Jesus Came, the Corn Mothers Went Away: Marriage, Sexuality, and Power in New Mexico, 1500–1846*. Stanford, CA: Stanford University Press, 1991.

Hackel, Steven W. *Children of Coyote, Missionaries of St. Francis: Indian-Spanish Relations in Colonial California, 1769–1850*. Chapel Hill: University of North Carolina Press, 2005.

———. *Junípero Serra: California's Founding Father*. New York: Hill and Wang, 2013.

Halsey, William M. *The Survival of American Innocence*. Notre Dame Studies in American Catholicism 2. Notre Dame, IN: University of Notre Dame Press, 1980.

Kauffman, Christopher J. *Tradition and Transformation in Catholic Culture: The Priests of Saint Sulpice in the United States from 1791 to the Present*. New York: Macmillan, 1988.

Keeley, Theresa. *Reagan's Gun-Toting Nuns: The Catholic Conflict over Cold War Human Rights Policy in Central America*. Ithaca, NY: Cornell University Press, 2020.

Kelly, Timothy. *Transformation of American Catholicism: The Pittsburgh Laity and the Second Vatican Council, 1950–1972*. Notre Dame, IN: University of Notre Dame Press, 2009.

Leavelle, Tracy Neal. *The Catholic Calumet: Colonial Conversations in French and Indian North America*. Early American Studies. Philadelphia: University of Pennsylvania Press, 2012.

Leo XIII, Pope. "*Longinqua*: Catholicism in the United States." Vatican, Jan. 6, 1895. https://www.vatican.va/content/leo-xiii/en/encyclicals/documents/hf_l-xiii_enc_06011895_longinqua.html.

———. "*Rerum Novarum*: On Capital and Labor." Vatican, May 15, 1891. https://www.vatican.va/content/leo-xiii/en/encyclicals/documents/hf_l-xiii_enc_15051891_rerum-novarum.html.

Luce, Henry R. "The American Century." *Diplomatic History* 23 (Spring 1999) 159–71. http://www-personal.umich.edu/~mlassite/discussions261/luce.pdf.

Massa, Mark S., SJ. *The American Catholic Revolution: How the Sixties Changed the Church Forever*. New York: Oxford University Press, 2014.

Matovina, Timothy. *Latino Catholicism: Transformation in America's Largest Church*. Princeton, NJ: Princeton University Press, 2011.

McCaffrey, Lawrence J. *The Irish Catholic Diaspora in America*. Rev. ed. Washington, DC: Catholic University of America Press, 1997.

McCartin, James P. *Prayers of the Faithful: The Shifting Spiritual Life of American Catholics*. Boston: Harvard University Press, 2010.

McDannell, Colleen. *Catholics in the Movies*. New York: Oxford University Press, 2007.

———. *The Spirit of Vatican II: A History of Catholic Reform in America*. New York: Basic, 2011.

McGreevy, John T. *Catholicism and American Freedom: A History*. New York: Norton, 2003.

McGuinness, Margaret M. *Called to Serve: A History of Nuns in America*. New York: New York University Press, 2013.

McShane, Joseph M., SJ. *Sufficiently Radical: Catholicism, Progressivism and the Bishops' Program of 1919*. Washington, DC: Catholic University of America Press, 1986.

Moore, James T. *Indian and Jesuit: A Seventeenth-Century Encounter*. Chicago: Loyola University Press, 1982.

Morris, Charles. *American Catholic: The Saints and Sinners Who Built America's Most Powerful Church*. New York: Random House, 1997.

National Conference of Catholic Bishops. *The Challenge of Peace: God's Promise and Our Response*. USCCB, May 3, 1983. https://www.usccb.org/upload/challenge-peace-gods-promise-our-response-1983.pdf.

O'Brien, David J. *Public Catholicism*. Maryknoll, NY: Orbis, 1996.

Orsi, Robert A. *The Madonna of 115th Street: Faith and Community in Italian Harlem*. New Haven, CT: Yale University Press, 1988.

O'Toole, James M. *The Faithful: A History of Catholics in America*. Cambridge, MA: Belknap, 2010.

Pasquier, Michael. *Fathers on the Frontier: French Missionaries and the Roman Catholic Priesthood in the United States, 1789–1870*. Religion in America. New York: Oxford University Press, 2010.

Paul VI, Pope. "*Humanae Vitae*." Vatican, July 25, 1968. https://www.vatican.va/content/paul-vi/en/encyclicals/documents/hf_p-vi_enc_25071968_humanae-vitae.html.

Smith, Anthony Burke. *The Look of Catholics: Portrayals in Popular Culture from the Great Depression to the Cold War*. CultureAmerica. Lawrence, KS: University Press of Kansas, 2010.

Taylor, Alan. *American Colonies: The Settling of North America*. Edited by Eric Foner. Penguin History of the United States 1. New York: Penguin, 2001.

Tentler, Leslie. *American Catholics: A History*. New Haven, CT: Yale University Press, 2020.

———. *Catholics and Contraception: An American History*. Cushwa Center Studies of Catholicism in Twentieth-Century America. Ithaca, NY: Cornell University Press, 2009.

United States Catholic Bishops. *Economic Justice for All: Pastoral Letter on Catholic Social Teaching and the U.S. Economy*. USCCB, 1986. https://www.usccb.org/upload/economic_justice_for_all.pdf.

Weber, David J. *The Spanish Frontier in North America*. Yale Western Americana. New Haven, CT: University Press, 1992.

Williams, Shannen Dee. *Subversive Habits: Black Catholic Nuns in the Long African Freedom Struggle*. Durham, NC: Duke University Press, 2022.

Section Two

The Story of Christianity Expressed in a Grand Church Family Mosaic:
An Evolutionary Tale of Evangelicalism

Chapter 5

Revivalism, Restorationism, and Reform in Antebellum America

BRANTLEY W. GASAWAY

BY THE MIDDLE OF the nineteenth century, White Protestants in America had many reasons to view their country as a substantially Christian nation. To be sure, the First Amendment of the Constitution, ratified in 1791, stipulated that the federal government could not legally "establish" any religion or particular church through providing it with unique recognition, privileges, or financial support. However, the First Amendment also promised that citizens possess the right to "free exercise" of religion. In an era of rapid geographic, demographic, and economic changes, White Christians across different denominations and sects—especially zealous evangelical Protestants—utilized this liberty and adopted new strategies not only to grow their respective churches but also to achieve their social and political goals. Their significant success resulted in antebellum America becoming a remarkably religious society. Both domestic and foreign observers regularly chronicled how "the ideals of evangelical Protestantism seemed to dominant national culture."[1] The noted French political philosopher Alexis de Tocqueville declared in the 1830s, "There is no country in the world where the Christian religion retains a greater influence over the souls of men than in America."[2] In the decades preceding the Civil War, the evangelical majority of White Protestants developed innovative tactics and exerted cultural power in their efforts to transform the United States into a broadly Christian civilization.

This chapter analyzes three primary, interconnected methods employed by these Protestants both to persuade individuals to become pious, passionate Christians and to Christianize American culture as a whole.

1. Smith, *Revivalism and Social Reform*, 37.
2. Alexis de Tocqueville, as quoted in Cole, *Social Ideas*, 12.

First, leaders planned and promoted religious revivals. Evangelists inspired hundreds of thousands of conversions and commitments to Christianity, which fueled the massive growth of churches and other religious organizations that depended upon voluntary support as a result of disestablishment. In addition, despite denominational differences, recurrent waves of revivals in the first half of the nineteenth century reinforced common Protestant evangelical attitudes and experiences that helped to create a shared national culture. Second, many Protestants sought to restore aspects of early Christianity that seemed abandoned or forgotten. Those associated with the ecclesiastical restorationist movement championed church unity and doctrinal purity by calling all Christians to return to the primitive, ideal example of the New Testament church. The restorationist impulse also prompted other prominent leaders to insist that Christians can and should seek moral perfectionism through entire sanctification by the Holy Spirit. Third, Protestants created scores of benevolent societies and participated in reform movements that focused on a range of personal vices and social problems. While encouraging virtuous character and aiding individuals in need, these enterprises also enabled evangelical Christians to shape public affairs and politics according to their moral vision for the nation. Throughout the antebellum era, this moral vision often included millennial expectations that energized White Protestants' revivalism, restorationism, and reform activities. They hoped and even anticipated that their efforts were preparing the way for Christ's second coming and the inauguration of his thousand-year reign on earth.

Although evangelical Protestants had created the largest and most powerful subculture in the United States by the middle third of the nineteenth century, theological and political controversies undermined their dreams of establishing a thoroughly Christian America. The veneer of widespread consensus regarding the authority of the Bible, the importance of revivals, the need for social reforms, and millennial aspirations could not mask increasingly contentious differences. Debates concerning the legitimacy of slavery produced the greatest crises, fracturing the major Protestant denominations and revealing doubts concerning the efficacy of revivals and religiously based social reform. This chapter concludes by analyzing the limits and legacy of the combination of revivalism, restorationism, and reforms within antebellum Evangelicalism.

Revivalism

As a new generation of White Protestant leaders explored how to win converts and influence culture in the early decades of the nineteenth century, revivalism became a prominent feature of American Christianity. Evangelicals believed that everyone needs a personal conversion to Christianity, marked by a spiritual rebirth resulting from conviction of one's sinfulness, faith in Christ's sacrificial death and God's forgiveness, and repentance. As a result, preachers designed revival meetings and tactics that could induce emotional conversion experiences and renew the religious passions of lukewarm Christians. Large gatherings and services—held in places ranging from frontier settings to small towns to the nation's largest urban centers—often occurred over several days and attracted Americans of all kinds. The evangelical Protestant groups most committed to revivalism, Methodists and Baptists in particular, experienced dramatic growth and emerged as the largest Christian denominations. In the 1730s and 1740s, a previous series of revivals had spread throughout the American colonies, which later observers labeled a "Great Awakening." Consequently, the continual promotion and occurrences of revivals from the late 1790s through the 1840s became known as the Second Great Awakening.

Protestant ministers during this period developed their revivalistic practices in the midst of several challenges and changes in the early, expanding republic. After the Revolutionary War, Americans needed to build not only a new political culture but also a new religious culture. Many denominations and individual congregations suffered from disorganization. Leaders worried that the hostile criticism of Deists such as Ethan Allen and Thomas Paine would erode people's commitment to historical Christianity. Not least, with the short-lived exceptions of a few states, the government would not officially sponsor any churches—they would have to rely upon persuasive means to gain members and financial support. To a good number of Christian leaders, the outlook appeared bleak. In 1798, for example, the Presbyterian General Assembly lamented the "general dereliction of religious principle and practice among our fellow citizens," as well as the "visible and prevailing impiety and contempt for the laws and institutions of religion."[3] The effects of migration and emerging economic transformations also began to raise questions for concerned White Protestants. As more and more settlers moved westward into new states and frontier territories, how could Christians evangelize, build institutions, and provide moral guidance to those living in rural areas and inchoate communities? As the destabilizing

---

3. Hudson, *Religion in America*, 131.

forces of the market revolution and industrialization began to draw people to larger cities and to exacerbate social problems, how could Christians sustain their churches and exert their moral authority?

Strategically planned revivals became the foundation for the successful responses of evangelical Protestants who were eager to reach people, to recruit converts, and to retain members. Because disestablishment created a type of religious marketplace in which groups had to contend for potential adherents, revivals represented a pragmatic, assertive, and creative missionary tool. In turn, leaders built upon revival gatherings in frontier areas to establish new congregations and to create denominational networks; in more settled communities and urban contexts, converts joined existing and expanding churches. As social institutions, local churches and other religious associations offered Americans who felt unsettled a sense of community, stability, and moral purpose. As Donald G. Mathews suggests, revivals and the consequent growth of churches during the Second Great Awakening produced "an organizing process that helped to give meaning and direction to people suffering in various degrees from the social strains of a nation on the move into new political, economic, and geographical areas."[4]

In addition, many nineteenth-century Protestant leaders embraced an evolving theological interpretation of revivals that both corresponded with the democratic spirit of the new nation and justified their evangelistic campaigns. Most notable preachers during the First Great Awakening—including Jonathan Edwards, George Whitefield, and Gilbert Tennent—had upheld the Calvinist doctrine that conversions resulted *only* from God's unconditional election of certain people for salvation. During the Second Great Awakening, however, more and more leaders embraced a practical or fully explicit Arminian understanding of conversion that emphasized humans' responsibility. People possess free will, they insisted, the ability to accept or to reject God's gracious offer of salvation. While Methodists and Free Will Baptists had been proclaiming this tenet since the mid-eighteenth century, influential New Englanders such as Yale theologian Nathaniel William Taylor and nationally known minister Lyman Beecher began to modify the strict Calvinism of their predecessors by stressing humans' free agency and choice. Charles Grandison Finney, the most famous advocate and architect of nineteenth-century revivalism, especially popularized perceptions of conversion as the responsibility of people themselves. "The fact is, sinners, that God requires you to turn [i.e., to convert], and what he requires of you, he cannot do for you. It must be your own voluntary act," Finney declared. "Do not wait then for him to do your duty, but do it immediately yourself,

---

4. Mathews, "Second Great Awakening," 27.

on pain of eternal death."[5] Revivalist messages that described salvation as available to anyone willing to convert aligned with the democratic ideals of individual liberty, optimistic autonomy, and egalitarianism within early nineteenth-century American culture. Just as important, the conviction that conversions result from voluntary human choices rather than from divine determination inspired preachers to try to stimulate revivals through sermons and strategies that would cause hearers to make such a decision.

While the shared evangelical impulse that animated the Second Great Awakening loosely connected many Protestant participants, separate series of revivals occurred in diverse regions, unfolded over different times, and developed divergent styles. In New England, the efforts of Yale College president Timothy Dwight at the end of the eighteenth century to combat religious apathy and Deist sympathies laid the foundation for subsequent revivals. Dwight's persistent chapel sermons defending the Christian faith and promoting experiential religion prompted the conversions of one-third of the student body in 1802. Many Yale graduates went on to work for revivalism as Congregational ministers. One acclaimed example was Asahel Nettleton, the region's most successful itinerant evangelist in the early nineteenth century. Though he remained a traditional Calvinist and later opposed Charles Finney's theology and techniques, Nettleton's solemn preaching and calls for repentance inspired an estimated thirty thousand conversions. Dwight's protégés Lyman Beecher and Nathaniel William Taylor became the most visible champions of New England revivalism. Claiming that he "was baptized into the revival spirit," Beecher played a central role in encouraging campaigns for conversions during his fifty-year career as first a Congregational and Presbyterian minister and then a seminary president in Cincinnati.[6] Taylor, one of the most influential theologians of his generation, provided sophisticated justifications for revivals. His attempt to synthesize Calvinist doctrines of God's sovereignty and humans' total depravity with a rationalistic defense of human responsibility and free will—known as the New Haven theology—provoked divisive debates with staunch Calvinists but also emboldened evangelical efforts to win converts. Through the 1820s, the periodic revivals in New England tended to be decorous affairs led by clergy within local churches.

Revivalism in the recently admitted states of Kentucky and Tennessee and other areas of the American frontier developed quite differently. Few, if any, churches and resident ministers existed to serve new settlements and scattered populations, and thus Protestant leaders organized camp meetings

5. Charles Finney, as quoted in Hambrick-Stowe, *Charles G. Finney*, 82.
6. Beecher, *Autobiography*, 1:45.

in order to evangelize and to exhort audiences. Motivated by some combination of spiritual need, sense of isolation, and curiosity, hundreds and sometimes thousands of people traveled to these multiday, outdoor religious gatherings. Participants often had emotional conversion experiences and dramatic physical responses during the many hours of fiery sermons, singing, and prayers. In 1800, several revivals led by Presbyterian minister James McCready and Methodist peers in southwestern Kentucky became some of the earliest camp meetings and inspired one of the greatest religious events in American history: the Cane Ridge (KY) Revival of 1801. At a time when the state's largest city of Lexington had just over two thousand residents, somewhere between ten thousand and twenty-five thousand people gathered at this weeklong camp meeting that included Presbyterian, Methodist, and Baptist preachers. The emotional intensity, hundreds of conversions, and eccentric bodily agitations of worshippers were viewed by many as outpourings of the Holy Spirit. Cane Ridge set the stage for thousands of fervent camp meetings over the following decades in rural areas throughout the country and the Western frontier. Methodists and Baptists especially used these types of revivals to grow their denominations, relying upon less formally trained and even lay preachers to offer populist, passionate evangelistic sermons. Methodists also effectively utilized their circuit-riding system, in which itinerant preachers regularly traveled by horseback around a particular geographic area, to participate in camp meetings and to organize churches in rural communities.

The culminating stage of the Second Great Awakening was largely shaped by the revival campaigns and convictions of Charles Finney, the "father of modern revivalism." After his own conversion in 1821 at the age of twenty-nine, Finney immediately abandoned his career as a lawyer in order to become an evangelist. He began his work as a missionary in western New York, a region undergoing massive social and economic changes with the completion of the Erie Canal in 1825. Finney's successful revivals in numerous towns gained national attention, as did his popularization of "new measures" to win converts. He forcefully and directly challenged sinners to repent and to change their own hearts; prayed for people by name; introduced a type of "altar call" by inviting those on the verge of conversion to come forward for prayer at an "anxious bench"; invited women to publicly pray and to testify; and held "protracted meetings" over many consecutive days. Finney's strategies proved both effective and controversial. Critics denounced his tacit Arminian theology and apparent use of emotional manipulation. Undaunted and unapologetic, Finney extended his reputation through larger, longer, and ecumenical preaching engagements throughout the Northeast, including New York, Philadelphia, Rochester, and Boston.

The 1835 publication of his *Lectures on Revivals of Religion* provided a summary of his methods and best-selling manual for other evangelists to follow. That year, Finney also accepted a professorial position at Oberlin College in Ohio, eventually becoming president in 1851. His example, writings, and influence through his work at Oberlin ensured that revivalism remained an enduring urban phenomenon and not merely associated with the frontier.[7]

The proliferation and popular appeal of revivals during the first half of the nineteenth century transformed America's religious landscape. While Congregationalists (heirs of seventeenth-century Puritans) and Anglicans (members of the Church of England) had been the largest colonial groups, by the 1850s Methodists and Baptists became predominant and together accounted for 70 percent of Protestant Christians. The number of Methodist churches soared from about seven hundred in 1790 to nearly twenty thousand in 1860; Baptist congregations grew from less than nine hundred to over twelve thousand; and Presbyterian churches increased from about seven hundred to more than six thousand. Collectively, evangelical Protestants across denominations accounted for approximately 40 percent of the American population.[8] To be sure, many Americans rejected and resisted revivalism: Old School Calvinists, liturgical Protestants, Unitarians, Catholics, and non-Christian groups. Nevertheless, revivals became a defining part of antebellum American culture, and evangelical Protestantism served as a significant bond of national unity. In the words of C. C. Goen, "The revivals and the multifaceted activities they generated laid the foundation for a religiously based nationalism that transcended sectional differences, tamed the 'barbarism' of the frontier, and heightened Americans' sense of fulfilling a special vocation in the purposes of the Almighty."[9] Indeed, prior to the Civil War, many Protestant leaders interpreted the success of revivals and growth of Evangelical Christianity as hopeful signs that God's millennial kingdom could well come soon in America.

Restorationism

Evangelical revivalism may have flourished in the soil of disestablishment, but the possibilities for religious freedom and the populist ethos of the early nineteenth century also allowed for significant religious diversity to arise. Common core convictions and cooperative evangelistic efforts did not prevent Protestant groups from disagreeing and competing for members.

---

7. Hambrick-Stowe, *Charles G. Finney*.
8. Smith, *Revivalism and Social Reform*, 22; Noll, *Civil War*, 12, 27.
9. Goen, *Broken Churches, Broken Nation*, 24; see also Noll, *Civil War*, 25–27.

Beyond mainstream denominations, an array of new and alternative religious movements also emerged.[10] In the midst of religious fervor and tumult, some leaders looked backwards for guidance to the beginnings of Christianity. They believed that restoring the beliefs and behaviors of the primitive first-century church as described in the New Testament offered solutions to religious conflicts and ideal models for Christian living. This restorationism, or Christian primitivism, took two distinct forms during the Second Great Awakening.[11]

The first type focused on ecclesiastical primitivism, returning to the simple nature of the early church. The urge to restore the pure essence of Christianity by renouncing extrabiblical creeds, denominational structures, and other church customs arose within a number of scattered groups. The two most important ones were led respectively by Barton W. Stone and Thomas and Alexander Campbell. As a Presbyterian minister, Stone helped to coordinate the 1801 Cane Ridge Revival. Two years later, however, he and several associates withdrew from the denomination and declared their intentions to abandon all "traditions of men." They adopted the plain title of "Christians" and the Bible as their only standard for faith and practice. Loosely led by Stone, this Christian movement attracted thousands of followers in Kentucky and southern Ohio over the following decades. Another Presbyterian minister in Pennsylvania, Thomas Campbell, followed a similar path. In 1809 he resigned from his synod and organized a nondenominational "Christian Association" that rejected all creeds and ecclesiastical institutions in favor of the New Testament as their only guide. "Where the Scriptures speak, we speak," the group insisted, and "where the Scriptures are silent, we are silent." Thomas's son Alexander eventually took leadership of their growing movement, which benefited from the successful revivalistic campaigns of Walter Scott. Reacting against religious diversity and divisiveness, both Stone and the Campbells believed that restoring the primitive Christianity depicted in the New Testament offered a basis for Christian union. In 1832 their affinities led to a merger under the interchangeable labels of "Christians" and "Disciples of Christ." Alexander Campbell began publishing *The Millennial Harbinger* with hopes that this restoration movement was preparing the way for Christ's kingdom. By 1850, the Disciples of Christ had grown to well over one hundred thousand members.[12]

---

10. Hatch, *Democratization of American Christianity*.

11. For an overview of different types of restorationism, or Christian primitivism, see Hughes, "Christian Primitivism as Perfectionism."

12. Williams et al., *Stone-Campbell Movement*, 20.

The most reviled yet ultimately most successful new religious movement that arose during the Second Great Awakening—the Church of Jesus Christ of Latter-day Saints—originated with a very different interpretation of ecclesiastical restoration. As a teenager in western New York, Joseph Smith Jr. felt confused by competing Christian groups conducting revivals. In the early 1820s, he claimed to have a series of visions in which God told him not to join any denomination, for all of their creeds were incorrect. Instead, Smith had been chosen as a prophet to restore "the only true and living church upon the face of the whole earth" (Doctrine and Covenants 1:30). He published the Book of Mormon, a supplementary scripture to the Bible, and reinstituted a priesthood, temple ordinances, and eventually polygamy ("plural marriage") based upon further divine revelations and Old Testament precedents. Popularly known as Mormonism, the Church of Jesus Christ of Latter-day Saints attracted many thousands of converts in the 1830s. Traditional Christians, however, denounced the movement as heretical and responded hostilely to successive Mormon communities in Ohio, Missouri, and Illinois. After a mob murdered Smith in 1844, his successor Brigham Young led a Mormon migration to Utah, where the Mormons sought to build their own unique millennial kingdom of God on earth.[13]

The second type of restorationism that developed as an even broader force among evangelical Protestants prior to the Civil War combined commitments to ethical and experiential primitivism. Proponents called for a renewed focus on biblical expectations for righteous living through the power of the Holy Spirit, especially highlighting the "baptism of the Holy Spirit" experienced by the earliest Christians on the day of Pentecost (Acts 2). Many also found inspiration in the teaching of John Wesley, the eighteenth-century founder of the Methodist movement, that Christians have the ability and the duty to attain holiness, or "Christian perfection" and "entire sanctification." The Methodist Phoebe Palmer emerged as a central figure in the holiness movement. After her own experience of entire sanctification in 1837, she inspired an array of Protestant leaders and laity to pursue perfection through renowned weekly meetings in New York City, best-selling books such as *The Way of Holiness* (1843), and preaching at camp meetings and other revivals. At the same time, Charles Finney, Oberlin College president Asa Mahan, and other associates also began to promote entire sanctification. Mahan published *Scripture Doctrine of Christian Perfection* in 1839, and Finney lectured regularly about the need for Christians to consecrate themselves fully to God and to pursue complete obedience to the moral law. "Perfect sanctification is the great blessing

---

13. Bowman, *Mormon People*.

promised throughout the Bible," he taught; and "perfect sanctification is the very object for which the Holy Spirit is promised."[14] Through the influence of Finney, Oberlin advocates, and prominent Methodists, a desire for holiness became a significant theme within Protestant Evangelicalism. "The whole nineteenth-century evangelical movement," Grant Wacker observes, "might well be defined as historic Protestant orthodoxy spiced with a tingling expectation that the power of the Holy Spirit, lost since the days of the apostles, was about to be restored."[15]

Social Reform

While the burgeoning holiness movement concentrated primarily on personal perfection, the bulk of antebellum Protestant Evangelicals also aspired to redeem American culture. They believed that God had given them a civilizing mission to help the needy, to redress social problems, and to imprint the nation with Christian morality. In the absence of government support, Protestants, especially in the Northeast, launched a wide range of voluntary charitable organizations and public reform campaigns that shaped American society and politics in the first half of the nineteenth century. The United States was expanding and changing rapidly, but the country had relatively weak national institutions. Benevolent societies and reform movements helped to form powerful local, regional, and often nationwide associations that united diverse Christians in new coalitions. Inspired by prominent leaders, many Evangelicals connected their own moral agency to broad social problems, extending their personal piety into public action. Different strategies emerged: some believed that social transformation would result best from an aggregate of converted and reformed individuals, while others focused on institutional and structural changes through political actions. In addition, northern Evangelicals more directly connected revivalism and social issues than did southern Christians. As enthusiastic Evangelicals channeled their energies into building a Christian civilization in line with their millennial hopes, revivals and reforms became closely associated during the Second Great Awakening.

Most of the early benevolent groups and movements originated among Congregationalists and Presbyterians influenced by New England revivalism and the concept of "disinterested benevolence" promoted by theologian Samuel Hopkins. Seeking to regulate America's religious and ethical progress,

---

14. Finney, *Lectures to Professing Christians*, 348, 352.

15. Grant Wacker, as quoted in Hughes, "Christian Primitivism as Perfectionism," 239. For more on perfectionism, see Smith, *Revivalism and Social Reform*, 103–47.

philanthropic Protestants formed missionary, education, humanitarian, and moral reform societies that collectively became known as the "benevolent empire." These parachurch organizations relied upon middle-class participants and elite benefactors such as New York businessmen Arthur and Lewis Tappan. Evangelical ministers also played critical roles, and no one in the early nineteenth century did more to promote the dual necessity of revivals and social reform than Lyman Beecher. "The great aim of the Christian Church in its relation to the present life is not only to renew the individual man, but also to reform human society," he believed.[16] Beecher helped to found and to direct numerous voluntary societies, which he envisioned acting as "a sort of disciplined moral militia" that would "devise ways and means of suppressing vice and guarding the public morals."[17] National organizations devoted to spreading Christian knowledge and virtue arose in the 1810s and 1820s, such as the American Bible Society, the American Home Missionary Society, the American Sunday School Union, and the American Tract Society. At the state and local level, a multitude of benevolent societies were founded to address specific issues and problems, including poverty, prostitution, prison reform, access to education, physical and mental disabilities, protecting the Sabbath, and alcoholic intemperance. On the whole, these charitable and social reform initiatives reflected the conservative vision of White Protestants for maintaining a Christian moral order.[18]

Beginning in the 1830s, the revivals of Charles Finney and the spread of perfectionist theology unleashed within broader evangelical circles a new wave of populist energy and more radical approaches to reform. Like Beecher, Finney urged Christians to work both for people's spiritual salvation and for social transformation. "The great business of the church is to reform the world—to put away every kind of sin," he declared. Thus Christians must endeavor "to reform individuals, communities, and governments."[19] Personally, Finney took a moderate approach to social reforms, supporting movements such as temperance and abolitionism but prioritizing individualistic and spiritual solutions. The primary, permanent cure for any and all sin is the conversion and sanctification of people, Finny asserted. He therefore warned against campaigns that competed with rather than complemented evangelism, arguing that reform efforts should remain "an appendage of a

---

16. Beecher, *Autobiography*, 1:253.

17. Abzug, *Cosmos Crumbling*, 45.

18. Young, *Bearing Witness against Sin*, 54–85. For an analysis of the conservative, imperial nature of the "benevolent empire," see Marty, *Righteous Empire*.

19. Charles Finney, as quoted in Dayton, *Discovering an Evangelical Heritage*, 67.

general revival of religion."[20] Nevertheless, Finney's Oberlin perfectionism, combined with his conviction that entirely sanctified Christians would increasingly conquer evil and eventually establish Christ's millennial kingdom, inspired many friends and followers to pursue radical social reforms. Similarly, even though the social actions of Phoebe Palmer and other Methodist leaders generally focused on humanitarian aid, their holiness teaching galvanized some in the Wesleyan perfectionist tradition to promote progressive public and political goals.

Perfectionist reformers raised the intensity of social movements by rejecting gradual, ameliorating changes and insisting upon an absolute, immediate end to evils and injustices. They extended expectations for holiness beyond personal conduct and into political concerns: not only individuals but also societies should perfectly obey God's moral law *without delay*. The largest and most contentious antebellum reform movements—temperance and abolition—were especially transformed by perfectionist zeal. Many early benevolent societies concerned about alcohol concentrated only on distilled liquor, advocated moderate consumption, and relied upon moral suasion. By the early 1830s, however, perfectionist temperance activists were promoting abstinence from all alcoholic beverages and legal prohibition, inspiring hundreds of thousands of personal pledges to teetotalism and eventually several state-level restrictions on public sales. A significant number of Finneyite and Wesleyan perfectionists directed even more energy into abolitionist campaigns. Influenced by William Lloyd Garrison's uncompromising demands for immediate emancipation, they condemned proposals for the gradual end of slavery as immoral toleration of social sin. Leaders such as Finney disciple Timothy Dwight Weld and the Wesleyan Methodists Orange Scott and Luther Lee worked as agents to promote antislavery societies and equal rights for Black Americans. Under Finney's influence, Oberlin College became a hub for abolitionism and other progressive evangelical activism. In addition to educating Black students, Oberlin was the first college to admit both male and female students in 1837. Women regularly had equal opportunities and important roles within the revival and reform movements associated with perfectionists, and this inchoate support for evangelical feminism contributed to the broader development of the early women's rights movement. In the decades prior to the Civil War, perfectionist Evangelicals often viewed the political platforms and

---

20. Charles Finney, as quoted in Cole, *Social Ideas*, 208. For more on Finney's opinions, see Moorhead, "Social Reform."

candidates of the Liberty or Free Soil Parties as most compatible with their hopes for radical social reform.[21]

Conclusion: The Limits and Legacy of Revivalism, Restorationism, and Reform

To the chagrin of antebellum Protestants, conflicts that presaged the Civil War—not the millennial kingdom of God—steadily grew in the 1850s. Evangelicals had created a synthesis of revivalism, restorationism, and reform that appeared for several decades as a promising basis for uniting the majority of Protestants and strengthening the status of America as a culturally Christian nation. Yet this foundation proved fragile and inadequate, particularly in the face of irreconcilable disagreements among Evangelicals themselves regarding the moral and political status of slavery. The leading denominations fractured primarily along regional lines, as southern Christians chafed at attempts by their northern brethren to discipline slaveholding ministers and missionaries. In the Methodist Episcopal Church, a faction of abolitionists grew impatient with the larger denomination's hesitancy to condemn slavery, and in 1843 they withdrew to form the Wesleyan Methodist Church. A year later, the remaining Methodists split into southern and northern bodies. Southern and northern Baptists separated and formed their own cooperative conventions in 1845. Presbyterians had already divided in 1837, with "Old School" members evicting "New School" Presbyterians for doctrinal departures from Calvinism related to revivalism. Debates over slavery led to a sectional separation within each group, the New School in 1857 and the Old School in 1861. These ecclesiastical divisions did more than undermine religious collaboration and the optimistic millennial visions of Evangelicals. They also severed an important bond of national unity, shattering many White Protestants' sense of common identity and purpose. In so doing, the denominational schisms foreshadowed and perhaps even provoked the southern political secession that led to the Civil War.[22]

In less conspicuous ways, controversies regarding slavery also further exposed and exacerbated competing interpretations among mid-nineteenth-century Evangelicals concerning the relationship between revivals and social reform. Should revivals essentially concentrate on personal spiritual conversions, affecting the public welfare only indirectly through the actions of redeemed individuals? Or should revivals also address social sins

21. Dayton, *Rediscovering an Evangelical Heritage*; Strong, *Perfectionist Politics*.
22. Goen, *Broken Churches, Broken Nation*; see also Noll, *Civil War*, 17–28.

and thus more directly serve as a catalyst for reform? Southern Christians had generally adopted the former view, influenced by Baptist convictions regarding the separation of church and state or Old School Presbyterians' view of the "spirituality of the church." Thus they avoided direct connections between religion and politics, promoting revivals without involving political questions about slavery. By the 1850s, intractable disagreements regarding abolition led more and more northern Evangelicals to also disassociate revivals from contentious political questions in order to maintain a unified focus on conversions. Protestant revivalism became increasingly socially conservative if not fully silent about social issues. The Great Revival of 1857–58, involving mass prayer meetings that spread from New York city throughout the nation, culminated this trend. Organizers explicitly prohibited participants from raising controversial topics such as slavery, prioritizing issues of personal piety while virtually ignoring questions of social evils and injustices. As a result, radical and perfectionist Evangelicals grew more doubtful concerning the effectiveness of revivalism as an instrument for social reform, and many shifted their attention and energies to political action.[23]

Although the combination of revivalism, restorationism, and reform prevalent among Evangelicals in the first half of the nineteenth century largely disappeared by the Civil War, each of these themes became a prominent feature of a subsequent movement within Protestantism. Socially conservative revivalism that focused on personal conversions and piety remained a defining characteristic of late nineteenth- and twentieth-century Evangelicalism. Renowned evangelists such as Dwight Moody, Billy Sunday, Aimee Semple McPherson, and Billy Graham followed many of the revival principles and practices popularized by Charles Finney.[24] In contrast, more theologically liberal Protestants adopted the emphasis upon social reform, particularly participants in the social gospel movement that arose in the late nineteenth century.[25] From within the holiness movement, a commitment to restorationism inspired the development of Pentecostalism, which sought to recover the charismatic gifts of the Holy Spirit experienced by the earliest Christians as described in the New Testament.[26] In the 1970s, a minority movement arose within evangelical circles that sought to recover a balanced concern for spiritual conversions and social activism. These contemporary progressive Evangelicals, or the evangelical left, have justified their political

23. Long, *Revival of 1857–58*, 93–126.
24. FitzGerald, *Evangelicals*.
25. Evans, *Social Gospel*.
26. Wacker, *Heaven Below*.

engagement by highlighting the examples of their antebellum predecessors who refused to divorce revivals and social reforms.[27] Thus the legacy of early and mid-nineteenth century Protestant Evangelicals continues to reverberate in American religion.

Bibliography

Abzug, Robert H. *Cosmos Crumbling: American Reform and the Religious Imagination.* New York: Oxford University Press, 1994.
Beecher, Lyman. *The Autobiography of Lyman Beecher.* 2 vols. Cambridge, MA: Belknap, 1961.
Bowman, Matthew. *The Mormon People: The Making of an American Faith.* New York: Random House, 2012.
Carwardine, Richard. *Transatlantic Revivalism: Popular Evangelicalism in Britain and American, 1790–1865.* Contributions in American History 75. Westport, CT: Greenwood, 1978.
Cole, Charles Chester. *The Social Ideas of the Northern Evangelists, 1826–1860.* New York: Columbia University Press, 1954.
Dayton, Donald W., with Douglas M. Strong. *Rediscovering an Evangelical Heritage: A Tradition and Trajectory of Integrating Piety and Justice.* 2nd ed. Grand Rapids: Baker Academic, 2014.
Evans, Christopher H. *The Social Gospel in American Religion: A History.* New York: NYU Press, 2017.
Finney, Charles. *Lectures to Professing Christians.* New York: Revell, 1879.
FitzGerald, Frances. *The Evangelicals: The Struggle to Shape America.* New York: Simon & Schuster, 2017.
Gasaway, Brantley W. *Progressive Evangelicals and the Pursuit of Social Justice.* Chapel Hill: University of North Carolina Press, 2014.
Goen, C. C. *Broken Churches, Broken Nation: Denominational Schisms and the Coming of the American Civil War.* Macon, GA: Mercer University Press, 1985.
Hambrick-Stowe, Charles E. *Charles G. Finney and the Spirit of American Evangelicalism.* Grand Rapids: Eerdmans, 1996.
Hatch, Nathan O. *The Democratization of American Christianity.* New Haven, CT: Yale University Press, 1989.
Hudson, Winthrop S. *Religion in America: An Historical Account of the Development of American Religious Life.* 3rd ed. New York: Scribner, 1981.
Hughes, Richard T. "Christian Primitivism as Perfectionism: From Anabaptists to Pentecostals." In *Reaching Beyond: Chapters in the History of Perfectionism*, edited by Stanley M. Burgess, 213–55. Peabody, MA: Hendrickson, 1986.
Long, Kathryn Teresa. *The Revival of 1857–58: Interpreting an American Religious Awakening.* Religion in America. New York: Oxford University Press, 1998.
Marty, Martin E. *Righteous Empire: The Protestant Experience in America.* New York: Dial, 1970.

---

27. Dayton with Strong, *Rediscovering an Evangelical Heritage*; Gasaway, *Progressive Evangelicals.*

Mathews, Donald G. "The Second Great Awakening as an Organizing Process, 1780–830: An Hypothesis." *American Quarterly* 21 (Spring 1969) 23–43.

Moorhead, James H. "Social Reform and the Divided Conscience of Antebellum Protestantism." *CH* 48 (Dec. 1979) 416–30.

Noll, Mark. *The Civil War as a Theological Crisis*. Steven and Janice Brose Lectures in the Civil War Era. Chapel Hill: University of North Carolina Press, 2006.

Smith, Timothy L. *Revivalism and Social Reform: American Protestantism on the Eve of the Civil War*. Baltimore: Johns Hopkins University Press, 1980.

Strong, Douglass M. *Perfectionist Politics: Abolitionism and the Religious Tensions of American Democracy*. Religion and Politics. Syracuse, NY: Syracuse University Press, 1999.

Wacker, Grant. *Heaven Below: Early Pentecostals and American Culture*. Cambridge, MA: Harvard University Press, 2001.

Williams, D. Newell, et al., eds. *The Stone-Campbell Movement: A Global History*. St. Louis: Chalice, 2013.

Young, Michael P. *Bearing Witness against Sin: The Evangelical Birth of the American Social Movement*. Chicago: University of Chicago Press, 2006.

Chapter 6

Called to Arouse, Warn, and Save

The American Fascination with Premillennial Dispensationalism

CHRISTOPHER H. EVANS

IN 1912, WALTER RAUSCHENBUSCH, the major figure of the social gospel movement in the United States, gave a hopeful assessment of the American religious landscape. Five years after his groundbreaking book *Christianity and the Social Crisis*, Rauschenbusch saw Protestant churches taking aggressive actions to combat the social evils of the era. Noting the number of Protestant denominations that had adopted social creeds, as well as the 1908 founding of the Federal Council of Churches, Rauschenbusch looked confidently to what he saw as a significant social awakening in the churches.[1] Even as he saw signs that churches were engaging the social-economic problems of the nation, Rauschenbusch also recognized that many Christians resisted his calls for social action. Among them was the Rev. I. M. Haldeman, pastor of the First Baptist Church of New York. Haldeman represented a conservative wing of American Protestantism that by the early 1920s would become known as Fundamentalism. For years, he had written pamphlets condemning theological liberalism and late nineteenth-century religious movements such as Christian Science and Theosophy. Now, Haldeman took aim at the most well-known proponent of social Christianity, accusing Rauschenbusch's work as anathema to the historic truths of Christianity.

While Haldeman objected to several aspects of Rauschenbusch's theology, his chief concern circled back to Rauschenbusch's failure to grasp the true meaning of the Bible. For Haldeman, Scripture didn't point to a Christianity that could save the world from its sins. Rather, the gospel pointed to a faith where people needed to be saved from a world of sin. "The world is to the Church in this age as a ship pounding to pieces on the rocks," he explained. "The Church is to the world in this age . . . as a life-saving service

1. Rauschenbusch, *Christianizing the Social Order*, 1–39.

on the shore, called to arouse, warn and save individuals from the growing wreck."[2] For Haldeman, the church's efforts to reform society were a waste of time, distracting Christians from their central mission of saving as many souls as possible before the second coming of Christ brought an end to the world.

I. M. Haldeman was one of numerous representatives of a strand of apocalyptic Christianity called premillennial dispensationalism. Emerging out of movements of British and North American Evangelicalism in the mid-nineteenth century, dispensationalism represented a movement rooted in historical forms of Christian apocalyptic thought, while also being a unique form of nineteenth-century evangelical theology. By the early twentieth century, the apocalyptic themes within dispensationalism not only shaped the theology of major figures in evangelical colleges, seminaries, and mission boards; they also crafted a practical template for interpreting Scripture that appealed to thousands of Americans on a grassroots level.

Throughout the twentieth century, dispensationalist ideas concerning the return of Christ and the end-times dominated the worldview of several high-profile evangelical leaders, and became part of the cultural fabric of countless churches throughout the US. In the twenty-first century, dispensationalist themes are deeply woven in popular culture, reflected in the popularity of books such as Tim LaHaye and Jerry Jenkins's *Left Behind* series, and in countless movies and television shows.[3]

Historically, church leaders, like Walter Rauschenbusch, attacked dispensationalists for promoting a theology of pessimism. A close examination of the history of this movement, however, moves beyond what some would dismiss merely as a "gloom and doom" theology. At the heart of the movement lies a unique theological movement that illuminates the history of American Evangelicalism, as well as a broader fascination with apocalyptic themes woven into the fabric of American history.

Origins

Christianity has always fostered strong apocalyptic sentiments. From the Greek, the term *apocalypse* means something that is hidden or concealed, and many Jewish and Christian Scriptures seem to offer clues that God will cast a final judgment upon evil forces on the earth. In early Christianity, the apostle Paul's first-century writings expressed a sentiment that the church might witness the return of Christ during Paul's lifetime.

---

2. Haldeman, *Prof. Rauschenbusch's "Christianity,"* 36.
3. Forbes, "Apocalypticism in the United States"; Hummel, *Rise and Fall*, 301–29.

Even as these apocalyptic beliefs died out in subsequent centuries, they never fully disappeared from church history. While verses from the four Gospels and Pauline texts contributed to apocalyptic speculation, historically the key apocalyptic Scriptures were Daniel from the Hebrew Bible and the final book in the Christian Bible, Revelation. Addressing different historical contexts and faith communities, these books inspired—and frustrated—generations of thinkers who saw them as holding the key to understanding God's ultimate plans for humanity. Written in the second century BCE, Daniel represented an example of Jewish apocalypticism that flourished in the centuries before the birth of Christ and that characterized segments of Judaism in the first century CE. Set in the time of the Babylonian exile of the sixth century BCE, Daniel is depicted as an exiled Jewish prophet in the court of the Babylonian king Nebuchadnezzar II. With its vivid depiction of dreams, prophecies, and its cryptic use of numerology to foretell God's final judgment, the book describes Daniel's perseverance amid persecution, while he remains steadfast in his faith. In the tradition of Jewish apocalypticism that emerged in the second century BCE, Daniel spoke a message of encouragement to a beleaguered people, offering hope that at the end of time, God would destroy the wicked and raise up persons who had faithfully endured centuries of persecution.[4]

Later Christian apocalyptic interpreters were drawn to Daniel, reading its prophecies through a christological lens. The book was often read alongside of the book of Revelation. Written in the late first century CE, that book tells of an exiled apostle named John who in the tradition of Daniel provides vivid accounts of God's final judgment. While many see the book allegorically, designed to offer Christians hope in the face of Roman persecution, Revelation sparked intense debate among centuries of Christian theologians who saw it as foretelling the second coming of Christ and God's final judgment upon humanity. Laying out a pattern of great political and military turmoil on earth, the book points to the rise of the antichrist and the battle of Armageddon, in which the forces of Christ defeat the forces of Satan. After a thousand years of peace, Satan wages a final battle against Christ, leading to a heavenly realm on earth, where the righteous in faith will dwell forever with God in peace and harmony.

> Then I saw a new heaven and a new earth: for the first heaven and the first earth were passed away; . . . and I heard a great voice from the throne saying, "Behold, the dwelling of God is with men. He will dwell with them, and they shall be his people, and God himself will be with them; he will wipe away every tear

---

4. See Boyer, *When Time Shall Be*, 26–33.

from their eyes, and death shall be no more, neither shall there be mourning, nor crying, nor pain any more, for the former things have passed away." (Rev 21:1, 3–4 RSV)

Revelation spoke of God's ultimate triumph over evil forces in the world. However, after Christianity became the official religion of the Roman Empire in the fourth century, apocalyptic impulses waned. In the medieval era, Christianity was seen as essential to preserving ecclesiastical and civil order. The end-times would occur sometime in the distant future, but the need for the church to provide one a path toward eternal life in the present was more important than belief that the second coming was imminent. Even with the sixteenth-century Reformation, most Protestant movements focused on the church's role in forging ecclesiastical and political unity—especially at a time when European Christian powers believed in the necessity of one state church.

Yet apocalyptic thought never disappeared entirely from church history. In the twelfth century, Joachim of Fiore, an Italian theologian, speculated on the appearance of the antichrist, postulating that the second coming of Christ would occur sometime in the thirteenth century.[5] Other medieval writers viewed the Crusades as evidence that Christ's return was imminent. While dominant Protestant movements of the sixteenth century, such as the Lutheran and Reformed, often downplayed this sort of end-time speculation, the splintering of Protestant movements into a variety of churches and sects touched off numerous apocalyptic movements in continental Europe and the British Isles in the sixteenth and seventeenth centuries. These movements would help sprout the rise of apocalyptic theologies in North American European colonies, particularly in the English colonies that later formed the United States.

Post- vs. Premillennialism

Dispensationalists frequently emphasized the uniqueness of their approach to interpreting Scripture. However, the movement fit well within a tradition of apocalyptic thought present in North America since its colonial settlement in the seventeenth and eighteenth centuries.[6] Historically, the United States has a strong tradition of civil religion, emphasizing God's role in guiding the affairs of the nation. Many cite the 1630 oration of John Winthrop, the founding governor of the Massachusetts Bay Colony, whose address

---

5. McGinn, *Antichrist*, 135–42.
6. Davidson, *Logic of Millennial Thought*.

to the colonists became woven into the fabric of a subsequent American civil religion. Reflecting the strong Puritan sentiments of the new colony, Winthrop spoke of the settlement in language steeped in biblical imagery. "We shall find that the God of Israel is upon us, . . . that men shall say of succeeding plantations, 'the Lord make it like that of New England.' For we must consider that we shall be a city upon a hill." While striking a hopeful note, Winthrop also warned of the consequences that awaited those who failed to live up to the covenant they were making with God. "The eyes of all people are upon us, so that if we shall deal falsely with our God in this work we have undertaken, and so cause him to withdraw his present help from us, we shall be made a story and a byword through the world. . . . We shall shame the faces of many of God's worthy servants, and cause their prayers to be turned into curses upon us till we be consumed out of the good land whither we are going."[7]

In a short oration, Winthrop sketched out two sides of eschatology that have dominated American Christianity ever since. Eschatology defines the branch of Christian theology commonly associated with God's final purposes for humanity. On one hand, Winthrop suggests a hopeful view of the future, one where churches might serve as leaven for converting people to Christianity. However, the other side of Winthrop's speech emphasizes the idea of judgment upon a people who are guilty of breaking God's covenant, choosing instead to live in sin. It is this latter view that centuries later would sprout apocalyptic beliefs that shaped premillennial dispensationalism.

Even as many colonial-era ministers believed that they might live to see the inauguration of a divine era of peace on earth, many also speculated on apocalyptic themes. New England clergy such as Cotton Mather and Jonathan Edwards regularly engaged in speculation regarding the end-times, drawing upon larger world events to justify their arguments.[8] One prominent New Englander, Samuel Sewell, read contemporary events through an apocalyptic lens. Keeping track of local and international occurrences. Sewell frequently turned to the Bible to interpret these events, often praying fervently for the Lord's coming.[9]

However, colonial theologians who read biblical texts like Revelation struggled with the question: If the second coming of Christ was indeed near, would it come about peacefully or through catastrophe? While many colonial ministers frequently changed their minds on this subject, theories of God's final judgment often depended on how one interpreted the book of

---

7. Evans, *Histories of American Christianity*, 21.
8. Silverman, *Cotton Mather*; Marsden, *Jonathan Edwards*.
9. Hall, "Mental World."

Revelation's meaning of the millennium. For many Protestants, especially in the aftermath of the American Revolution, American independence ushered in a period of new possibilities where many believed that the nation's churches would play a unique role in bringing about the kingdom of God on earth. The spirit of revivalism that accompanied the Second Great Awakening led many new religious movements to emphasize that they were doing nothing less than restoring primitive Christianity to American shores. Free from the polluting European influences of popery, monarchy, and political aristocracy, evangelical Protestantism took on the task of perfecting society, advocating for a range of reforms, including creating public schools, promoting temperance reform, supporting women's rights, and abolishing slavery.[10]

This strand of nineteenth-century Evangelicalism is frequently termed postmillennialism. Represented by revivalist preachers like Charles Finney, postmillennial theology stressed that America might build the kingdom of God on earth, in advance of Christ's second coming. Yet the antebellum era also saw the emergence of new sects that stressed the opposite perspective. Known as premillennialism, these Evangelicals did not necessarily reject the importance of social reform. However, they could not reconcile a world of peace coming before God's final judgment. The most prominent of these antebellum groups was led by an upstate New York farmer, William Miller. Focusing on the books of Daniel and Revelation, Miller devised a chronology that predicted the return of Christ and the end of the world, first in 1843 and then in 1844. The failure of this event to materialize ended Miller's movement, but it led to the growth of new apocalyptic movements.[11] While the nineteenth century witnessed the emergence of several churches with strong apocalyptic theologies, including the Seventh-day Adventists and Jehovah's Witnesses, dispensationalism found a home in a range of Protestant sects and churches.

The Dispensationalist Turn

Dispensationalism emerged as a unique third-way response to various forms of nineteenth-century evangelical Protestant eschatology. On one hand, it rejected the optimistic eschatology associated with postmillennial Evangelicalism, yet it also spurned the idea of tying down Christ's second coming to a specific date. Dispensationalism was a form of apocalyptic thought that came across to adherents as both biblical and logical. The movement's origins came from a Church of Ireland clergyman, John Nelson Darby, who

10. See Smith, *Revivalism and Social Reform*.
11. Numbers and Butler, *Disappointed*.

formulated the template for dispensationalist thought that carries down to our day. Darby came to believe that all churches were apostate and devoid of biblical teaching, and in the 1830s he helped found a British sect, the Plymouth Brethren. Like other premillennialists of his era, Darby borrowed ideas from past and contemporary strands of apocalyptic thought. Yet Darby not only avoided the problems of date-setting that plagued William Miller; he crafted a theology that for subsequent generations of followers became a road map for interpreting the whole of Scripture.

Darby's understanding of the end-times emphasized three themes that later generations of dispensationalist thinkers built upon.[12] First, although he avoided date-setting, Darby stressed the idea that earthly conditions would grow worse before Christ's return. Dispensationalists since Darby emphasized the idea that earthly conditions—whether reflected in a lack of individual morality or in broader ecological, cultural, or political calamities—pointed to the likelihood of Christ's second coming. This theme is in line with earlier movements of premillennialist thinkers; however, Darby's successors saw this inevitability not as an excuse to retreat from the world but as underscoring the need for Christians to convert as many people as possible before Christ's return. As I. M. Haldeman noted, "The mission of the Church is not to cry peace in a world which, by the grace of God alone, simply exists under a pronounced, but suspended sentence." Rather, the church served "as the ark was in the days before the flood, a witness of the world's condemnation, a warning of judgment to come."[13] Outside of the apocalyptic texts of Daniel and Revelation, dispensationalists could find many scriptural texts in support of the view that the world would end soon, including from Jesus's own words. Mark 13 and Matt 24 are two chapters often cited by dispensationalists, depicting Jesus warning his disciples about a final judgment that is known only by God, admonishing his followers to be ready for this occurrence. These chapters, where Jesus speaks of a world filled with lawlessness, greed, and many false prophets provided Darby and subsequent generations of dispensationalists a clear biblical mandate for believing that the world was to end soon—even as one was never sure of a precise date.

A second theme of Darby that became a centerpiece for later dispensationalist beliefs was the idea that the unifying message of Scripture focused upon God's covenant with the Jewish nation. Once again, Darby was not unique in espousing arguments that believed that a characteristic

---

12. For further details on Darby, see the following sources: Burnham, *Story of Conflict*, 14–43, 113–36; Hummel, *Rise and Fall*, 19–49.

13. Haldeman, *Prof. Rauschenbuch's "Christianity,"* 52.

of the end-times would be some sort of physical and spiritual restoration of the Jews. Citing God's unique covenant with Israel, Darby believed that the Bible's central message focused upon the redemption of the Jews as well as righteous gentiles as part of scriptural prophecy. Represented in the founding of the Plymouth Brethren, the true church was a remnant of the faithful who rejected the false teachings and prophecies of those bodies that called themselves churches.[14]

Instead of setting dates for Christ's return, Darby devised a theological system that used the Bible to map out a pathway that showed believers how God acted in specific time periods, or dispensations. Stretching from the Genesis account of humanity's creation; the story of the rise and fall of Israel; and leading to the baptism, ministry, death, and resurrection of Christ, Darby noted humanity's repeated failure to stay faithful to God. He saw the establishment of the church at Pentecost (Acts 2) as inaugurating the still-unfulfilled dispensation, frequently dubbed the age of the Holy Spirit, or the church age. For Darby and later dispensationalists, most churches would fall into apostasy, but the true church would be represented by those who turned to Christ for their salvation. Unlike postmillennialists who believed that churches could make the world a righteous place, Darby and successive generations of dispensationalists saw a world steeped in sin where human efforts at building a godly kingdom on earth were futile. In refuting Walter Rauschenbusch, I. M. Haldeman cautioned, God "makes no provision" to save society, but "occupies himself thenceforward with warning the individual soul of its need of salvation."[15]

Finally, Darby is best known for one innovation that he believed would mark the end of the Holy Spirit or church age, with the inauguration of the events leading to the return of Christ. Darby cited a verse from 1 Thess 4:17, where Paul wrote, "Then we who are alive, who are left, shall be caught up together with them in the clouds, to meet the Lord in the air: and so we shall always be with the Lord" (RSV). This event when believers would disappear suddenly and be taken up in the clouds to be with Jesus became known as the rapture. This doctrine is key to understanding not only dispensationalism as a theological system, but also its ongoing appeal to many Christians who emphasize the importance of personal salvation, in order to be taken up to heaven before the final judgment occurs on earth.

Following the rapture, a series of events would unfold that completed the cycle of dispensationalist belief. The rapture removed from earth those true Christians (usually a fairly small number) who manifested saving

---

14. Hummel, *Rise and Fall*, 9–11.
15. Haldeman, *Prof. Rauschenbusch's "Christianity,"* 30.

faith in Christ. This event would then lead to a seven-year period, called the tribulation, that would witness the rise of the antichrist. At the end of this period, Christ would return with his saints in heaven and, along with those who had turned to Christ during the tribulation, wage the battle of Armageddon, where Christ would defeat the forces of Satan. Following descriptions in Revelation, this defeat would inaugurate a millennium of a thousand years of peace, at the end of which Satan would wage one final battle and be defeated by Christ. This last defeat would lead to the final dispensation of eternal peace, whereby Christ would dwell forever with his church in heaven.

John Nelson Darby carved out a unique theology that not only stressed the apocalyptic character of the Bible, but also saw both Testaments telling a unique story of redemption for God's chosen people—embracing both Jews and gentiles.

Jesus Is Coming

Initially, many American Protestant theologians rejected dispensationalism, as it violated the spirit of postmillennial Evangelicalism that believed conversion might usher in a godly kingdom on earth. Despite criticism from many church leaders, dispensationalist theology offered followers a clear guide to interpreting what may have seemed like cryptic biblical texts, while avoiding the problems faced by those, like William Miller, who set precise dates. Even though Darby stayed away from date-setting, successive generations of dispensationalist believers still could look for clues to judge whether the world was creeping closer to the rapture and the beginning of the tribulation that would lead to Christ's second coming.

Before the Civil War, Darby's theories found an audience among some Evangelicals outside of the small circle of those in the Plymouth Brethren. However, after the war dispensationalism (or Darbyism, as it was initially referred to) grew in popularity among many Evangelicals in North America. Part of its appeal rested in the fact that the Civil War and its aftermath seemed to affirm for many Protestants that world conditions were not improving. The death and destruction of the war, and the social-political turmoil that gripped the US in the 1870s and 1880s, gave dispensationalist beliefs a growing popular audience. However, dispensationalism also spread because it provided opportunities for many people to do their own exegetical work of the Bible. After the Civil War, a series of Bible prophecy conferences were held in Ontario and the upper Midwest that brought together dispensationalist practitioners to study Scripture to discern biblical signs of the end-times. Additionally, prominent post–Civil War Protestants, notably Dwight Lyman Moody and missionary leader A. J. Pierson, were converted to dispensationalist teaching.

Although Darby remained a significant figure until his death in 1882, his ideas were finding new expression in a spate of popular publications. Part of the appeal of dispensationalism is that it not only encouraged a close reading of Scripture, but also emphasized—keeping with the root meaning of the word *apocalypse*—that the Bible represented hidden knowledge waiting for the faithful to uncover. As Boston minister Adoniram Judson Gordon noted in 1889, "Scripture is like a dissected map, whose scattered parts we must fit together if we would discover what is the divine pattern of the ages."[16]

Since Darby, many have claimed to have solved the puzzle of the end-times presented in Scripture. One of the most important late nineteenth-century books that spread dispensationalist ideas was written by a Chicago businessman, William Blackstone. With the gripping title *Jesus Is Coming*, Blackstone's volume went through multiple editions since it was first published in 1878.[17] Setting a template for later books on the topic, Blackstone provided readers a book chock-full of scriptural references and charts, showing believers a clear road map through the Bible and explaining the major arcs of dispensationalism, including the rapture, the tribulation, and God's final judgments upon a sinful world where only righteous Christians would survive. Like others in the movement, Blackstone emphasized that one could not determine the exact time when the rapture would occur. However, he also encouraged believers to pay attention to current events for signs. At a time when the US was experiencing high levels of immigration of non-Protestants from Eastern and Southern Europe, Blackstone saw increasing signs of the Antichrist's emergence in new political movements, manifested in "the godless, lawless trio of communism, socialism and nihilism, so alarmingly permeating the nations to-day."[18]

Blackstone also amplified a theme from Darby emphasizing the unique covenant that God maintained with the Jews. Throughout church history, many theologians speculated on the relationship of apocalyptic themes with the conversion of the Jews preceding a final judgment. Palestine carried particular significance in the minds of those who promoted dispensationalism, with many seeing the establishment of a Jewish homeland as essential

---

16. Adoniram Judson Gordon, *Behold He Cometh*; reprinted in Carpenter, *Premillennial Second Coming*, 63.

17. Sutton, *American Apocalypse*, 8–10.

18. Blackstone, *Jesus Is Coming*, 149.

for understanding the prophecies in the book of Revelation. By the 1890s, Blackstone became an advocate for the fledging Zionist movement—an advocacy that dispensationalists feverishly supported throughout the twentieth century. Not only would the so-called church age be a time when the world would see a rise of apostate churches; it also heightened speculation that one sure sign of the end-times would be a restoration of the people of Israel. Since Darby, many dispensationalists have argued that God never abandoned his special covenant with the Jewish people, and the permanency of that bond is emphasized in both the Old and New Testaments. "Other nations come and go, but Israel remains," Blackstone observed, "and their wonderful preservation, as a distinct people, through all the persecutions, vicissitudes and wanderings of the past eighteen centuries . . . is a standing miracle, attesting the truth of God's word, and assuring us of His purposes in their future history."[19]

One unfortunate aspect among some dispensationalists was that their support for the idea of a Jewish homeland also left many susceptible to popular beliefs that saw Jews as part of an international conspiracy of global domination. These fears were stoked by the appearance at the dawn of the twentieth century of a book that promoted this argument, *The Protocols of the Elders of Zion*. This anti-Semitic work confirmed for several dispensationalists that signs were pointing to the convergence of global interests that foretold of the coming days of judgment before Christ's return.[20]

William Blackstone was only one of several authors to write on dispensationalist prophecies in the late nineteenth and early twentieth centuries. The widespread appeal of dispensationalism was confirmed with the 1909 publication of Cyrus Scofield's annotated version of the King James Bible, the Scofield Reference Bible. Originally published by Oxford University Press, the Scofield Bible became one of that publisher's biggest selling books in the twentieth century with sales exceeding ten million copies.[21] The Scofield Bible's appeal was reinforced by its annotations and diagrams that gave a comprehensive view of how different Scriptures pointed to the inevitability of the rapture, and its publication signaled the ways dispensationalism would flourish as a form of popular theology throughout the twentieth century.

---

19. Blackstone, *Jesus Is Coming*, 107.
20. Weber, *Living in the Shadow*, 154–57.
21. Boyer, *When Time Shall Be*, 98.

Signs of the Times

American Protestant biblicism of the nineteenth century carried a strong belief that the Bible's secrets could be uncovered, and this populist spirit animated many to see the Bible as a codebook that needed to be studiously scrutinized to be fully deciphered. From Genesis to Revelation, the Bible told a singular story of redemption through Christ, and thanks to media like film and television, dispensationalist beliefs spread deep into American culture throughout the twentieth century. Although many evangelical Protestants debated the merits of dispensationalist theology, various forms of this movement easily grafted themselves on numerous forms of American Christianity.

Much of the history of twentieth-century US Protestantism has often been told as a conflict between conservatives (Fundamentalists) and liberals (modernists). However, the term *Fundamentalist* not only fails to capture the diverse iterations of evangelical Protestantism that have emerged since 1900; it also doesn't reflect the ways that dispensationalist ideas have interpenetrated a disparate range of churches, including Fundamentalist, holiness, and Pentecostal, as well as mainline Protestant denominations. A common thread that links these disparate movements together is a shared belief that dispensationalism pointed to a world on the precipice of a final judgment, where faith in Christ would allow persons to escape these divine punishments.

Although many Evangelicals who identified as Fundamentalists rejected dispensationalism as unscriptural, the movement's popularity led to the creation of numerous Christian colleges, Bible schools, and seminaries. The most prominent of these was Dallas Theological Seminary, an institution founded in 1924 that played a key role throughout the twentieth century in training ministers, missionaries, and teachers in a brand of what one historian calls "scholastic dispensationalism."[22]

Dispensationalists often warned their followers that while current events might point to the coming rapture, one needed to be careful not to repeat the mistakes of William Miller by setting a precise time line. At the same time, events in the mid-twentieth century signaled to some that the countdown to the last days might have already commenced. The establishment of the state of Israel in 1948 became especially significant in this speculation, as this event appeared to many as a fulfillment of Bible prophecy. After 1948, many dispensationalists scrutinized world events to argue that the world's end was imminent. The most popular work that tied together

---

22. Hummel, *Rise and Fall*, 182–88.

dispensationalist themes to world events in the mid-twentieth century was Hal Lindsey's best-selling book *The Late Great Planet Earth*. Originally published in 1970, *The Late Great Planet Earth* became one of the best-selling books of the 1970s.

While he emphasized to readers that he was drawing his arguments directly from the Bible, Lindsey was very much in the succession of earlier dispensationalist authors such as John Darby, William Blackstone, I. M. Haldeman, and Cyrus Scofield. Pointing to texts in Daniel and Revelation, he looked to global events of the mid-twentieth century—from the establishment of the state of Israel to the rise of the Soviet Union—as proof that the end-times were approaching. Even as Lindsey wrote dispassionately about these biblical prophecies, the book's concluding chapter ends with a plea to the unconverted to accept Jesus before the rapture occurs.

The success of *The Late Great Planet Earth* was the first of many works that garnered wide audiences—both inside and outside evangelical communities. With Lindsey's success came a spate of rapture books, novelizations, and films depicting the events leading up to the rapture, the tribulation, and the battle of Armageddon. In 1972, Donald Thompson, an evangelical filmmaker from Iowa, produced the first in a series of popular rapture films, *A Thief in the Night*. These films coupled with authors like Lindsey set the stage for the popularity of the *Left Behind* novels by Jerry Jenkins and Tim LaHaye of the late twentieth and early twenty-first centuries.

Historian Daniel Hummel observes that most of these late twentieth-century dispensationalist popularizers ignored the details of how this theological system developed in the nineteenth and early twentieth centuries.[23] However, an earlier dispensationalist like I. M. Haldeman might very well recognize the biblical and theological plotlines of these contemporary books and films. Consistent with the message of Hal Lindsey and Tim LaHaye, Haldeman warned his readers that the Christian always needed to be ready because one never knew when Christ might return. "Let us understand that every moment the platform is being put together for the concluding acts in the drama of time; that all things in Heaven and in earth are moving forward to the Consummation; . . . His coming for us is as liable and imminent now, as any moment when He bade His disciples to watch and wait; and that in our ears as in theirs, He utters the solemn admonition: 'What I say unto you, I say unto all, "WATCH."'"[24]

---

23. Hummel, *Rise and Fall*, 301–19.
24. Haldeman, *Coming of Christ*, 325.

Conclusion: Dispensationalism as Popular Theology

Walter Rauschenbusch wrote that if one were to compare his theology to I. M. Haldeman's, "he will face two kinds of Christianity and can make his choice."[25] While dispensationalism historically struggled to establish permanent theological traditions, its adherents likely outnumbered the followers of the progressive theologies espoused by figures like Rauschenbusch. At a time in the early twenty-first century when many demographic studies point to Christianity's decline in the US, American beliefs in the end-times remain rampant. A 2022 Pew study noted that 39 percent of US adults believe that the world will end in their lifetimes.[26] Further, while historically dispensationalist beliefs rested primarily within segments of White American Evangelicalism, today these beliefs are flourishing in global Christian movements, particularly in the rapidly growing Pentecostal churches in Latin America, Africa, and Asia.[27]

At the conclusion of *The Late Great Planet Earth*, Lindsey cautioned readers that the imminence of Christ's coming did not exempt Christians from living fully in the world. "Far from being pessimistic and dropping out of life, we should be rejoicing in the knowledge that Christ may return any moment for us. This should spur us on to share the good news of salvation in Christ with as many as possible."[28] While historical events come and go, dispensationalist theology has provided adherents with a view of the future that offers a secure biblical foundation for their beliefs—even as imminent prophecies of the end-times fail to materialize.

Amid a changing landscape of current events and political crises, the basic formula used by premillennial dispensationalists has changed little since the mid-nineteenth century. Throughout its history, dispensationalism has been attacked by numerous critics. However, efforts to challenge believers as lunatics, feeble minded, or simply misguided miss an important point. Dispensationalist beliefs didn't catch on because they seemed far fetched. They have caught on because they helped believers make sense of the Bible. The movement is a pertinent example of Martin Luther's doctrine of the priesthood of all believers, whereby individuals are encouraged to interpret the Bible outside of priestly authority. In a nation like the US where the Bible is taken seriously, persons like John Nelson Darby, William Blackstone, I. M. Haldeman, Cyrus Scofield, Hal Lindsey, and Tim LaHaye

25. Rauschenbusch, *Christianizing the Social Order*, 56n1.
26. Diamant, "About Four-in-Ten U.S. Adults."
27. For examples, see Mollett, "Apocalypticism and Popular Culture"; Green et al., *All Things New*; Shin, "Influence of the Bible."
28. Lindsey with Carlson, *Late Great Planet Earth*, 187.

succeeded in transforming cryptic biblical passages into a narrative that made sense of the Bible, while heightening one's commitment to their faith.

Dispensationalism has played a vital role in shaping the history of American Evangelicalism. On one hand, it fits well into David Bebbington's quadrilateral for defining Evangelicalism as a movement anchored historically in biblicism, crucicentrism, personal conversion, and mission and outreach.[29] On the other hand, dispensationalists' tendency to rely on current events as a theological bellwether has also made the movement prone to embrace conspiracy theories that have little to do with classic definitions of being an Evangelical, such as Bebbington's.[30]

Ultimately, dispensationalism's popularity in the US probably owes its appeal not just to its use of the Bible, but to its eschatology that promises believers that no matter what happens to the world, they will be rewarded for their perseverance. As one prominent dispensationalist from the early twentieth century, Arno Gaebelein, summarized, despite the judgments that a sinful world would face, for those who keep the faith "the earth's jubilee will come. . . . And Peace on earth at last."[31]

Historically, such a promise has brought comfort to many who rest their Christian faith on such a hope.

Bibliography

Barkun, Michael. *A Culture of Conspiracy: Apocalyptic Visions in Contemporary America*. 2nd ed. Comparative Studies in Religion and Society. Berkeley: University of California Press, 2013.

Bebbington, David. *Evangelicalism in Modern Britain: A History from the 1730 to the 1980s*. London: Unwin Hyman, 1989.

Blackstone, William E. *Jesus Is Coming*. Rev. ed. London: Revell, 1898.

Boyer, Paul. *When Time Shall Be No More: Prophecy Belief in Modern American Culture*. Cambridge, MA: Belknap, 1992.

Burnham, Jonathan D. *A Story of Conflict: The Controversial Relationship between Benjamin Wills Newton and John Nelson Darby*. Carlisle, UK: Paternoster, 2004.

Carpenter, Joel A., ed. *The Premillennial Second Coming: Two Early Champions*. New York, 1988.

Davidson, James West. *The Logic of Millennial Thought: Eighteen Century New England*. New Haven, CT: Yale University Press, 1977.

Diamant, Jeff. "About Four-in-Ten U.S. Adults Believe Humanity Is 'Living in the End Times.'" Pew Research Center, Dec. 8, 2022, https://www.pewresearch.org/short-reads/2022/12/08/about-four-in-ten-u-s-adults-believe-humanity-is-living-in-the-end-times/.

    29. Bebbington, *Evangelicalism in Modern Britain*.

    30. Barkun, *Culture of Conspiracy*.

    31. Gaebelein, *League of Nations*, 49–50.

Evans, Christopher H. *Histories of American Christianity*. Waco: Baylor University Press, 2013.

Forbes, Bruce David. "Apocalypticism in the United States." In *Twentieth-Century Global Christianity*, edited by Mary Farrell Bednarowski, 211–30. A People's History of Christianity. Minneapolis: Fortress, 2008.

Gaebelein, Arno Clemon. *League of Nations in Light of the Bible*. New York: Our Hope, 192[?].

Green, Gene L., et al., eds. *All Things New: Eschatology in the Majority World*. Carlisle, UK: Langham, 2019.

Haldeman, I. M. *The Coming of Christ: Both Pre-Millennial and Imminent*. New York: Cook, 1906.

———. *Prof. Rauschenbusch's "Christianity and the Social Crisis."* New York: Cook, 1911 [?].

Hall, David C. "The Mental World of Samuel Sewell." *Proceedings of the Massachusetts Historical Society* 92 (1980) 21–44.

Hummel, Daniel G. *The Rise and Fall of Dispensationalism: How the Evangelical Battle over the End Times Shaped a Nation*. Grand Rapids: Eerdmans, 2023.

Lindsey, Hal, with C. C. Carlson. *The Late Great Planet Earth*. Grand Rapids: Zondervan, 1970.

Marsden, George M. *Jonathan Edwards: A Life*. New Haven, CT: Yale University Press, 2003.

McGinn, Bernard. *Antichrist: Two Thousand Years of the Human Fascination with Evil*. San Francisco: Harper, 1994.

Mollett, Margaret Mollett. "Apocalypticism and Popular Culture in South Africa." *R&T* 19 (2012) 219–36.

Numbers, Ronald L., and Jonathan M. Butler. *The Disappointed: Millerism and Millenarianism in the Nineteenth Century*. Bloomington: Indiana University Press, 1987.

Rauschenbusch, Walter. *Christianizing the Social Order*. New York: Macmillan, 1912.

Shin, Hyunte. "The Influence of the Bible in Shaping the Negative Viewpoint of Korean Christian towards Nature." *ExpTim* 132 (2021) 211–22.

Silverman, Kenneth. *The Life and Times of Cotton Mather*. New York: Harper & Row, 1984.

Smith, Timothy L. *Revivalism and Social Reform in Mid-Nineteenth-Century America*. New York: Abingdon, 1957.

Sutton, Matthew Avery. *American Apocalypse: A History of Modern Evangelicalism*. Cambridge, MA: Belknap, 2014.

Weber, Timothy P. *Living in the Shadow of the Second Coming: American Premillennialism, 1875–1982*. Grand Rapids: Academie, 1983.

Chapter 7

North American Pentecostalisms

ALLISON KACH-YAWNGHWE

PENTECOSTALISM BEGAN AS A fringe restoration movement among radical Evangelicals just over a century ago. Since its inception, Pentecostalism's accessible message, experiential spirituality, and theological innovations have been adopted, adapted, and transmitted by diverse racial-ethnic communities across the globe, making it the fastest growing arm of Christianity today. In North America, Pentecostalism emerged as a convergence of nineteenth-century socioreligious movements including African American slave religion, holiness teaching, Keswick spirituality, premillennial dispensationalism, the divine healing movement, and restorationism. This chapter explores Pentecostalism's North American antecedents, origins, early growth and expansion, divisions and formal organization, adoption into mainstream Evangelicalism, and ongoing surges of fresh revival. A dominant presence in North American Christianity, the Pentecostal movement shapes contemporary Christian belief and practice, invigorates local and global Christianity, claims millions of intercultural members throughout the US and Canada, and receives renewal through its growing immigrant membership.

An Apostolic Return: A Root with Many Branches

North American Pentecostalism is a root with many branches, the oldest belonging to African American slave religion. Embodied, participatory, and expressive liturgies centered around preaching, singing, and prayer. Intrinsically African, the "spontaneous responses to the sermon, shouting, stomping, singing, sighing, dancing, swaying, clapping, humming, and an entire array of kinesthetic activities" and forms of worship, including spirituals, were an expression of a spiritual liberty that evaded the participants' physical reality.[1] Southern revivalist camp meetings adopted the traditions and forms of African American spirituality that quickly made their way into radical evangelical, and at times racially segregated, practice and parlance.[2] After Emancipation in 1863, African Americans joined the era's urban migration, bringing their unique and vibrant religious expressions with them to urban churches.

A driving force in nineteenth-century revivalism, Black and White holiness groups came to represent much of the emerging transatlantic spirituality that would direct Pentecostalism. The Wesleyan holiness tradition harkens back to John Wesley and the Pietism, the seventeenth-century revival of personal piety and holy living, that shaped him. In 1738, Wesley experienced a strange warming of the heart during a Moravian worship service in Aldersgate Street, London. From this, Wesley believed that God had made him completely holy, having eradicated all sin from his soul through Christ's atoning sacrifice and perfect love. This experience developed into the Wesleyan doctrine of "entire sanctification" accomplished by God's second work of grace, or "second blessing," that proceeded from salvation and affected holiness in a Christian's life.

The core of this message was popularized through the ministry and teaching of Phoebe Palmer nearly one hundred years after Wesley's Aldersgate experience. In 1835, Palmer and her sister, Sarah Langford, began hosting home meetings to devote themselves to seeking God's holiness to receive "entire sanctification," an experience they both claimed. First attended only by women, these "Tuesday Meetings" began attracting men. The "mixed crowd" ruffled social norms of the day and garnered much criticism, but the "second blessing" continued to flow. Palmer and her husband Walter were invited to preach at holiness camp meetings in Canada, the US, and England. Her book, *The Way of Holiness* (1843), and magazine, *A Guide to Holiness*, reached a wide readership and influenced emerging holiness leaders to pursue, as Palmer put it, "the witness of the Spirit, that my heart is the temple of an indwelling God."[3]

With the holiness movement well underway in the northern US, Canada, and England, the message reached the southern US with the end of the Civil War. Palmer's ministry and the National Camp Meeting Association founded in 1867 inspired and intersected emerging African American holiness groups in the southern US that received the message through the ministries of Joanna Patterson Moore, a White preacher, and Amanda Berry

---

1. Vondey, "Making of Black Liturgy," 153–54.
2. Raboteau, *Slave Religion*, 72.
3. Palmer, *Way of Holiness*, 130.

Smith, a Black missionary.[4] Leaders from Black Methodist and Baptist churches in the Arkansas Delta adopted the holiness teaching and preached a Wesleyan message of instant sanctification, God's physical protection, and divine healing. As was the case in White holiness circles, leaders and adherents in pursuit and promotion of entire sanctification found their loyalties shift from traditional denominations to holiness associations.[5] William Christian, Charles Harrison Mason, Charles Price Jones, and Lizzie Woods eventually left their Baptist denominations to found new African American holiness churches. The Church of the Living God and the Church of God in Christ united followers into thriving Bible bands that pursued keeping the "body pure and the soul sinless."[6]

Another distinct arm of the holiness movement, undoubtedly influenced by Wesleyan holiness ideas, found its home in Charles Finney and Oberlin perfectionism. Both Palmer's and Finney's teachings rested on a conversion experience, or "first work of grace," followed by a second crisis and resolution in the "second work of grace." The definitions of this "second blessing" differed significantly and informed one's self-understanding and practice of faith. Finney taught that the "second blessing" marked the beginning of one's lifelong journey toward unattainable holiness, rather than the Wesleyan belief that God affirmed its completion. Christian effort, therefore, to live holy remained an occupation of those who followed Finney's reformed holiness teachings, while Wesleyan holiness followers attempted to see their life and ministries in the world as flowing from God's perfect kingdom through their sinless lives. It was into this belief that the baptism of the Holy Spirit was believed to be the "power for service." While the cross-pollination of Wesleyan and Reformed holiness teachings abounded, their theological distinctions of holiness and divergent beliefs in the work and gifts of the Holy Spirit would become a dividing line of the soon-to-arrive Pentecost.

An interdenominational innovation of the late nineteenth century still active today, the Keswick "higher life" movement blended the Wesleyan and Reformed holiness positions of personal holiness, Christian service, and premillennialism into an annual Bible conference that drew transatlantic speakers, attendees, and missionaries. Beginning in 1875 in Keswick, England, the convention was inspired by the ministry and writings of US Presbyterian William E. Boardman and his associates, Quakers R. Pearsall Smith and Hannah Whitall Smith. Boardman's *The Higher Christian Life*

---

4. Giggie, "Making."
5. Synan, *Holiness-Pentecostal Tradition*, 39.
6. Giggie, "Making," 169.

(1858) and Hannah Whitall Smith's *The Christian's Secret to a Happy Life* (1875) infused the convention. Keswick's distinct holiness teachings originally focused on holy living or the "higher life" free from sin through receiving the "second blessing" or "infilling of the Holy Spirit." Keswick teaching eventually distinguished itself from the Wesleyan doctrine of eradication of original sin and provided a more moderate Calvinist interpretation that supported the Reformed idea of the baptism of the Holy Spirit as an empowerment for service.[7]

Running through these same streams of radical Evangelicalism of the early nineteenth century was the teaching of John Nelson Darby. A founding member of the Plymouth Brethren in Dublin, Ireland, in 1825, Darby developed a teaching on the end-times, return of Christ, and pre-tribulation rapture that would become known as premillennial dispensationalism. Darby's teaching promoted an eschatological urgency that invigorated world missions. Propelled by widescale prophecy belief and promulgated by transatlantic conferences, like the annual Niagara Bible Conference, the Keswick Convention, the Northfield Conference, and newly established Bible institutes of prominent premillennialists D. L. Moody, A. J. Gordon, and A. B. Simpson, premillennial dispensationalism became entwined with the development of radical evangelical and holiness belief.[8] While Darby's ideas were nothing new, his systematization of Bible prophecy to create distinct dispensations, or "ages," that explained God's "timetable" seen throughout Scripture made premillennialism accessible for anyone who could read the Bible. To Christians at the close of the nineteenth century, Darby's teaching provided a practical road map for Christian service, faith, and relation to the world. Inspired with hope to hasten Christ's return, premillennialists sought to preach the gospel to all creatures and embodied a vision for world mission best summed up in the era's watchword: "the evangelization of the world in this generation."

Ultimately, the reception and diffusion of these "new" teachings were part of a broader restorationist impulse of the era. By a return to the apostolic age, restorationist groups claimed direct descent from primitive, first-century Christianity, ahistorically bypassing the nearly two millennia of church history that preceded their revelations. Divine healing and Spirit baptism, both practiced and promoted by the holiness movement, were clear signs of God working in power and purpose in individual lives and through the church. Wesleyan holiness groups held onto their pursuit of the Holy Spirit for entire sanctification. Restorationists like John Alexander Dowie

---

7. Marsden, *Fundamentalism and American Culture*, 77–78.
8. Boyer, *When Time Shall Be*, x, 103.

and Frank Sanford extended the benefits of Christian perfection to include to God's ability to heal physical ailments. Testimonies of healing abounded, and many holiness and future Pentecostal leaders entered the ministry in response to their healings. Healing homes, originally founded in Switzerland, began popping up in the US and Canada to provide a more permanent structure for those seeking God's divine intervention. Divine healing, a central tenet of the emerging "fourfold gospel" credited to A. B. Simpson, was widely accepted among radical Evangelicals who held to premillennial and holiness teachings that proclaimed Christ as Savior, Baptizer, Healer, and soon-coming King. An increasing expectation of miracles and gifts needed for effective evangelism fostered a renewed and reimagined idyllic apostolic age being restored in the "last days."[9]

Apostolic Faith and Pentecost Restored: North American Origins

Until the turn of the twentieth century, receiving the gift of tongues had been an uncommon occurrence in evangelical circles. Tongues appeared more as an unintended consequence of intense spiritual encounter than a gift taught or sought like the "second blessing" of Spirit baptism. A prominent aspect of the Acts 2 narrative of the day of Pentecost, tongue speaking, or *xenolalia*, was understood to be a gift of a known foreign language for missionary service. And while the phenomenon had been reported at the 1801 Cane Ridge Revival in Kentucky, in Edward Irving's meetings in 1830s London, and among D. L. Moody's London YMCA audience in 1875, it was not until the height of the holiness movement that the gifts of tongues came to spiritual prominence.[10] In 1895, seventeen-year-old Jennie Glassey was baptized in the Holy Spirit at Full Gospel Tabernacle in St. Louis, Missouri, and reportedly spoke in multiple African dialects. Walter and Frances Black, Glassey's pastors, followed in the experience, and the three set out for Sierra Leone as divinely equipped missionaries.[11]

Glassey's testimony aroused a new interest in this missionary gift among restorationists like Frank W. Sanford. Sanford's acquaintance with Jennie Glassey furthered his own conviction that God was restoring the gift of tongues. His publication of her testimony in his newspaper, *Tongues of Fire*, spread the message to his readership. At his Bible school and church, The Holy Ghost and Us, at Shiloh near Durham, Maine, he taught on Spirit baptism and tongues as present in the Acts 2 day of Pentecost narrative and

9. Anderson, *Spreading Fires*, 18.
10. Synan, *Holiness-Pentecostal Tradition*, 87–88.
11. McGee, *Miracles, Missions*, 69–73.

encouraged students to seek God for the restoration of these gifts. As early as January 1, 1900, some of Sanford's Bible students displayed this spiritual gift during prayer meetings known as "tarrying meetings" over the new year where they waited in expectation for extended times for God to meet them in power.

One seeker witness to the tongue speaking at Shiloh, who was profoundly influenced by Sanford's restorationism, was a former Methodist preacher turned independent holiness itinerant from Kansas, Charles Fox Parham. After an experience of divine healing, Parham and Sarah, his wife, opened a healing home in Topeka in 1898. In 1900, he took a small group of Bible students on a holiness pilgrimage, making stops at Zion City, Nyack College, and Shiloh.[12] Parham gleaned from Sanford's methods and teachings for six months, and upon his return to Kansas he opened Bethel Bible School and promoted the study of the scriptural basis for tongue speaking. Parham perpetuated the teaching that tongues were languages given by God for missionary service, but he also formulated a new teaching—tongue speaking as the physical proof of Spirit baptism and essential for normal Christian living.[13] It was this theological innovation and imperative that would inspire and define early Pentecostalism. For Parham's students, it inspired them to search the Scriptures for proof of tongues speaking. Then, on New Year's Eve 1900, Agnes Ozman began speaking in tongues after what she described as a Spirit baptism.

After Parham relocated his Bible school to Houston, it was another student, William J. Seymour, who would go down in Pentecostal history. Lucy Farrow, the first recorded African American woman to have spoken in tongues and nanny to Parham's children, invited Seymour to pastor her church in Houston.[14] Farrow had told Seymour about tongue speaking and introduced him to Parham.[15] Allowed to listen to classes from a seat outside the door, Seymour imbibed Parham's teachings for a number of weeks despite Parham's personal racism and commitment to uphold Jim Crow. Then, in February of 1906, Mrs. Neely Terry invited Seymour to replace her as pastor at her Black holiness church in Los Angeles. Accepting the invitation, Seymour set off for LA by way of Alma White's "Pillar of Fire" in Denver, Colorado.[16] Seymour's welcome at Terry's church was short lived when after a few nights of his preaching, the interim leader Julia Hutchins had him

---

12. Espinosa, *William J. Seymour*, 45.
13. McGee, *Miracles, Missions*, 74–76.
14. Alexander, *Women of Azusa Street*, 39–46.
15. Robeck, "Lucy F. Farrow."
16. Synan, *Holiness-Pentecostal Tradition*, 95.

locked out on account of his erroneous message of tongues as the sign of Spirit baptism.

Seymour began prayer meetings in the home of church member Edward Lee, where he had been staying. He continued sharing his message that melded tongues as "initial evidence," the new birth, a radical egalitarian vision of God's kingdom, and power manifested through holy believers with a small group that gathered for prayer.[17] The group grew, and after a move to a larger home they were joined by the first White participants, the Osterbergs and Frank Bartelman. Then, on April 6, 1906, multiple members began speaking in tongues shortly after Seymour's friends Lucy Farrow and Joseph Warren arrived from Houston to help him in the ministry.[18] The news of Spirit baptism and powerful manifestations, including the gift of tongues, divine healing, and an awe-inspiring sense of God's presence spread among holiness circles. An interracial congregation of holiness hungry women and men gathered to hear, see, participate, and receive the Spirit baptism and tongue speaking. The revival swelled. The Apostolic Faith Mission, more commonly known as the Azusa Street Revival led by William J. Seymour, would become one of the most influential starting points of North American Pentecostalisms, and its global iterations spread through Azusa missionaries' pioneering efforts and established missionary networks.[19]

Seven months after the revival began in Lost Angeles, another notable movement of Spirit baptism with tongue speaking took place in North America through the ministry of British immigrant Ellen Hebden. The daughter of an Anglican clergyman, Ellen had a "second blessing" experience in her teens and was mentored by Elizabeth Baxter, the renowned faith healer and founder of London's Bethshan healing home. Ellen married James Hebden, and after having a family, their shared missionary calling led them to relocate to Jamaica and on to Toronto. The Hebdens founded the East End Mission in May 1906 as a hybrid healing home and rescue mission. It was here that their healing and holiness ministry gave way to the first known Pentecostal revival in Canada independent of, or at most indirectly influenced by, Azusa Street.[20]

In November 1906, Ellen's longing to receive more power to heal the sick drove her to prayer, during which she experienced a profound Holy Spirit baptism and tongue speaking. After sharing with James and others at the mission, "between seventy and eighty others" had a similar experience by

---

17. Espinosa, *William J. Seymour*.
18. Robeck, *Azusa Street Mission*, 65.
19. Giggie, "Making."
20. A. S. Stewart, "Quenching the Spirit," 41.

April 1907.[21] Word spread across Toronto and through the well-established holiness and newly forming Pentecostal networks in the US and Canada. Seekers of Spirit baptism, many who had already been to Azusa, began to descend on the East End Mission hoping to receive tongues themselves and to observe the meetings.[22] The White, middle-class, and British-influenced East End Mission differed significantly from the diverse socioeconomic, interracial crowds that flocked to encounter God and hear Seymour's well-articulated teachings that would give shape to early Pentecostal doctrine. And while Ellen Hebden and the "Canadian Azusa" reflect a unique expression of Pentecostalism in North America, Hebden would ultimately look to Seymour and Azusa as the leaders of the movement, providing insight as to how Azusa went on to exert lasting influence in the development of Pentecostalism.

A Diversity of Tongues: Early Developments and Expansion

Within the first few years of the Pentecostal revival, the new movement was blossoming in diverse communities all over the continent and globe, even as Seymour and Hebden's ministries declined.[23] Distinct forms of worship emerged—a cappella hymns sung by exuberant worshippers; biblical preaching, prophecy, testimonies, and exhortation from leaders or attendees; prayer and laying on of hands for the sick and those seeking Spirit baptism; extended hours of quiet, waiting prayer, or "tarrying," to receive the baptism of the Holy Spirit; outbursts of joy and shouts of amen, hallelujah, and speaking in tongues—modeling the egalitarian ethos of the personal, indwelling, empowering, gift-giving Holy Spirit available to all Christians. Spirit baptism became the only requirement for ministry, leveling the harvest field and transforming passive recipients into active participants of the burgeoning grassroots movement. Largely nameless to the pages of history, independent itinerant evangelists, female and male, from diverse racial-ethnic backgrounds, crisscrossed the US and Canada by foot, horse, wagon, and train holding brush arbor and cottage prayer meetings, preaching on street corners, gathering seekers of Spirit baptism in homes, and planting churches throughout the continent.

Within a few years the Azusa and Toronto ministries died down and the fervor shifted to new centers in more formally organized Pentecostal ministries in Kansas, led by Gaston B. Cashwell; Chicago, led by William

---

21. A. S. Stewart, "Quenching the Spirit," 41.
22. Miller, "Canadian 'Azusa.'"
23. Di Giacomo, "Pentecostal and Charismatic Christianity," 18–19.

Durham; and Oregon, led by Florence Crawford.[24] In California, the first known Latino Pentecostals like Abundio and Rosa Lopez, Genaro and Romanita Carbajal de Valenzuela, and Susie Villa Valdez pioneered local Spanish Pentecostal missions, preached "Pentecost" in labor camps, and reached out to prostitutes on skid row.[25] In Canada, the Hebdens' mission spread to rural communities, leading to new missions in Ontario towns like Ingersoll, where future Canadian evangelist and founder of the International Church of the Foursquare Gospel, Aimee Semple McPherson, was born again and met her first husband, Robert Semple.[26] The Pentecostal movement arrived in Winnipeg, Manitoba, in 1907 by way of Chicago. A. H. Argue brought the experience home after he was successfully baptized in the Holy Spirit and spoke in tongues after weeks of tarrying at Durham's North Avenue Mission. Italian immigrants in the US, Luigi Francescon, Giacomo Lombardi, and Pietro Ottolini, were Spirit baptized at Durham's mission in Chicago. They formed a strong partnership with the preexistent Italian Pentecostal movement in Canada and transported the Pentecostal message back to Italy and on to Brazil.[27]

Pentecostalism also grew by absorbing entire churches or through the attrition of members from holiness and radical evangelical churches who embraced the experience of tongues at the expense of belonging. If church leaders had experienced "Pentecost," they attempted to lead their congregations and associations to adopt the new teaching of tongues as the evidence of Spirit baptism, often resulting in opposition by those who had not experienced tongues or who were leery of the new doctrine. As in the case of the Church of God in Christ, Charles H. Mason's own baptism at Azusa, and appeal to the churches to join Pentecostalism, was met with opposition from longtime friend and cofounder Charles Price Jones. Mason's conviction led to a split, with the few churches that followed Mason becoming the first official Pentecostal denomination in the US in 1907. If leaders rejected Azusa and opposed the message, there were other consequences. A. B. Simpson, whose teaching had laid much of the ground work for the emergence of Pentecostalism, officially opposed Azusa's manifestations and message. Personal experiences and a Pentecostal revival at Nyack College inspired numerous members and missionaries to depart the denomination in favor of the Holy Spirit and speaking in tongues.[28] And despite his discouragement

24. Espinosa, *William J. Seymour*, 18.
25. Espinosa, *Latino Pentecostals*, 40, 56.
26. A. Stewart, "Canadian Azusa."
27. Di Giacomo, "Identity and Change," 85, 88.
28. E. W. Blumhofer, *Assemblies of God*, 27.

of tongue speaking, the Missionary Alliance became an important network that populated Pentecostalism at home and facilitated its global transmission through robust mission infrastructure.

The missionary nature of the early Pentecostal movement was an essential ingredient to its growth and development at home and abroad. Countless experienced missionaries at home on furlough received Spirit baptism and power at Azusa, Toronto, Chicago, and other places and took it back to evangelize both non-Christian and mission communities. George Berg from India, Antoinette Moomau from China, and B. Berntsen from China were among the many missionaries who left Azusa speaking in tongues.[29] Herbert Randall, on furlough from Egypt and H. L. Lawler from China, were Spirit baptized in Toronto.[30] For others like Minnie Abrams, missionary at Pandita Ramabai's Mukti Mission in India, missionaries did not need to return to North America to receive the Spirit baptism they had already been expecting and experiencing. Her pre-Azusa writings on "The Baptism of the Holy Ghost and Fire" were confirmed by the Welsh and North American revivals and ultimately converged with the expanding "Apostolic Faith" movement.[31]

Alongside this reinvigoration that played out in foreign missions was a new wave of first-time missionaries inspired and sent out from early Pentecostal centers in Canada and the US. The reception of missionary tongues and spiritual gifts became a powerful justification removing barriers that kept willing workers from doing their part to evangelize the world. Lucy Farrow, William Seymour's old friend from Houston, was one of many African American missionaries who went out from Azusa Street to Liberia and Angola. Alfred and Lillian Garr, believed to have been equipped with the Bengali language, made their way to India and then to Hong Kong.[32] Charles Chawner, the first Canadian Pentecostal missionary, went to South Africa from the East End Mission. Thomas and Louise Hindle were sent from Toronto to Hong Kong and on to Mongolia. Single women, long the backbone of foreign missions, were instrumental in the spread of the Pentecostal experience. Women like Barbara Johnston, the first Canadian Pentecostal missionary to India, or the Canadian Alice Wood, first Pentecostal missionary to Argentina, were sent out to start new churches and join existing mission

---

29. Anderson, "Azusa Street Revival," 114.
30. Miller, "Canadian 'Azusa,'" 12.
31. McGee, "Baptism of Holy Ghost."
32. Anderson, "Azusa Street Revival," 113.

works.[33] Within just a few years, this new wave of Spirit-empowered missionaries were active in Africa, Asia, Central and South America.[34]

The restoration of the apostolic age, complete with the gift of missionary tongues to fast-track preaching, worldwide conversion, and Christ's return, was the new ticket to overseas missions. And while there were some supernatural stories of tongue speaking being understood by local people, reports from expectant missionaries began expressing disappointment and disillusionment when it turned out that their hearers couldn't understand their tongues. With these less than apostolic realities, it took only a few years for the belief and expectation of missionary tongues to fall out of popularity and all but disappear from Pentecostal periodicals. Instead of calling tongues and the restoration of "Pentecost" into question, an interpretation was adopted, tongue speaking becoming widely understood as *glossolalia*, unknown tongues understood only by God. Still a sign of the power of God's indwelling Spirit in the believer, glossolalia's overshadowing of its progenitor, xenolalia, was another innovation of the pragmatic Pentecostal experience. Evangelists and missionaries continued to spread the Pentecostal message and speak in tongues, known or unknown, underscoring the reality that the gift of tongues, with its divine purpose, was only one of many driving forces behind the movement's growth.

United by the Spirit, Divided by Necessity

The first generation of North American Pentecostals united around their shared spiritual experience of Spirit baptism; biblical interpretations of evangelism, mission, and eschatology; and the radical egalitarian reception and administration of the spiritual gifts. The new Pentecostals believed the gift of the Holy Spirit was given to restore and unite the end-time church. Following the leadership of the Holy Spirit over human-made organizations, the independent impulse of the early movement saw pioneers opposing any attempt to institutionalization, believing that it would result in the movement's death.[35] Rejected and ridiculed as an aberration by the radical evangelical and mainline churches from which they came, early Pentecostals proved their endurance and forged unified family-like alliances and diverse Pentecostal networks that would become the scaffolding of a thriving global movement. It was not long, however, that doctrinal differences, theological disputes, and internal racism and misogyny common to the era propelled

33. Courtney, "Barbara Johnston."
34. Anderson, "Azusa Street Revival," 116.
35. Kydd, "Canadian Pentecostalism," 293.

many pioneers toward homogenous organization, belief, and practice at the expense of the interracial, egalitarian ethos reflective of the day of Pentecost.

While Pentecostalism was itself a fracture from the holiness movement, the rumblings of a significant theological rift emerged during the Worldwide Apostolic Camp Meeting in Arroyo Seco, California, in April 1913. Although the camp meeting had been organized with the intent to unify the Pentecostal movement in North America, Canadian R. E. McAlister delivered a message on baptizing in Jesus's name only that was anything but unifying. Inspired by William Durham's "finished work theology," McAlister, Frank Ewart, Garfield T. Haywood, and Franklin Small would go on to develop oneness, or "Jesus only," Pentecostalism.[36] Dubbed the "new issue" at the time, oneness Pentecostalism rejected Trinitarian theology, leading to their break away from the recently formed Assemblies of God in 1916. Oneness denominations founded in the US include the historically interracial Pentecostal Assemblies of the World, the White United Pentecostal Church International, the Latino Apostolic Assembly of the Faith in Christ Jesus, and the Latino United Pentecostal Church. In Canada, the Pentecostal Assemblies of Canada (PAOC) was founded as a oneness body in 1919 by R. E. McAlister. But by 1920, the PAOC had disbanded and joined the Trinitarian Assemblies of God in the US, prompting Frank Small to found the Apostolic Church of Pentecost and remain true to his oneness convictions. Preachers in western Canada had originally affiliated regionally with the Assemblies of God in the US and remained with the AG until the 1924 reestablishment and separation of the PAOC.

Other early divisions and their resulting denominational formations were racially motivated and led to a reinstitution of segregation. The traditionally African American Church of God in Christ, the first official Pentecostal denomination incorporated in 1909, was the first interracial church to reckon with enduring racism. Having been the only licensing body of the early movement, it was home to Black and White ministers and churches alike. By 1914, a large group of White pastors and preachers separated themselves from the Church of God in Christ to join other White preachers from independent churches and networks to form the Assemblies of God (AG) in April 1914. By 1920, other traditional interracial denominations like the Pentecostal Assemblies of the World, the Pentecostal Holiness Church, and the Church of God (Cleveland) had organized along racial lines. White churches, like the AG, inhibited the ordination of African American pastors and missionaries, prompting the creation of new African

---

36. Reed, *In Jesus' Name*, 2.

American-led denominations.[37] Latino, Asian, and Indigenous Pentecostals found institutional homes in White-led denominations like the AG and the PAOC that allowed them a measure of linguistic, cultural, and ethnic autonomy while still providing administrative oversight. In recent years, however, ethnic minority Pentecostals have moved toward self-determination and independence from dominant cultural systems, leading to the formation of new networks, like the Christian Aboriginal Fellowship of Canada, and the acknowledgment of the historical significance and religious-cultural contribution of minority Pentecostals to North American Christianity.

Divisions over women's leadership and ordination followed a similarly ambiguous path. Spirit-empowered women were visible in early Pentecostalism as evangelists, preachers, missionaries, church planters, and pioneers. The move to formal institutional structures reified gender barriers, bias, and scriptural restrictions on women's leadership in the church characteristic of contemporary North American society and conservative Protestantism of the era. Ordained as missionaries and evangelists in the Church of God in Christ and the Pentecostal Holiness Church before and after they joined the Pentecostal movement, women rarely pastored churches.[38] And even though the Assemblies of God licenced women as assistant pastors in 1920 and granted them full ordination in 1935, the male-dominated administration served a conservative constituency that held to more traditional gender roles. Aimee Semple McPherson was an exception to the dearth of formal female leadership in North American Pentecostalism. McPherson's successful evangelistic ministry allowed her to leave the AG to found her own International Church of the Foursquare Gospel in 1923. For most Pentecostal women called into ministry, the justification of their Spirit baptism has allowed them freedom to exercise their gifts and serve others faithfully even if their denominations have not endorsed their invaluable contribution and informal leadership.

A Move to Mainstream and New Waves of Apostolic Faith

Throughout the mid-twentieth century, North American Pentecostalisms experienced steady growth through conversion, immigration, and waves of revivals that transformed existing churches and welcomed Christians from other denominations. In the interwar and postwar years, an influx of European migration led to the growth of a diversity of ethnic Pentecostal churches, most notably Swedish and German. The German branch of the

37. Daniels, "North American Pentecostalism," 78.
38. E. Blumhofer, "Women in Pentecostalism," 1:402.

PAOC in Alberta, for example, flourished with growing membership and new churches from 1940 to 1980. Alongside the renewed vitality provided by these ethnic offshoots, North American Pentecostalism had gained the once-lost social respect and position. These "fundamentalists with a difference" had successfully moved from a fringe movement of fanatics into fellowship with the increasingly culturally dominant US Evangelicalism.[39] Thanks to their upward mobility, institutional permanence, and alliance with the National Association of Evangelicals in the US (1943) and the Evangelical Fellowship of Canada (1960), classical Pentecostalism expressed through the AG and PAOC had become mainstream in the socioreligious consciousness of most North American Christians.

It was in this context that new waves of Pentecostal-inspired revival simultaneously brought renewal to and threatened the established Pentecostal denominations. The healing and Latter Rain movements of the 1940s attracted spiritually hungry Pentecostals to itinerant tent meeting–style revivals. Healing evangelists like Oral Roberts, William Branham, and Kathryn Kuhlman demonstrated God's healing power for a modern audience. In North Battleford, Saskatchewan, the Latter Rain movement emerged under the leadership of former PAOC and Foursquare pastors and a score of Sharon Bible college students who began to prophecy and practice the laying on of hands. Both of these movements were officially rejected by classical Pentecostal denominations, but the opposition did not hinder Pentecostal church members from attending and being influenced by the vibrancy of the teaching and the renewed experiential Christianity that they offered.

In the late 1960s and 1970s, the charismatic renewal signaled another return to the Holy Spirit's power and gifts present in primitive Christianity. Beginning with Spirit baptisms among leaders and members of traditional Protestant and Catholic churches, the renewal was quickly condemned as counterfeit by classical Pentecostals. Marked by ecstatic spiritual experiences, the reception of spiritual gifts of tongues, healing, and prophecy, and new forms of worship that transformed existing churches, the renewal inspired the formation of new churches like the Vineyard. And despite denominational rejection, Pentecostal churches welcomed new non-Christian converts and mainline Protestants swept up by the charismatic renewal who were looking for churches to join. Seen by many as a "new Pentecost" that seemed to be at last succeeding in uniting and touching churches from all denominations, the renewal drew on the same restorationist yearnings that had motivated the Pentecostal movement six decades earlier.

---

39. E. W. Blumhofer, *Restoring the Faith*, 4.

Echoes of the charismatic renewal and Pentecostal revival continue to sound through ongoing restorationist impulses in North American Christianity. New teachings progressing from Pentecostal doctrines and practices, such as the word of faith movement, the prosperity message, spiritual warfare, and Seven Mountains of Society gain traction and followers from within Pentecostal movements.[40] More recent and small-scale movements are brokered by new independent networks and maintained by traditionally Pentecostal-charismatic ministries like the International House of Prayer, Catch the Fire, Bethel Church, Iris Global, Global Harvest, and countless others. Revivals like the Toronto Blessing of the 1990s, the 2008 Lakeland Revival, or the 2023 Asbury Revival inspire apostolic retrievals long lost since Azusa, the East End Mission, and, ultimately, the day of Pentecost.

Conclusion

The Spirit-baptized and empowered life that was earnestly sought by a fledgling group of faithful African American holiness seekers led by William Seymour in Los Angeles and by Ellen Hebden alone in her prayer closet is now a part of a diverse global movement thriving in the Majority World. North American Pentecostalism is continually revived by steady streams of migration that bring fresh waves of Global South Pentecostalisms and a missionary zeal intent on seeing God's transforming power at work in the post-Christian West. And while the shifting demographics of all Christians in Canada and the US present challenges, Pentecostals' hope remains fixed in the Holy Spirit's ability to empower them as witnesses equipped to usher in the still long-awaited global revival and the return of Christ. Today, North American Pentecostalism is more visibly diverse and diffuse, reflective of the increasing pluralism of the US and Canada. To Pentecostals, however, it is a sign of God's power in their midst restoring the day of Pentecost and prophetically affirming the unity of every tribe, nation, and tongue in the eschaton.

Bibliography

Alexander, Estrelda. *The Women of Azusa Street*. Cleveland: Pilgrim, 2005.

Anderson, Allan. "The Azusa Street Revival and the Emergence of Pentecostal Missions in the Early Twentieth Century." *Transformation* 23 (2006) 107–18.

———. *Spreading Fires: The Missionary Nature of Early Pentecostalism*. Maryknoll, NY: Orbis, 2007.

---

40. See Bowler, *Blessed*.

Blumhofer, Edith. "Women in Pentecostalism." In *Encyclopedia of Women and Religion in North America*, edited by Rosemary Skinner Keller et al., 1:394–407. Bloomington: Indiana University Press, 2006.

Blumhofer, Edith Waldvogel. *The Assemblies of God: A Popular History*. Springfield, MO: Radiant, 1985.

———. *Restoring the Faith: The Assemblies of God, Pentecostalism, and American Culture*. Urbana: University of Illinois Press, 1993.

Bowler, Kate. *Blessed: A History of the American Prosperity Gospel*. New York: Oxford University Press, 2013.

Boyer, Paul S. *When Time Shall Be No More: Prophecy Belief in Modern American Culture*. Studies in Cultural History. Cambridge, MA: Belknap, 1992.

Courtney, Caleb. "Barbara Johnston of Sarnia, Ontario: The First Canadian Pentecostal Missionary to India." *Canadian Journal of Pentecostal-Charismatic Christianity* 8 (2017) 1–18. http://journal.twu.ca/index.php/CJPC/article/view/189/143.

Daniels, David D. "North American Pentecostalism." In *The Cambridge Companion to Pentecostalism*, edited by Cecil Robeck Jr. and Amos Yong, 73–92. Cambridge Companions to Religion. Cambridge: Cambridge University Press, 2014.

Di Giacomo, Michael. "Identity and Change: The Story of the Italian-Canadian Pentecostal Community." *Canadian Journal of Pentecostal-Charismatic Christianity* 2 (2011) 83–130. http://journal.twu.ca/index.php/CJPC/article/view/40/35.

———. "Pentecostal and Charismatic Christianity in Canada: Its Origins, Development, and Distinct Culture." In *Canadian Pentecostalism Transition and Transformation*, edited by Michael Wilkinson, 15–38. McGill-Queen's Studies in the History of Religion, 2nd ser., 49. Montreal: McGill-Queen's University Press, 2009.

Espinosa, Gastón. *Latino Pentecostals in America: Faith and Politics in Action*. Cambridge, MA: Harvard University Press, 2014.

———. *William J. Seymour and the Origins of Global Pentecostalism: A Biography and Documentary History*. Durham, NC: Duke University Press, 2014.

Giggie, John M. "The Making of the African American Holiness Movement." In *After Redemption: Jim Crow and the Transformation of African American Religion in the Delta, 1875–1915*, edited by John M. Giggie, 165–93. Oxford University Press, 2007.

Kydd, Ronald. "Canadian Pentecostalism and the Evangelical Impulse." In *Aspects of the Canadian Evangelical Experience*, edited by George A. Rawlyk, 289–300. Montreal: McGill-Queen's University Press, 1997.

Marsden, George M. *Fundamentalism and American Culture: The Shaping of Twentieth Century Evangelicalism, 1870–1925*. New York: Oxford University Press, 1980.

McGee, Gary B. "'Baptism of the Holy Ghost & Fire!' The Mission Legacy of Minnie F. Abrams." *Missiology* 27 (Oct. 1999) 515–22.

———. *Miracles, Missions, and American Pentecostalism*. American Society of Missiology 45. Maryknoll, NY: Orbis, 2010.

Miller, Thomas William. "The Canadian 'Azusa': The Hebden Mission in Toronto." *Pneuma* 8 (Jan. 1986) 5–29.

Palmer, Phoebe. *The Way of Holiness: With Notes by the Way; Being a Narrative of Experience Resulting from a Determination to Be a Bible Christian*. New York: Piercy and Reed, 1843.

Raboteau, Albert J. *Slave Religion: The "Invisible Institution" in the Antebellum South*. Updated ed. Oxford: Oxford University Press, 2004.

Reed, David A. *"In Jesus' Name": The History and Beliefs of Oneness Pentecostals.* Journal of Pentecostal Theology Supplement Series. Blandford Forum, UK: Deo, 2008.

Robeck, Cecil M., Jr. *The Azusa Street Mission and Revival.* Thomas Nelson, 2018.

———. "Lucy F. Farrow." In *The New International Dictionary of Pentecostal and Charismatic Movements*, edited by Stanley M. Burgess and Eduard M. van der Maas, 632–33. Rev. and expanded ed. Grand Rapids: Zondervan, 2003.

Stewart, Adam. "A Canadian Azusa? The Implications of the Hebden Mission for Pentecostal Historiography." In *Winds from the North: Canadian Contributions to the Pentecostal Movement*, edited by Michael Wilkinson and Peter Althouse, 17–37. Religion in the Americas 10. Leiden, Neth.: Brill, 2010.

Stewart, Adam Scott. "Quenching the Spirit: A Transformation of Religious Identity and Experience in Three Canadian Pentecostal Churches." PhD diss., University of Waterloo, 2012.

Synan, Vinson. *The Holiness-Pentecostal Tradition: Charismatic Movements in the Twentieth Century.* 2nd ed. Grand Rapids: Eerdmans, 1997.

Vondey, Wolfgang. "The Making of a Black Liturgy: Pentecostal Worship and Spirituality from African Slave Narratives to American Cityscapes." *Black Theology* 10 (Mar. 2012) 147–68.

Chapter 8

Before Modern Feminism

Protestant Women in the Twentieth Century

PRISCILLA POPE-LEVISON

The nineteenth century will stand out in history as "the discoverer of woman" and it is for the womanhood of this twentieth century to prove what this discovery shall mean. No longer cramped by the old-time notions of a woman's very narrow sphere, our girls today find wide open doors for culture and education and travel. They may enter business if they choose, and the professions are inviting them. But in no realm of activity does the door swing wider than to Christian service. The Church is recognizing the necessity of the labor of trained, capable, spiritual women, and today she offers a magnificent opening for her consecrated daughters.

—IVA DURHAM VENNARD, "APPEAL TO YOUNG WOMEN"

THESE WORDS, PENNED IN 1906 by Iva Durham Vennard (1871–1945), Methodist deaconess and founder of two religious training schools, encapsulated the hope many held for a new century with wider opportunities for women everywhere and especially in the church. Vennard predicted that women would finally move beyond their "very narrow sphere" of nurturing, serving, and creating a serene, even religious, atmosphere in the home as a bulwark against men's exigencies in the public sphere. The term *separate spheres* describes the distinction between male and female roles in American culture at the time. It was a "dichotomized view of male and female nature and function wherein men, economics, and politics were associated with the public spheres and women, children, religion, and morality with the private sphere."[1] An advocate of separate spheres, Albert Leake, ramped up the rhetoric to grandiose proportions when, in his 1918 publication *The Vocational Education of Girls and Women*, he insisted that women's homemaking had a direct impact on the nation: "Notwithstanding the new avenues of employment opening up to them [women] in industrial, commercial, and professional life . . . homemaking is and will become more and more the one industry the character of which will determine the caliber of the nation."[2]

Within three years of her prediction, however, Vennard was forced by Methodist clergymen to resign as principal of Epworth Evangelistic Institute, a deaconess training school in St. Louis. Her detractors objected to her hiring women to teach courses in theology and Bible, training women in evangelism rather than religious education, and supposedly training women preachers under the guise of deaconesses. The opposition reached a crisis point when she returned from maternity leave to find a new regime installed at Epworth. Her detractors justified the overhaul by appealing to the separate spheres ideology: "Methodist preachers do not want deaconesses who study theology. We can attend to that ourselves. We want women as helpers who will work with the children, care for the sick, and visit the poor. If our deaconesses are trained in theology they will become critical of the preachers, and that will be the end of the deaconess movement."[3]

This scenario illustrates the push-pull of gender issues within American Protestantism at the turn of the twentieth century. They surfaced, for example, in votes cast at the quadrennial General Conferences of the Methodist Episcopal Church (MEC) from 1872 to the 1920s. In 1880, male delegates voted to rescind all local preacher licenses previously issued to women. The same vote also banned women from all but a few church leadership positions, and it slammed the door shut on women's ordination. Then in 1888, as an appeasement of sorts, the office of deaconess was established. Subsequent General Conferences dallied around gender issues for another four decades before voting in 1924, forty-four years later, to restore women's local preacher licenses. Methodist women would then have to wait another three decades for the vote in 1956 to approve full clergy rights for women, the same year the mainline Presbyterian Church ordained its first woman minister.

1. Taves, "Women and Gender," 263.
2. Leake, *Vocational Education*, v–vi.
3. Bowie, *Alabaster and Spikenard*, 145.

Protestant Women in the Twentieth-Century Church

Deaconesses

The deaconess movement caught on in American Protestantism in the late 1880s, and for the next four decades, scores of women signed on for one to two years of a theological education combined with practical training before they began full-time church work as teachers, nurses, evangelists, pastors, pastor's assistants, settlement workers, missionaries, visitors, or Bible teachers. Nearly all Protestant denominations—from Lutheran to Baptist, Episcopal to Congregational—sponsored some iteration of the movement, yet it found its greatest success in the numbers of deaconesses and breadth of institutions within the Wesleyan family. The 1888 MEC discipline outlined these duties for deaconesses: minister to the poor, visit the sick, pray with the dying, care for the orphan, seek the wandering, comfort the sorrowing, save the sinning, and relinquishing wholly all other pursuits, devote themselves, in a general way, to such forms of Christian labor as may be suited to their abilities.[4]

As structural inroads in the 1920s opened up more opportunities for women in pastoral ministry, many deaconess institutions, particularly the training schools, became obsolete. Enrollment at the flagship institution, the Chicago Training School, for instance, peaked in 1910 with 256 matriculated students; it eventually merged with nearby Garrett Bible Institute in 1934. During the same time period, women's enrollment increased in other types of educational institutions that led to secular careers. Many women became credentialed to do the same work as a deaconess—nursing, teaching, social work, and (eventually) ministry—yet as salaried professionals.

Evangelists

The two most prominent women evangelists in the twentieth century were Aimee Semple McPherson (1890–1944) and Kathryn Kuhlman (1907–76). McPherson made her way from Canada down the Eastern Seaboard in 1918, holding meetings in a forty-foot by eighty-foot tent. She settled eventually in Los Angeles, where her ministry and influence flourished, as did the audience in Angelus Temple, whose 5,300-seat auditorium filled up three times every Sunday and every evening for services. She claimed to have been the first woman to preach a sermon over the radio on February 6, 1924, only eighteen months after the nation's first broadcast station

---

4. Methodist Episcopal Church, *Doctrines and Discipline*, 213.

opened. She went on to install a radio station in Angelus Temple, and at 7:00 a.m. every morning, the station broadcast *The Sunshine Hour*, which she performed live when in Los Angeles. Even after her mysterious and highly contested kidnapping disappearance in 1926, her impact remained such that in the 1934 California gubernatorial campaign, she catalyzed her followers to help defeat the Democratic candidate, Upton Sinclair, whom she believed supported atheism and Communism.

Kathryn Kuhlman, as a teenager, joined her older sister and brother-in-law for their summer tent meeting season in the Pacific Northwest. What she had intended for the summer turned into a five-year apprenticeship in evangelism. In 1928, Kathryn and pianist Helen Gulliford formed an evangelistic partnership that would last ten years, known as "God's Girls"; A two-week revival in Denver in 1933 resulted in the organization of a church, the Denver Revival Tabernacle, as well as a radio ministry. Eventually, she moved on to Franklin, Pennsylvania, where she began *Heart-to-Heart*, a religious radio program that was regularly broadcast for over forty years. When she settled in Pittsburgh, she held healing services first in Carnegie Hall, then in the sanctuary of the downtown First Presbyterian Church. Her popular, long-running television program on CBS, *I Believe in Miracles*, also served as the title of her book, which sold over a million copies.

Ministers

When the twentieth century dawned, the denominations recognizing women ministers with the same rights and status as men were very few—the Quakers, Congregationalists, Unitarians, Universalists, Wesleyan Methodists, Methodist Protestants, and Church of God (Anderson, Indiana). In 1907, when the Northern Baptists (now the American Baptists) formed a denomination, they affirmed women's ordination. The following year, when the Church of the Nazarene was established by merging several Wesleyan/holiness churches, women comprised 13 percent of the ministers.

A sign of growing national interest in women ministers was the founding in 1919 of the American Association of Women Preachers (AAWP) by MEC minister Madeline Southard. Membership in AAWP was open to any woman who had been called to preach, and by 1923, that included 189 members from sixteen denominations spread across twenty-nine states. In 1925, Southard "lamented that the church seemed to be the last to yield to the growing spirit of what she called 'sex-democracy.' Women were serving society in many ways, but they were still not allowed to serve the ecclesiastical world."[5]

---

5. Zikmund, "Protestant Women's Ordination Movement," 2:949.

Beginning in the 1950s, more Protestant denominations began to ordain women, such as the African Methodist Episcopal Church (1948), Christian Methodist Episcopal Church (1954), Presbyterian Church in the USA (1956), MEC (1956), Southern Baptist Church (1964), Episcopal Church (1976), and Evangelical Lutheran Church in America (1987). Some of these denominations with an episcopal polity also consecrate women as bishops.

Church Founders

Some women tired of waiting for leadership opportunities to open up in their church, so they launched their own, like Alma White. Alma married a Methodist minister, Kent White, and preached often in his pulpit while also leading evangelistic meetings throughout Colorado. At the time, prominent clergymen were strengthening their opposition to women in ministry and refused to let her speak in their churches. The Whites settled in Denver, where they set up an independent mission and opened a training school for their workers. Despite Kent's resistance, in 1901, Alma formally organized the mission into a church, known as the Pillar of Fire. Because she was now leading a multicampus church with oversight over forty pastors and evangelists across four states, she set up her own ordination with a sympathetic Quaker minister. The Pillar of Fire's membership continued to expand through evangelistic meetings and the distribution of gospel literature in cities throughout the United States and even into Great Britain. To mark her authority over the now international church, in 1918, at the age of fifty-six, she set up a consecration service to become one of the first US women bishops. She also founded a self-sufficient community for church members in New Jersey, which included a school for every age, from elementary through college.

Ida Bell Robinson followed a similar trajectory. She did street evangelism in Philadelphia under the auspices of the United Holy Church of America, a Black holiness denomination. In 1919, she was ordained an elder and appointed to a small mission church, where she was successful in pastoral ministry and itinerant evangelism. In her estimation, however, women's prospects within the denomination were decreasing as male leaders repetitively debated women's ordination. This situation conflicted with a divine promise she had received, "that He would do a great work through the women as time passed on." In January 1924, she spent ten days in prayer and fasting, during which time she heard God's call to "come out on Mount Sinai," so that "I will use you to loose the women."[6] Immediately she set up a

---

6. See the pamphlet prepared by the church's historian for the sixty-fifth anniversary of the church: Bell, *History of Mt. Sinai*, 3.

new church, the Mount Sinai Holy Church of America, and was consecrated a bishop the following year. At its founding, women comprised six of nine members of the board of elders and held the top four denominational offices. When she died at the age of fifty-four, the membership had increased to eighty-four churches and more than 160 ordained ministers of whom 75 percent were women.

In 1927, McPherson launched the largest church founded by a woman, the International Church of the Foursquare Gospel. Several years earlier, she had opened a coeducational Bible school, Lighthouse of International Foursquare Evangelism or LIFE. After graduation, many students, more women than men, went out to organize Angelus Temple branch churches in other cities. Currently, the denomination has nearly nine million members worshipping in more than 67,000 churches in 135 countries.

The accomplishments of these women church leaders occurred during a time of relative intransigence toward women in ministry, when mainline denominations only begrudgingly allowed laywomen to vote in church conferences, when a handful of women attended seminary, and when women's ordination seemed a pipe dream. Nevertheless, these women persevered in the face of continual dismissal by family and ministerial foes. They endured despite constantly battling those who considered their cause illegitimate. By standing in the pulpit, presiding at the communion table, and laying on hands to ordain ministers, they provided a visible witness—a century ago—of women church leaders in American Christianity.

Protestant Women and the Bible

Many treatises, penned by supporters and detractors of women's right to preach, even women's ordination, had been authored throughout the nineteenth century. The most controversial was the Woman's Bible, published in two volumes, 1885 and 1888, and spearheaded by suffrage advocate Elisabeth Cady Stanton. Stanton believed that the supreme impediment to women's advancement was the widespread, long-standing belief that women's subordination was divinely ordained by an infallible Bible. To counteract this reigning opinion, advocated by clergymen and sanctioned by church tradition, she organized the Woman's Bible, so that women, in particular, would be able to assess critically the most influential and highly regarded text in Western civilization. Her guiding hermeneutical assumption, which was greatly influenced by the interpretive strategy known as historical criticism, was that biblical texts were written and edited by men, not by God; therefore, these texts were open to interpretation, criticism, even rejection. For this two-volume project, she recruited only female biblical and classical scholars to write comments on biblical references to women in general, a particular woman, female animals—in short, anything remotely related to the female sex.

Other Protestant women in the twentieth century continued to call out patriarchy in the Bible. Katherine Bushnell, medical missionary, temperance worker, and Woman's Christian Temperance Union social purity lecturer, had witnessed firsthand manifold injustices perpetrated against women in her extensive travels, from China to Wisconsin lumber camps. Because she believed that patriarchal biblical interpretations were at the root of these injustices, she aimed to reinterpret the Bible as liberative for women. This purpose guided the writing of her correspondence course on women in the Bible, begun in 1908 and self-published in 1916 as *God's Word to Women: One Hundred Bible Studies on Woman's Place in the Divine Economy*.

Alma White supported male and female equality on biblical grounds, and she advocated for gender equality in every realm of society—political, religious, familial, social, and economic. She grounded this belief in her interpretation of the Genesis creation stories. "In the beginning God gave men and women copartnership and control of all that He had created. But His order has been reversed and woman has become man's servant or slave, and as a result the social fabric is going to pieces and the world is well-nigh wrecked. Before lasting peace can be expected, woman must be accorded the place designed for her."[7] She sometimes published her biblical interpretations in poetic form in her periodical, *Woman's Chains*.

> If social evils they'd correct,
> Men on this subject should reflect,
> And learn from Genesis, the Book
> Where God would now have all men look.
>
> 'Tis there equality is taught
> For which the women long have sought;
> To this end then we will contend
> Till men their rights to them extend.
>
> A helpmeet not alone was she,
> But man's own equal she should be,—
> In partnership with him to rule
> O'er everything on God's footstool.

---

7. White, *Woman's Chains*, 41.

When Satan would them both deceive
He came first to our mother Eve;
And by his subtlety and power
He captured her in that dark hour.

Secure her first, he would prefer,
So as not to risk losing her;
She was the stronger citadel,
And what she'd do he could not tell.

So at the task the tempter went,
That her escape he might prevent;
The man heard all that Satan said,
And into sin he, too, was led.[8]

The methods utilized by these biblical interpreters, especially Stanton and the Woman's Bible female editorial board, were picked up by second-wave biblical scholars in the 1970s. They critiqued the Bible as a patriarchal document that discriminated against women. After all, men dominated the cultures in which the Bible was written; men, perhaps without exception, wrote it; men ultimately selected the canonical texts included in it; men, until recently, translated it; and men have comprised the vast majority of its interpreters. As a result, they approached the Bible with "a hermeneutics of suspicion," to apply a prominent phrase from Elisabeth Schüssler Fiorenza, because it has functioned historically to oppress women. They also focused on texts about women, even when they exist on the periphery of the biblical narrative. The critical principle in this endeavor is to promote and ensure "the full humanity of women. Whatever denies, diminishes, or distorts the full humanity of women, is therefore, appraised as not redemptive. . . . What does promote the full humanity of women is of the Holy."[9]

Protestant Women and Theological Education

Women's theological education flourished in the first decades of the twentieth century not in theological seminaries, but in religious training schools, like Moody Bible Institute, Boston Missionary Training School (now Gordon-Conwell), St. Paul Bible College. At first, these schools welcomed women into their classrooms and trained them to be pastors, evangelists, Bible teachers, and missionaries. Women were not assigned gender-segregated vocational

---

8. White, *Woman's Chains*, 81–82.
9. Ruether, *Sexism and God-Talk*, 18–19.

tracks but were educated together with men in the same classrooms, learning Bible study and practical work. After the first generation of students were graduated, however, women were increasingly relegated to a different curriculum, focusing on home economics rather than a theological education.

The course of study in deaconess training schools was similar to that for male ministerial candidates in that it focused on the core theological disciplines. Deaconesses studied the Bible, book by book, with corresponding maps and geographical diagrams; became conversant with ancient Jewish and Christian authors; mastered theological movements and ecclesial leaders in successive generations of church history; learned about theological doctrines from creation to glorification; and became experts in their denomination's history and doctrine. Some deaconesses even enrolled in classes at nearby seminaries to learn biblical languages.

A few women matriculated in theological seminaries, like Amy Lee Stockton, a protégé of John Marvin Dean, a Baptist minister who founded Northern Baptist Seminary outside of Chicago. Dean established a fund to cover her seminary educational costs and enrolled her as the very first student when the seminary opened. As the lone woman in her class, she felt like a misfit, as she described in her autobiography: "My thoughts revert to an afternoon when I sat at my desk quite discouraged. I was homesick. I felt somewhat inadequate to the requirements. My fellow students were all men and they rather resented a woman invading their world." Nevertheless, she persevered, completed her degree, and went on to preach nationwide for more than sixty years. In 1950, she received an honorary doctor of divinity degree from her alma mater.

Women enrolled in seminaries in greater numbers during the later decades of the twentieth century. In the early 1970s, the percentage of women among all seminary students was around 10 percent; that number increased to 35 percent by 2000. Women faculty were increasingly hired to teach in seminaries; in 1971, women represented 3 percent of all faculty, and by 2000, the number had grown to 20 percent.[10] The first woman hired to teach theology full-time at the seminary level was Georgia Harkness, a Methodist minister who, in 1939, became professor of applied theology at Garrett Biblical Institute, now Garrett-Evangelical Theological Seminary. She was also a leader in the ecumenical movement, and at the first meeting of the World Council of Churches in 1948, she debated Karl Barth on women's roles in the church.

With more women students and faculty, reflection on women's experience as a primary source of theology blossomed. A central question

---

10. McLean, "Women in Theological Education," 2:925.

developed from this reflection, namely, "Whose experience constitutes women's experience?" White feminists argued initially that despite vast differences in contexts, there remains a shared experience of women's oppression and powerlessness. This claim has been denounced by women of Color who find that it trivializes and negates differences. Even as "universal" an experience as motherhood differs substantially due to myriad factors, such as race, class, location, sexuality, and ability. As women of Color engaged increasingly in theological reflection, they coined new names to set their theology apart from the first generation of feminist theologians, such as *womanism* for Black women's theology and *mujerista* for Hispanic women's theology.

Protestant Women and Voluntary Organizations

Missionary Societies

While male church leaders equivocated over gender issues in most Protestant denominations, women forged ahead on their own to establish voluntary religious organizations separate from men's. From the 1870s to 1890s, women in a number of denominations had established their own home and foreign missionary organizations, including eight within Methodism alone. These organizations opened up myriad opportunities for women missionaries to preach, teach, and plant churches on the mission field, the very activities that women were not authorized to do in their home congregations. Due to the substantial influx of women missionaries supported by these organizations, the Protestant missionary force sent from America grew exponentially. Of the six thousand foreign missionaries at the turn of the twentieth century, women comprised roughly two-thirds, and women would continue to outnumber men by two to one throughout much of the twentieth century, with even greater numerical strength in nondenominational faith missions. A leading spokeswoman during the 1910 Woman's Missionary Jubilee was Helen Barrett Montgomery (1861–1934), a Baptist leader with a string of accomplishments: author of the best-selling study book *Western Women in Eastern Lands*, in honor of the jubilee; first woman to translate the New Testament; first woman elected to the Rochester, New York, school board; and first woman elected president of a mainline denomination, the Northern Baptist Convention.[11]

---

11. Robert, "Protestant Women Missionaries," 2:834–39.

WCTU

The Woman's Christian Temperance Union (WCTU) was the largest woman's organization in the United States at the beginning of the twentieth century with a membership approaching two hundred thousand. From its start in the Women's Temperance Crusade of 1873–74 to its expanse into a "Do Everything" policy under Frances Willard's nearly twenty-year presidency (1879–98), the WCTU provided women with their own, separate institution for societal and ecclesial reform. The organization tackled pivotal reforms of the day, such as women's suffrage, health, and dress reform; equal pay for equal work; the eradication of prostitution; an eight-hour workday; and women's equality in church polity. Due in large measure to the WCTU's advocacy, the Eighteenth Amendment to the US Constitution was passed in 1919, which ushered in the Prohibition era. Fourteen years later, in 1933, this amendment was repealed.

The WCTU's Social Purity Department labored to dismantle the gendered double standard that judged sin differently depending upon whether a man or a woman committed it; in other words, the same sin was considered more serious, even less forgivable, if done by a woman. This belief was traced to the story of original sin—often described as Eve's sin (Gen 3:13)—which validated women's suppression. Southard, a WCTU worker and national speaker on social purity, found church members, like the male religious leaders in the biblical story of the adulterous woman (John 8:1–11), to be "merciless toward a woman who takes a single false step."[12] She interpreted Jesus's refusal to condemn the woman as his putting an end to the double standard once and for all. In this regard, she presaged second-wave feminism's indictment of the contemporary church and American society for what she considered a theological fallacy.

Feminist theologians later in the century would revise the doctrine of sin, one that has been particularly destructive to women given its link to Eve and original sin. As Rosemary Radford Ruether writes, because of Eve's culpability in the fall, "she [woman] is now, within fallen history, subjected to the male as her superior. This subjugation is not a sin against her, but her punishment for her sin. It is the expression of divine justice."[13] Valerie Saiving articulated that the traditional definition of sin as pride or will to power in an individual is inadequate, especially for women. Instead, she argued that pride in oneself provides an antidote to women's sin of self-deprecation.[14]

---

12. Southard, *White Slave Traffic*, 78.
13. Ruether, *Sexism and God-Talk*, 97.
14. Saiving, "Human Situation," 37.

NACW

Founded in 1896, the National Association for Colored Women (NACW) was an amalgam of two previous organizations: the Colored Women's League and the National Federation of Afro-American Women. Its early leaders included nationally prominent "race women," who were committed to the uplift of their race, like Ida B. Wells-Barnett (1862–1931), Nannie Helen Burroughs (1879–1961), and Mary Church Terrell (1863–1954), the first NACW president. The motto they adopted, "Lifting as They Climb," set out the club's altruistic purpose toward all Black Americans. In a speech given in 1900, Terrell explained the motto: "In no way could we live up to such a sentiment better than by coming into a closer touch with the masses of women, by whom, whether we will or not, the world will always judge the womanhood of our race. *Even though we wish to shun them, and hold ourselves entirely aloof from them*, we cannot escape the consequences of their acts. . . . We are bound by the ties of race and sex."[15] This strategy would be criticized by womanist theologians in later decades for its conformity to middle-class White values.

The NACW's membership and leadership was comprised of church-women who came together to address social, cultural, and educational needs of the Black community through the club's various departments—prison and jail work, sewing circles, and history and literature. NACW women also engaged in fundraising for hospitals, orphanages, kindergartens, vocational schools, and retirement homes for Black communities, as well as a college scholarship fund for Black women. In political advocacy, they worked to dismantle the segregated transportation system, to put an end to lynching, and to support women's suffrage.

Mary McLeod Bethune, the eighth NACW president, went on to establish the National Council of Negro Women (NCNW) in 1935 to expand the impact and representation of Black women nationally and internationally. NCNW brought together delegates from a number of organizations in order to coordinate and strengthen their work collectively. Bethune, who was motivated in all her endeavors by her Christian faith, founded a private school, now named Bethune-Cookman University, became an advisor to President Roosevelt, supported the United Nations Charter, and cofounded the United Negro College Fund.

---

15. Sieglinde Lemke, introduction to Elizabeth Lindsay Davis, *Lifting as They Climb*, xix, as quoted in Jones, *Quest for Equality*, 144; emphasis original.

Protestant Women and Social Issues

Suffrage

Agitation for women's suffrage came to the fore in the late nineteenth century, particularly as more women analyzed underlying factors of alcoholism, which led to interest in enacting legislation to ameliorate damaging social conditions of poverty, overcrowding, and dangerous labor conditions, to name a few. Protestant women helped to lead the suffrage movement to its eventual success, like the Rev. Dr. Anna Howard Shaw, Susan B. Anthony's chosen protégé. Shaw was a physician, a graduate of Boston University School of Theology, and the first ordained woman minister in the Methodist Protestant Church. She became president of the National American Woman Suffrage Association (NAWSA) and led it from 1904 to 1915. In its 1913 parade in Washington, DC, the NAWSA required Black women to march separately so as not to offend southern White women supporters. Ida Wells-Barnett refused and stood on the parade sidelines, joining the march only toward the end, once the Chicago contingent of White women had passed by. Wells-Barnett had founded a Black women's suffrage organization in Chicago, the Alpha Suffrage Club, and organized members to elect candidates who would best serve the Black community. The club's work helped to pass women's suffrage in Illinois in 1913. In 1920, the Nineteenth Amendment, which gave women in the US the right to vote, was ratified.

Race

Protestant women were active in myriad ways in the movement for racial justice throughout the twentieth century. Wells-Barnett was an early leader. She was born a slave and was emancipated with her family when she was three years old. Being raised in the southern Black Methodist Church, she developed early on a deep spirituality and a strong sense of Christian duty made visible in high moral standards and in doing good works. These commitments coalesced in the courage, persistence, and creative maladjustment she applied to her advocacy of the anti-lynching movement. From 1892, when her close friend Thomas Moss was lynched in Memphis, Wells-Barnett become a national and international critic of lynching, both in speech and in journalism. Her unrelenting commitment to racial justice, however, met with heavy resistance.

After she published a newspaper article exposing inequalities in the Black schools in Memphis, she lost her teaching job. The conflict grew more violent after she wrote an editorial about interracial relationships. While she was out of town, the office of the *Free Speech*, a newspaper of which she was part owner, was vandalized and demolished, and lynching threats were published against her in another newspaper. In 2020, Wells-Barnett was posthumously awarded a citation by the Pulitzer Prize Board "for her outstanding and courageous reporting on the horrific and vicious violence against African Americans during the era of lynching."[16]

Rosa Parks became the mother of the civil rights movement, as many refer to her, in December 1955, when she refused to give up her bus seat to a White man in Montgomery, Alabama. She was active at the time in the local NAACP, serving as secretary, and she had attended civil rights training workshops. She was also a member of the African Methodist Episcopal Church (AME), known as the Freedom Church, due to its many petitions against slavery during the abolition movement. Parks had grown up at home and in church singing hymns about freedom, like "Woke Up This Morning with My Mind Stayed on Jesus" and "O Freedom Over Me." Later in life, Parks became an AME deaconess, the highest position for a laywoman in the denomination.

White women also braved opposition in the work of racial justice. Church of the Nazarene evangelist, pastor, and church planter Mary Lee Cagle accepted invitations to preach in Black churches in Alabama during Jim Crow, even though her family and White friends disapproved. This excerpt from her autobiography describes one of her interracial meetings as well as the criticism she faced:

> She was given a pressing invitation by the colored people to come to their church and preach for them, which she was glad to do, as she had known many of them from her childhood when they had worked for her father on the farm. . . . Some of her relatives opposed her preaching for them; but she felt it was of the Lord and said that she must go, and she did. It was a day long to be remembered by her as she preached the Word of God to them and saw their black faces light up with the blessings of heaven. When the ones who objected saw the results they gladly withdrew all objections.[17]

After the Nineteenth Amendment passed, Jessie Daniel Ames (1883–1972), an active Methodist laywoman, turned her focus to racial justice. In 1921, she became director of the Texas Council of the Commission on Interracial Cooperation (CIC), then moved to Atlanta in 1929 to become

---

16. See https://www.pulitzer.org/prize-winners-by-year/2020.
17. Cagle, *Life and Work*, 62.

the national director of the CIC Women's Committee. The following year, she founded the Association of Southern Women for the Prevention of Lynching to galvanize White women to end racial violence and executions. She traveled through southern states, where lynching occurred most often, in an effort to organize local chapters, frequently connecting first through Protestant women's missionary societies.

Racial justice work was also done behind the scenes by women like Josephine Beckwith (1908–2008). She gained a vision for racial transformation while growing up in an integrated neighborhood in Kansas City, Kansas, and later as a college student active in the Methodist Student Movement's interracial meetings in the 1930s. With the combined support of Blacks and Whites, she broke the color barrier in 1939 to enroll as a graduate student at the National College for Christian Workers in Kansas City, Missouri. After graduation, Beckwith directed several church-based community centers until, in 1958, she was appointed director of the Bethlehem Community Center in Savannah, Georgia. In her annual report the following year, she tied her work in the community center work to racial transformation: "Some of the neighbors refuse to accept us but see daily people of a different skin color come into our building to lead a group, meet with a committee, or bring friends for a tour. A philosophy based on our Christian principles which includes respect for those of a different race or creed must be a leavening force in this community."[18] Until she died at the age of one hundred, Beckwith worked to transform relationships between Blacks and Whites.

Conclusion

"The Church is recognizing the necessity of the labor of trained, capable, spiritual women, and today she offers a magnificent opening for her consecrated daughters." Did Vennard's words come to pass by century's end? One answer is yes, when looking at the wide-open opportunities in many Protestant churches for women to serve in the full range of ministerial roles. Women students' enrollment in theological education currently is well over 50 percent, and women faculty number close to 25 percent. Another answer is no, when looking at the largest Protestant church, the Southern Baptist Church, which no longer ordains women and advances a separate spheres ideology, now known as complementarianism. From these two perspectives, it is clear that the push-pull of gender issues in the Protestant Church continues into the twenty-first century.

18. Schueneman, "Leavening Force," 893–94.

Bibliography

Bell, Minerva. *Brief History of Mt. Sinai*. Teaneck, NJ: Self-published, 1986.
Bendroth, Margaret Lamberts, and Virginia Lieson Brereton, eds. *Women and Twentieth-Century Protestantism*. Urbana: University of Illinois Press, 2002.
Bowie, Mary Ella. *Alabaster and Spikenard: The Life of Iva Durham Vennard, D.D., Founder of Chicago Evangelistic Institute*. Chicago: Chicago Evangelistic Institute Press, 1947.
Cagle, Mary Lee. *Life and Work of Mary Lee Cagle: An Autobiography*. Kansas City, MO: Nazarene, 1928.
Jones, Beverly Washington. *Quest for Equality: The Life and Writings of Mary Eliza Church Terrell, 1863–1954*. Vol. 13 of *Black Women in United States History*. Brooklyn, NY: Carlson, 1990.
Keller, Rosemary Skinner, and Rosemary Radford Ruether, eds. *In Our Own Voices: Four Centuries of American Women's Religious Writing*. San Francisco: HarperOne, 1995.
Leake, Albert H. *The Vocational Education of Girls and Women*. New York: Macmillan, 1918.
McLean, Jeanne P. "Women in Theological Education." In *Encyclopedia of Women and Religion in North America*, edited by Rosemary Skinner Keller et al., 2:923–30. Bloomington: Indiana University Press, 2006.
Methodist Episcopal Church. *The Doctrines and Discipline of the Church*. Repr., Trenton, NJ: MEC, 2016. First published 1888.
Robert, Dana. "Protestant Women Missionaries: Foreign and Home." In *Encyclopedia of Women and Religion in North America*, edited by Rosemary Skinner Keller et al., 2:834–43. Bloomington: Indiana University Press, 2006.
Ruether, Rosemary Radford. *Sexism and God-Talk*. Boston: Beacon, 1993.
Saiving, Valerie. "The Human Situation: A Feminine View." In *Womanspirit Rising: A Feminist Reader in Religion*, edited by Carol P. Christ and Judith Plaskow, 25–42. San Francisco: HarperOne, 1992.
Schueneman, Mary K. "A Leavening Force: African American Women and Christian Mission in the Civil Rights Era." *CH* 81 (Dec. 2012) 873–902.
Southard, M. Madeline. *The White Slave Traffic versus the American Home*. Louisville: Pentecostal, 1914.
Taves, Ann. "Women and Gender in American Religion(s)." *RelSRev* 18 (Oct. 1992) 263–70.
Vennard, Iva Durham. "An Appeal to Young Women." *Inasmuch* (Nov. 1906) 8.
White, Alma. *Woman's Chains*. Zarephath, NJ: Pillar of Fire, 1943.
Zikmund, Barbara Brown. "The Protestant Women's Ordination Movement." In *Encyclopedia of Women and Religion in North America*, edited by Rosemary Skinner Keller et al., 2:940–50. Bloomington: Indiana University Press, 2006.

Chapter 9

Between Faith and Doubt

The American Protestant Intellectual Mind

DAVID MISLIN

IN 2005, SHORTLY BEFORE he died, the United Church of Christ minister William Sloane Coffin Jr. published *Letters to a Young Doubter*. The book, which marked the final publication of Coffin's career, consisted of his musings to an imagined correspondent, a "bright college student" like those he counseled during his tenure as Yale University chaplain during the 1960s.¹ In the letters, Coffin urged this young doubter to cultivate his faith, despite the intellectual and moral questions about religion raised by his education. The letters, not surprisingly, revealed much about Coffin's religious perspective. His admission that he came to Christianity after reading the works of theologians reflected his conviction that faith had an intellectual component.² His advice that the fictional student attend church "with a profound and critical humility" that allowed him "to question all things earthly while being open to intuitions of some things heavenly" captured another key belief: religious understanding would never be complete, and uncertainty would remain.³

Coffin was a towering figure in American Protestantism. The nephew of the president of Union Theological Seminary, he rose to prominence as a civil rights and anti-war activist during the 1960s. Later in his career, he became pastor of the prestigious Riverside Church in New York City, following in the footsteps of some of the most famous Protestant ministers of the twentieth century. There, he espoused support for abortion rights and the gay rights movement, causes he embraced in *Letters to a Young Doubter*.⁴

1. Coffin, *Letters to Young Doubter*, x.
2. Coffin, *Letters to Young Doubter*, 37.
3. Coffin, *Letters to Young Doubter*, 61.
4. See Goldstein, *William Sloane Coffin Jr.*

Far more significant than its political statements was the way the book allowed Coffin to situate himself in a long tradition of American Protestant thought. It was telling that the young doubter was a college student at a prestigious institution. Skepticism about Christianity was long associated with educated elites who found the tradition's claims intellectually untenable. But Coffin's insistence on the compatibility of Christian faith with a sophisticated intellectual mind—even when reconciling the two meant harboring doubts—drew on an equally rich tradition of Protestant thought.

From the earliest days of the colonial era, American Protestants have concerned themselves with the mind, and generations of theologians and ministers have sought to assure churchgoers of the reasonable nature of Christian faith. Importantly, this has been true across the ideological spectrum of Protestantism. Conservative traditionalists, including early leaders of the fundamentalist movement, proved no less emphatic than progressive innovators in their insistence on the accord between their beliefs and reason.

But it is among the latter group where the American experience has proved distinctive. Unlike in Europe, where engagement with intellectual trends of the eighteenth and nineteenth centuries pushed many people away from Christianity, Protestants in the United States repeatedly found ways to reconcile faith with the intellectual currents of the day.[5] The liberal tradition, to which William Sloane Coffin belonged, offered two key innovations: that Christian revelation is best understood as a progressive unfolding of truth, and that this evolving development of religious knowledge leaves room for doubt as part of a healthy religious life.

A Reasonable Faith

The presumption of affinity between a religious life and the life of the mind has deep roots in Protestant Christianity. A core principle of the Reformation was that any person could read and understand the Bible without the interpretative intervention of church tradition or authority. In practice, the interpretation of religious ideas remained the work of clergy and theologians in many of the new Protestant denominations. But the expectation that Christianity would align with and be understood by human reason was embedded in the Protestant tradition from its earliest days.[6]

This commitment to the intellect was present in the English colonies in the future United States from the outset. Though the Puritans who settled in New England in the early 1600s considered reason to be secondary to

---

5. Hollinger, *After Cloven Tongues*, 3–4.
6. Dorrien, *Imagining Progressive Religion*, xv.

scriptural revelation as a source of religious knowledge, they nevertheless espoused a religious message that appealed to the intellect. As the historian E. Brooks Holifield has written, sermons regularly introduced churchgoers to complex theological ideas, and "America's first learned class consisted largely of Protestant clergy."[7] The earliest institutions of higher learning in England's North American colonies were established primarily to train ministers, and the clergy were experts not only in theology but in philosophical and scientific ideas as well. Like their European counterparts, Puritan ministers saw little discord among these domains of thought.[8]

During the 1700s, the belief that Christianity should appeal to the mind gained wider currency in the American colonies. This development reflected broader trends of Enlightenment thought, which privileged reason and humanity's capacity for knowledge. Some groups, like the Deists, found this high view of human reason incompatible with Christian faith.[9] Many other Protestants, however, identified new ways to emphasize the affinity of Christianity and reason. The tradition of natural theology grew popular, with its promise that "reason, reflecting on either the visible world or the workings of the human mind, could produce evidence for the existence of a transcendent God apart from the revelation in scripture or the tradition of the church."[10] Eighteenth-century thinkers thus went further than their Puritan predecessors in making reason a key vehicle for attaining knowledge of God. This same emphasis on reason guided ministers like Jonathan Edwards, who argued that a reasoned reflection on nature revealed both complexity and order. This combination, he argued, offered intellectual proof of the existence of God.[11]

Protestants' appeal to the intellect proved so ubiquitous that it was embraced even by new splinter groups whose leaders rejected existing churches as being elitist in their emphasis on the importance of theology. Methodists and Baptists, who gained popularity amid the religious revivals of the late 1700s and early 1800s, offered a simpler religious message of salvation that did not revolve around debates about theological nuances. But they argued that it was the very simplicity of their teachings that made them seem reasonable.[12]

---

7. Holifield, *Theology in America*, 1.
8. Holifield, *Theology in America*, 1–2, 25.
9. Hutchison, *Modernist Impulse*, 14–15.
10. Holifield, *Theology in America*, 5.
11. Holifield, *Theology in America*, 107.
12. Holifield, *Theology in America*, 19.

By the early 1800s, the presumption of Christianity's intellectual reasonableness had become commonplace in the newly independent United States. In the decades that followed, Protestant theology across denominations was grounded in commonsense philosophy. This tradition, as defined by one historian, was characterized by its reassurance that "God's truth was a single unified order." It also held, in the spirit of the Reformation, that "all persons of common sense were capable of knowing that truth."[13] This confidence in the easy interpretation of Christianity and a simple view of the world would soon be shaken, however.

New Intellectual Challenges to Christianity

The middle decades of the nineteenth century brought significant challenges to the belief in the natural accord between Christianity and an intellectual life. Evolutionary theories, especially Darwin's theory of natural selection, posed the first challenge. At the most basic level, these ideas conflicted with a straightforward reading of Scripture, calling into question the seven-day creation narrative. But evolutionary theory disturbed even the multitude of Protestants whose faith did not demand a literal reading of Genesis. Rather, the substantive challenge came from the way that evolution seemingly undermined the argument from design, which had been commonplace for over a century and had been popularized by the English clergyman William Paley. For decades, Paley's arguments about nature had provided a cornerstone for Protestant arguments for the reasonableness of Christianity. Drawing on his writing, American Protestants noted the fact that all living things were well suited to their natural environment. This, they argued, demonstrated the existence of a wise, divine Creator, who had taken great care in designing every aspect of the natural world. Evolutionary theories provided an alternative explanation for the apparent order of creation—one that had no need of God.[14]

The second major intellectual challenge came from new approaches to scholarship about the Bible. These methods originated in Germany and reached the United States in the second half of the nineteenth century. New scholarship employed close textual analysis and rigorous historical contextualization and called into question many of common justifications of biblical accuracy. Jesus's apparent prediction of the destruction of the Jerusalem temple in the Gospel of Matthew had long been cited as proof of his divinity. Scholars now argued that the text had been written *after* the temple's

---

13. Marsden, *Fundamentalism and American Culture*, 14.
14. Roberts, *Darwinism and the Divine*, 8–12.

destruction, however, calling into question Scripture's internal proofs of its accuracy. Moreover, scholarship suggested that biblical books were written later or earlier than their writers suggested, or by different authors entirely. These developments appeared to undermine Protestants' long-standing insistence that Scripture was readily interpretable by ordinary readers. They suggested that Christianity was not the straightforward, reasonable tradition it had long presented itself to be.[15]

Some Protestant leaders simply denied the validity of the new biblical scholarship and evolutionary theories. Even as they rejected these ideas, however, they grounded their arguments in appeals to the intellect and stressed the reasonableness of orthodox Christianity. Theologians like A. A. Hodge and Benjamin Warfield of Princeton Theological Seminary argued for the inerrancy of Scripture. They appealed to logic in their assertions that Protestantism demanded acceptance of a plain-sense reading of biblical narratives.[16]

Many skeptical churchgoers were unmoved by the arguments emerging from Princeton Seminary. To them, Christianity had ceased to offer an intellectually reasonable worldview. Ministers, especially those who led educated congregations in urban areas, recognized the effect of this newfound skepticism in their pews. Congregants fell away, often reluctantly, because they could not accept religious ideas that seemed irrational. The failure to reconcile Christian faith with new ideas had produced a spiritual crisis.[17]

A New Theology

Unwilling countenance the decline of Christianity, Protestant theologians searched for new ways to demonstrate that their faith tradition could still resonate with an intellectual mind. This project began haltingly in the mid-nineteenth century. The Connecticut Congregationalist minister Horace Bushnell urged the importance of reconciling Christianity with new scholarship, though it had not yet become clear just how deeply the work of scholars would challenge core Christian tenets. At Yale University, which had its origins as a bastion of orthodox theological thought, a cohort of faculty sought to demonstrate that "Christians could be well-educated and engaged with crucial issues of the times and still believe in God."[18] This tentative work of the 1840s and 1850s would become the major project of

---

15. Holifield, *Theology in America*, 188–89.
16. Dorrien, *Imagining Progressive Religion*, 344–49.
17. Mislin, *Saving Faith*, 22–23.
18. Stevenson, *Scholarly Means*, 4.

American Protestants in the decades that followed. The final decades of the nineteenth century would establish a lasting template for the relationship between Protestant Christianity and the intellectual mind.[19]

By the 1880s, a new effort to secure Christianity's intellectual basis took form in what became known as the "new theology." One of the first expressions of the new set of ideas was the 1883 book *The Freedom of Faith*, a collection of sermons preached by the New England Congregationalist minister Theodore T. Munger. The sermons had a twofold purpose: first, to acknowledge the increasingly popular critique that orthodox Protestantism was incompatible with modern intellectual life; second, to offer new interpretations of traditional Christian beliefs that would make them seem reasonable.

The problem with the older tradition of Protestant theology, Munger declared, was precisely that "it insists on a presentation of doctrines in such a way as perpetually to challenge the reason." The issue was not one of minor incongruences here or there. Rather, orthodox Protestantism vexed the educated intellect at every turn. This mattered to Munger because, like most American Protestants, he thought highly of the mind. The act of reasoning constituted "the fundamental action of human nature." Thus, it was necessary for Christianity not only to "sit easily on the mind" but also to go further and "ally itself" with the mind "in all its normal action." Christianity could not demand the suspension of reason.[20]

Fortunately, Munger argued, it was still possible for Christianity to ally itself with the intellectual mind. Because "the mind of man" was made "in the image" of "the mind of God," it followed that humans were capable "of similar processes of thought and feeling."[21] Theology, properly articulated, would allow a reasoned approach to Christian teaching. In the series of sermons, Munger offered numerous examples of how this might be done. The new theology emphasized the "inspiration" of Scripture. But it also addressed biblical scholarship by reading "the Scriptures as literature" that reflected the reality "that the Scriptures were written by living men, whose life entered into their writings."[22] Likewise, the new theology denied the possibility of "antagonism between the kingdoms of faith, and natural law."[23] He argued that the "method of creation" proposed by evolutionary theory proved beneficial to Christian faith. It offered "a closer and more vital

19. Stevenson, *Scholarly Means*, 11.
20. Munger, *Freedom of Faith*, 11.
21. Munger, *Freedom of Faith*, 13.
22. Munger, *Freedom of Faith*, 16.
23. Munger, *Freedom of Faith*, 25.

relation between God and creation" by showing an ongoing divine presence in the natural world.[24]

The new theology did more than simply resolve the apparent intellectual inconsistencies between Christianity and modern thought, Munger argued. It demonstrated greater alignment between Christian teaching and modern values. In a discussion of the doctrine of judgment, he complained that traditional theology moved judgment "to a future world, thus placing the wide and mysterious gulf of time between actions and their motives." In contrast to this logically questionable view of divine judgment, Munger posited an ongoing process of justice that was "confined to this world." What was clear in all aspects of Munger's writing on the new theology was his conviction that new scholarship would in fact make Christianity more appealing to the intellect for both scientific and moral reasons.[25]

During the 1880s and 1890s, American Protestants of greater prominence than Munger embraced the new theology and championed the effort to show Christianity's appeal to the modern, educated mind. The Ohio pastor Washington Gladden, a Methodist-turned-Congregationalist who had built a strong reputation through his editorial work at widely read periodicals, offered a similar message in his sermons, articles, and books. Like Munger (with whom he frequently corresponded), Gladden privileged the workings of the intellect by suggesting that the mind transcended the purely physical. Thought was not simply "the motion in the tissues of my brain," and "spiritual activity" was not the same as "mental activity." Given the inherently spiritual nature of the mind, it followed that Christianity should not seem inimical to the conclusions drawn by the intellect.[26]

Gladden popularized many of the same ideas Munger had put forth in *The Freedom of Faith*. The Ohio clergyman embraced theories of evolution, echoing Munger's assertion that new ideas of science in fact rendered Christian theology more intellectually reasonable. Far from dismantling the argument from design, evolution had offered a new mode of design more befitting of a benevolent deity. Noting the widely held perception that Paley's original argument bad "been completely overthrown by the theory of evolution,"[27] Gladden nevertheless argued that Darwin's theory "furnishes a proof of intelligence far more impressive than any that Paley ever dreamed of."[28] Gladden also noted addition benefits of new efforts to

24. Munger, *Freedom of Faith*, 26.
25. Munger, *Freedom of Faith*, 340.
26. Gladden, *Burning Questions*, 141.
27. Gladden, *Burning Questions*, 12.
28. Gladden, *Burning Questions*, 17.

reconcile Protestant teaching and reason. "Theology is becoming more and more ethical," he concluded, by "dropping those dogmas, such as original sin and unconditional election, which confound our moral sense."[29] The new theology, with its critical rejection of traditional doctrines that no longer aligned with reason, not only rendered Christianity more logical but more ethical as well.

Perhaps the most significant endorsement of the new theology came from Lyman Abbott. During the 1890s, Abbott served as the pastor of the Plymouth Church in Brooklyn, one of the most prestigious pulpits in the United States. More significantly, he was also the editor of the weekly periodical *The Outlook*, and through its pages he reached tens of thousands of readers nationwide. Abbott wrote that this new approach to religion represented a crucial tool to "maintain faith by expressing it in terms which are more intelligible and credible" than what had historically been taught.[30] The benefit of the new theology was its rigor that aligned with a century that brought, as he saw it, "a new era of intellectual activity"[31] and "an era of individual and independent thinking" in all matters, including religious ones.[32] "It is the spirit of original investigation, characteristic of the age, applied to the elucidation of the problems of religious thought and life," he concluded.[33] On specific theological ideas, Abbott joined his contemporaries in suggesting the new theology made Christian teachings more appealing to the rational mind. Echoing Gladden's and Munger's arguments that evolutionary theory suggested a constant divine presence in the world, Abbott suggested that such a view made miracles far more comprehensible. By being a constant presence in nature, God did not need to suspend any natural laws to accomplish the miraculous. Miracles were simply "unexpected or unusual acts of power and wisdom for spiritual ends" that were entirely reasonable actions of a God who was engaged in the world.[34]

It is important to recognize that Munger, Gladden, and Abbott ultimately sought to do more than defend Christianity's alignment with the intellectual trends of their day. They wanted to prove that Christian thought would *always* align with the human knowledge. To support this assertion, they emphasized the idea of progressive revelation—that is, the belief that knowledge about theological matters had grown (and would continue to

---

29. Gladden, *Burning Questions*, 233.
30. Abbott, *Evolution of Christianity*, iv.
31. Abbott, *Evolution of Christianity*, 97.
32. Abbott, *Evolution of Christianity*, 97–98.
33. Abbott, *Evolution of Christianity*, 106.
34. Abbott, *Evolution of Christianity*, 113.

grow) deeper and clearer as humanity's knowledge expanded. The Bible, Munger declared, was not a completed set of texts. Rather, it was a "continuing unfolding revelation of God" and a "book of eternal laws and facts that are evolving their truth and reality in the process of history."[35]

Munger's framing clearly revealed the careful balancing act this theological perspective required. On the one hand, progressive revelation by its nature needed to leave room for further development. On the other hand, however, it risked a kind of relativism that could sweep away the historical foundations of Christianity. Abbott used the analogy of a veil to reconcile this tension. "Revelation is unveiling," he wrote, "but the veil is over the mind of the pupil." He explained that "the heavens are not veiled from the pupil, but the pupil is veiled, so that he cannot comprehend... until education has removed the veil and so revealed the truth."[36] It was a tricky needle to thread, but it was worth it. Progressive revelation offered the assurance that Protestant theology could evolve to always appeal to the intellectual mind. "As man grows in spiritual and intellectual capacity," Abbott assured readers, "his apprehension of the infinite grows also."[37] Cultivation of the mind—both as individuals and by humanity as a whole—would strengthen religious faith.

Fundamentalists vs. Modernists in the Twentieth Century

In the early decades of the twentieth century, the liberalism of the new theology and the conservatism espoused at places like Princeton Seminary coalesced into two distinct movements. The defenders of orthodoxy began to define themselves as Fundamentalists. The name reflected their desire to preserve what they believed to be essential aspects of Christian theology that liberal thinkers had been too quick to discard in their desire to accommodate their faith to contemporary intellectual currents.

Like earlier efforts to defend traditional Christian orthodoxy, a key project of the movement was to demonstrate the affinity of Fundamentalism with the intellect. As the historian George M. Marsden has written, for all the ways that Fundamentalists at times reflected the "anti-intellectual characteristics" of their "revivalist heritage"—and despite contemporary and subsequent characterizations of the movement as such—they nevertheless

---

35. Munger, *Freedom of Faith*, 21.
36. Abbott, *Evolution of Christianity*, 21.
37. Abbott, *Evolution of Christianity*, 59.

"stood in an intellectual tradition that had the highest regard for one understanding of scientific method and proper rationality."[38]

The fundamentalist appeal to reason was exemplified by another Princeton Seminary professor, J. Gresham Machen. In lectures and articles, Machen blasted liberals for sacrificing tradition to expediency in their effort to accommodate Christianity to contemporary intellectual culture. "The liberal attempt at reconciling Christianity with modern science has really relinquished everything distinctive of Christianity," Machen wrote,[39] adding that "in trying to bribe off the enemy by those concessions which the enemy most desires, the apologist has really abandoned what he started out to defend."[40] Moreover, he believed that modernists had abandoned rigorous intellectual methods just as much as they had abandoned real Christianity. According to Machen, liberals dismissed historical facts about Christian tradition that could be empirically proved. "It is not the Christianity of the New Testament which is in conflict with modern science," he declared, but rather it was "the supposed Christianity of the modern liberal Church."[41] By working so hard to accommodate Christianity to modern intellectual culture, liberals had set aside the very things that made it demonstrable to the religious mind.

Like their intellectual forebears that championed the new theology, modernists insisted that their religious outlook was the more reasonable one. Machen's great intellectual rival, the University of Chicago professor Shailer Mathews, noted that "theological orthodoxy no longer appeals to thousands of men and women,"[42] adding, "Dogmatic Christianity has succeeded in demonstrating . . . that it has no message for the world's new needs."[43] Rather than resonating with the needs of the day—including intellectual ones—Fundamentalism simply insisted on biblical inerrancy and repeated that "he who believes in evolution cannot believe in God."[44] In contrast to Fundamentalists' insistence on traditional theological understandings, Mathews affirmed a progressive conception of revelation. Scripture was not "final in itself" as a source of religious truths. Rather, it offered "a door through which one enters the earlier stages of the Christian religion" and thus "opens the way for using the fullest intellectual equipment

38. Marsden, *Fundamentalism and American Culture*, 7; see also 174–75.
39. Machen, *Christianity and Liberalism*, 7.
40. Machen, *Christianity and Liberalism*, 8.
41. Machen, *Christianity and Liberalism*, 7.
42. Mathews, *Faith of Modernism*, 10–11.
43. Mathews, *Faith of Modernism*, 11.
44. Mathews, *Faith of Modernism*, 10.

in understanding not only the Bible but the total religious movement," ultimately providing "a new conviction of the worth of that religion."[45] For Mathews, progressive revelation made even the most outmoded aspects of Scripture intellectually useful.

Unlike the conflicts of the 1880s and 1890s, the debates between Fundamentalists and modernists in the 1920s often took place away from major cities and academic centers. Questions about the compatibility of religion and reason took on new urgency in towns and small cities across the United States. Such was the case in 1925, when the Congregationalist minister Walter Thomas Lockwood warned his churchgoers in Boise, Idaho, of a "generation of youth who are in open rebellion against the orthodox creeds and theologies." They were inspired by developments in science that had "given us a new worldview," as well as by the "historical method of studying the religions of the past." Even in the small western city of twenty thousand people, there were Christians who chose to be "intellectually honest" with themselves and thus could no longer "share in our creedal statements and professed religious belief." In Lockwood's view, churches could either "translate religion into the terms of modern knowledge," or by default join "with those who are making the fight against modern scholarship, science and freedom of belief." The fault lines of Christianity had become defined by issues related to intellectual life.[46]

Lockwood affirmed the concept of progressive revelation. Echoing other modernists, he identified its presence in the pages of the Bible itself, given that Scripture chronicled "a religious people whose religious ideas" were "in the very process of evolution."[47] In language that certainly would have appealed to churchgoers in the small but rapidly growing western town, Lockwood likened much of Christian theology to a small building that had outlived its usefulness and was replaced by a larger structure. Yet there was much in the substance of biblical tradition—the social message of the Ten Commandments and the ethical teaching of the prophets—that might be rebuilt "on these new foundations of scientific fact."[48]

Like the generation that popularized the new theology, Lockwood recognized that accommodating Christianity to the intellectual currents of the time demanded a reconsideration of key theological concepts. What was different was how many concepts he proved willing to reject. Whereas someone like Abbott could rework his definition of miracles to align with

---

45. Mathews, *Faith of Modernism*, 49.
46. Lockwood, *Religious Renaissance*, 7.
47. Lockwood, *Religious Renaissance*, 14.
48. Lockwood, *Religious Renaissance*, 10.

his conception of God's constant presence in nature, Lockwood adamantly denied the miraculous. To have intellectual credibility, liberal Protestants needed to be "frank and honest and say that science knows no magic or miracle."[49] Yet, as he insisted that Protestants set aside religious ideas that no longer seemed reasonable, he urged them to find new ones that aligned with the intellectual currents of the time. One of the "grave dangers of liberalism," Lockwood warned, was its tendency "to tear down without rebuilding." It was reckless "to destroy faith in an infallible Bible and not give back a richer Bible" and to "take away the virgin birth as a guarantee of divinity without giving in its stead a rational basis for life's divinity."[50]

Lockwood offered the modernist approach distilled to its essence: Christians needed to set aside aspects of their tradition that did not seem reasonable, but they had an equally urgent obligation to offer new ideas that aligned with the modern intellectual mind. Yet, his sermons seemed almost intended to prove the validity of Fundamentalists' critiques. Once liberals began adapting their theology to the intellectual currents of the time, little in Christian tradition remained safe. The cost of accommodation was a commitment to make a continuing project of it.

A Faith of Doubt

There was an additional—and significant—consequence of the approach to the intellect that liberal Protestants adopted at the end of the nineteenth century, and it was a direct outgrowth of the reliance on progressive revelation. If understandings of Christianity constantly evolved with developments of human knowledge, it followed that even the most intellectually sophisticated Protestant thinkers remained shrouded in Lyman Abbott's proverbial veil. For Protestant theologians of the late nineteenth and twentieth centuries, that realization prompted a new recognition that doubt would remain part of the thinking believer's religious life.

Historically, American Protestants had approached issues of doubt in one of two ways. In many Protestant traditions, ranging from New England Puritanism to the revivalism of the Second Great Awakening, doubt was something to be passed through on the way to faith. Conversion narratives stressed periods of mental uncertainty that were eventually overcome through newfound conviction. Too much skepticism, however, was viewed as harmful to personal morality and the social cohesiveness of society. Figures

---

49. Lockwood, *Religious Renaissance*, 10.
50. Lockwood, *Religious Renaissance*, 37.

like Thomas Paine represented cautionary tales of people whose religious uncertainty inspired a destabilizing critique of established institutions.[51]

Though skepticism remained reasonably commonplace during the first half of the nineteenth century, it drew the consistent rebuke of religious leaders. Churchgoers felt a strong impulse to keep their questions to themselves. For their part, Protestant ministers continued to assure their congregants that any intellectual doubts they harbored could be resolved through close study of Scripture. By the century's final decades, that guidance no longer seemed useful.[52]

New conceptions of doubt emerged in the writings of Protestant thinkers who championed the new theology. While he conceded "there is danger in skepticism," Lyman Abbott nevertheless insisted that the "greater danger" lay "in trying to think something which is not really thinkable." Even Jesus would agree, he surmised, noting that "the master never condemned honest doubt."[53] One editorial in *The Outlook*, the periodical edited by Abbott, proclaimed that "unquestioning faith is not a Christian grace" and uncritical credulity represented "a greater foe to Christ and his cause than skepticism."[54]

Washington Gladden likewise offered a defense of doubt in sermons that he preached beginning in the 1880s. He noted that the intellectual currents of the time had proved vexing to "honest inquirers" seeking religious truth, and he conceded that clarity on many questions seemed unlikely to be forthcoming. Like Abbott, Gladden insisted that doubt could be a marker of a healthy religious life, provided it was not expressed in a cynical spirit. He declared that the "honest scrutiny of the foundations of faith is far more pleasing to God than the blind and bigoted credulousness of many an orthodox confessor."[55]

This affirmation that intellectual doubt would continue to coexist with faith grew more commonplace among liberal Protestants in the early twentieth century. Religious leaders increasingly recognized the importance of conveying this attitude to churchgoers. Francis J. McConnell, a Methodist bishop who served as the president of the interdenominational Federal Council of Churches in the late 1920s, saw value in a religious outlook that was willing "to leave some problems unsolved."[56] There was a place "in

---

51. Mislin, *Saving Faith*, 21–26.
52. Grasso, *Skepticism and American Faith*, 6–8.
53. Abbott, *Evolution of Christianity*, 36.
54. *Outlook*, "Value of Doubt," 245–46.
55. Mislin, *Saving Faith*, 14.
56. McConnell, *Personal Christianity*, 129.

Christian experience for legitimate suspension of judgment" that allowed doubts to linger. He urged his ministerial colleagues to emphasize the legitimacy of doubt in order to prevent good Christians "from leaving the Church because of supposed agnosticism."[57]

This perspective on doubt was also embraced by Harry Emerson Fosdick, the Baptist minister who enjoyed a significant platform as the first pastor of New York's interdenominational Riverside Church and the weekly broadcasts of his sermons on national radio. Though he was less theologically rigorous (and less consistent) than other liberals, he echoed their affirmations that intellectual uncertainty was a welcome part of the religious experience. "Religion at its best is not a cramped cell for the intellect, but a mind-stretcher," he noted in one essay,[58] and the goal was to accept the "all-embracing mystery" as the basis for greater insight.[59] In fact, he offered doubt as the panacea for the divisions within Protestantism that had emerged, in part, from liberals' embrace of uncertainty. "In the present juncture of religious affairs," Fosdick wrote, "few things are more needed than fundamentalists with some honest doubts about fundamentalism and modernists with some searching misgivings about modernism."[60]

Even in Boise, far away from the cosmopolitan centers of the East Coast, Walter Lockwood took to his pulpit and blasted clergy who obfuscated to "lead the church blindfolded past certain religious doubts." Far better, he argued, would be to acknowledge the very real sources of those doubts. Doing so would allow ministers and their congregants to "stand up and be counted for intelligence and reason in matters of religious belief." For Lockwood, too, doubt reflected a healthy religious and intellectual life. In words that echoed Gladden's, he urged that doubt was far less detrimental to faith than the effort to "try to believe something you cannot believe."[61]

Liberal Protestants had reached consensus that a religious message that affirmed the intellect was one that must welcome doubt.

A Lasting Legacy

The template that took form between the 1880s and the 1920s continued to define American Protestantism for the remainder of the twentieth century. In the major denominations, the liberal voices who held increasing sway

57. McConnell, *Personal Christianity*, 131.
58. Fosdick, *Adventurous Religion*, 209.
59 Fosdick, *Adventurous Religion*, 210.
60. Fosdick, *Adventurous Religion*, 258–59.
61. Lockwood, *Religious Renaissance*, 9, 11.

continued to emphasize the harmony between Christianity and modern intellectual life. Fundamentalists—and conservative Evangelicals more broadly—continued to claim that their theological perspective was the more logical, reasonable one by sustaining traditional theological interpretations rather than continually accommodating religion to the larger culture.

William Sloane Coffin's 2005 book was thus the encapsulation of ideas about religion and the mind that were quintessentially products of American Protestantism. In creating a correspondent who was a bright, curious college student, Coffin affirmed the centuries-old Protestant conviction that reason should support Christian faith. For all his liberal theological and social commitments, his emphasis on this point reflected the values of conservative Protestants as well. For all their differences, liberal and orthodox, Fundamentalist and modernist alike presumed the necessity of Christianity's appeal.

Yet, when Coffin assured his hypothetical undergraduate correspondent that "a religious faith despite doubts is far stronger than one without doubts," he captured an important element of American Protestant thought.[62] Intellectual Christians were people who sought to expand their minds, and that could only happen if they accepted their uncertainty. That widespread affirmation of uncertainty was a key innovation of Protestants in the nineteenth- and twentieth-century United States.

Bibliography

Abbott, Lyman. *The Evolution of Christianity*. Boston: Houghton, Mifflin, 1892.

Coffin, William Sloane. *Letters to a Young Doubter*. Louisville: Westminster John Knox, 2005.

Dorrien, Gary. *Imagining Progressive Religion, 1805–1900*. Vol. 1 of *The Making of American Liberal Theology*. Louisville: Westminster John Knox, 2001.

Fosdick, Harry Emerson. *Adventurous Religion and Other Essays*. New York: Harper and Brothers, 1926.

Gladden, Washington. *Burning Questions of the Life That Now Is and of That Which Is to Come*. New York: Century, 1891.

Goldstein, Warren. *William Sloane Coffin Jr.: A Holy Impatience*. New Haven, CT: Yale University Press, 2008.

Grasso, Christopher. *Skepticism and American Faith: From Revolution to the Civil War*. New York: Oxford University Press, 2018.

Holifield, E. Brooks. *Theology in America: Christian Thought from the Age of the Puritans to the Civil War*. New Haven, CT: Yale University Press, 2003.

Hollinger, David A. *After Cloven Tongues of Fire: Protestant Liberalism in Modern American Culture*. Princeton, NJ: Princeton University Press, 2013.

---

62. Coffin, *Letters to Young Doubter*, x.

Hutchison, William R. *The Modernist Impulse in American Protestantism*. Rev. ed. Durham, NC: Duke University Press, 1992.

Lockwood, Walter Thomas. *The Religious Renaissance*. Boise: Strawn, 1925.

Machem, John Gresham. *Christianity and Liberalism*. New York: MacMillan, 1923.

Marsden, George M. *Fundamentalism and American Culture*. 2nd ed. New York: Oxford University Press, 2006.

Mathews, Shailer. *The Faith of Modernism*. New York: MacMillan, 1924.

McConnell, Francis J. *Personal Christianity: Instruments and Ends in the Kingdom of God*. New York: Revell, 1914.

Mislin, David. *Saving Faith: Making Religious Pluralism an American Value at the Dawn of the Secular Age*. Ithaca: Cornell University Press, 2015.

Munger, Theodore T. *The Freedom of Faith*. Boston: Houghton, Mifflin, 1883.

Outlook. "The Value of Doubt." *Outlook* 56 (May 19, 1897) 224–46.

Roberts, Jon H. *Darwinism and the Divine in America: Protestant Intellectuals and Organic Evolution, 1859–1900*. Erasmus Institute. Notre Dame: University of Notre Dame Press, 2001.

Stevenson, Louise L. *Scholarly Means to Evangelical Ends: The New Haven Scholars and the Transformation of Higher Learning in America, 1830–1890*. New Studies in American Intellectual and Cultural History. Baltimore: Johns Hopkins University Press, 1986.

Chapter 10

The Social Gospel in Canada

GORDON L. HEATH

THE ENGLISH-SPEAKING WORLD OF the Victorian Era saw some of the most fantastic advances in human history. Urbanization and industrialization, as well as scientific advances in mathematics, chemistry, biology, and metallurgy had led to remarkable and steady gains in science, travel, government, and industry. The list of inventions boggles the mind: steam engines, light bulbs, telephones, typewriters, and undersea cables are just a few of the plethora of developments that improved the human condition by leaps and bounds.

Yet the advances in science were not always matched by the living conditions of the poor and marginalized. The irony was that the same industry and advances that led to social improvements also contributed to widespread suffering. By the end of the nineteenth century and into the early twentieth century, living and working conditions, especially in crowded urban slums filled to overflowing with new arrivals from waves of immigration, were no better than they had been in the eighteenth century. In fact, due to horrible overcrowding, lack of proper sewers, and unsafe factories, conditions were arguably worse. The vision among the churches for the newly minted nation was expressed in Ps 72:8: "He shall have dominion also from sea to sea" (KJV). Yet by the late nineteenth century, many Christians were appalled by such atrocious conditions and considered it to be scandalous that there could be such horrors in nations that identified as Christian. And those passionate about alleviating such suffering were often a part of what is coined the social gospel.

A number of interrelated motives animated proponents of the social gospel. There was a deep sense of compassion for the suffering of the poor and marginalized, and a justice-fueled drive to see their plight alleviated and things made right. It was assumed that the only way forward was for the ethics of Jesus to permeate all aspects of society. The impulse to act as Jesus in all areas of social life mirrored the seemingly simple question asked by Charles M. Sheldon in his best-selling late-nineteenth-century novel *In His Steps: What Would Jesus Do?* In the words of Shalier Matthews in 1921, the social gospel was aimed at "the application of the teaching of Jesus and the total message of the Christian salvation to society, the economic life, and social institutions such as the state, the family, as well as to individuals."[1] The title of Phyllis Airhart's recent book *The Church with the Soul of a Nation* is a pithy way of saying virtually the same thing—the church existed to transform all aspects of Canada into a model Christian nation. Finally, motivating some was the conviction that the Christian faith needed to adjust to the modern world, or it would fade into irrelevance. Thus, for some, to save the faith meant that old assumptions of theology and social engagement were to be jettisoned if they were deemed to be unscientific and/or unhelpful.

Origins

While the social gospel origins can be traced to British figures such as Thomas Chalmers (1780–1847), John Frederick Denison Maurice (1805–72), and Charles Kingsley (1819–75), and Americans Josiah Strong (1847–1916), Washington Gladden (1836–1918), and Walter Rauschenbusch (1861–1918), the focus of this chapter is on the movement in Canada. The reason for the attention on Canada and not its much larger neighbor to the south is that the Canadian experience has at least three unique factors. First, its British and imperial identity made it quite distinct from the American republic to the south. Second, the large presence of Catholics—leading to what Hugh MacLennan coined the "Two Solitudes"—created a national divide between English Protestant and French Roman Catholic unknown in the United States.[2] Third, one further factor that made for a unique Canadian experience was that of nascent nationhood. Confederation had occurred quite recently in 1867, and the churches were ardently united in the nation-building ethos; it was a young nation in the making and, so the argument went, what better time to shape its identity and telos than in its earliest years. For those invigorated by the optimism of the social gospel, it was a time ripe for the realization of the kingdom of God in the here and now.

This chapter narrows the focus on the social gospel in Canada to the mainline Protestant churches. Roughly 40 percent of the country identified as Roman Catholic, and, while social activists in Catholic Canada were motivated by such factors as Pope Leo XIII's encyclical *Rerum Novarum* (1891), there were enough differences between Catholics and Protestants to justify a

1. Hopkins, *Rise of Social Gospel*, 3.
2. Although a significant number of Catholics were Irish and thus English speaking.

focus solely on the Protestant experience. That being the case, unless noted otherwise, reference to the churches is to the Methodists, Presbyterians, Anglicans, Baptists, and (after 1925) the United Church of Canada (UCC).[3]

What follows is a description of the Canadian movement's key persons, ideals, and organizations, as well as a number of examples to illustrate the engagement of social gospel concerns with a host of social ills. It will also trace the rise and fall of the movement, along with comments on its detractors and legacy. But first a few words on the nation-building ethos of the churches are in order.

Nation-Builders

The Protestant churches in the Anglo-Saxon world at the end of the nineteenth century and the first half of the twentieth century wielded an influence on society unlike any other institution, and they had taken upon themselves the identity of nation-builders.[4] While nation-building meant many things, at the very least it meant building a united, democratic, distinctly Christian (mainly Protestant) nation that increasingly exhibited the influence of the growth of the kingdom of God in social relations. Commitment to nation-building meant that all the means of the church—services, sermons, organizations, and literature—were marshaled to that end.[5] In Canada, that nation-building ethos was fused to repeated calls for social reform.

In the 1890s to the 1930s the "spirit of reform" was abroad in Canada.[6] Calls for reform in Canada were virtually all rooted in the initiatives of the churches, and "until the 1930s almost every facet of social investigation and social policymaking fell under the aegis of Christian leadership."[7] Presbyterians, Anglicans, and Baptists focused on proposed solutions to social ills, but "Methodists welcomed the social gospel with a fervour unmatched elsewhere."[8] That social gospel impulse among Methodists was carried into the United Church in 1925.

---

3. Those denominations were predominantly British background and represented around 85 percent of all Protestants in Canada. The United Church of Canada was formed in 1925 through a union of the Methodists, Congregationalists, and two-thirds of Presbyterians.

4. For the Canadian experience, see Airhart, "Ordering a New Nation."

5. Heath, "Forming Sound Public Opinion."

6. Allen, *Social Passion*, 3.

7. Christie and Gauvreau, *Full-Orbed Christianity*, xi.

8. Grant, *Church in Canadian Era*, 102.

Presbyterians had their reformed vision for social transformation. Anglicans and Baptists—though on different ends of the spectrum on a variety of issues—also sought to see the ideals of the kingdom impact the social order. Yet the radical Methodist calls for social reform extended back to a fervency reflected in the life and ministry of its founder John Wesley.[9] While some (such as William and Catherine Booth, who birthed the Salvation Army) believed that Methodism had lost its way when it came to ministering to the poor, there remained an ethos of social concern especially within Methodism (and the UCC) that resonated with the spirit of the social gospel.

Points of Contention

It is important to note that some argue that Methodism's embracing of the social gospel was an indication of significant and troubling shifts within Methodism. The claim is that in order to gain respectability Methodism became secularized when it abandoned its evangelical theological moorings and historic revivalism.[10] Yet others argue that what took place was a necessary reorientation and reimagining of Methodism away from past notions of camp meeting revivalism, individual salvation, and theological dogma to forging a "new model of piety" that could engage the modern world in a meaningful way.[11] Those debates could be applied in certain cases to those in other denominations who were likewise supportive of the social gospel.

The waxing and waning of the social gospel has also been debated, with some arguing that the movement was in decline by the late 1920s.[12] Others argue that the years 1900 to 1940 "represented the apogee of the cultural authority of the churches."[13] The early 1920s to the early 1960s have even been described as the "long social gospel era" for American churches.[14] There could be an argument made that the "long social gospel era" was the case for the Canadian context, for by the 1960s Canadian Christian identity—and the churches' powerful place within it—had begun to unravel.[15]

Part of the difficulty of assessing claims made about the social gospel is that there was no one kind of social gospeler. The social gospel movement

---

9. Marquardt, *John Wesley's Social Ethics*.
10. Marshall, *Secularizing the Faith*.
11. Airhart, *Serving the Present Age*, ch. 4.
12. Allen, *Social Passion*.
13. Christie and Gauvreau, *Full-Orbed Christianity*, xii.
14. Evans, *Social Gospel*, 4.
15. Clarke and Macdonald, *Leaving Christianity*.

was far from a uniform movement, and the range of theological views extended from conservative (traditional theological orthodoxy) to liberal (a departure from traditional theological orthodoxy). There was also a range of political and economic views extending from left to right. For instance, for some, the Marxist vision for state control of industry seemed like the solution to workplace exploitation, yet to others such appeals sounded too much like the rhetoric coming from Communist Russia. Richard Allen's taxonomy of three streams within the social gospel is widely recognized and is helpful for describing a movement marked by divergent views.[16] He argues that there were:

1. Conservatives, those closest to traditional Evangelicalism, stressing personal salvation and sin as personal acts
2. Radicals, those who believed that society was so evil and pervaded with injustice that there could be no personal salvation without social salvation
3. Progressives, those between the other two

Those three groups were not always in agreement, and those divisions weakened the movement.

Key Convictions

The church had been founding and supporting ministries for the poor and downtrodden since its inception, so in that sense there was nothing new about the social gospel concern for those languishing in slums and unsafe working conditions. The social gospel movement started in nineteenth-century seminaries and among a small number of pastors, and, by the early twentieth century, it had become much more commonplace and even mainstream in mainline denominations. What made the social gospel a new and unique movement was not only its concern for the blight caused by the worst aspects of modern industrialization and urbanization, but also its theological DNA comprised of an amalgam of a social salvation, the social teachings of Jesus, postmillennial optimism, a realized kingdom of God, and what was often coined the "brotherhood of man."

What would have been fairly common across the spectrum was a heightened sense of optimism, marked by a postmillennial expectation of the advancement of the kingdom of God in preparation for Christ's return. Conflated with that optimism was a potent mix of social Darwinism, racial

16. Allen, *Social Passion*.

superiority, and imperial advancement—a *Zeitgeist* that assumed the advances of the Anglo-Saxons was a providential progression of Christianity and civilization. It was also a time when notions of Christendom were common, and the Christianizing of the social order was a matter of lining up the social order with the Christian identity of the nation.

Some social gospel proponents found a Marxist critique of industry, capitalism, and the plight of labor to be helpful for getting at the root of social ills. In fact, some openly identified as democratic socialists. At a time of heightened fear of revolution and unrest, those links with a Marxist critique of capitalism gave ammunition to opponents, thus opening themselves (and the movement) to critics accusing social gospel reformers as being in cahoots with Communism.

The social gospel was often tied to a new theology that in many cases was a departure from historic orthodoxy. Those who departed from traditional doctrine were coined *modernists* (adjusted doctrine to the modern world) or *liberals* (liberated from religious tradition and dogma).[17] While those on the left and right of the theological spectrum were motivated by the plight of the poor and downtrodden, what did lead to serious theological conflict was the social gospel emphasis on social sin. Critics of nineteenth-century Christianity claimed that injustices were so deeply imbedded in social structures that they could no longer be solved by trying to save one person at a time, as revivalists and evangelists had done for generations. What was needed, it was argued, was a concerted effort for social salvation—the application of the Christian faith to social ills to Christianize the social order. A unique reading of the parable of the good Samaritan provides a vivid sense of the church's responsibility to move beyond merely helping one person at a time if the dismantling of larger social injustices was the aim. Rauschenbusch wrote: "The good Samaritan did not go after the robbers with a shot gun but looked after the wounded and helpless man by the wayside. But if hundreds of good Samaritans travelling the same road should find thousands of bruised men groaning to them they would not be such very good Samaritans if they did not organize a vigilance committee to stop the manufacturing of wounded men."[18]

Key Figures

There were a number of key Canadian figures that not only drew upon American material such as Rauschenbusch's *Christianity and the Social*

17. Marsden, *Understanding Fundamentalism and Evangelicalism*.
18. Rauschenbusch, *Christianity and Social Crisis*, 305.

Crisis (1907) or the American Federal Council of Churches' *The Social Creed of the Churches* (1908), but also social gospel material indigenized for the Canadian context. A close reading of the sources allows one to discern the mix of cultural influences and theological assumptions undergirding the social gospel movement. Of course, the degree to which people held such views varied from one end of the theological spectrum to the other.

Among the plethora of rank-and-file proponents of the social gospel in the Canadian churches, a few well-known figures stand out as representative of the movement. Samuel Dwight Chown (1853–1933), a Methodist minister and key denominational administrator, including the role of general superintendent of the Methodist Church, played an instrumental role navigating the advancement of the social gospel within the denomination, as well as carrying the social gospel ethos into the United Church after church union in 1925.

James Shaver Woodsworth (1874–1942) was a Methodist minister who eventually turned to politics to advance the aims of the social gospel. His two key written works, *Strangers within Our Gates* (1909) and *My Neighbour* (1911), reveal his heartfelt concern for the integration of immigrants into Canadian life but also his problematic views of race tied to Anglo-Saxon national identity. He was an ardent supporter of the labor movement, especially in the western Canadian turmoil of the postwar years. He was one of the Methodist leaders on the radical end of the spectrum, rejecting "not just traditional Christian institutions but also much of conventional Christian theology."[19] He was critical in the task of advancing a Christian socialism and helping to start a new political party entitled Co-operative Commonwealth Federation (CCF).

Salem Bland (1859–1950), Methodist minister and professor at Wesley College, was another radical supporter of the social gospel. Bland faced intense criticism through what has been coined "heresy trials" for his unorthodox views (in that he was not alone—there were other such trials in Methodism and other denominations).[20] His book *The New Christianity: or The Religion of the New Age* (1920) provides a glimpse of some of the more modernist or liberal sentiments animating the social gospel. The following comments on the need for the faith to change with the times were troubling for those on the conservative end of the theological spectrum: "Protestantism must pass away. It is too rootedly individualistic, too sectarian, to be the prevailing religion of a collectivist age. It is passing away before our eyes. Everywhere it reveals the marks of decay or of transformation. It must

---

19. Mills, *Fool for Christ*, 253.
20. Allen, *Salem Bland*, 57–67, 287–93.

change or die."[21] His commentary on the need for a socialist critique of (and solution for) social ills was also deemed to be troubling, especially in light of the reports of horrors coming out of Soviet Russia: "Does Christianity mean Socialism? It means infinitely more than Socialism. It means Socialism plus a deeper, diviner brotherhood than even Socialism seeks. It abhors inequality."[22]

A widely popular but less radical Presbyterian (later United Church) figure was a minister and novelist. In fact, Charles William Gordon (1860–1937)—pen name Ralph Connor—provides in his novels such as *The Sky Pilot* (1899) a sense of the social gospel's vision for moral reform and social regeneration, as well as a new type of pastor, one attuned to issues and methods not traditionally considered to be pastoral.

Countless women were also active in the movement.[23] Perhaps the best-known female proponent of social gospel reforms was activist Nellie McClung (1873–1951). She was an author and politician who advocated for a host of reforms, including the right of women to be able to vote as well as hold public office. She was a firm advocate that the Christian faith included the mandate to engage with social issues for the purpose of promoting justice and elevating suffering.[24] And, as one author notes, she wrote widely, and her literature acted as a pulpit to carry out social activism.[25]

McClung was just one of the "Famous Five."[26] McClung, Louise McKinnney, Henrietta Muir Edwards, Emily Murphy, and Irene Parlby were animated by the Christian faith as they sought to eliminate social ills, especially ones that harmed women and children. Thus, their efforts were directed to temperance and prohibition (for alcohol was seen to be a primary cause of abuse and poverty), the elimination of prostitution, and the creation of new laws that supported children and families. They played a key role in organizations such as the Woman's Christian Temperance Union and the National Council of Women in Canada.

Structures and Ministries

The range of activities motivated by the social gospel was impressive. Ministries for the homeless, poor, oppressed, ill, exploited, and disenfranchised

21. Bland, *New Christianity*, 96–97.
22. Bland, *New Christianity*, 34.
23. Stebner, "More than Maternal Feminists."
24. Warne, "Nellie McClung's Social Gospel."
25. Warne, *Literature as Pulpit*.
26. Smith, *Famous Five*.

were ubiquitous. The following provides a brief representative sample of how the social gospel was lived out in the churches.

The social gospel movement had a vision for pastors that made them central in the mission of Christianizing the social order. Along with traditional functions such as preaching, visiting, marrying, and burying, they were expected to be experts on matters traditionally outside the purview of parish life. For instance, the minister "was expected to be a student of the social sciences and scientific agriculture, a coordinator and interpreter of community social services, a social activist, and a knowledgeable expert in the design of state social legislation, as well as a powerfully emotive revival preacher."[27] Those priorities were encapsulated in statements coming out of events such as the interdenominational Social Service Congress in Ottawa in March 1914, an event Richard Allen deems to be one of the best places to see "the range of activity and concern of the social gospel."[28]

At the heart of the movement was the marshaling of the attention and resources of local churches and denominations. Organizational structures (fused to the work of evangelism, as the titles indicate) were established to carry out research, educate church members, and aid in the carrying out of reforms. Denominational structures such as the Presbyterian Board of Social Service and Evangelism (1900), Methodist Department of Evangelism and Social Service (1902), and United Church Board of Evangelism and Social Service (1925) were all critical to the advance of social gospel priorities.

Statements and resolutions made it to general assemblies for ratification, and those official positions were intended to chart a course for the coming years. Some of the statements could be relatively short, such as the one-page Maritime Baptist statement of 1921. That brief statement listed a wide range of issues for the church to address, such as ensuring a safe and wholesome upbringing for children, equal opportunity for all in society, proper allocation of resources, right stewardship of property, one day off a week for workers, equal pay for equal work for men and women, care for widowed mothers, and a partnership in industry between employers and employees.[29]

Statements and documents expanded exponentially. One of the most comprehensive summaries and explorations of the churches' role in society can be seen in *Church, Nation and World Order* (1944), a document produced by the United Church's Commission on Church, Nation and World Order, a commission under the aegis of the Board of Evangelism and Social Service. The eighty-eight-page document took four years to create and was

---

27. Christie and Gauvreau, *Full-Orbed Christianity*, xiv.
28. Allen, *Social Passion*, 18.
29. Feltmate, "Help Should Be Greatest," 1–2.

produced by forty-five clergy and laity, with further input from dozens of members in regional study groups in every province (as well as Newfoundland). The document is a prime example of a church taking the time to prepare a thoughtful and comprehensive guide to the church's engagement with a plethora of social issues. It affirmed the role of the church in shaping both domestic and international issues, making it clear that the "church speaks" because the fundamental and foundational issues of the world were primarily spiritual in nature and no amount of laws or structures would succeed without the church tending to the root spiritual issues.[30] The issues dealt with in the document ranged widely, including matters related to employment, labor and capital, agriculture, economic aid for child care, social insurance and security, public and private ownership, finances, preservation of family life, delinquency and crime, race, arts and culture, religious education, and religious freedom, along with arguments for why and how the church should engage in such issues. What is noteworthy for the purpose of this chapter is that much of the progressive and/or reimagining discourse in the churches—be they United Church, Anglican, Presbyterian, and Baptist—was mirrored in the report.

That host of issues to be addressed led to the churches being at the forefront of the advancement of the study of social sciences in universities.[31] The need for the new discipline was considered to be obvious, for the nature and extent of social ills required the sharpest minds and the most up-to-date research to chart a path of effective reform. As Nancy Christie and Michael Gauvreau note, "Protestant clergy were . . . instrumental in utilizing the most-up-to-date methods of social investigation to pave the way for the application of expert knowledge to the formulation of social legislation, thereby helping transform the scope and responsibilities of the modern state."[32]

Another area of concern was ministry among the waves of new Canadians, especially those suffering horribly in the slums and shantytowns of rapidly growing cities. Planting churches and evangelizing new arrivals was deemed to be essential, but along with that more traditional church activity was a host of ministries to those suffering in extreme poverty, facing harsh abuse, freezing in cold weather, dying of untreated illnesses, and living in a new world of a strange culture and foreign language. Government services

---

30. United Church of Canada, Commission on Church, *Church, Nation and World Order*, 11–14.

31. Helmes-Hayes, *Perfect Sociology*.

32. Christie and Gauvreau, *Full-Orbed Christianity*, xiii.

were limited, and the work of the social gospel–inspired churches was a mainstay of care for the needy.

One of the most radical (and alarming, for some) responses to postwar problems was the establishment of labor churches.[33] Methodist Rev. William Ivens (1878–1957) was one key figure who wanted the church to respond quickly and kindly to the plight of workers, and in the midst of social unrest in the Canadian West (marked by such events as the infamous Winnipeg General Strike, 1919) he started a labor church in Winnipeg. Others followed, with eventually a total of 660 labor church members in six cities in 1921 (Toronto, 2; Winnipeg, 547; Calgary, 25; Edmonton, 13; Brandon, 57; St. Boniface, 16). While Ivens and others were planting labor churches in Canada, the Russian Revolution was in full swing with all its attendant horrors, and many were worried about the spread of Communism to Canada. The radical nature of the churches, and public fear of Communism, contributed to the demise of the labor church movement by the end of the 1920s.

A number of reformers moved from church leadership to politics, partly to avoid theological scrutiny in heresy trials of the more radical social gospel proponents, partly to avoid what they felt was a slow church held captive by special monied interests, but also especially because they believed that a move from the pulpit to parliament made complete sense. Ivens was one such person, as was Woodsworth. Along with entering into the already existing political parties in parliament was the formation of new entities such as the Co-operative Commonwealth Federation (CCF), formed in 1934 with a distinctly social gospel–oriented political platform. If the goal was to Christianize the social order, so the logic went, what better way to do that than to shape the formation of Christian laws.

The reach of the social gospel extended into wartime efforts and postwar international relations. The Great War (1914–18) was seen as an opportunity to apply a more radical approach to state control of industry and morals for the Christianization of the nation. It was anticipated that the wartime sacrifices would lead to a renewed and reinvigorated Christianity and nation, and the "war to end all wars" would usher in a new world order.

The conflict was framed in the language of purging and renewal. Since the latter part of the nineteenth century the moral condition of British society had been cause for concern. Churches called for national days of prayer and repentance. Simultaneously there was a call among churches for daily spiritual renewal and revival to wage war against national sins to transform the nascent nation into a truly Christian Canada. Robert A. Wright argues

---

33. Cole-Arnal, "Prairie Labour Churches"; Vipond, "Blessed Are the Peacemakers"; Turkstra, "Social Gospel in City."

that the churches hoped that the war would contribute to many of their social reform aims: the elimination of oppression, an increased spirit of sacrifice among citizens, the establishment of a more cooperative and less exploitive way of doing business, and a removal of class barriers.[34] In that way the social gospel agenda and war effort were fused.

Interestingly, the fusion of the war effort and the social gospel was quickly abandoned in the postwar years. The social gospel was a vital element to the postwar shift to pacifism and support for international organizations for peace such as the League of Nations. Many social gospel supporters of the Allied cause experienced remorse for their wartime enthusiasm, for in the 1920s the hatred and profiteering of war made support for past—and any future—war seem untenable.

Legacy

Some argue that by the late 1920s the social gospel impulse had waned. Others argue that it continued into the 1930s, or even into the late 1940s or 1950s. However, what is agreed upon is that the movement played an important role in the Canadian Protestant churches and the life of the nation.[35]

On the micro level, countless individuals who needed help received it, and impoverished families gained hope when government offered none. On the macro level, the legacy is mixed. On the negative side of the ledger, "the social gospel failed either to change the attitudes of the business community or to retain the allegiance of working men to the church."[36] The aims to usher in a Christian Canada marked by a realized kingdom of God failed. In fact, in the post-World War Two decades the country quickly moved away from identifying at all as a Christian nation. The assumptions and discourse of the social gospel were fused with notions of Christendom, but a Christian society as once imagined in the "sea to sea" language of Ps 72:8 is now a bygone world. There is also a sense of irony about the social gospel. It was a movement that sought to Christianize all aspects of society, but its success in getting governments to take on social services offered by the churches contributed to secularizing social services. Increasingly, due to the success

---

34. Wright, "Canadian Protestant Tradition," 143–45.

35. The international impact of the social gospel on a grand scale can be seen in the global movement for racial justice, movements against military juntas such as minjung theology (Korea) or liberation theology (Central America), or even the formation of international organizations such as the United Nations.

36. Grant, *Church in Canadian Era*, 103.

of advocating for government to be more Christian, the churches became less and less of a factor in the elevation of suffering and promoting of justice.

The theological innovation of the new theology associated with the social gospel created problems for conservative denominations. Pastors lost their posts and livelihood due to their departure from orthodox doctrine. Baptists in Ontario split over theological modernism. The link between theological liberalism and the social gospel led to decades of conservative Christians staying away from social reforms for fear of being—or of being labeled—liberal. That loss of a social conscience was challenged later by C. F. Henry's *The Uneasy Conscience of Modern Fundamentalism* (1947), but the guilt by association would not easily be undone.

However, on the positive side of the ledger, the Christianizing impulses of the social gospel contributed to many aspects of Canadian life that are now considered to be a part of Canadian identity. Universal healthcare, welfare, unemployment insurance, old age security, government retirement pension, better access to education, female suffrage, labor legislation, workplace codes, and other improvements of social conditions—all in some way and to greater or lesser degree can be traced to the social gospel impulse of the early twentieth century. Even the modern-day New Democratic Party—a leftist and certainly not self-identifying Christian party—that advocates for social justice has its roots in its earliest Christian iteration, the CCF. One of the greatest achievements of the social gospel could be how it helped society transition into the modern world. As John Webster Grant argues, the social gospel played a vital role in "a transitional stage between the old rural moralism and the new urban sophistication."[37]

Bibliography

Airhart, Phyllis. *A Church with the Soul of a Nation: Making and Remaking the United Church of Canada*. Montreal: McGill-Queen's University Press, 2014.

———. "Ordering a New Nation and Reordering Protestantism, 1867–1914." In *The Canadian Protestant Experience, 1760–1990*, edited by George A. Rawlyk, 98–138. Burlington, Can.: Welch, 1990.

———. *Serving the Present Age: Revivalism, Progressivism, and the Methodist Tradition in Canada*. Montreal: McGill-Queen's University Press, 1992.

Allen, Richard. *Salem Bland: A Canadian Odyssey*. Vol. 1 of *The View from Murney Tower: Salem Bland, the Late-Victorian Controversies, and the Search for a New Christianity*. Toronto: University of Toronto Press, 2008.

———. *The Social Passion: Religion and Social Reform in Canada 1914–28*. Toronto: University of Toronto Press, 1990.

37. Grant, *Church in Canadian Era*, 103.

Bland, Salem Goldworth. *The New Christianity—or, The Religion of the New Age*. Toronto: McClelland & Stewart, 1920.

Christie, Nancy, and Michael Gauvreau. *A Full-Orbed Christianity: The Protestant Churches and Social Welfare in Canada, 1900–1940*. Montreal: McGill-Queen's University Press, 1996.

Clarke, Bran, and Stuart Macdonald. *Leaving Christianity: Changing Allegiances in Canada since 1945*. Montreal: McGill-Queen's University Press, 2017.

Cole-Arnal, Oscar L. "The Prairie Labour Churches: The Methodist Input." *RevScRel* 34 (2005) 3–26.

Connor, Ralph. *The Sky Pilot*. Toronto: Westminster, 1899.

Evans, Christopher H. *The Social Gospel in American Religion: A History*. New York: New York University Press, 2017.

Feltmate, Darrell. "'Help Should Be Greatest Where the Need Is Most': The Social Gospel Platform of the United Baptist Convention of the Maritime Provinces, 1921." MA thesis, Acadia University, 1993.

Grant, John Webster. *The Church in the Canadian Era*. Repr., Vancouver: Regent College Press, 1988.

Heath, Gordon L. "'Forming Sound Public Opinion': The Late Victorian Canadian Protestant Press and Nation-Building." *Journal of the Canadian Church Historical Society* 48 (2006) 109–59.

Helmes-Hayes, Rick. *"The Perfect Sociology, Perfectly Applied": Sociology and the Social Gospel in Canada's English-Language Universities, 1900–1930*. Saskatoon, Can.: University of Saskatchewan, 2013.

Hopkins, C. Howard. *The Rise of the Social Gospel in American Protestantism, 1865–1915*. New Haven, CT: Yale University Press, 1967.

Marquardt, Manfred. *John Wesley's Social Ethics: Praxis and Principles*. Translated by John E. Steely and W. Stephen Gunter. Eugene, OR: Wipf and Stock, 2000.

Marsden, George. *Understanding Fundamentalism and Evangelicalism*. Grand Rapids: Eerdmans, 1991.

Marshall, David B. *Secularizing the Faith: Canadian Protestant Clergy and the Crisis of Belief*. Heritage Series. Toronto: University of Toronto Press, 1992.

Mills, Allen. *Fool for Christ: The Political Thought of J. S. Woodsworth*. Toronto: University of Toronto Press, 1991.

Rauschenbusch, Walter. *Christianity and the Social Crisis*. New York: Macmillan, 1908.

Sheldon, Charles M. *In His Steps: What Would Jesus Do?* Chicago: Chicago Advance, 1897.

Smith, Barbara. *The Famous Five: Canada's Crusaders for Women's Rights*. Victoria: Heritage, 2019.

Stebner, Eleanor J. "More Than Maternal Feminists and Good Samaritans: Women and the Social Gospel in Canada." In *Gender and the Social Gospel*, edited by Carolyn De Swarte Gifford and Wendy J. Deichmann Edwards, 53–70. Urbana: University of Illinois Press, 2003.

Turkstra, Melissa. "Social Gospel in the City: Rev. W. E. Gilroy and Hamilton Clergymen Respond to Labour Issues, 1911–1918." *Urban History Review* 37 (Fall 2008) 21–35.

United Church of Canada, Commission on Church. *Church, Nation and World Order*. London, Can.: United Church of Canada, 1944.

Vipond, Mary. "Blessed Are the Peacemakers: The Labour Question in Canadian Social Gospel Fiction." *Journal of Canadian Studies* 10 (1975) 32–43.

Warne, Randi R. *Literature as Pulpit: The Christian Social Activism of Nellie McClung.* Kitchener, Can.: Wilfrid Laurier University Press, 2014.

———. "Nellie McClung's Social Gospel." In *Changing Roles of Women within the Christian Church in Canada,* edited by Elizabeth Gillan Muir and Marilyn Fardig Whiteley, 338–54. Toronto: University of Toronto Press, 1995.

Wright, Robert A. "The Canadian Protestant Tradition, 1914–1945." In *The Canadian Protestant Experience, 1760–1990,* edited by George A. Rawlyk, 139–97. Montreal: McGill-Queen's University Press, 1994.

Section Three

The Story of Christianity Encounters Twenty-First-Century Issues: Immigration and the Future of North American Christianity

Chapter 11

North American Christianities
A West Coast Perspective

Patricia O'Connell Killen

CHRISTIANITIES ON THE PACIFIC edge of North America have never fit comfortably into the conventional US narrative of Christianity on the continent. That story unfolds from east to west; focuses primarily on the experience of White Christians of the English Reformation denominations; and in popular versions, attributes US power and wealth to the nation's having realized its divinely ordained manifest destiny.[1] Through that narrative lens, the West Coast presents a problem and a puzzle. Despite sustained effort, historic Protestant denominations never achieved the size and influence on the Pacific edge that they held in regions to the east. Neither did Roman Catholicism, though it achieved a healthy presence. American-born sectarian groups became robust. New forms of Christianity incubated on the Pacific edge proliferated, and Judaism and other world faiths more than sustained themselves. Since Christianity's arrival on the West Coast, an uncomfortably large number of people have contentedly spent their lives disconnected from religious institutions. The size and grandeur of the Pacific edge both beguiled and disturbed those who arrived, leaving many with the intimation that it was, perhaps, a religious force of its own.

The religious profile also is puzzling: Why has this religious configuration of the West Coast persisted, even after significant population increase and development over two-plus centuries? Does it reflect an institutional immaturity to be expected of a region that came late to Euro-American settlement, an immaturity that will change with time and population

---

1. This chapter explores the West Coast from the southern border of California to the northern border of British Columbia. It focuses primarily on the United States but uses data from British Columbia with its religious and historical connections to the Pacific Northwest. The English Reformation denominations are Episcopalian (Anglican in Canada), Congregationalist, Baptist, Presbyterian, Quaker, and Methodist.

growth? (That happened in Texas between its 1836 rebellion against Mexico and folding into the Baptist south by 1890.)[2] Or are the distinct religious configuration and sensibility of the Pacific edge lasting regional features? To date the religious character of the Pacific edge has remained remarkably resilient through significant population increase and accelerating national and global shifts that influence religion.[3] Through this time there have been winners and losers among organized religious bodies in their contest for members, but minimal expansion in the proportion of the total population involved in institutional religion.

Christianities on the West Coast are part of a regional religious configuration that has been more unlike the nation's than that of any other region. On the Pacific edge broader changes and movements affecting religion in the US became visible sooner, and so the history of Christianities here has long pointed toward the future fortunes of Christianities across the country. The West Coast story is one of an ongoing experiment in fidelity to the Christian message in a post-Christian, postmodern context.

The Open Religious Environment of the West Coast

From earliest Euro-American presence, most people in what today we know as the Canadian province of British Columbia and the US states of Washington, Oregon, and California have remained outside the doors of church, synagogue, temple, or mosque.[4] This pattern persisted despite significant population increase, most of it driven by in-migration. While low institutional religious participation features in the history of Christianities in most of the territory west of the hundredth meridian (with Latter-day Saints in Utah and heavily Catholic locations at the southern edge the exception), the rates have been markedly lower on the West Coast, with Oregon, Washington, and British Columbia having the lowest.[5] California trails the northern segment slightly, its still very low rates tempered by its historically larger

---

2. Pritchard, "Western Religious History," 418–25.

3. Stump, "Regional Migration," 302; Zelinsky, "Approach to Religious Geography," 163–64, 193. Every region of the US and Canada has its own religious configuration and characteristic religious practices and sensibilities that influence the contours of religion and society. Regional religious profiles and characteristic sensibilities are forged and change in a dynamic interplay among local realities and broader national and global trends.

4. This chapter does not address other world religious heritages that are an important part of the Pacific-edge context, including those of American Indians and First Nations peoples.

5. Szasz, *Religion*, 3–5.

Hispanic Catholic population and larger in-migration of Christians and peoples of other world faiths. In 1950 California, Oregon, and Washington had the lowest religious adherence rates in the nation, leading one cultural geographer to describe the West Coast as having "'the least recognizable [religious] personality."[6] Additionally, the minority who are institutionally religiously involved have been spread across many groups.[7]

With low levels of institutional religious involvement and distribution of the institutionally involved across many groups, no single organized religious denomination has ever succeeded in becoming the dominant religious referent group along the West Coast.[8] The absence of a dominant religious referent group makes religion weak as a force of social control. It also complicates individual religious identity and belonging. With no single group alongside or over against which to define oneself, forging and sustaining religious identity and belonging becomes a lifelong project of the individual.[9]

The entire Pacific edge has always had a large population of "unchurched" or "unaffiliated," those who do not participate in organized religious communities for whatever reasons. At the turn of the twenty-first century, however, the Pacific Northwest stood out for its large number of "nones," those who, when asked, "What is your religion, if any?," respond "none." In the 2001 American Religious Identification Survey, more adults in Oregon and Washington responded "none" (25 percent) than anywhere else in the United States. In those two states "nones" comprised a population twice that of the then–single largest Christian denomination in the Pacific Northwest, the Roman Catholic Church. In California 19 percent of the adult population answered the question with "none."[10] In British Columbia in 2001, 34.6 percent of the population identified as having no religion.[11]

The 2017 Pacific Northwest Social Survey found that an estimated 49 percent of British Columbians, and 44 percent of residents in Washington and Oregon said they had no religion. "Nones" are the largest single religious

6. Szasz, *Religion*, 99.

7. Killen and Shibley, "Surveying the Religious Landscape," 30.

8. While the Pacific edge has lacked a dominant religious denomination to this point, such as Baptists were in the South or Catholics and Lutherans in the Upper Midwest, the region's culture has a Christian-based character easily recognizable to Indians, First Nation peoples, and immigrant communities of other world faiths.

9. Killen, introduction to *Religion and Public Life*, 11; Killen and Shibley, "Surveying the Religious Landscape," 28–46; Killen, "Questing for Home," 144–49.

10. Killen and Shibley, "Surveying the Religious Landscape," 28–29; American Religious Identification Survey 2001, 40.

11. See https://doi.org/10.25318/1710000901-eng.

group in British Columbia. In Oregon and Washington the "nones" at 44 percent lag slightly behind the portion of the population that identifies as Christian, 46 percent. (Identification as Christian is not equivalent to participating in any organized form of Christianity.)[12] The number of "nones" has increased across the US and Canada since 1990, and so the "nones" of British Columbia, Washington, and Oregon are no longer outliers. Whether they were the vanguard of a process of secularization underway across the continent remains a subject of lively discussion.[13]

Cumulatively these features—most people outside the doors of religious institutions, those inside the doors divided among many groups, a significant population of "nones," the absence of a single dominant religious reference group—contribute to and reinforce what I have described elsewhere as an "open religious environment," with a "highly elastic religious reality," one "where boundaries and identities are fluid, where energy and movements coalesce and then dissolve." An open environment is "alternately indifferent or inviting to religion, an obstacle or opportunity, a refuge or revelation." In an open environment religion is highly responsive to broader disruptive changes and trends and exhibits simultaneous contradictory tendencies, e.g., cooperation among religious bodies and extreme separation, deep commitment to religious participation and total disinterest in all things religious, expansive spiritual exploration and rigid assent to a belief system. What religion in an open environment lacks is a sturdy, moderate middle.[14]

California's open environment and larger population has made it a more prolific incubator of novel forms of Christianity and spirituality than the states and province to its north. Historian Eldon Ernst highlights the challenges of an open environment to religious communities:

> How do old traditions persevere, become shaped, and in turn make a public impact, along with continually emerging new religious movements and groups in a society where traditions and conventionalities acquiesce to the new and innovative, where all religious traditions must live with almost unprecedented equality, where no religious tradition or denomination enjoys hegemony, where there is no quasi establishment, where there is no mainstream but only many streams of various sizes flowing every which way?[15]

12. Killen, "Questing for Home," 142–43; Wilkins-LaFlamme, "Second to None," 100.

13. Silk, "Outlier to Advance Guard," 135–37.

14. Killen, introduction to *Religion and Public Life*, 10.

15. Ernst, "Emergence of California," 35.

In this open religious environment most individuals are free to explore or bypass spiritual pursuits on their own terms; fewer people on the West Coast than elsewhere experience the restraining effects of ascriptive factors such as family and ethnic identity on their religious choices, and those ascriptive factors are weaker in the region.[16] In an open environment, individuals and communities have "considerable freedom to experiment and innovate," should they choose to do so.[17]

The Fortunes of Christianities in an Open Religious Environment

Four features in the history of Christianities on the West Coast shed light on their fortunes in an open religious environment. Each form of Christianity found its own way on the West Coast while at the same time navigating intra-denominational and national events and movements that affected religion across the continent. Global encounter is the first feature. Christianities arrived on the West Coast as part of a great powers contest for domination; they remain embedded in global encounter. The second is the close relationship between the structure of the economy and the fortunes of religious communities. The affinity between material practices and religious sensibility has been on full display on the West Coast, where economic disruption eroded the plausibility of specific versions of Christianity and contributed to denominational growth and decline. The third theme is creativity in a context of constraint. Creativity allowed historic Protestant bodies, the Catholic Church, and Jewish communities to influence society beyond what their numbers would have suggested was possible, allowed sectarian groups to thrive, and propelled the incubation of new forms of Christianity that competed for members in the open environment. The fourth theme is spiritual experience outside the doors of religious institutions. The natural environment is the most prominent site of such spiritual experience, and the size, scale, and beauty of nature on the Pacific edge make it a reality to be reckoned with.

Global Encounter

Christianities arrived on the West Coast of North America in the mid-eighteenth century with the start of continuous European and American

---

16. Killen, "Questing for Home," 144–47.
17. Killen, introduction to *Religion and Public Life*, 11.

presence. Growth in global demand for furs spurred this chapter in the contest among world powers for control of the seas and possession of the lands, resources, and peoples of the Americas that began in the late 1400s. In the century between Christianity's arrival and the United States taking sole possession of the Oregon Country (1846) and uncontested possession of California (1848), Spain, France, Great Britain, Russia, and the US had established settlements and laid claim to the vast and resource rich lands of the Pacific edge.[18]

Orientation toward the Pacific and Asia was and remains a defining regional feature. Control of West Coast ports meant dominance of the Pacific and of trade routes to Asia. The ocean's size and prevailing winds necessitated ports mid-ocean as well, hence the outsized importance of Hawaii. Until the twentieth century, travel between San Francisco and Victoria, BC, or Astoria, Oregon, was by way of Hawaii.[19] The final phase of the contest for dominance of the Pacific that brought Christianities to the West Coast ended in 1898 when the US took possession of the Philippines from Spain.

Born in global contest, West Coast Christianities have a plural origin in the multiple forms of Christianity that arrived with the fur traders, merchants, soldiers, settlers, fortune seekers, and missionaries. United States Protestants were late to the scene. To the south the story begins with the Spanish who brought to Alta California their Catholicism and an *encomienda* system that subjected Native peoples to forced labor and taxation. To the north the story begins in a culturally mixed fur-trade society, with Russian Orthodox, French, French Canadian, Métis, Iroquois Catholics, English Anglicans, and Presbyterians coexisting among themselves and with Hawaiians, Asians, and Indigenous peoples. The cultural exchange that was a defining feature of the eighteenth- and nineteenth-century fur-trade Pacific world included regular communication among Indigenous peoples on different continents.[20] The origin story lacks the trope of a quest for religious freedom.

Russian Orthodox and Spanish Catholic priests were present on the West Coast from the 1750s. Protestant clergy arrived in the north in 1834, with a brief sojourn by Anglican cleric Henry Beaver at the Hudson's Bay

---

18. The US was a relative newcomer to the contest among global powers but rose quickly. The US took possession of Oregon through a treaty with Great Britain, ending the joint occupancy agreement that begin in 1818. Uncontested possession of California came in 1848 by treaty and monetary payment after the end of the US invasion of northern Mexican territory in 1846 and the war that ensued between 1846 and 1848.

19. The American Board of Commissioners of Foreign Missions considered the Oregon Country part of the Hawaii Mission.

20. Maffley-Kipp, "Eastward Ho," 137.

Company's Fort Vancouver, and the arrival of the first US Protestant ministers, Methodist Jason Lee and, shortly after, Presbyterian Marcus Whitman. Inspired by the Second Great Awakening to win the world for Christ, both men's religious fervor intertwined with a commitment to US manifest destiny. Largely unsuccessful at converting Indians and foreigners to their version of Christianity and Victorian mores and habits and appalled by the ethnically mixed fur-trade society they encountered, Lee and Whitman redirected much of their energies to recruiting US settlers to secure Oregon for the United States. French Canadian Catholic priests Francis Norbert Blanchet and Modeste Demers, both familiar with the fur-trade culture, arrived from Montreal in 1838, to care for former HBC employees and to evangelize the Native populations throughout the Columbia District. Their work was part of the Roman Catholic Church's project to establish institutional structures of Catholicism around the globe and to nurture Indigenous clergy.[21] Protestant ministers became active in California with the Gold Rush of 1848.

From the mid-1840s into the 1920s, when racist and anti-foreign nativism reached a fever pitch across the United States, Christianities on the West Coast displayed both the dark potency of mixing the gospel with notions of White racial superiority and efforts to counter it. That mix justified violent subjugation of Indian nations, the effects still felt in Indian and First Nation communities. Oregon officially became a federal territory in 1848, and its government enacted racial separation and forbade entry to African Americans. Blacks, Hawaiians, Asians, and Métis were not counted in the 1848 territorial census. Hawaiians departed Oregon, south to pilot ships in California's harbors or north into British Columbia after territorial governor Joseph Lane rejected their petition for citizenship based on the color of their skin.[22] Immigrants from East and South Asia were subject to ongoing racial discrimination that flared into violence when White workers felt insecure economically. Mexicans who remained in California after the US took possession, and Métis in the Oregon Territory were targeted. In the late 1880s anti-Asian sentiment flared in Oregon and Washington, leading to confiscation of Chinese-owned properties and the forced physical removal of the Chinese, including Christians, from Tacoma and Seattle. Presbyterian

---

21. Schoenberg, *History of Catholic Church*, 94. In 1846 Rome erected the Archdiocese of Oregon City, only the second archdiocese in the continental United States. At the time the entire Oregon Country had only twelve priests and roughly six thousand Catholics, most of them French Canadian, Métis, and Indian converts. Only after the transcontinental railroad to Puget Sound would Catholics arriving from the US and Europe match their numbers.

22. Duncan, *Minority without Champion*, 16–18.

and Methodist clergy spoke out against anti-Chinese riots and violence. Some took part in home guard units that defended Chinese neighborhoods; some carried guns as insurance against the ire of congregants.[23] In the first decades of the twentieth century the Ku Klux Klan grew larger in Oregon than anywhere outside the South other than Indiana; sometimes members stood in their robes at the rear of Portland churches to monitor sermons.[24] The heady mix of US manifest destiny, colonialism, racism, and anti-foreign sentiment was strong along the entire West Coast into the late twentieth century. Racist and anti-foreign sentiments have not disappeared. In recent decades diverse populations present since earliest settlement have begun to be written into state histories, correcting narratives long told through a White American Protestant lens.

Christians and immigrants of other world faiths never stopped arriving on the West Coast. The vitality and survival of historic forms of Protestantism, Catholicism, and some sectarian groups have depended on this continuous in-migration. Among those coming to the West Coast from points east, only African American Christians increase in participation in local congregations after arrival. White Protestants, whether from Europe, the US, or Canada, are the most likely to cease participating.[25] The steady loss of large numbers of Caucasians moving to the West Coast from points east in the US generated a humorous trope shared among clergy for more than a century, that the Rocky Mountains are white because migrants tossed their congregational transfer papers to lighten their loads, to which some added that the air of the Rockies is "too rare for prayer."[26]

Throughout the twentieth century and into the twenty-first, increasing numbers of Asian Christians of all nationalities have continued to settle along the West Coast. By 1984, six different forms of Arab Christianity were active in California.[27] The largest urban areas along the West Coast, Vancouver, BC, and Los Angeles are centers of global Christianity. At the turn of the twenty-first century, the Catholic Archdiocese of Los Angeles listed "ninety-three different ethnic groups in its parishes" and offered Mass in "forty-two different languages."[28]

The dependence of West Coast religious bodies on ongoing in-migration has now reached a new stage. Immigrant priests from Mexico,

23. Buerge and Rochester, *Roots and Branches*, 153–54.
24. Soden, *Outsiders in Promised Land*, 101–8.
25. Quinn, "Religion in the American West," 153–54, 160.
26. Killen, introduction to *Religion and Public Life*, 9.
27. Quinn, "Religion in the American West," 148.
28. Szasz, *Religion*, 197.

Vietnam, Africa, and India now staff increasing numbers of diocesan parishes along the West Coast. The number of Protestant missionary clergy from Asia and Africa working in the region also has grown. In some subregions, Asian Christians have become the majority population in denominations. Asian Methodists sustain that denomination in British Columbia, and Jason Byassee and colleagues argue that in Vancouver, BC, Christianity is an Asian religion.[29] In subregions of some dioceses, Hispanic Catholics are approaching or at majority status. On the West Coast various forms of Christianity grapple with living into the practice of being globally diverse faith communities.

Economic Structures and Religious Fortunes

From the beginning, Christianities on the West Coast have had to adapt to rapid economic change. Perhaps the most consequential in the nineteenth century was the discovery of gold in California, followed in short order by gold and silver strikes in Oregon, Washington, British Columbia, and Alaska. The precious metal strikes cemented the region's extractive economy, accelerated intra-regional migration and in-migration, and destabilized fledgling social institutions. Mining, as would be the case for timber, fishing, and some agricultural work, drives migration, creating a lasting challenge for religious communities. Each migration severs social relationships and confronts people who migrate with the task of building new relationships in a different place. Repeated migration weakens networks, including individuals' connections with religious communities.

Between the 1850s and 1990s clergy and histories recorded distress over mobility and the seeming indifference it bred. In 1854, Fr. James Croke reported to Archbishop Francis Norbert Blanchet of Oregon City, on the prospects for a parish in southern Oregon: "Catholics [here] are so few and in general so lukewarm . . . [that for a priest to work among them] he must become personally acquainted with them, must follow their motions from place to place, particularly here at the mines where the population is so uncertain and floating."[30] A Methodist history recounts a woman filling out a visitor card at a Methodist Church in Seattle early in the 1960s and telling the pastor who visited that she had not resumed her participation as a Methodist after moving to Seattle because she never thought she would stay, though she had been in Seattle for thirty-seven years.[31]

29. Byassee et al., *Christianity*.
30. O'Hara, *Pioneer Catholic History*, 167.
31. Howell, *Methodism in the Northwest*, 159–60.

Many clerics saw such mobility making people "'indifferent' to religion."[32] In 1881, the Anglican bishop of the Crown Colony of British Columbia complained of the "constitutional religious apathy" of "the people of the whole Pacific slope."[33] In his 1898 annual report on St. Leo Parish, Tacoma, Washington, Rev. Peter Hylebos responded to the question on the number of parishioners with "They come and go—impossible to keep track" and characterized parish organizations as "only in quasi existence, too many members left for the mines and other diggings."[34] A 1902 Northern Baptist publication described Western Washington as "religiously destitute."[35] And in the 1980s historian Jeffrey Burns "summarized the history of Roman Catholicism in the Pacific States as 'the difficult task of inspiring an indifferent people to devotion.'"[36]

Most extractive industries attract primarily men who are single or physically distant from their spouses and families.[37] Participation in extractive industries generally works against participation in organized religion. The opportunity to wash one's clothes takes priority over attending a service, should one be available. Participation in extractive industries undercuts the plausibility of a common "Christian" teaching, that steady habits lead to reward.[38]

When individuals' experiences undercut what they have held as Christian teaching, new forms of Christianity find opportunity. The rapid growth of Pentecostalism along the West Coast after the Azusa Street (Los Angeles) Revival of 1906–8 provides one example. Pentecostalism privileges inner experience and makes the Spirit's power accessible without need for mediation by clergy. Pentecostal religious experience is self-verifying, providing an interior, and so portable, moral compass with which individuals can navigate life. The movement grew initially on the West Coast among those surviving at the economic margins through hard manual labor, especially during the throes of the Great Depression. Disconnected from social and familial networks and with their daily lives subject to the vagaries of booms and busts in the economy, Pentecostalism supported and sustained them.[39] In the 1960s the movement's teaching of direct, visceral experience

32. Killen, "Christianity," 6.
33. McNally, "Victoria," 23; Marks, *Infidels and the Damn Churches*, 6.
34. Killen, "Geography of Minority Religion," 54.
35. Szasz, *Religion*, 5.
36. Burns, "Building the Best," 15.
37. Maffley-Kipp, *Religion and Society*, 150–51.
38. Maffley-Kipp, "Eastward Ho," 119–24.
39. Szasz, *Religion*, 82–84, 87–88, 111–16.

of the Spirit grew through the charismatic movement in many historic denominations, including Catholicism.

Early leaders of the movement spread their teaching through new communication technologies. Aimee Semple McPherson, founder of the Foursquare Gospel Church, wed a growing Fundamentalism with emerging mass media and a profound sense of the character and needs of Los Angeles in a mix a that made her the "first 'superstar' of American popular religion."[40]

An open religious environment supports faster emergence and spread of new forms of Christianity that align better with how people make a living and spend their lives. During the 1960s, as Donald Miller relates in *Reinventing American Protestantism*, California incubated three early post-denominational churches that spread throughout the West and then nationally, Calvary Chapel, Hope Chapel, and Vineyard Christian Fellowship. These groups, as do more recent emergent Christianities, attract people seeking community, moral clarity, and visceral experience of transcendence. Casually clad clergy, sermons delivered informally and targeted at practical instructions for living, worship that evokes mass religious experience, supported affinity groups, and a structure seemingly more horizontal than hierarchal drew members from historic denominations and newcomers to the Pacific edge. In the decades following, cities up and down the West Coast saw the rise and fall and often rebirth of megachurch congregations, with most, like Mark Driscoll's Mars Hill in Seattle, led by charismatic pastors. Many of these congregations teach traditional gender roles, trust in God, and the goodness of economic prosperity. Participants in these congregations are often in-migrants, separated from family educationally, economically, and geographically.

Newer forms of Evangelicalism have thrived on the West Coast, in part by adapting to it.[41] A recent study by Christopher James of 105 new, refounded, or relocated congregations in Seattle between 2001 and 2014 identified shared features that contributed to their success. The list included "cultivating embodied, experiential, everyday spirituality."[42] New congregations provide community, teaching, and networks of support in a more culturally familiar format, one that aligns with the life and experience of workers in a global knowledge economy. These congregations also offer the opportunity to be part of something new, and building something new has long been a powerful attractor to religious participation on the West Coast. At the turn of the twentieth century, the Rev. Mark Matthews, like most

---

40. Szasz, *Religion*, 111–12.
41. Shibley, "Contemporary Evangelicals," 85–86.
42. James, *Church Planting*, 11.

clergy of the time an in-migrant to the region, used multipoint gathering places and other new strategies to grow First Presbyterian in Seattle into the largest Presbyterian congregation in the nation.[43]

Creativity in a Context of Constraint

Different Christianities respond to the constraints of an open religious environment differently. Long-established and emergent forms of Christian Evangelicalism see a large pool of potential members in the open environment. For denominations of the magisterial Reformation (including the Roman Catholic Church), whose theological identities obligate engagement directed to the welfare of the broader society, the open religious environment has presented a particular challenge: how to promote broader social welfare in a context in which they lacked the numbers and social influence they had in East into the 1960s. Through a combination of pragmatic realism, adaptability, and creative innovation, they developed effective strategies for promoting broader social welfare and made lasting contributions exceeding what their numbers warranted.

Historic denominations began by providing worship, pastoral care, and material assistance to residents, in-migrants from the US, and immigrants from other nations, thereby taking advantage of being among the earliest institutions to form in cities and towns. Churches, synagogues, and temples were sources of community, mutual aid, and access to social networks. Some congregations and parishes had strong ethnic identities; others were "American." They continue to serve immigrants and the poor, through direct services and sponsoring low-income housing. Like generations before them, some in-migrants to the West Coast seek community in congregations, especially when the move has dislocated them from family and friend networks. As a 2018 focus group participant, Fiona, "a Chinese millennial Catholic from California," put it about life after moving to Seattle: "it was hard to find community and the community I ended up in and really not branching out of is my church community."[44]

The historic churches established social welfare institutions that were the first in most subregions. Hospitals, orphanages, homes for the mentally ill and the elderly, and schools were all founded and run primarily by vowed Catholic religious communities, but also by Protestant deaconesses, lay missioners, and faith-inspired volunteers, many into the second half of the twentieth century. The wider population, including those not inclined to be

43. Soden, *Reverend Mark Matthews*, 49–50.
44. Killen, "Questing for Home," 149.

religiously active, valued these services and contributed to them. In 1866, Caroline Leighton, wife of a customs agent in the Washington Territory, noted in her journal that a Scots-Presbyterian stage depot manager maintained a donation box to collect funds for a school run by Roman Catholic sisters.[45] A quite visible example of the effectiveness of historic Christianities in influencing the larger society is the number of faith-founded colleges and universities on the West Coast that have broad regional impact.[46]

The constraint of minority status and the commitment to social welfare led historic denominations on the West Coast to practice ecumenical and interfaith cooperation more than a century before it became a practice elsewhere in North America.[47] Protestants, Catholics, and Jews developed practical strategies for cooperating with each other and with those beyond the doors of religious institutions to advance faith-inspired activity intended to improve civic life and social welfare. Cross-faith cooperation and the need to draw on the good will of the unchurched led to the practice of translating faith-motivated legislative proposals into the language of the common welfare and good business. In 1924 this strategy led to an interfaith alliance of businessmen, Protestant religious leaders, and a Jewish rabbi, heavily funded by two local wealthy Catholic entrepreneurs, that drove the defeat of the Ku Klux Klan–sponsored Initiative 49 to ban parochial schools in Washington State. The Friends of Educational Freedom, the formal name of the alliance, argued that it violated the American sense of "fair play," "would brand the state of Washington before the nation as the home of cranks and bigots," and would lead the capital investment necessary to "develop our natural resources" to dry up. The initiative failed at the ballot box.[48]

Another example of ecumenical and interfaith collaboration that reached beyond organized religious communities was *Challenge*, a program aired on Seattle's KOMO television station in 1960 that ran for fourteen years, attracting an audience of three hundred thousand each week. On the program Fr. William Treacy, Rabbi Raphael Levine, and a Protestant minister, originally Dr. Martin Goslin, "discussed issues that divided them in a lively, rational, and amiable manner."[49] Among the topics covered were a Catholic president in the White House, open housing in Seattle, and celebrating Christmas in public schools.

45. Leighton, *West Coast Journeys*, 72–73.
46. Szasz, *Religion*, 20–21.
47. Szasz, *Religion*, 6–7, 11.
48. Killen, "Geography of Minority Religion," 62.
49. Killen, "Geography of Minority Religion," 66–67.

This kind of cooperation continues and has become more interfaith. The Sikh community of Richmond, BC, for example, works with a dwindling United Church of Canada congregation in downtown Vancouver to keep its well-established free meal program going.[50]

During World War II, some historic denominations awakened to race and ethnicity, and became more vocal about social justice. Some Catholic priests entered the internment camps with their Japanese parishioners; Protestant congregations set up regular relationships with groups of internees and provided supplies. Quakers worked in the camps. Religious leaders took on the task of imagining a just postwar world.[51] Some became leaders in the movement against nuclear weapons that grew from the bombing of Hiroshima and Nagasaki (home of the oldest Japanese Christian community). Seattle Archbishop Raymond Hunthausen became an outspoken leader in this movement, even withholding a portion of his taxes in protest.

During the 1960s and 1970s churches were the sites where minorities could safely present their case seeking support and advocacy on economic, policy, and political issues, for example, collective bargaining for farm workers in California, Washington, and Idaho, or legislation to restore to Indians in Washington and Oregon the freedom to exercise their treaty rights to fish at their historic sites. West Coast churches were active in sanctuary movements, and denominations developed renewed migrant ministries.

Pacific-edge churches led in bringing Christian perspectives to environmental issues. The Presbytery of Oregon adopted a statement on the environment that became the model for the national Presbyterian statement. The Roman Catholic bishops whose dioceses abutted the Columbia River developed and published a joint pastoral letter on the Columbia, which became a model for a later pastoral by Catholic bishops around the Great Lakes.[52] By the 1990s, however, it had become more difficult to pass denominational statements on social issues, and the broader public influence of such statements declined. As tensions increased over issues such as rights of sexual minorities, abortion, reparations, global warming, and immigrants, growing numbers of congregations left denominations. The West Coast's open religious environment made it easier to sever denominational ties.

Historic forms of Catholic and Protestant Christianity are in decline on the West Coast and have been since the 1970s. While all have some thriving congregations, in general these denominations do not draw like new forms of

---

50. Killen, "Questing for Home," 158.

51. Szasz, *Religion*, 96–98.

52. Szasz, *Religion*, 95–98, 180–82; Killen and Shibley, "Surveying the Religious Landscape," 48.

Evangelicalism, whose constellations of teaching, worship, and organization resonate more widely with those whose lives are shaped by the knowledge economy and mass culture. Evangelicalism, broadly defined, is now considered by some scholars the dominant form of Christianity in the region.

Spiritual Experience beyond Institutions

In this third decade of the twenty-first century, features long part of West Coast Christianity are now more visible nationally. The reconfiguration of religion in North America that has been underway for half a century is toward a more open religious environment. Hence, simultaneous, disparate religious realities should not be surprising—the growth of muscular White Christian nationalism; deep engagement on the part of individual congregations and some denominations with issues of racial justice, protection of sexual minorities, and environmental activism; a steady decline in the number of those who find a Christian theistic vision plausible; a proliferation of emergent forms of Christianity; and falling rates of institutional religious participation. Christianity as a global religion is now more visible across the continent. All Christianities now capitalize on affinity with the ways people make a living and participate in mass culture, some by aligning with it in their form of worship and ministry, others by offering alternatives to it. Shrinking denominations continue to minister. Creative leadership has become the watchword for clergy. Christianities across the nation now negotiate a context like that of the West Coast from the beginning, one lacking an overarching story that unites people.

As forms of Christianity continue to evolve in an open environment, it is important to pay attention to the meaning and impact of spiritual experience beyond the doors of institutional religion for what it reveals about the human person and prospects for viable civic community. On the West Coast, the natural environment has been the most prominent site of transcendent experience beyond faith communities.[53] In its power to crush and destroy as readily as elevate and inspire, nature on the Pacific edge decenters and relocates the human person. For some, like the naturalist John Muir, the experience leads to richer understandings of the meaning of the human person in creation and how to live as part of it.[54] For others it reinforces social rootlessness, disconnection and a sense of aimlessness, shadow effects on individuals of an open environment.

---

53. Killen, introduction to *Religion and Public Life*, 10–11; Bramadat, "Reverential Naturalism in Cascadia," 23–34.

54. Szasz, *Religion*, 65.

That the West Coast's nature continues to beguile and disturb was evident in recent interviews with religious leaders. One liberal Protestant pastor in Portland, Oregon, saw the natural world competing with congregational commitment, noting that core families announced they would miss the next week because they were going hiking, and did so in a way expectant of strong affirmation for their choice. Another pastor related experiences in nature that revised and deepened their understanding of Christian theology and made them more open to the power of other religious paths. A rabbi put best a theme echoed by many pastors, that there was something about the West Coast that led congregants to "want meaning" but with "fewer obligations and commitments."[55]

Like every location on the planet, the West Coast now grapples with the ravages of climate change, change that is undoing the environment so many have found to be a source of spiritual sustenance and, among Christians, a stimulus to theological reflection on the gospel. Whether the impulse to care for the earth will overcome resistance to the constraints of obligation that an open religious environment nourishes and the fractured nature of American civic life remains to be seen.

Bibliography

Bramadat, Paul. "Reverential Naturalism in Cascadia: From the Fancy to the Sublime." In *Religion at the Edge: Nature, Spirituality, and Secularity in the Pacific Northwest*, edited by Paul Bramadat et al., 23–40. Vancouver: University of British Columbia Press, 2022.

Buerge, David M., and Junius Rochester. *Roots and Branches: The Religious Heritage of Washington State*. Seattle: Church Council of Greater Seattle, 1988.

Burns, Jeffrey M. "Building the Best: A History of Catholic Parish Life in the Pacific States." In *The Pacific, Intermountain West, and Midwest States*, edited by Jay P. Dolan, 1–136. Vol. 2 of *The American Catholic Parish: A History from 1850 to the Present*. New York: Paulist, 1987.

Byassee, Jason, et al. *Christianity: An Asian Religion in Vancouver*. Eugene, OR: Cascade, 2023.

Duncan, Janice K. *Minority without a Champion: Kanakas on the Pacific Coast, 1788–1850*. Portland: Oregon Historical Society, 1972.

Ernst, Eldon G. "The Emergence of California in American Religious Historiography." *Religion and American Culture: A Journal of Interpretation* 11 (Winter 2001) 31–52.

Finke, Roger, and Rodney Stark. *The Churching of America, 1776–1990*. New Brunswick, NJ: Rutgers University Press, 1992.

Frankiel, Sandra Sizer. *California's Spiritual Frontiers: Religious Alternatives in Anglo-Protestantism, 1850–1910*. Berkeley: University of California Press, 1988.

---

55. Killen, "Questing for Home," 155.

Howell, Erle. *Methodism in the Northwest.* Pacific Northwest Conference Historical Society. Nashville: Parthenon, 1966.
James, Christopher B. *Church Planting in Post-Christian Soil: Theology and Practice.* New York: Oxford University Press, 2018.
Killen, Patricia O'Connell. "Christianity in the Western United States." Pacific Lutheran Theological Seminary *SPAN* (Summer 2002) 6–7, 25, 28.
———. "The Geography of a Minority Religion: Catholicism in the Pacific Northwest." *U.S. Catholic Historian* 18 (Summer 2000) 51–71.
———. Introduction to *Religion and Public Life in the Pacific Northwest: The "None" Zone*, edited by Patricia O'Connell Killen and Mark Silk, 9–20. Religion by Region 1. Walnut Creek, CA: AltaMira, 2004.
———. "Memory, Novelty, and Possibility in This Place." In *Cascadia: The Elusive Utopia; Exploring the Spirit of the Pacific Northwest*, edited by Douglas Todd, 65–85. Vancouver: Ronsdale, 2008.
———. "Questing for Home: Place, Spirit and Religious Community in the Pacific Northwest." In *Religion at the Edge: Nature, Spirituality, and Secularity in the Pacific Northwest*, edited by Paul Bramadat et al., 141–62. Vancouver: University of British Columbia Press, 2022.
Killen, Patricia O'Connell, and Mark A Shibley. "Surveying the Religious Landscape: Historical Trends and Current Patterns in Oregon, Washington, and Alaska." In *Religion and Public Life in the Pacific Northwest: The "None" Zone*, edited by Patricia O'Connell Killen and Mark Silk, 25–50. Religion by Region 1. Walnut Creek, CA: AltaMira, 2004.
Leighton, Caroline C. *West Coast Journeys, 1865–1879; The Travelogue of a Remarkable Woman.* Introduction and notes by David M. Buerge. Seattle: Sasquatch, 1995.
Maffley-Kipp, Laurie F. "Eastward Ho! American Religion from the Perspective of the Pacific Rim." In *Retelling U.S. Religious History*, edited by Thomas A. Tweed, 127–48. Berkeley: University of California Press, 1992.
———. *Religion and Society in Frontier California.* Yale Historical Publications. New Haven, CT: Yale University Press, 1994.
Marks, Lynne. *Infidels and the Damn Churches: Irreligion and Religion in Settler British Columbia.* Vancouver: University of British Columbia Press, 2017.
McNally, Vincent J. "Victoria: An American Diocese in Canada." *Canadian Catholic Historical Association Historical Studies* 57 (1990) 7–28.
Miller, Donald E. *Reinventing American Protestantism.* Berkeley: University of California Press, 1997.
O'Connell, Nicholas. *On Sacred Ground: The Spirit of Place in Pacific Northwest Literature.* Seattle: University of Washington Press, 2003.
O'Hara, Edwin Vincent. *Pioneer Catholic History of Oregon.* Patterson, NJ: St. Anthony Guild, 1939.
Pritchard, Linda K. "A Comparative Approach to Western Religious History: Texas as a Case Study, 1845–1890." *Western Historical Quarterly* 19 (1988) 416–29.
Quinn, D. Michael. "Religion in the American West." In *Under an Open Sky: Rethinking America's Western Past*, edited by William Cronon et al., 145–66. New York: Norton, 1992.
Schoenberg, Wilfred P., SJ. *A History of the Catholic Church in the Pacific Northwest, 1743–1988.* Washington, DC: Pastoral, 1987.

Shibley, Mark A. "Contemporary Evangelicals: Born-Again and World Affirming." *Annals of the American Association of Political and Social Sciences* 558 (July 1998) 67–87.

Silk, Mark. "From Outlier to Advance Guard: Cascadia in Its North American Context." In *Religion at the Edge: Nature, Spirituality, and Secularity in the Pacific Northwest*, edited by Paul Bramadat et al., 125–40. Vancouver: University of British Columbia Press, 2022.

Soden, Dale E. *Outsiders in a Promised Land: Religious Activists in Pacific Northwest History.* Corvallis: Oregon State University Press, 2015.

———. *The Reverend Mark Matthews: An Activist in the Progressive Era.* Seattle: University of Washington Press, 2001.

Stump, Roger W. "Regional Migration and Religious Commitment in the United States." *JSSR* 23 (1984) 292–303.

Szasz, Ferenc Morton. *Religion in the Modern American West.* Tucson: University of Arizona Press, 2000.

Taylor, Quintard. *In Search of the Racial Frontier: African Americans in the American West, 1528–1990.* New York: Norton, 1998.

Wellman, James K., Jr. *Evangelical vs. Liberal: The Clash of Christian Cultures in the Pacific Northwest.* New York: Oxford University Press, 2008.

Wilkins-Laflamme, Sarah. "Second to None: Religious Nonaffiliation in the Pacific Northwest." In *Religion at the Edge: Nature, Spirituality, and Secularity in the Pacific Northwest*, edited by Paul Bramadat et al., 100–124. Vancouver: University of British Columbia Press, 2022.

Zelinsky, Wilbur. "An Approach to the Religious Geography of the United States: Patterns of Church Membership in 1952." *Annals of the Association of American Geographers* 51 (June 1961) 139–93.

Chapter 12

God to Texas

A Selective Tale of Christianity from the South

JEREMY HEGI

IN MAY 2023, THE Eighty-Eighth Regular Session of the Texas Legislature ended. Texas governor Greg Abbott signed several bills into law that reflected the newest stage in the United States' culture wars and dominated media headlines. For example, Senate Bill 14 banned puberty blockers and hormone therapy for children under eighteen.[1] Senate Bill 17 banned diversity, equity, and inclusion offices in Texas's public universities and colleges. Beyond these bills, legislators put forward several explicitly religious pieces of legislation that would test the boundaries of religious disestablishment in the US. Senate Bill 1515 would require a copy of the Ten Commandments to be posted in every public school room in Texas; Senate Bill 1396 sought to designate time for prayer and Scripture reading in public schools; and Senate Bill 1556 would allow public school employees to engage in religious expression while working.[2] While none of these pieces of legislation passed, Governor Abbott did sign Senate Bill 763 into law. This bill allowed uncertified religious chaplains to replace trained, professional counselors in K–12 public schools in Texas.[3]

For decades, conservative Christian Republicans have dominated both chambers of the state legislature and the offices of the governor, lieutenant governor, and attorney general in Texas. The legislation I listed above, which reflects the political and religious positions of many conservative Christians living in Texas, should not surprise the reader. Indeed, at first glance, if a person were to examine the religious demographic data of Texas, their findings would seem consistent with the religious and political makeup of the

---

1. *Texas Tribune* Staff, "Regular 2023 Legislative Session."
2. Byrd, "Ten Commandments Bill Fails."
3. Parra, "Bill Allowing Religious Chaplains."

legislature. In 2020, Southern Baptists, non-denominational Evangelicals, and United Methodists combined numbered roughly 6.9 million people, making up 41 percent of the state's religious adherents and constituting 23 percent of the state's population. Roman Catholics accounted for 36 percent of the state's religious adherents, and constituted 20 percent of the state's overall population with 5.9 million people.[4]

Several of Texas's municipalities reflect this reality, with a church on almost every street corner. For example, go to Lubbock, Texas, and drive down Thirty-Fourth Street or Fiftieth Street, two of the main thoroughfares in that city. You will see various churches with large buildings and names like Highland Baptist Church, Sunset Church of Christ, Oakwood Wesleyan Fellowship (formerly Oakwood United Methodist Church), or Our Lady of Guadalupe Catholic Church. These churches reflect the same conservative Christianity that defines Texas's politics. Based on the narrative I have constructed up to this point, the case of Texas's religious identity seems simple and easy to define. Conservative Christianity, represented by traditional White and Hispanic Christian institutions and denominations, dominates the state. It is an open-and-shut case.

Such a surface-level reading of Texas's religious identity, however, is shortsighted as it would miss the complex, diverse, and vibrant reality of Christian expression and practice throughout the state. Return to Lubbock and pay attention to the strip malls that populate the sides of these roads between the big churches listed above. A different picture quickly emerges altogether. You see churches with names like the Church of God of the First Born, Iglesia Cultura Cristiana Lubbock, Redeemed Christian Church of God Tree of Restoration, Lubbock Korean Baptist Church, and Lubbock Chinese Church, tucked between bookshops, tattoo parlors, taquerias, and nail salons. Not to be left behind, Lubbock also has a Coptic Orthodox church, Greek Orthodox church, Russian Orthodox church, and Malankara Mar Thoma Syrian church.[5] Rather than representing the groups that have made up Texas's racial and ethnic identity of Hispanic, Black, and White settlers since its founding as a distinct political entity as the Republic of Texas in 1836, these churches are made up of immigrants from the Global South: places like Nigeria, South Korea, China, and Southern India.

This situation is not unique to Lubbock. Much larger Texas cities such as El Paso, Dallas, San Antonio, and Houston are experiencing an influx of

---

4. "Group Detail Data by Nation, State, County, and Metro," in US Religion Census, "Maps and Data Files."

5. "Group Detail Data by Nation, State, County, and Metro," in US Religion Census, "Maps and Data Files."

immigrants from the Global South at a much larger scale.⁶ A closer look at Texas's most prominent Christian traditions further complicates the situation. While Southern Baptists and Roman Catholics ally with each other over social issues like abortion, they find themselves at odds with each other over other complex issues such as immigration.⁷ When it comes to Christianity in Texas, things are much more complicated than they seem at first glance.

In this chapter, I narrate the dynamic story of Christianity in Texas by asking two questions: What is happening now, and how did we get here? In doing so, I show that the history of Christianity in Texas offers a counter-story to the narratives of American Christianity that commonly focus on New England. Rather than beginning with established Protestant churches with a primarily British heritage that eventually led to disestablishment after the American Revolution, the story of Christianity in Texas begins with a weak Spanish colonial Catholicism that finds itself quickly challenged by an influx of Anglo-evangelical Protestant settlers from the American South who brought enslaved Africans, many of them Christians, to the area. Whether Catholic, Baptist, or Methodist, early Texas Christians would struggle to learn how to live beside new settlers who brought new expressions of Christianity to their republic (and later their state) without enjoying the advantages of established state support. In this way, Texas began forming its religious identity in the free-for-all religious marketplace, and a contentious Christian pluralism emerged.

Christian pluralism defines Texas's religious identity through the nineteenth, twentieth, and twenty-first centuries as wave after wave of migrants who have famously said "gone to Texas" have brought God to Texas with them.⁸ They came from other states in the US, places like Mexico, Germany, France, Norway, Sweden, Bohemia, and Moravia. More recently, they come from the broad regions of the Global South: Asia, Africa, and Latin America. Each group brought and continues to bring its unique expression of Christianity to Texas. Rather than being a settled story that ends with the domination of one form of conservative Christianity over the state, the story of Christianity in Texas continues to be written as new immigrants continue to bring God to Texas.

---

6. White et al., *Texas Migration*, 2.
7. See Wuthnow, *Rough Country*, 356–61, 427–32.
8. Campbell, *Gone to Texas*, xi.

Christianity and Immigration in Texas History[9]

Since its beginning, Christianity has been a missionary faith. Historically, this missionary activity has expressed itself through two broad patterns:

1. Apostolic, or missionary individuals, sent out from the church with a missionary vocation
2. Migrations of Christians into new places who carried their faith with them[10]

Christianity's entrance into Texas represents both these impulses, though within the framework of the Spanish empire and colonialism intertwined with the institution of the Roman Catholic Church.

The first Spanish explorers and conquistadors made their way through the region eventually known as Texas in the seventeenth century. It was not until the end of the century in 1690 that the first permanent Spanish settlement, Mission San Francisco de los Tejas, appeared in central Texas near present-day San Antonio. The mission was the first of several in Texas run by Roman Catholic Franciscan priests who were paid by the Spanish Crown. In partnership with local Spanish soldiers who occupied nearby presidios, or garrisoned forts, these Franciscan missions had three purposes. First, missionaries planned to proselytize Native Americans who lived in Texas and, in doing so, bring them out of a nomadic way of life into settlements near the missions. Second, missionaries worked to assimilate Native Americans into Spanish culture and a way of life that would turn them into loyal tax-paying subjects of the Spanish king. Third, the missions, and the presidios alongside them, would help cement Spanish claims on the region against those of other nations attempting to settle there, especially France.[11] While missionaries were concerned about the spiritual condition of local Native Americans, their motivations were also bound up with their loyalty to Spain. By 1794, though the Franciscans had established a chain of thirty-six missions, they had little success among Native Americans in Texas, except for the Coahuiltencan people in the San Antonio area.[12]

Christianity struggled during the first hundred years of its existence in Texas. The Spanish government invested little time and effort in the area, and

---

9. This section outlines the only basic contours of the history of Christianity in Texas regarding people migration.

10. See Hanciles, *Beyond Christendom*, 377–80; Sunquist, *Unexpected Christian Century*, 135–52.

11. Campbell, *Gone to Texas*, 31.

12. Breazeale, "Negotiating Catholicism," 105.

Native Americans resisted Franciscan efforts to Christianize them. At the end of the century, the Franciscans turned over their missions to be secularized under government control, leaving 3,169 Spanish-speaking inhabitants in Texas loyal to the Roman Catholic Church.[13] Most of these individuals lived along the Rio Grande Valley, from modern-day Brownsville to Laredo, and up to San Antonio, along the trail of Franciscan missions.[14] In the years that led up to Texas independence in 1836, the Catholic Church largely abandoned faithful Catholics in this area. After the Franciscan departure, churches fell into ruin, and communities had little to no pastoral support or education. This situation did not change until 1847 when the Catholic Church organized the Diocese of Galveston to look after its parishioners in Southern Texas.[15] Despite their infrequent contact with priests and the poor religious education that resulted from the little support they received, most early Catholics in the region held their faith deeply to the point that a visiting priest would be overwhelmed with requests to administer sacraments like baptism, marriage, take confession, anoint the sick, or perform Mass.[16]

The sparsity of Catholic clergy during this period left an indelible mark on Roman Catholicism in Texas. It helped establish a critical component of Texas's religious identity. The maintenance of religious belief was the responsibility of lay practitioners in the absence of clergy. As a result, Catholic churches in Texas developed a long-lasting tradition of lay leadership, activism, and practices (such as home altars and prayer groups) that persisted into the twenty-first century.[17] After Texas became a part of the US, the Roman Catholic Church in Texas became primarily populated by Mexican Americans when waves of immigrants entered the state from Mexico. Though many Mexican Catholic clergy came with the immigrants, they left Mexico because of anticlerical sentiment during periods of political unrest in the country. Their main concern was finding a way to return home rather than root themselves in Texas to minister to communities of Mexican Catholics in Texas.

Mexican American Catholic communities were also largely neglected by American Catholic clergy. While Mexican Catholics had learned to depend on lay initiative in the absence of clergy, American Catholics, who were also immigrants with strongholds in the midwestern and northeastern US, became defined by the ethnic parish with a heavy emphasis on the central

13. Campbell, *Gone to Texas*, 72.
14. Wright, "Religious Change," 23.
15. Wuthnow, *Rough Country*, 112.
16. Wright, "Religious Change," 34.
17. Sagarena, "Migration," 57.

authority of the episcopacy. As the twentieth century progressed, these two visions of Catholicism came into tension with each other as the American Catholic Church made its way into the southwestern United States.

It was not until the 1940s that the American Catholic Church began its first focused efforts to work among Mexican American communities. The most successful programs focused on lay leadership and initiative, such as the Cursillo movement.[18] This movement helped engender a strong sense of social activism among Mexican American Catholics whom the African American civil rights movement of the 1950s and 1960s further inspired. By the end of the 1960s, Chicano activism arose, which championed Mexican American identity in the face of intense pressure to assimilate into American culture and the American Catholic Church.[19] It was only after Vatican II in the mid-1960s, with reforms like the vernacular Mass and inclusion of other cultural elements in religious life (such as an acceptance of the veneration of the Virgin of Guadalupe), that the American Catholic Church was able to make further inroads with Mexican American communities in Texas.[20]

Christianity's initial introduction to Texas through mission efforts enmeshed in colonial expansion failed to establish the religion across the region. It did, however, succeed in creating a sense of independence and a tradition of lay leadership among those Catholic communities that existed in the Rio Grande Valley and up to San Antonio. Christianity's second introduction to the area occurred via the mass migration of evangelical Protestants from the American South. Like their Catholic predecessors, they would also champion lay independence and initiative in their expression of Christianity.

In 1821, after Mexico won its independence from Spain, the new nation created an immigration initiative to attract settlers to its holdings north of the Rio Grande River, modern-day Texas. While the Mexican government hoped the new initiative would attract Mexican, European, and American settlers, most immigrants came from the southern US. Between 1821 and 1830, approximately ten thousand White Americans immigrated to Texas. They brought enslaved African Americans to work in cotton plantations on the massive land grants owned by people like Stephen F. Austin.[21] These two groups also brought their expressions of Christianity with them. White settlers came with Baptist and Methodist versions of Christianity that grew out of the revivalism of the Second Great Awakening. They focused

---

18. For more, see Sagarena, "Migration," 62–65.
19. Wuthnow, *Rough Country*, 11.
20. Sagarena, "Migration," 66.
21. Campbell, *Gone to Texas*, 96.

on lay leadership and initiative with an emphasis on personal salvation that further enhanced the sense of independence and individualism that was coming to define religious life in Texas.[22] African Americans participated in the publicly segregated religious life common in the southern US, while also practicing an inculturated version of the faith away from the prying eyes of their enslavers, what scholars often refer to as "the Invisible Institution."[23] During the antebellum period, the Invisible Institution became a way for African Americans to make sense out of, bring meaning to, and find hope despite the oppression and suffering they faced.

Following Texas's independence in 1836, free and enslaved settlers from the southern US continued to stream into the state. New groups of Europeans, who were mostly Catholic, also began to immigrate to the new republic: Irish immigrants settled outside Corpus Christi; Germans in New Braunfels and Fredericksburg; and Swiss, Belgians, and the French in the Hill Country outside of San Antonio.[24] By the time the republic had been admitted into the US as a state, Texas had a population of 212,592. In a little over a decade, this number almost tripled to 604,215 on the eve of the Civil War in 1860.[25] Even with the chaos of the Civil War and the Reconstruction that followed, immigrants continued to stream into the state. By 1920, the population of the state ballooned to 4,663,228 people, a 671-percent increase over its population just prior to the Civil War.[26]

During this period and into the twentieth century, three forms of Christianity came to dominate religious life in Texas. First, White Southern Baptists became the most significant expression of Protestantism in the state. By the early 2000s, more than twice as many Southern Baptists as anywhere else in the US would live in the state, with some of the largest Southern Baptist congregations located in Dallas and Houston.[27] They became so populous and ingrained in Texas life that Southern Baptists represented an almost de facto religious establishment in the state. As I outlined in the introduction, Southern Baptists' theological conservatism often moves outside the confines of their congregations to influence Texas's social and political landscape.[28]

22. Wuthnow, *Rough Country*, 9.
23. For more, see Raboteau, *Canaan Land*, 42–60.
24. Breazeale, "Negotiating Catholicism," 108–9.
25. Wuthnow, *Rough Country*, 8.
26. Rozek, *Come to Texas*, 190.
27. Wuthnow, *Rough Country*, 5.
28. Leonard, "Southern Crossroads," 36.

Second, among African Americans, Baptists represent the most significant religious demographic through three groups: the National Baptist Convention, USA; the National Baptist Convention in America; and the Progressive National Baptist Convent. African American Baptist identity in Texas often expressed itself through a socially conscious charismatic spirituality. Regionally, both White and African American Baptists became concentrated in the Panhandle, north, and east regions of Texas.[29]

Third, despite little support from the American Catholic Church, Roman Catholics continued to grow in the state through immigration to Texas. Toward the end of the nineteenth century, in 1890, there were roughly 100,000 Catholics in Texas. By 1916, this number quadrupled to 402,874 members who were mainly Mexican American.[30] Though they continued to be concentrated in the Rio Grande Valley and the area around San Antonio, Catholics also began making inroads into Protestant strongholds and the state's largest cities, like Houston, Fort Worth, and Dallas. Despite being concentrated in different parts of the state, Protestants could not easily dismiss the importance of the growing Catholic presence. Likewise, as Catholics settled across the state during the twentieth century, they often had to work with Protestants and contend with them over social and political issues that each group passionately championed.

By the end of the twentieth century, waves of migration resulted in a robust White Southern Baptist Christianity that stood in tension with African American and Catholic Christianities. The religious identity of the state seemed to be set, especially regarding the social and political power that conservative Baptists enjoyed in the state. After the Immigration and Nationality Act of 1965, however, groups of new immigrants would come to Texas and bring new expressions of Christianity. These people practiced and understood Christianity in ways that did not neatly fit the traditional Baptist and Catholic identities that had defined Texas's religious identity in the past. As an immigrant state, Texas's Christian identity would continue to morph as more migrants brought God to Texas.

Christianity, Immigration, and Religious Change in Twenty-First-Century Texas

Houston is one of the most exciting food cities in Texas. The metropolis boasts a dizzying array of restaurants from every cultural background imaginable. For example, Crawfish and Noodles is a flagship restaurant in the

---

29. See Leonard, "The Southern Crossroads," 39, 41 for demographic maps.
30. Wuthnow, *Rough Country*, 113.

Viet-Cajun fusion food phenomenon that has popped up along the Texas Gulf Coast. When Vietnamese refugees made their way to Texas in 1975 after Saigon's fall and the Vietnam War's end, they brought their culinary traditions with them. The refugees had trouble, however, when it came to finding fresh Vietnamese ingredients along the Texas Gulf Coast in the 1970s. So, they did the next best thing. Rather than using river prawns in cooking, they turned to crawfish, a viable alternative in Texas. Lemongrass and other herbs and spices commonly used in Vietnamese cooking were out of reach of them, so they explored local Cajun spices in their new home to find close substitutes.[31] What resulted was a distinctive fusion of Cajun and Vietnamese cooking that could be the product only of human migration and ingenuity. Since new, contextualized forms of fusion food emerged in this immigrant community, how would other aspects of their lives, particularly the Catholicism that many Vietnamese brought with them, be impacted by their new home and, in turn, how would they impact the Catholicism that they found waiting for them?

People of Vietnamese descent are not the only individuals adapting their way of life to the Texas Gulf Coast. Roughly 1.6 million immigrants, mainly from the Global South (Latin America, Asia, and Africa), the new demographic heartlands of world Christianity, call Houston home.[32] Just as they have brought their culinary traditions with them, they have also brought their expressions of the Christian faith. From Mexican Catholic churches that have close ties to parishes in Monterrey, Mexico; to the Chinese Gospel Church, the largest Chinese Protestant church in Houston; and the Redeemed Christian Church of God, an outgrowth of one of the most significant megachurch movements in Nigeria, the city has become a quilted mosaic of global Christianity stitched together in one metropolitan area. As the city with the second fastest population growth, by number, in the US, these immigrant communities will have an increasing impact on the religious identity of Houston.[33]

What has happened in Houston represents what has been happening more broadly in Texas over the last several decades. In 2020, the population in Texas grew to 29 million from 25 million in 2010, a change of about 4 million people in ten years, making it the fastest-growing state in the US. International immigration accounts for 20.8 percent of this population increase, about 830,000 people. Looking at the total population of Texas, roughly 4.9 million immigrants compose 17 percent of the state's population, making it

---

31. For more, see Chang, "Shrimp & Crawfish."
32. Capps and Soto, *Profile*, 1.
33. Potter, *State of the State*, 8.

the second largest immigrant population in the US.[34] These growth trends will continue as Texas gains around 250,000 new residents each year through domestic migration and international immigration.[35] By 2060, demographers predict that the state's population will grow to just over 44 million.[36]

These numbers help demonstrate that Texas is a rapidly diversifying state, impacting every aspect of the state's social fabric: cities, rural areas, politics, economy, culture, and religion. The White population of Texas, once a majority, is now a minority in the state behind Hispanic/Latino Texans and is becoming less defined by its nineteenth and twentieth-century Christian identity.[37] The new Latino majority, once predominantly Catholic, is embracing Protestant Christianity at a high rate, impacting the identity and politics of one of the oldest communities in the state. African American Christians, who have long primarily been a part of Baptist forms of Christianity, are finding faith alternatives in new expressions of Christianity coming to Texas with the African Christian diaspora. This story reflects the experience of the earliest Texans: new waves of immigrants are bringing their expressions with them to impact the region's religious identity. This time, however, immigrants from the Global South are bringing new expressions of Christianity that challenge long-established Protestant and Catholic patterns of the faith. In this section, I pay particular attention to Christianity among Texas's Latino population as a salient example of rapid changes in the state's religious landscape.

The largest group of immigrants to Texas during the twenty-first century has continued to be from Latin America. As a result of this steady stream of immigration, Latinos constitute 39 percent of the state's population, making Texas the state with the third largest Hispanic population in the US.[38] Historically, Mexico has been the dominant country of origin for Latino immigrants to Texas. From 1965 to 2015, over sixteen million Mexicans migrated to the US, one of the largest mass migrations in history.[39] Since the beginning of the twenty-first century, however, Mexican immigration has declined. For example, in 2005, 69,275 individuals immigrated to Texas from Mexico. Eight years later, in 2013, this number fell by more than

---

34. American Immigration Council, *Immigrants in Texas*.

35. White et al., *Texas Migration*, 1.

36. Potter, *State of the State*, 30.

37. See Adriano, "Hispanics Are Now Largest." I interchange the terms *Latino* and *Hispanic*. For more on the complexity of using a single term to describe all individuals from Latin America, see Mulder et al., *Latino Protestants*, 13–14.

38. Pew Research Center, "Latinos in 2016 Election," para. 2.

39. Krogstad, "5 Facts," para. 1.

half to 34,204.[40] Despite the decrease in immigrants from Mexico, migrants from the Latin American countries of El Salvador, Guatemala, and Honduras have increased to the point that they help offset the lack of Mexican migrants. For example, in 2015, Mexico deported 150,000 unauthorized immigrants from the three countries attempting to travel through the country to the US, a 44 percent increase over the previous year. Taken together, El Salvador, Guatemala, and Honduras account for almost all of Mexico's deportations in 2015, roughly 97 percent.[41] The result of the steady influx of Latinos into Texas has resulted in the recent demographic shift I mentioned above: Hispanics are now the largest demographic group in Texas. As these demographic shifts take place, they impact Texas's religious identity.

Many Christians coming to Texas from Latin America in the twenty-first century are Catholic. The steady flow of Hispanic Catholics into America has helped drive a regional shift in the US. Where the Northeast and the Midwest were once strongholds of Catholicism in the country, today the center of the faith has moved toward the South and West regions of the US.[42] Forty-two percent of Catholics in Texas are first-generation immigrants while 16 percent have at least one parent who is an immigrant.[43] According to the Pew Research Center, the majority of Catholic Texans have a strong belief in God, and they see faith and religion as a defining aspect of their lives.[44] An increasing number of Hispanic Catholics in Texas, especially among recent immigrants, have also incorporated charismatic practices into their religious life, characterized by glossolalia (speaking in tongues), healing, and seeking ecstatic religious experiences.[45]

Politically, less than half of Texas Catholics (45 percent) identify as Democrats and 29 percent as Republicans. Most of them (67 percent), however, identify themselves as politically conservative or moderate. While 55 percent believe that abortion should be illegal, 70 percent believe that homosexuality should be accepted, and 52 percent strongly favor same-sex marriage.[46] In other words, Catholic Texans do not readily line up with one or the other of the major political parties in the US on their social stances.

---

40. White et al., *Origins of Immigrants*, 8.
41. Krogstad, "5 Facts," para. 1.
42. Lipka, "Catholic America."
43. Pew Research Center, "Catholics in Texas," para. 4.
44. Pew Research Center, "Catholics in Texas," paras. 10–11.
45. Leonard, "Southern Crossroads," 31. For an in-depth discussion of charismatic Catholicism, see Hartch, *Latin American Christianity*, 114–17.
46. Lindsey, "At the Crossroads," 16–18.

They are sympathetic toward LGBTQ individuals and have a passion for issues related to immigration in the US, but they strongly oppose abortion.

Despite not fitting in neatly with the political positions of the Democratic party, they long courted, counted on, and even took for granted the Hispanic community in Texas when it comes to voting. Thus, political pundits were stunned after the 2020 United States presidential election when Zapata County along the Rio Grande River voted for Republican candidate Donald Trump over the Democratic nominee, Joe Biden. In the past, the counties along the Rio Grande River south of San Antonio had been strongholds of Hispanic Catholicism in Texas and the Texas Democratic party. In the 2016 election, Maverick, Webb, Zapata, Starr, Hidalgo, and Cameron Counties voted overwhelmingly for then-Democratic presidential candidate Hilary Clinton. Clinton beat out Trump by an average of 45.5 percentage points across the region.[47] In 2020, Trump made significant inroads into the area by gaining an average of 35.15 percentage points over his previous performance in 2016.[48] Why did individuals in these predominantly Catholic Hispanic communities who had previously voted for Democratic candidates vote for a presidential candidate who made a strong stance against immigration a central plank of his political platform? One part of the answer to this question has to do with a religious shift taking place within the Hispanic community.

Since the late 2000s, Latinos have become the fastest-growing group of evangelical and Pentecostal/charismatic Protestants in the US, which is remarkable considering the decline of Christianity in North America in general. In 2007, 19 percent of the Hispanic community identified as Protestant, and this increased to 22 percent by 2014.[49] By 2020, 30 percent of Latinos identified as Protestant.[50] This group is growing so fast that by 2030, scholars predict that half of all Latinos in the country will be Protestant. Three factors help account for this:

1. High fertility rates
2. Conversion from Roman Catholicism
3. Immigration from countries that have high percentages of Protestants, especially Guatemala and El Salvador[51]

---

47. Murphy and Batheja, "See Which Counties."
48. Astudillo, "Texas 2020 Election Results."
49. Mulder et al., *Latino Protestants in America*, 2.
50. Espinosa, "Latinos Shifting Republican," 392.
51. Mulder et al., *Latino Protestants in America*, 3.

Indeed, while fewer than 10 percent of Catholic priests in the US are Hispanic, recent studies of Latino Protestant churches have demonstrated that 80 percent of Hispanic pastors who start new churches are first-generation immigrants.[52]

When immigrants from Latin America make their way to the US, they are more likely to find pastors who can speak Spanish, identify with them, and who can help them navigate their new cultural context in evangelical Protestant churches than Catholic churches. Moreover, because of the flexibility of evangelical church polity, Latino immigrants have opportunities to participate in the leadership structures of Protestant congregations. In a broader cultural context that often vilifies immigrants who must reestablish their social and economic fortunes in a new country, these leadership opportunities give them a place in their new community that helps them build social capital. Finally, heightened religious experiences in Pentecostal/charismatic contexts, over and against Catholic contexts, draw Latino immigrants into Protestantism. Experientially-focused worship services that help individuals feel that they have a direct connection to Jesus through the Holy Spirit aid new migrants in finding an anchoring point in their unsettled state. By the late 2000s, for every Latino who comes to the US as a Catholic, four leave the church, resulting in an estimated six hundred thousand Hispanic Catholics joining evangelical Protestant churches annually.[53]

Latino Protestants demonstrate higher rates of religiosity—in church attendance, Bible reading, and prayer—than their Anglo–Protestant and Hispanic Catholic counterparts. They are also more likely than Catholics to vote for Republican candidates. As I discussed earlier in the chapter, Hispanic Catholics have a long tradition of engaging in social justice issues, especially immigration and poverty. Protestant theology focuses on a personal relationship with God and individualism, especially among its evangelical and Pentecostal/charismatic expressions. Republican arguments about social life focusing on personal responsibility and their stances on issues like abortion and same-sex marriage appeal to Latino Protestants.[54] In a recent Pew survey, half of Latino Protestants said they would vote for Republican candidates. At the same time, 59 percent of Hispanic Catholics indicated that they would vote for Democrats. In Texas, this shift has resulted in the election of the first Mexican-born woman, Mayra Flores, to serve as a member of Congress representing Texas's thirty-fourth congressional district located in the Rio Grande Valley. Flores, a Pentecostal Christian,

---

52. Winter, "Fastest-Growing Group," para. 5.
53. Mulder et al., *Latino Protestants in America*, 10.
54. Mulder et al., *Latino Protestants in America*, 20–21.

centered her campaign on three values, "faith, family and country," with the slogan "Make America Godly Again."[55] She is one of the few Republicans ever to represent the Rio Grande Valley in Congress.

The preceding discussion raises several questions about the future of the Hispanic community and the shape of Christianity in the state. How do defections from the Catholic Church to evangelical Protestantism affect Latino communities and families? Historically, the Catholic Church has been a center of social life and cultural traditions in Hispanic communities. As Latinos leave Catholicism, how will their leaving affect their identities and sense of belonging to a distinct ethnic community in Texas? Does this shift encourage Latinos to assimilate into a way of life that reflects the White culture that has dominated Texas for so long? Finally, as White Southern Baptists continue to decline in the state, will Latino evangelical Protestants take their place—especially in terms of continuing to fortify conservative culture and power in the state? These questions, among others, demand more investigation as the future of Christianity in Texas continues to unfold.

Conclusion

Popular portrayals of Texas's history and contemporary character are rife with stories of the Alamo, cowboys, cattle drives, oil, and conservative politics. These narratives obfuscate a fundamental truth: Texas is an immigrant state. Whether it concerns Spanish Franciscans, Baptist settlers, enslaved African Americans, or Vietnamese Catholics, Christianity in Texas is closely tied to its immigrant identity. Each new wave of immigrants has arrived with unique expressions of faith and has had to adapt to the rough, independent spirit that has long characterized Texas's culture. Immigrant arrival has also changed the state's cultural and religious identity.

European colonialism introduced Christianity to the region. Anglo-American immigration helped establish a dominant Southern Baptist ethos that would define much of Texas's social and political character in the late nineteenth and twentieth centuries. However, in the twenty-first century, sustained waves of immigration from Latin America, along with newcomers from Asia and Africa, are once again reshaping the character of Christianity in the region. These demographic shifts reflect a broader trend in the US, where the country is becoming more Christian through migration while less Christian as White Americans leave the faith.[56] As a result, the US can

---

55. Molina, "Ahead of Midterms," paras. 1, 3.
56. Sunquist, *Unexpected Christian Century*, 147.

still maintain its status as the country with the most Christians in the world, but the future of Christianity in the country remains uncertain.[57]

The story of immigrants bringing God to Texas is dynamic and ongoing. If current immigration and demographic trends continue, the future of Christianity in Texas will likely be characterized by conservatism, charismatic practices, and Latino identity. This projection, however, is not set in stone. The evolving nature of Texas's religious landscape suggests that Christianity will continue to change, adapt, and take on new forms as new waves of immigrants shape its expression. Texas's religious identity is far from being monolithic. Its diversity reflects the complex interplay of culture, history, and migration. While the story of Christianity in Texas defies traditional narratives on the history of American Christianity, it is still an American story that serves as a microcosm of the ever-changing religious tapestry of the US as a whole.

Bibliography

Adriano, José Luis. "Hispanics Are Now the Largest Demographic Group in Texas, Census Data Confirms." *Dallas Morning News*, June 22, 2023. https://www.dallasnews.com/news/texas/2023/06/22/census-data-confirms-hispanics-are-now-the-largest-demographic-group-in-texas/.

American Immigration Council. *Immigrants in Texas*. American Immigration Council, Aug. 6, 2020. https://www.americanimmigrationcouncil.org/sites/default/files/research/immigrants_in_texas.pdf.

Astudillo, Carla. "Here Are the Texas 2020 Election Results." *Texas Tribune*, Dec. 1, 2020. https://apps.texastribune.org/features/2020/general-election-results/.

Breazeale, Kathlyn. "Negotiating Catholicism: Religious Identity vs. Regional Citizenship." In *Religion and Public Life in the Southern Crossroads: Showdown States*, edited by William Lindsey and Mark Silk, 103–25. Religion and Region 5. Walnut Creek, CA: AltaMira, 2005.

Byrd, Don. "Ten Commandments Bill Fails, Chaplain in Schools Measure Passes as Legislative Session in Texas Ends." Baptist Joint Committee, June 5, 2023. https://bjconline.org/texas-legislative-session-060523/.

Campbell, Randolph B. *Gone to Texas: A History of the Lone Star State*. 3rd ed. New York: Oxford University Press, 2018.

Capps, Randy, and Ariel G. Ruiz Soto. *A Profile of Houston's Diverse Immigrant Population in a Rapidly Changing Policy Landscape*. Migration Policy Institution, Sept. 2018. https://www.migrationpolicy.org/sites/default/files/publications/HoustonImmigrantsProfile_FinalWeb.pdf.

Chang, David, presenter. *Ugly Delicious*. Season 1, episode 4, "Shrimp & Crawfish." Aired Feb. 23, 2018, on Netflix. https://www.netflix.com/watch/80191116.

---

57. Zurlo, *Global Christianity*, 304.

Espinosa, Gastón. "Latinos Shifting Republican? Evangelical, Pentecostal, and Catholic Charismatic Voting in the 2020 Election in the U.S., Florida and Texas." *Pneuma* 44 (2022) 380–414.

Hanciles, Jehu J. *Beyond Christendom: Globalization, African Migration, and the Transformation of the West*. Maryknoll, NY: Orbis, 2008.

Hartch, Todd. *The Rebirth of Latin American Christianity*. New York: Oxford University Press, 2014.

Krogstad, Jens Manuel. "5 Facts about Mexico and Immigration to the U.S." Pew Research Center, Feb. 11, 2016. https://www.pewresearch.org/short-reads/2016/02/11/mexico-and-immigration-to-us/.

Leonard, Bill. "The Southern Crossroads: Religion and Demography." In *Religion and Public Life in the Southern Crossroads: Showdown States*, edited by William Lindsey and Mark Silk, 27–53. Religion and Region 5. Walnut Creek, CA: AltaMira, 2005.

Lindsey, William. "At the Crossroads." Introduction to *Religion and Public Life in the Southern Crossroads: Showdown States*, edited by William Lindsey and Mark Silk, 9–22. Religion and Region 5. Walnut Creek, CA: AltaMira, 2005.

Lipka, Michael. "A Closer Look at Catholic America." Pew Research Center, Sept. 14, 2015. https://www.pewresearch.org/short-reads/2015/09/14/a-closer-look-at-catholic-america/.

Molina, Alejandra. "Ahead of Midterms, Faith Plays Central Role in Republican Efforts to Win Latino Votes." *Religion News Service*, Oct. 31, 2002. https://religionnews.com/2022/10/31/ahead-of-midterms-faith-plays-central-role-in-republican-efforts-to-win-latino-votes/.

Mulder, Mark T., et al. *Latino Protestants in America: Growing and Diverse*. New York: Rowman & Littlefield, 2017.

Murphy, Ryan, and Aman Batheja. "See Which Counties in Texas Trump and Clinton Won." *Texas Tribune*, Nov. 9, 2016. https://www.texastribune.org/2016/11/09/see-which-counties-texas-trump-and-clinton-won/.

Parra, Ariana. "Bill Allowing Religious Chaplains in Public Schools Goes to Gov.'s Desk for Signing." *KFOX14*, May 25, 2023. https://kfoxtv.com/newsletter-daily/bill-allowing-religious-chaplains-in-public-schools-goes-to-governors-desk-for-signing-texas-legislation-greg-abbott-senate-bill-763-separation-of-church-and-state.

Pew Research Center. "Catholics Who Are in Texas." Pew Research Center, n.d. https://www.pewresearch.org/religion/religious-landscape-study/state/texas/religious-tradition/catholic/#demographic-information.

———. "Latinos in the 2016 Election: Texas." Pew Research Center, Jan. 19, 2016, https://www.pewresearch.org/hispanic/fact-sheet/latinos-in-the-2016-election-texas/.

Potter, Lloyd. *State of the State: Texas Demographic Trends and Characteristics*. Texas Demographic Center, May 23, 2023. https://demographics.texas.gov/Resources/Presentations/DDUC/2023/2023_05_23_StateTexasDemographicTrends.pdf.

Raboteau, Albert J. *Canaan Land: A Religious History of African Americans*. Religion in American Life. New York: Oxford University Press, 2001.

Rozek, Barbara J. *Come to Texas: Attracting Immigrants, 1865–1915*. College Station: Texas A&M University Press, 2003.

Sagarena, Roberto Lint. "Migration and Mexican American Religious Life, 1848–2000." In *Immigration and Religion in America: Comparative and Historical Perspectives*, edited by Richard Alba et al., 56–70. New York: New York University Press, 2008.

Sunquist, Scott W. *The Unexpected Christian Century: The Reversal and Transformation of Global Christianity, 1900–2000*. Grand Rapids: Baker Academic, 2015.

Texas Tribune Staff. "The Regular 2023 Legislative Session Is Over. Here's How the Most Consequential Bills Fared." *Texas Tribune*, May 18, 2023; updated June 20, 2023. https://www.texastribune.org/2023/05/18/texas-legislature-bills-pass-fail/.

US Religion Census. "Maps and Data Files for 2020." US Religion Census, last updated June 23, 2023. https://www.usreligioncensus.org/node/1639.

White, Steve, et al. *Origins of Immigrants to Texas*. Texas Demographic Center, May 2015. https://demographics.texas.gov/Resources/Publications/2015/2015_05_Origins.pdf.

———. *Texas Migration*. Texas Demographic Center, Jan. 2017. https://demographics.texas.gov/Resources/publications/2017/2017_01_11_TexasMigration.pdf.

Winter, Meaghan. "The Fastest-Growing Group of American Evangelicals." *Atlantic*, July 26, 2021. https://www.theatlantic.com/culture/archive/2021/07/latinos-will-determine-future-american-evangelicalism/619551/.

Wright, Robert E. "Religious Change along the Mexican Border, 1852–1876." *USCH* 39 (2021) 23–48.

Wuthnow, Robert. *Rough Country: How Texas Became America's Most Powerful Bible-Belt State*. Princeton, NJ: Princeton University Press, 2014.

Zurlo, Gina. *Global Christianity: A Guide to the World's Largest Religion from Afghanistan to Zimbabwe*. Grand Rapids: Zondervan Academic, 2022.

Chapter 13

Unintended Consequences

Refugee Resettlement in the United States

CINDY M. WU

BHADRA RAI HAD BEEN living in a refugee camp in Nepal for only two months when his sister became deathly ill.[1] Bhadra's father—part Buddhist, part Hindu—employed healing rituals and cast away evil spirits, to no avail. A man in the camp told Bhadra's father about Jesus, urging the family to believe upon the name of Jesus so the girl could be saved. Bhadra's family had never heard about Jesus in their native Bhutan. In desperation, they believed—and the sister lived. This miraculous healing was the catalyst for Bhadra's family's faith journey, but it came at a cost—other family members immediately shunned them, for now they belonged to the lowliest caste, the Christian caste.

A few years later, in 2008, Bhadra and his sister were approved for resettlement in Houston, Texas. They stepped off the plane with a combined cash reserve of two US dollars. For the first three weeks, they cried every day, wondering how they would make a new life for themselves on their own. Out of such scarcity and insecurity, the path Bhadra's life would eventually take is hard to imagine.

Migration Realities

Over the past century, human migration has accelerated. According to the United Nations, today more people—281 million or about 3.6 percent of the world's population—live outside their country of origin than ever before.[2]

---

1. Interview by author with Bhadra Rai on Zoom, Mar. 14, 2023.
2. See "About Migration and Human Rights" at https://www.ohchr.org/en/migration.

The main driver for migration is opportunity, but a significant number—35 million—are refugees who have been forcibly displaced from their homes.[3]

Since 1975, the United States has resettled over 3.5 million refugees.[4] This number tells a dramatic story—a story about conflict, loss, migration, integration, assimilation, success, and pain. Most of the refugees resettled by the US have been Christians, among them, persecuted Christian minority groups like Bhadra's family. Refugees are changing the landscape of the country—and of the church. Many native-born American Christians are either unaware of or not paying enough attention to this reality.

This chapter seeks to offer a glimpse into how refugee resettlement to the United States is shaping the demographics of the church through the stories of diverse refugee populations being resettled in Houston, one of America's largest resettlement cities. Readers will be invited to consider how the migration of refugees to the US is confronting and reshaping approaches to ministry, with the focus on Evangelicals. Finally, this chapter will contemplate future challenges and opportunities for followers of Jesus as the number of refugees continues to increase and the world comes to our doorstep.

Addressing the Global Refugee Crisis

The first international effort for refugees was precipitated by World War I (1914–18). Beginning in 1921 under the League of Nations, governments came together to offer refuge for war-displaced victims. In 1950, the office of the United Nations High Commissioner for Refugees (UNHCR) was created to address the even larger-scale refugee populations produced by World War II (1939–45).

UNHCR was initially established as a temporary body to address the needs of forcibly displaced Europeans in the aftermath of World War II, specifically "events occurring before 1 January 1951."[5] In 1951, an international standard for defining refugee status and rights was put forth at a special United Nations conference held in Geneva, Switzerland. Conferees signed a multilateral treaty called the Refugee Convention, which recognized the inherent right of every human being to seek protection and defined *refugee* as "someone who is unable or unwilling to return to his/her country of origin owing to a well-founded fear of being persecuted for reasons of race, religion, nationality, membership of a particular social group, or political

---

3. See https://www.unhcr.org/refugee-statistics/; accessed Apr. 28, 2023.
4. See https://www.unrefugees.org/refugee-facts/usa/; accessed Dec. 8, 2023.
5. United Nations Conference, "Status of Refugees," ch. 1, art. 1.A.2.

opinion. A refugee is outside of his country of origin."[6] A 1966 protocol removed the original geographic and temporal limitation of the convention, thus making refugee protection more expansive, as reflected today.[7] UNHCR is the primary international refugee protection body, but other players include thousands of international humanitarian organizations.

Before 1980 the United States did not enact a formal refugee welcome program. In the aftermath of the Korean War and Southeast Asian conflicts in countries like Vietnam and Cambodia in the 1970s, the US government created an ad hoc Refugee Task Force with temporary funding through which hundreds of thousands of Southeast Asian refugees were resettled. These refugees came through presidential action and were privately sponsored by churches and individuals.

The first comprehensive plan for refugee resettlement was the Refugee Act, passed with unanimous support by Congress in late 1979, and later codified by President Jimmy Carter in 1980.[8] The Refugee Act standardized and streamlined resettlement services, resulting in today's Refugee Admissions Program. This life-saving program allows tens of thousands of refugees every year to seek legal residence in the United States; while this number sounds high, in any given year, fewer than 1 percent of all refugees globally are granted resettlement.

Refugee Numbers Skyrocket in the Twenty-First Century

At the turn of the century, the number of global refugees hovered between ten and twelve million, and it held steady until 2013, even dropping below nine million in 2005. Then in 2014, the global refugee population spiked 23 percent in one year, increasing yearly in subsequent years until it skyrocketed in 2022 to over twenty-six million. UNHCR projects over thirty-five million refugees under their mandate by the end of fiscal year 2023. Wars and civil unrest in Syria, Afghanistan, Ukraine, Sudan, and Venezuela have contributed to the sudden rise in numbers, not to mention the continuous outflow of migrants from protracted situations in East Africa and Southeast Asia.

In the United States, the resettlement program has long been viewed as a life-saving humanitarian program, enjoying bipartisan support since its inception. Resettlement numbers are subject to impact by national tragedies, such as the 9/11 attack, or by global events, such as COVID-19, which restricted international travel. Between the years 2017 and 2021, however,

6. United Nations Conference, "Status of Refugees," ch. 1, art. 1.A.2.
7. General Assembly, "Protocol," art. 1.
8. See National Archives Foundation, "Refugee Act of 1980."

polarizing politics played a role in dropping the admissions ceiling to the lowest in the history of US resettlement, a move that decimated the resettlement program. During that time, among the most negatively impacted were some of the world's most severely persecuted Christians.

The graph below displays the numbers of refugees who were admitted to the US between 1975 and 2022, in tens of thousands. The admissions ceiling has averaged ninety thousand persons per year since 1980, while on average seventy thousand refugees per year have actually been resettled since 1975.⁹

X Axis = Refugees Admitted; Y Axis= Fiscal Year. Graph created by author.

In recent years, we have seen an increase in Muslim arrivals, but, as mentioned above, historically the US has always received more Christian refugees, including Christians who have been persecuted for their faith identity, whether Orthodox Iraqis fleeing ISIS, Karen (Burmese) tribal groups facing brutal repression, or Sudanese Christians fleeing civil war. While the degree of adversity faced by refugees is heartbreaking, consider what God is doing. Within the framework of God's sovereignty, Christians can catch sight of missional opportunities and lessons to be learned.

---

9. See https://www.wrapsnet.org/admissions-and-arrivals/; accessed May 10, 2023.

Bhutanese Nepali Church Grows in Exile

Since the 1980s, the Lhotshampa (ethnic Nepalis) have faced expulsion by the Bhutanese government in a mass exile that today is considered one of the most protracted and neglected refugee crises in the world. Of the nearly one hundred thousand Bhutanese refugees resettled around the world, 85 percent have come to the United States. Among them is Bhadra Rai, to whose story we now return.

Bhadra and his sister arrived in Houston with little to their name. They were fortunate to meet Christians who assisted with their integration. Over time, more Bhutanese Nepali refugees were resettled in Houston, about five thousand in just a few years' time, and Bhadra, a young man of many talents who speaks six languages, found himself called into a leadership position among his community.

In 2009 Bhadra planted Canaan Bhutanese Church, borrowing church space from a White pastor with a vision for investing in Indigenous immigrant leaders, a man who became a mentor and godfather to Bhadra. Canaan Church quickly grew larger than their aging host church. By Bhadra's estimation, about 80 percent of the Bhutanese Nepalis at Canaan coming to faith in Christ did so while in Houston (a phenomenon occurring among Bhutanese Nepalis in other cities in the US).[10] Though most Bhutanese Nepalis have a Pentecostal background, many also claim Baptist identity because those were the churches who initially shared space with them.

Bhadra went to work. He galvanized his congregation to welcome incoming Bhutanese Nepali refugees and provided care within his community to recent converts and Hindus alike. In 2011, he became the treasurer for the Bhutanese Nepali Churches of America, through which he had the opportunity to attend his first global leadership conference. In 2016 he founded the Global Nepali-Speaking Christian Fellowship, a network with diaspora members in Denmark, Australia, Norway, and Canada, to name a few countries. He also publishes and updates an impressive US and Canada directory of state and provincial leaders and individual churches.

In 2002 the first church led by a native Nepali pastor was planted in the US. In 2009, when Bhadra started Canaan, there were three Bhutanese Nepali churches; in 2016, there were 177; in 2022, Bhadra accounted for approximately 290 congregations in thirty-one states. The explosion of Bhutanese Nepali churches is a mighty work of the Holy Spirit.

---

10. Information in this section was gleaned from interviews by the author with prominent Bhutanese Nepali church leaders around the US on Zoom, Mar. 14–Apr. 10, 2023.

The concentration of Bhutanese Nepali Christians in the United States is currently located in the Midwest (Cincinnati and Columbus, Ohio) and in Harrisburg, Pennsylvania. Bhadra was happily settled in Houston, but with more friends and family members coming to the US, the pull to reunite with them eventually led him out of Houston in 2021 to Harrisburg, which is now home to over five thousand Bhutanese Nepalis and nineteen Indigenous churches. Family reunification, comprehensive social services, and employment opportunities are strong pulls for refugees to make a secondary migration within the US. As a result of this mass secondary migration of Bhutanese, Houston, which once maintained a sizable Bhutanese population, is left with only a dozen families (a similar pattern occurred with the Burmese population in Houston, many of whom also moved to the Midwest for job opportunity).

In Nepal, there are still seven thousand refugees in camps, with fifteen to twenty churches within the camps. It is almost impossible for refugees to visit Bhutan, but those within are allowed to travel out, and the global networks have made it possible for those pastors to attend conferences and receive training and encouragement. Bhadra's dream is to someday hold a conference in Bhutan; in the meantime, Bhutanese Nepali leaders stay strongly connected with diaspora in Nepal, India, and Bhutan.

Bhadra's journey has been nearly unimaginable. For one who was forcibly displaced at age ten, living in and out of a refugee camp for fifteen years, for one who started his elementary education in the camp and is now leading a global network of pastors, his path to prominence among his people has been remarkable. He has encountered challenges along the way but also much support from Christians within his Houston community. Bolstered by the rapid emergence of Indigenous churches led by Indigenous leaders, the global Bhutanese church continues to gain momentum.

Transforming One of America's Largest Cities

Countless visitors to Houston, Texas, have been surprised to learn the city is much more than cowboys and oil. Houston is, in fact, a cosmopolitan city with first-class arts, education, and food, as well as the world's largest medical center. Over the past five years, various reports have placed Houston at the top of the list of most diverse cities in the United States. The latest census suggests that the nation's trajectory toward a majority-minority country by 2043—in which no group, namely Whites, will make up a majority—is moving faster than predicted; Houston is already there.

Sociologist Stephen Klineberg of the Kinder Institute at Rice University labels Houston a "prophetic city," one by which the nation can forecast demographic trends in the United States based on what is happening in the Greater Houston area.[11] Based on forty years of tracking and analyzing urban data, his Kinder Area Study—the longest-running longitudinal study of any major city in the country—allows Klineberg to state with confidence that Houston is ahead of the curve in terms of immigration trends. The study also measures attitudes toward immigration, and the research team has found that "on virtually every relevant measure of attitudes and beliefs, Harris County Anglos have been expressing more comfort with the region's burgeoning diversity and more support for the new immigration," while "strong early concerns about the impact of undocumented immigrants in the region are fading rapidly."[12] Since 1995, fears over legal immigration (like resettlement) have been diminishing; views toward increased immigration trend positive; and diversity is seen as a strength for Houston.

One contribution to Houston's diversity is refugee welcome. As one of the top refugee-receiving cities in the United States—and hence the world—over the past decade, resettlement has contributed to Houston's proliferation of languages and cultures, thriving food scene, and ranking as America's most diverse city. Between 2016 and 2018, in the early years of the Donald Trump presidency, unprecedented anti-refugee rhetoric and policies were employed at the national level, yet support for resettlement actually increased among Houston-area residents.

In the late 1970s, the United States received large numbers of Southeast Asian refugees fleeing wars. Many of those refugees came to Houston, resulting in what is now one of the largest Vietnamese communities in the United States. Besides the Vietnamese, Houston has received large numbers of refugees from Myanmar (Burma), Bhutan, the Democratic Republic of Congo, Somalia, Iran, and, more recently, Afghanistan.[13] While Houston is perhaps most famous for evangelical icons like Joel Osteen's Lakewood Church and large Southern Baptist megachurches—including the nation's largest, Second Baptist Church—it is Catholics who constitute the largest Christian population in Houston, represented by the large number of Latinos and Vietnamese refugees who resided or immigrated here decades ago.

11. Klineberg, *Prophetic City*.
12. Klineberg, *Prophetic City*, 212.
13. Houston also receives many Latinos, especially Cubans and Central Americans, but these come under asylum programs different from the refugee admissions program. This is a technical difference explaining why although Houston has a large Hispanic immigrant population, they are not included in this list.

Today Houston continues to be home to many refugees. It has one of the largest refugee consortiums in the nation, with hundreds of nonprofits and churches involved in refugee welcome. While every major city has its unpleasant aspects, personal conversations with refugees will reveal that many new Americans appreciate Houston's friendly people, innovative spirit, job opportunities, affordable housing (comparatively), and diversity. Some even enjoy the weather! Many former refugees have become well-known business, political, and community leaders. Refugee presence has transformed on-the-ground ministries as well, as increasing numbers of refugees come from places of extreme persecution, places missionaries have a difficult time entering to do the type of ministry they could only dream of doing.

Migration Key to Christian Expansion

From the birth of the church, starting with Jesus's disciples, migration—even forced migration—has been key to the expansion of the faith. Global Christianity would not exist without migration. African scholar Jehu Hanciles argues that "migration has been an indispensable element in the advancement of the Christian faith," even more central than missionary activity or imperial design.[14] And yet, at what cost? Theologian Chris Wright reminds us that God is not uninvolved or disinterested in the pain and suffering of migrants. We are to try to "see our contemporary movements in light of God's story . . . and perceive the kingdom of God at work like yeast, or a mustard seed, or a net . . . to help us understand."[15] The kingdom of God is a mystery.

Theologian Peter C. Phan posits that the very character of the church is as a community of migrants; migration is both a permanent reality and the security for the church's existence.[16] At a time when Christian affiliation is in decline in the United States, in line with the trend in the West over the past century, could it be possible, as theologian Susanna Snyder proclaims, that "the United States is, in effect, being re-Christianized by migration"?[17] The decline of Christianity in the US, converting it into a so-called "post-Christian" nation, seems inevitable and obvious if the focus is on the White majority church. However, underneath lies a burgeoning immigrant faith movement that includes some of the world's most diverse, most marginalized, and most

14. Hanciles, *Migration*, 1.
15. Wright, "Shared Human Condition," loc. 2719.
16. Phan, "Christianity as Institutional Migrant," 10.
17. Snyder, "Faces of Migration," 226–27.

persecuted believers, believers who embody a Jas 1 kind of faith (trials and suffering) and a Rev 7 vision (every tribe and tongue).

The US must acknowledge the microcosm of global Christianity that exists within the nation and ask, "What is God doing?"[18] Western, especially American, Christianity not only is no longer the juggernaut it was in terms of producing theologians and systematic theologies and missionaries, it is also on the receiving end of concern and alarm from Majority World Christians who see the US as having lost its "anointing." Historically, the US has been the nation that sends the most missionaries, but now we also *receive* the most missionaries, largely from Majority World nations coming to minister among the immigrant populations here. Those to whom the US exported a particular brand of Christianity are now coming to the States, and they are revitalizing the church. We observe a decline in Christian affiliation in our country and simultaneously see growth, diversity, and vibrancy among immigrant communities, including refugee faith communities. As one of the most religiously diverse countries in the world, the United States has Latino immigration to thank for our global standing as the country with the highest number of Christians.[19] The current concern is that Christianity in the US will shrink in proportion and population; perhaps immigration (including refugee resettlement) will be key to addressing that concern.

Missiologist Sam George, who serves as the catalyst for diasporas for the Lausanne movement, describes Christianity as a faith that was "born to travel."[20] Thus, "the contemporary mission praxis is from everywhere to everywhere, multilateral, multidirectional, sending as well as receiving, with a polycentric global network requiring it to be conceived as polycentrifugal and polycentripetal flow."[21] This multidirectional movement is about more than physical relocation; it includes our posture and heart toward one another. It requires an openness and willingness to learn from one another, especially from those in the margins and those historically powerless. Contemporary mission praxis must invite global voices because Christianity is a global religion.

Emerging Challenges and Opportunities

In recent decades, religious scholars have been increasingly scrutinizing past missionary methods, often unfortunately tainted by colonialism and

18. Snyder, "Faces of Migration," 231.
19. Zurlo, *Global Christianity*, 304.
20. George, "Motus Dei," 179.
21. George, "Motus Dei," 178.

paternalism. This type of historical and self-reflective critique has forced re-examination of approaches to ministry to the marginalized. Refugees have indeed changed the demographics of the church in the US; beyond that, their presence is reshaping our missionary methods. This final section will explore emerging challenges and opportunities, which, while not exclusive to refugee populations, are uniquely informed by two factors that define refugees: migration and persecution. These topics were raised by the dozen or so US-born and refugee Christian leaders interviewed for this chapter.

Generational Gaps

Generational gaps occur in all cultures. Bhutanese Nepali pastor Norbu Tamang of Columbus, Ohio, cites challenges facing his community as new Americans. The immediate barrier they encounter when they arrive is lack of proficiency in the English language and lack of exposure to Western culture. Once the younger generation starts developing fluency in English and serves as translators for their parents, it changes the power dynamics in the family. This is especially difficult for families belonging to honor/shame cultures, from which the majority of refugees in the US come.

Pastor Norbu shares that his people are intimidated by advanced technology, American laws and regulations, and navigating the health-care system. Along with this, refugees are often assigned to strenuous, menial jobs in warehouses with little or no benefits, making them physically and mentally exhausted. Living through persecution leaves trauma scars on all members of the family, but especially on those who were the primary applicants or whoever bore most responsibility in the resettlement process. Older generations often do not seek mental health care for their trauma because of stigmatization, and the effects of trauma get passed on to their children. For the younger generation of Bhutanese Nepalis, issues like alcohol and drug abuse, gambling in casinos, and divorce are slowly taking a grip on their close-knit community.

Culturally and socially speaking, the more conservative Bhutanese Nepalis are not accustomed to the free culture of open relationships, LGBTQ issues, and American race relations. The younger generation, however, is more justice minded, and the frequent lack of shared passions and values drives generations apart. Compounding all this with disintegration with family members back home contributes to depression within the Bhutanese Nepali community; so far, Pastor Norbu knows of 250+ who have committed suicide. Normalizing and funding mental health care could be a lifeline for many immigrant populations, and much more so for those who have experienced extreme trauma.

Ecumenical Cooperation

Newly arrived Christian refugees will encounter other Christian refugees with parallel stories of displacement and loss, but the similarities stop short once it comes to the expression of their Christian faith. Many Christian refugees come from rather homogeneous and monocultural backgrounds; for example, their entire tribe may claim the same religious and ethnic identity. When they encounter Christians from other backgrounds, there may be dissonance and avoidance. Given that resettlement services typically do not segregate or cater to group preferences, it is vital for refugees to willingly engage with other groups for the sake of their integration. Overcoming ingrained patterns and cultural mores is challenging at the beginning. However, over time, many refugees understand the role of cooperation and compromise in a pluralistic society.

Christian groups have historically been at the forefront of refugee welcome. A generous hospitality is often combined with a subconscious or overt agenda to "convert" Christian refugees to a more Western style or tradition. This is usually done with good intentions but does not honor refugees' difference or acknowledge the diversity of God's people. To be sure, all Christians hold imperfect beliefs; learning to hold the tension of difference is key to building bridges while welcoming refugees.

Contemporary mission praxis should focus on collaboration over sponsorship models of the past when working with immigrants. This includes sharing space—and sharing power. Two angles of collaboration should be considered: with refugees and with other groups serving refugees. Evangelicals in particular struggle to set aside differences in theological convictions when working with self-identified Christians holding divergent views. Evangelical faith-based groups who mobilize from a broad spectrum must learn to prioritize areas of unity and harmony, especially when in any given month a large city like Houston may welcome Congolese Seventh-day Adventists, Pentecostal Cubans, Orthodox Eritreans, and Arab Baptists all at once. This provides tremendous opportunity to experience God in new ways and witness the fullness of the gospel across cultures.

Discipleship and Education

Refugee pastors not only take on the spiritual duties related to ministry, but they also tend to the acute needs of their community, especially of newly arrived refugees. They are often called upon to fulfill case management work such as helping newcomers register for social services. This places strain on leaders, resulting in raising up Indigenous leaders too quickly; meanwhile, the needs of the congregation are so urgent, there is not enough time for discipleship. Christians who fled countries with low access to theological education find that basic discipleship programs are very expensive as they often take place outside of their home country.

Refugees experience disruption to their education. Many church leaders lack robust theological training, having to piece together their education over time rather than enroll in a continuous multiyear program. They are caught up in the demands of learning English (if applicable) and finding employment to support themselves or their families and, often, fund the ministry. Few refugee pastors have a doctorate or even a master's degree, as it is prohibitive, both in time and money, to pursue such training. Local churches could provide theological education, but a challenge would be contextualization, both culturally and experientially. Refugees, because of their suffering, often have lived experience of what is only theoretical for native-born Americans, who would benefit greatly from sitting under the teaching of refugees and learning from their faith tested by fire.

Reaching the Least Reached

A recent phenomenon in Houston is the influx of Central Asian or Persian refugees, primarily single Iranian men (Muslim or Christian), along with Afghans, both singles and families, and overwhelmingly Muslim with rare exceptions. Although Christianity in Iran is under 2 percent of the population, Iran is currently recognized as the country with the fastest growing church in the world. Many of those suffering persecution for their faith in Iran are taking a circuitous route to Houston, where there has been for many years a sizable Persian population that continues to grow due to refugee resettlement.[22] Local ministry workers estimate that Houston has the second largest Persian population in the US (the largest is in Los Angeles). It is not uncommon for Persians to claim double identification as

---

22. A common pathway to resettlement for Iranians, especially single males, in recent years has been through Nauru and Manus Island, in Oceania, where migrants were held for a lengthy period in detention camps. According to the Migration Policy Institute, up to 50 percent of refugees from Iran over the past decade identify as Christian.

Christians and Zoroastrian or Shia Muslim. There is both the religious and cultural identity, as well as the tie to historical identity. In Houston, many Persians become Westernized and secularized, and over time, believers may downplay their need for spirituality because their material needs are being met. Discipling and training Persian leaders builds potential to equip the world's fastest growing church; use of technology has facilitated mobilization and made resources available to believers in Iran.

Another Central Asian group with a growing population in Houston is Afghans. In August 2021, Kabul fell rapidly to the Taliban while the US was tapering off its military presence in Afghanistan. Afghans fleeing the takeover boarded airplanes within hours, some with nothing packed, not even personal identification. The United States received seventy-six thousand Afghans in the months to come; some were already in process of applying for resettlement and some had had no intention of leaving at all. Many of those who fled arrived in Houston—about eight thousand, a staggering number for any city to receive in one year, and not counting the thousands who had come prior, resulting in what is now one of the largest Afghan communities in the United States. The Christian population in Afghanistan is extremely low, as low as 0.02 percent.[23] Among the Afghans, Jesus is appearing in dreams and visions, and many Afghans are hearing about Jesus through locals who welcome them. US-based missionaries from around the country have moved to Houston to intentionally befriend Afghans. They want to disciple and develop believers like Asma (a pseudonym) and her husband, who became followers of Christ while living in Afghanistan. During the evacuation, they were separated, and the husband remains in Central Asia, hoping to reunite with his wife soon through the US resettlement program. Other believers, like Omi (a pseudonym), worked with Western nongovernmental organizations in Afghanistan; today, Omi has no hope of ever returning. Despite their personal hardship, believers like them have a vision for what God is doing among the Afghan diaspora. Their presence in the US is expanding the global church in historic and strategic ways.

Every Tribe and Tongue

A common assumption is that once in the US, refugees will bond over their shared displacement. However, tribal instincts tend to remain, if not intensify, in a new homeland, especially if there is perceived inequality over allocation of services and resources. It is important for cross-cultural workers

---

23. See https://joshuaproject.net/countries_photos/AF; accessed May 10, 2023.

to be aware of rival distinctions between groups, that boundaries are drawn not by political maps but by history and culture.

In addition to sociohistorical knowledge, understanding worldview and culture types is also vital to ministry among refugees. Integration happens at a different pace for different groups, and having local friends who are compassionate about culture shock and who can look beyond surface behaviors is a great asset. Within each ethnic or cultural community, power dynamics, family unity, and leadership structures impact receptivity to the gospel, and these are important factors to consider.

Churches must be mindful to not elevate spiritual needs and minimize material ones; this tendency to bifurcate spiritual and humanitarian aspects of refugee care betrays the holistic approach appreciated by people who have endured immense loss. These communities desire justice, advocacy, and empowerment as well as spiritual nurture, and local friends can leverage their power and privilege to benefit refugees whose voices are often quenched. Both refugee communities and native-born welcomers do well to embrace trauma healing, a topic that is unfortunately often taboo on both sides. Without a theology of suffering, the pain and loss experienced by refugees can seem capricious or meaningless, but an understanding of God's sovereignty paired with healing can restore hope.

Hospitality and Mutuality

Analysis of the blind spots of past missionary methods will reveal a problem with prepositions: Is ministry "to" refugees, "for" refugees, or, better yet, "with" and "beyond" refugees?[24] By considering prepositions, workers are immediately challenged to question whether their missionary methods empower or oppress. Snyder states, "Recognizing and supporting the agency and dignity of migrants requires an acting with and alongside, rather than action for or to. Paternalism and a sense of do-gooding largesse can all too easily creep in, particularly among those of us who are Anglo."[25]

Refugees are often treated as an object of conversion, a pawn in a political game, or leverage for religious ends, the last being described by the Lausanne movement in their guidelines for action and witness to refugees as "deplorable."[26] Refugees are sometimes romanticized ("They are always

---

24. George and Adeney, *Refugee Diaspora*, utilizes a diaspora missiology framework to illustrate ministries as mission to refugees, mission through refugees, and mission beyond refugees.

25. Snyder, "Faces of Migration," 236.

26. Consultation on World Evangelization, "Christian Witness to Refugees," art. 5,

joyful and grateful even though they are poor") or infantilized ("They cannot survive without our help") or demonized ("They are dangerous and a threat"). Instead, what can refugees teach us? In particular, the presence of Christian refugees in the country draws attention to the persecuted church. Those who have endured trials and suffering because of their faith identity have much to teach and inspire. In a global church context, all are teachers, and all are learners. Seeing others as equal and fostering two-way relationships engender an appropriate mutuality that offers dignity and respect. Hospitality involves opening our homes to the stranger, but it also hints at the posture of our hearts toward others, at our having a hospitable attitude of welcome.

A final thought on hospitality and mutuality: In the past decade, Muslim refugee resettlement has increased. Is the church making room for non-Christians? Will Christians fight for religious freedom for non-Christian groups? Non-Christian and non-Protestant groups sharpen us and challenge us to embrace both our global human and global Christian families. Nothing like an outsider's view helps reveal prejudice and confront preconceived notions. Furthermore, sometimes non-Christians set an example of devotion that we lack—will we allow their devoutness to convict us?[27]

Conclusion: Unintended Consequences?

Ultimately the end of all mission is a Rev 7 vision of "a great multitude that no one could count, from every nation, tribe, people and language, standing before the throne and before the Lamb" (Rev 7:9 NIV). A great multitude from many nations and tribes is already in the United States—and they are changing the landscape of our country and the church permanently because of migration. The motif of the migrant holds deep theological significance, for both Christian individuals as temporal sojourners and the church as a "pilgrim on the march toward the *Eschaton*."[28] The apostle Paul reminds us that our citizenship is in heaven and that we eagerly await our Savior there (Phil 3:20). This world is not our home, so may we share it with those God brings to our land.

Like the biblical character Joseph, many refugees eventually experience beauty from ashes, good from harm. Without minimizing their suffering, we wonder if God intended forced migration "for good to accomplish what is now being done, the saving of many lives" (Gen 50:20 NIV). Many

---

"Guidelines for Responsible Christian Action," para. 1.

27. Levitt, *God Needs No Passport*, 16–18.

28. Phan, "Christianity as Institutional Migrant," 23.

refugees are coming to faith in the United States, or if already Christians they are sharing their faith so others can be saved. God saved the life of a little girl in a Nepalese camp so her family could come to saving faith, and a little boy ended up as a global leader. The movement of God through migrants cannot be overlooked.

Bibliography

Consultation on World Evangelization. "Christian Witness to Refugees." Lausanne, June 16–27, 1980. Lausanne Occasional Paper 5. https://lausanne.org/content/lop/lop-5.

General Assembly, The. "Protocol Relating to the Status of Refugees." United Nations, Dec. 16, 1966. https://www.ohchr.org/en/instruments-mechanisms/instruments/protocol-relating-status-refugees.

George, Sam. "Motus Dei (The Move of God): A Theology and Missiology for a Moving World." In *Global Migration and Christian Faith: Implications for Identity and Mission*, edited by M. Daniel Carroll R. and Vincent E. Bacote, 166–81. Eugene, OR: Cascade, 2021.

George, Sam, and Miriam Adeney, eds. *Refugee Diaspora: Missions amid the Greatest Humanitarian Crisis of our Times*. Littleton, CO: William Carey, 2018.

Hanciles, Jehu J. *Migration and the Making of Global Christianity*. Grand Rapids: Eerdmans, 2021.

Klineberg, Stephen L. *Prophetic City: Houston on the Cusp of a Changing America*. New York: Avid Reader, 2020.

Levitt, Peggy. *God Needs No Passport: Immigrants and the Changing American Religious Landscape*. New York: New, 2009.

National Archives Foundation. "Refugee Act of 1980." National Archives Foundation, n.d. https://www.archivesfoundation.org/documents/refugee-act-1980/.

Phan, Peter C. "Christianity as an Institutional Migrant: Historical, Theological, and Ethical Perspectives." In *Christianities in Migration: The Global Perspective*, edited by Elaine Padilla and Peter C. Phan, 9–36. Christianities of the World. London: Palgrave McMillan, 2015.

Snyder, Susanna. "Faces of Migration: US Christianity in the Twenty-First Century." In *Christianities in Migration: The Global Perspective*, edited by Elaine Padilla and Peter C. Phan. Christianities of the World. London: Palgrave McMillan, 2015.

United Nations Conference of Plenipotentiaries on the Status of Refugees and Stateless Persons Convened under General Assembly Resolution 429 (V) of 14 December 1950. "Convention Relating to the Status of Refugees." United Nations, July 28, 1951. https://www.ohchr.org/en/instruments-mechanisms/instruments/convention-relating-status-refugees.

Wright, Chris. "A Shared Human Condition: An Old Testament Refugee Perspective." In *Refugee Diaspora: Missions amid the Greatest Humanitarian Crisis of our Times*, edited by Sam George and Miriam Adeney, loc. 2693–874. Littleton: William Carey, 2018. Kindle.

Zurlo, Gina A. *Global Christianity: A Guide to the World's Largest Religion from Afghanistan to Zimbabwe*. Grand Rapids: Zondervan Academic, 2022.

Chapter 14

Evangelicals and Systems of Domination
A Call for Reformation

JAMES K. WELLMAN JR.

> To a great extent, the evangelical church in America supported the status quo. It supported slavery; it supported segregation; it preached against any attempt of the black man to stand on his own two feet. And where there were those who sought to communicate the gospel to black people, it was always done in a way to make sure that they stayed cool. "We will preach the gospel to those folks so they won't riot; we will preach the gospel to them so that we can keep the lid on the garbage pail."
>
> —SKINNER, "URBANA"

I'VE BEEN THINKING ABOUT American Evangelicalism for much of my career. I coauthored a recent book on American megachurches called *High on God: How Megachurches Won the Heart of America*. Katie Corcoran, Kate Stockly, and I found that American megachurches are communities of evangelical faith that dutifully serve their attendees, present a gospel for all, and often anchor some of the most powerful ministries in their cities and towns. Critics have complained that megachurches subvert the gospel; we found otherwise. And yet, after thinking about the recent state of the American evangelical movement, I had to think beyond our megachurch research. I read a wide array of informed writing on the American evangelical movement, and my concerns only grew.

Megachurches tend to cover and blur some of the major tendencies in Evangelicalism, and for good reason. In megachurches, numbers matter, maintaining members and money is critical, thus contentious issues are ignored and downplayed, which often neuters the cultural and political demands of the faith to maintain an ability to attract crowds. For this essay, I found Tom Skinner's 1970 Urbana jeremiad an enlightening reminder about the spiritual conditions of the White evangelical church in America.[1] Indeed, below the surface of flash, charisma, and blessings, forms of racism, greed, and White nationalism linger as the shadows of the White evangelical Christian church. If reforming is possible, one must face one's sins to do so. At this point, I am doubtful that the present evangelical movement can hear "another side" on theological and public issues at all—they've turned their back on critics—taking a page from Donald Trump, their new messiah. A large swath of American Evangelicalism has become a political vehicle for "winning" and a form of spiritual vengeance against "liberals," whether Christian or not. Thus, I propose a new reading of the American evangelical church, based on new data, which includes critiques and warnings. Large swaths of American Evangelicalism seek to build a form of Christian nationalism that is a grave danger to our American democracy.

Religious and political movements have been known to repent and turn around. I hope the North American evangelical churches will repent. I go to one that has not been politicized and corrupted by power. The present evangelical Christian church needs prophets to confront its errors, and leaders who care and seek to mend differences rather than to separate. Christians, in this frame, are called peacemakers and in my language *covenantal pluralists*.[2] Covenantal pluralists take their faith seriously, and they seek a higher ground of wisdom, charity, and peace for all. They know that their version of truth is limited by their own past and confined by their experience in the world. This is what I call a *cosmopolitan point of view* that knows that one has only their own perspective on what is true about their faith or their country. Thus, this essay will be a critical take on the recent developments with the American evangelical church, which I call its political and cultural corruption. I end the essay with hope and a vision of a *covenantal pluralism* that I think can bring peace rather than conflict. We need to look at the hard truths of where we've been, where we are, and come back with courage to bear witness to the common good and well-being of all people no matter their race, class, sexuality, nation, or religion.

1. See Skinner, "Urbana."
2. See Seiple and Hoover, *Religious Literacy, Pluralism*, 1.

Evangelicalism and of Systems of Domination

Tom Skinner's 1970 jeremiad at Urbana remains as relevant today as it was back then. In many ways, very little has changed in the American evangelical culture. Skinner would not be surprised that Donald Trump became president in 2016 nor that he was nearly reelected with a wide majority of the White evangelical vote in 2020. And even now, if Trump isn't in jail, he will likely be nominated as the Republican candidate for the presidency in 2024. What this clarifies is that for many Evangelicals, forms of patriarchy, racism, and greed remain deeply entangled in their souls, beliefs, and organizations. I believe this not only needs to be faced but also to be explained. How can a financially corrupt, serial sexual offender be the leading candidate for one of America's major political parties? The answer is the support of White American evangelical Christians. By large majorities American Evangelicals support Trump now more than ever, and a similar majority of evangelical voters will likely support him in 2024. Why do they support an accused rapist, a financial loser, and someone who has very little interest in them or in governing the country on any sort of normal basis? Tom Skinner's 1970 jeremiad is a prophetic witness to the madness of our time. I argue that Skinner (who died in 1994) knew the deeply racist nature of America, and so would not have been surprised that Donald Trump may very well be our president again in 2024. Whiteness in America is intimately linked to patriarchal power, racism, and religious nationalism. Reform starts only by facing our deepest prejudices.

In 1970, Tom Skinner's fifty-eight-minute talk at Urbana was startling excavation aimed squarely at the sins and corruptions of the American evangelical spirit. His speech contextualized himself, America's sins of racism and classism, White Evangelicals, and his own deep understanding of a gospel that promised no simple answer, and yet gave freedom to all, including Tom Skinner. Skinner explained that as a young Black man, "I had twenty-two notches on the handle of my knife, which meant that my blade had gone into the bodies of twenty-two people, and I didn't care. All that mattered to me was that Tom Skinner got what he wanted, and how he got it made absolutely no difference." Skinner was no innocent. He was raised in mid-century Black Harlem of that period, with a 40-percent poverty rate, where rats "chewed Black babies to death," and no White man would come or go. But what changed him was not a "White Christ," lulling around with the angels, someone "who would not survive in my neighborhood . . . rather [Jesus] was a gutsy contemporary, radical revolutionary, with hair on his chest and dirt under his fingernails." For Skinner, the premise of "Scripture is that the human order is archaic, impractical; it is no good, it is infested with demonic power, with sin, racism, hate, envy, jealousy, and worldliness. And the whole purpose of Christ coming into the world was to overthrow the demonic human system and to establish his own kingdom in the hearts of men." Skinner followed this radical line of reasoning with his formal pronouncement: "I must renounce any attempt to wed Jesus Christ off to the American system. I disassociate myself from any argument that says God is on our side . . . that God is a capitalist, that God is a militarist, that God is the worker behind our system." And, as Skinner later said, commenting about Jesus's crucifixion, "Three days later Jesus Christ pulled off one of the great political coups of all time: he got up out of the grave . . . to establish a new order that is not built on man." Skinner concludes by saying Jesus came to "proclaim liberation to the captive, preach sight to the blind, set at liberty them that are bruised, go into the world, and tell men who are bound mentally, spiritually, and physically, 'The liberator has come!'"[3]

Anthea Butler's recent book on *White Evangelical Racism: The Politics of Morality in America* (2021) draws up the racial curtain on White Evangelicalism in America. Butler hails Skinner as a man of integrity and faith. Butler, as a fellow African American, started out in the evangelical camp though she has since walked away. Her book is a stunning refutation of the bad faith in her former community. It is the work of a heartbroken and head-spinning history of the corruption and final collapse of a racist movement called White Evangelicalism. As an African American she critiques the movement and rejects it as a failed racist train wreck. But her rejection does not stop her from seeking to understand the tradition. Indeed, it motivated her to seek to explain it more thoroughly, the roots of Black prejudice in the tradition and the kind of White nationalism it has enabled and produced. For her, any explanation that argues that racism is ancillary to White Evangelicalism is suspect. Butler declares that for White Christianity, racism is "not a disqualification,"[4] but indeed an expectation in the American Christian tradition. Billy Graham fought against integration in the South, Whites came out against integration, civil rights, and interracial marriage. Butler declares in American religion "Christianity is a race."[5]

For Butler, racism becomes the turnkey for how much White Evangelicals despise "the other," whether it's immigrants, Muslims, or the LGBTQ community. For her, all these groups are targets—at best, sinners; at worst, people who must be removed or deported and forced to keep their beliefs and practices to themselves. To be evangelical in the US is another

---

3. Skinner, "Urbana."
4. Butler, *White Evangelical Racism*, 7.
5. Butler, *White Evangelical Racism*, 9.

way of saying that one is White—ethnicity, nationality, and religion become the master key to the lock of privilege, pride, and power in the United States. Surely, some of us may say that any marking of a group is a form of prejudice itself. After all, there are many Evangelicals whom I have seen invite fellowship with these so-called despised groups, not only to convert them, but simply because that is what Christian hospitality expects. And, in my own experience, I know many who in the White evangelical community who are inclusive.[6] And yet, positionality is critical. Being an African American woman changes everything, and that is just the point. As a White male cisgender heterosexual and a US citizen, I embody a privilege and I am accepted in these communities no matter what, even though I despise this kind of perverse rejection of differences based on religion, sexuality, ethnicity, or nationality. I can pass, and I have this privilege in nearly any context. Anthea Butler does not, and she maintains her dignity by exposing a vile prejudice operating as a religion.

As I prepared for this work on Evangelicals, I read Thomas Kidd's *Who Is an Evangelical?* Kidd is a fair and thorough scholar, almost to the point where one doesn't recognize Kidd's own strong convictions. He is an Evangelical, and toward the end of the book he attempts to be critical of the movement. But the contrast to Butler is staggering. Kidd's first instinct is to protect Evangelicalism. He argues with pride that the well-known White pastor John Piper publicly refused to vote for Donald Trump in 2016, even as 81 percent of White Evangelicals did. Kidd also notes that, in 1995, his Southern Baptist Convention *finally* apologized for being slave owners. And—yes, slavery is wrong. And yet, their robust support of Trump as president, a known philander, bigot, and tyrant is somehow okay. Indeed, Kidd seems disappointed that Donald Trump won the 2016 election, with his now-famous 81 percent of American evangelical vote. Kidd notes that "something had *apparently* broken in the White evangelicals' community." Kidd's critique of Trump focuses on his personal morality: "A framed cover of the soft-core pornographic *Playboy* featuring Trump hung on the wall."[7] To rationalize this choice by Evangelicals, Kidd mentions Trump's promise to choose pro-life Supreme Court judges. Kidd argues that many Evangelicals voted for "Trump in spite of his personal characteristics, supposing that he would be better on evangelical concerns like abortion and judges, or on the economy."[8] Kidd asks the question on the second to last page, "Perhaps I am naïve to hope that there remains a core of practicing orthodox evangelicals

---

6. See Wellman, *Evangelical vs. Liberal* and *High on God*.
7. Kidd, *Who Is an Evangelical*, 145; emphasis added.
8. Kidd, *Who Is an Evangelical*, 149.

who really do care more about salvation and spiritual matters than access to Republican power."[9] In Kidd's work, there is little concern or critique for Trump's racist and bigoted belief systems. Kidd focuses on right belief and right reading of the Scripture, as well as a few pages on ethical and moral clauses in the American evangelical common culture. Kidd confirms Butler's comment that Black Evangelicals are at best taken for granted in the White evangelical world, and at worst ignored and viewed as second-class citizens.

Butler's work picks up on this "color-blind gospel," which, on first take, may seem to be an unbiased perspective, that is, to enter all interactions without prejudice. And yet, as we know from nearly every experience we have in social contacts, we are each full of biases, based on all sort of factors that motivate human reactions. Indeed, Butler confirms these prejudices by her own felt consistent need to "emulate whiteness."[10] And even more profoundly, Tom Skinner took from his own African American cultural figures what it meant to be a Black, to be proud, to be a man: "Understand that for those of us who live in the Black community, it was not the Evangelical who came and taught us our worth and dignity as Black men. It was not the Bible-believing Fundamentalist who stood up and told us that Black was beautiful. It was not the Evangelical who preached to us that we should stand on our two feet and be men, be proud that Black was beautiful and that God could work his life out through our redeemed blackness. Rather, it took Malcolm X, Stokely Carmichael, Rap Brown, and the brothers to declare to us our dignity. God will not be without a witness."[11]

White and Black American Christians live in entirely different worlds. Jemar Tisby, an African American historian of American Christianity, argues in his important book *The Color of Compromise: The Truth about the American Church's Complicity in Racism* that there is a stunning contrast between American Christian Whites and Blacks. As Tisby sums it up, both White and Black Christians generally believe that "a personal relationship with Jesus Christ is necessary for saving faith."[12] But that is where the agreements stop, particularly when it comes to the wealth gap between the races: "Sixty-two percent of white evangelicals attribute poverty among black people to a lack of motivation, while 31 percent of black Christians said the same. And just 27 percent of White evangelicals attribute the wealth gap to racial discrimination, while 72 percent of Blacks cite discrimination as a major

---

9. Kidd, *Who Is an Evangelical*, 155.
10. Butler, *White Evangelical Racism*, 20.
11. Skinner, "Urbana."
12. Tisby, *Color of Compromise*, 176.

cause of the discrepancy."[13] Indeed, at once, two groups are practicing the same religion—Christianity—in the same country but experiencing their lives in terms of poverty and wealth in dramatically different ways. But how does this translate into White/Black interactions? There are clearly radical differences, which are judged based on dramatically different perspectives, that tell the story of these two groups and shape how they live, how well they live, and what they think of one another. And the key variable continues to be race, with class as a subset of the assumptions gathered around these two groups. Whites assume that Blacks are not up to the task of making it in a "White" world, and Blacks come to recognize that the White world is simply *a different world*. Imagine, just for a moment, if American Whites awakened to the fact that Blacks were indeed even more religious and active in their Christian faith than Whites, and yet they were dramatically cut off from financial success simply because of their skin color—a difference that has undercut Black success for more than a hundred and fifty years, ever since emancipation. What is the single variable here? Race. And from it has come discrimination and violence against American Blacks, many of whom are descendants from the era of slavery. The heinous nature of slavery is brutally simple—the South took advantage of a group of immigrants from Africa, turning them into objects of manipulation for their pleasure and their profit—for no less than 170 years. And so, many Whites act as if this form of human servitude would have no long-term consequences. Southern Whites fought a Civil War to preserve this criminal enterprise to use this group for their leisure and satisfaction. After the Civil War Whites continued to subjugate the African American population by limiting their chances economically, culturally, politically, and socially. And all of this could be changed in a moment, particularly if White Evangelicals would simply wake up to those who are their brothers and sisters and say: *You are our brothers and sisters in the faith. We injured you for 170 years, and you are deserving of our repentance and our economic and political reparations.* Listen to Thomas Kidd, one of the leading experts on White Evangelicalism. Kidd details the cost of the 81 percent of White Evangelicals voting for Donald Trump—a man who is a known misogynist and racist:

> Eighty-one percent. The damage caused by evangelical white voter's support for Trump is substantial, leading many women and people of color to question the fundamental integrity of the movement. In the aftermath of the election, stories proliferated about blacks, Hispanics, and other people leaving evangelical churches and dropping the evangelical label. The 81 percent

---

13. Tisby, *Color of Compromise*, 176.

figure has renewed a sometimes-acrimonious debate among scholars about what the term evangelical really means. Meanwhile, pollsters and the media have produced countless stories about how white evangelical keep supporting Trump in the face of virtually any controversy.[14]

Plainly speaking, White Evangelicalism is a racially driven political interest group that has adopted a religious label to hide their larceny. Evangelicals should decide whether they want to be identified more officially as a *hate group*. I don't identify as an Evangelical, but I do attend an evangelical church for family reasons, and generally find *my* group more open to critique. Nonetheless, I don't think I would be honest if I didn't suggest identifying White Evangelicals in this way.

"God will not be without a witness." Skinner's point is to wake White people up and to say, "Drop the pretense, White Evangelicals. You are no longer worthy of the name you claim—the church of Jesus Christ. This One who lived and died for the truth did not compromise with the orders of his society. A society with every level of privilege as well as slaves and servants." Some of my White friends may say, "Well, Jim, so you think you are truly the righteous one." And I would say, "No, I am as much a fake Christian as the next White male in our society. I am a sin-sick sinner of a man. I like my privilege as much as the next rich White man. But at least I am willing to call a fake a fake; White Christianity has and is doing terrible harm to the name of Christ. We, I, us, must repent of our deep racism toward our sisters and brothers of Color." Some might say, "Well, they have had every chance to lift themselves up." And then I would drop on them these statistics of Black male education, opportunity, and income—all diminished in context of White privilege. The bootstrap theory is simply a lie: Tom Skinner had it right in 1970, and the fact that these differences remain today is an even greater form of outrage than in his time:

> But, you see, this bootstrap theory is one of the most damnable lies being preached in America today. There is no such thing as pulling oneself up by the bootstraps. Nobody pulls himself up by the bootstraps. Any of us who are anything at all are there because somebody opened some doors, somebody gave us some breaks, somebody provided some opportunities. In the case of Black people, it is difficult to pull yourself up by the bootstraps when somebody keeps cutting the straps. My nationalist friends said to me, "Tom, it's a fine thing that you're a brilliant student. It's a fine thing that you show the brilliant qualifications of

---

14. Kidd, *Who Is an Evangelical*, 149.

leadership. But if you've got any ideas of making it in our kind of society, you'd better think again." And here's what they'd say: "This is the White man's world, and in his world, he controls things from the top to the bottom. He might allow you to be a jazz player, a rock-and-roll singer, or the janitor in his building. But he will not allow you to compete with him on an open basis to make a tangible contribution to society. He does not consider you to be his equal. You may be able to make $30,000 a year and move into the best of communities, but as soon as you move out there, they're going to protest so loudly, you will never make it. If you do succeed in moving, there will those who put up their 'For Sale' signs and run. And among those people who will sell their homes will be those Bible-toting Christians who say 'Christ is the answer.'"[15]

But instead of true and humble repentance we hear of more threats and challenges by White evangelical culture to take over our country in the name of Christ, by using any means necessary. Philip Gorski and Samuel Perry's recent book *The Flag and the Cross: White Christian Nationalism and the Threat to American Democracy* (2022) is an startling and exquisitely well-documented evaluation of the agenda of the most contemporary players in the world of White Christian nationalism in the United States. In a sense, this, too, is yet another subculture within the American White church—a subculture that is more than ready to take the kid gloves off and to go to war with American democracy, for the sake of Jesus Christ, but in a form of violence and racism that we have not seen before.

The Daunting Threat of White Christian Nationalism

I have studied and taught on religious nationalism for some time now, and I've seen the consequences and results of religious nationalism in other countries, what happens to minorities, to wit—Muslims in India, Rohingya in Myanmar, or the work of evangelical Christians in Brazil that have led to the persecution of Afro-Brazilian religions. Religious nationalism creates terror for cultures and is a pox on democracy. Gorski and Perry's *The Flag and the Cross* argues that American Christian nationalists have plans, a strategy, and they will not be stopped by words, no matter how convicting. Gorski and Perry's recent research shows that any thought of peacemaking or what we call *covenantal pluralism*, the gift of Roger Williams—is dead to most American Evangelicals. Many contemporary White Evangelicals find

---

15 Skinner, "Urbana."

this type of liberal thinking as a weakness and lack of conviction. Faith is now a forcing mechanism, and because one believes that their religion is true, forcing faith is now accepted as right, good, and appropriate not only in countries like Saudi Arabia or Pakistan but in budding movements inside the US: "The characteristics we link with white Christian nationalism could all be considered component of what's commonly called 'populism,' an orientation or ideology that pits corrupt 'elites' against virtuous common folk. Its components are, among other things, scapegoating of minorities; distrust of science, the media, and 'establishment' politicians; corresponding trust in strongman leaders; and conspiratorial thinking. White Christian nationalism unites all these elements. As a result, it is one of the strongest currents within American right-wing populism and one the main drivers of political polarization."[16]

One of the major movements in right wing populism is a distrust of experts and a trust in a strongman leader—Donald Trump. Trump is believed rather than experts in medicine, politics, or religion. This trust in "the" leader is followed by a concomitant distrust in all experts. This occurred during the coronavirus outbreak, many refusing to listen to the medical community, which was led by conspiratorial thinking about the origins of the virus. Not surprisingly, as one narrows the "leaders" one believes, it decreases one's "circle of empathy" and increases faith in the leader who confirms one's prejudices. This happens in broader areas of politics and the economy, as leaders promote the belief in free market ideals (found almost exclusively among Whites) and a belief in free market capitalism, which is often identified as the crown jewel of White Americans.

White American conservative Christians deny that "Jesus was a socialist." Distorting all notions of the actual historical context of Jesus's ministry that show him practicing a communal way of life, in which giving and receiving are based on need and generosity from those who have to those without. Jesus gives his followers the Lord's Prayer, which at its heart practices a common daily practice of "Give us this day our daily bread." In its stead, many American Christians substitute an ethic of scarcity, where one should get as much as one can and save it for oneself. As Gorski and Perry explain, "To follow Jesus and love America is to love individualism and libertarian freedom, expressed in allegiance to capitalism and unequivocal rejection of socialism."[17] And this is noticeably a White phenomenon in the United States, in which White America "conflates racial, religious, and national identity . . . and pines for cultural and political power that

16. Gorski and Perry, *Flag and Cross*, 28.
17. Gorski and Perry, *Flag and Cross*, 40.

demographic and cultural shifts have increasingly threatened."[18] Indeed, in November 2020, roughly 20 percent of White Evangelicals [who were surveyed] believed the US Constitution was divinely inspired, and "nearly 80 percent affirmed constitutional originalism."[19]

"The MAGA narrative is not only secularized white Christian nationalism; it is a reactionary version. In the Puritans' Promised Land narrative, recall, blood was the master metaphor linking blood belonging (race), blood sacrifice (religion), and blood conquest (nation)."[20] In this vein, Christian nationalism is a form of taking back order for the sake of a righteous cause, which is who and what White people do. Thus, outsiders, individuals outside those who are White Christian and US citizens, can be ignored, or worse—righteous order can be and should be taken by force. Listening to another side is seen as compromise and a waste of time, and minorities are troublemakers or worse: "White violence is the ultimate source of order; Black or leftist violence, by contrast, is the ultimate source of disorder."[21] The politicization of Christian identity is not only claiming a membership in a political group or an ideological tribe, but also "defending a certain 'way of life.'"[22] This also means the need for conspiracy thinking: "In religious versions of the QAnon theory, moreover, Trump is often cast in the role of an avenging Christ, who would punish the pederasts on a day of judgment known as the 'the Storm.'"[23]

"White Christian nationalism is a form of what is often called *ethnonationalism*. It defines national belonging in terms of race, religions, and native birth. Liberal democracy rests on what is called *civic nationalism*. It defines the nation in terms of values, laws, and institutions."[24] Chris Seiple and I suggested a system in which *covenantal pluralism* and *faithful patriotism* are the ideal types of democratic cultural, civic, and state organizations. I put it at the center of a mapping of this alternative worldview, on which we plotted various cultures and countries, assuming that nationalism was the most typical of how nation-states organized themselves, on a grid that has four parts. In the top left quadrant, we placed religious nationalism, with Saudi Arabia, Russia, Pakistan, Turkey, Egypt, India, and to a lesser extent, the United States as featured in the top left quadrant. In the upper right

18. Gorski and Perry, *Flag and Cross*, 43–44.
19. Gorski and Perry, *Flag and Cross*, 44.
20. Gorski and Perry, *Flag and Cross*, 85.
21. Gorski and Perry, *Flag and Cross*, 102.
22. Gorski and Perry, *Flag and Cross*, 107.
23. Gorski and Perry, *Flag and Cross*, 113.
24. Gorski and Perry, *Flag and Cross*, 114.

quadrant, we plotted secular nationalist states, featuring North Korea and China. In the lower right quadrant, the ideal type is secular internationalism, featuring France, Germany, and England, with the United Nations as an ideal of what it means to live in democracy and international relations at the heart of an ideal that claims a national identity in relationships of both peace and cooperation with others. The lower left quadrant was what we have called *spiritual cosmopolitanism*; to some extent, with tongue in cheek, I feature California as an ideal type—combining pluralism and patriotism in cooperation and mutual learning. At its heart it is what we call *covenantal pluralism* and *faithful patriotism*. Here we are drawing on Roger Williams's early work in the US, which stressed a cautionary tale about government, a need to trust and respect difference and pluralism—recognizing the temptation of provincialism and nationalism. The two together are the siren calls of tyrants, whether religious or secular, who suffocate freedom, draw power to themselves, and force secularism and/or religion on populations. The road less taken and the one more fragile than others is *spiritual internationalism*, and here I placed Canada as a potential embodiment of this ideal—a nation that is deeply committed to pluralism, multiple religions, and European forms of deep pluralism. A country that assumes a pluralistic democracy with provinces that are diverse, ethnically, religiously, and culturally, Canada seems to give us all a lesson in covenantal pluralism, where patriotism is important but decentered, and the willingness to shift and change depends on the need of the other.

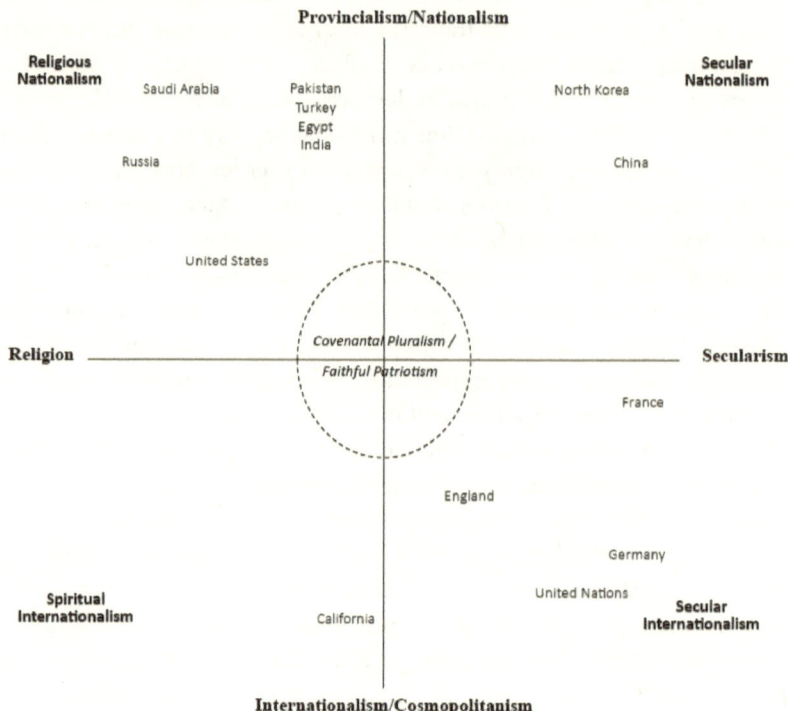

Figure 1: Religion, Nationalism, and Internationalism

Why is this mapping helpful? I think it gives us a sense that, in fact, nations can change dramatically. Few would have thought a generation ago that the United States would be so close to breaking apart due to a religious and political demagogue like Donald Trump. As a careful observer of the culture, religion, and politics of the United States, I was shocked by the rapid nature of Trump's ability to change the trajectory of the US. And even now, we don't know the fate of the country. Russell Moore, a longtime Southern Baptist leader, and one who held on tightly to the independence and pluralism within the Southern Baptist Convention, was simply dumbstruck by the ease with which the convention took a rightward turn and a sudden and deep passion for the White Christian nationalism of Donald Trump. As Moore laments:

> My situation was especially public, but it wasn't especially unusual. The issues—political fusion with Trumpism, Christian nationalism, white-identity backlash, the dismissing of issues such as abuse as "social justice" secularism, and several others—are (some of them or all of them) dividing almost every

church, almost every family, almost every friendship I know. Every institution—from the presidency to local churches to family dining room tables—seems to be in crisis, almost to the point of breakdown. Whereas at the beginning of my ministry parents used to seek my counsel about their young-adult children walking away from the faith, I was now more likely to hear from committed younger Christians wondering how to connect with parents who were politically radicalized by conspiracy theories. I was less likely to hear about wayward children going out into "the real world" and losing their faith as I was to hear about wayward parents retreating into an imaginary world and losing their minds. After a near-decade of American evangelical Christianity defined almost wholly in the public view with Trumpism or racism or the predatory sexual or financial or psychological power dynamics of countless leaders, the outside world didn't seem to be judging us by "secular" standards as by our own. Weighed in those balances, we were found wanting. Our kingdom was divided and couldn't stand.[25]

Moore, a national leader of deep respect in the Baptist family, was dismissed by his Southern Baptist convention in large part because he would not bow to Trump, to Trump's form of religious and political nationalism. What followed was predictable: Southern Baptists proceeded to cover up one institutional sin after another, whether in terms of sexual exploitation or other shenanigans of its leadership. Moore, who had been an esteemed leader, was dismissed in part because he would not bow to a new Republican right-wing and White supremacist leadership, which touted President Trump and had no interest in fair play, or in pluralism or covenants of difference.

Conclusion and Confession

I never predicted that a form of parochial and racist religious nationalism would be the potential fate of American Protestant Evangelicalism in the United States. Clearly, I was not truly aware of the depth of racism in our county, hoping against hope it would somehow go away. People of Color in our country knew better. Canada marks a different historical trajectory with an elemental covenantal pluralism at its heart and a faithful patriotism that is humble and progressive. The United States needs to wake up to the corrosive elements of racism, parochialism, and nationalism before it is too late. Our sisters and brothers to the North give us hope and a vision. I would

25. Moore, *Losing Our Religion*, 11.

argue if you are not concerned and troubled by recent events, then you are not paying attention. Americans take for granted that our democracy and our freedoms are guaranteed and that nothing can change that fact. The truth is when it comes to political systems, nothing is guaranteed. My fear is that the conservative evangelical religious nationalists are working hard to subvert our system and most of us are on vacation, believing that nothing and no one will "change our way of life." Many would say Donald Trump is a harmless and an idiotic figure whose only interest is money, power, and women. Some of this is true. Trump, for most of his life, has simply taken advantage of opportunities that have dropped into his lap. His one skill is exploiting these advantages and using them to gain power for the growth of his kingdom and wealth. Trump is a master exploiter of weakness. He sees in the White American evangelical community an easy mark. The faith of American Christianity is in disarray.

I'll finish by making a fullhearted plea for the reform of American Evangelicalism and American Christianity. The faith's reputation is in shambles. Few outside the Christian community have any respect for who and what we've become. What should we do? Repent. Repent for our cynicism about race, money, sexuality, and politics. Let us look to our Canadian friends up North as exemplars. I remain a Christian. I still believe in the Christ of Scripture. I am neither an Evangelical nor a liberal Christian. Jesus came to redeem us from sin, selfishness, and greed. Too often American Christians make selfishness and greed the heart of their faith. It's a sham. I still think the Christ of Scripture leads us into life and life abundant. How? Christian America needs to repent of her sins; refuse selfishness; respect others' sexualities; and seek to understand the other in all their difference, period. We must remember that we are all one in Christ's body—to damage or hurt the other is to damage and destroy the body of Christ. We are to humble ourselves before God. Judge no one. Forgive all. Work on our own character. Repent of greed and selfishness. Accept all humans as born in the image of God. God is the judge, we are not. Seek the common good, not our own. Care for the environment; it is God's body. Care for all people, gay, straight, Black, White. All people, no matter what. Give away your life and wealth for the sake of the common good. Christian America must repent. This is my hope.

Bibliography

Butler, Anthea. *White Evangelical Racism: The Politics of Morality in America*. Chapel Hill: University of North Carolina Press, 2021.

Gorski, Philip S., and Samuel L. Perry. *The Flag and the Cross: White Christian Nationalism and the Threat to American Democracy.* Oxford: Oxford University Press, 2022.

Kidd, Thomas S. *Who Is an Evangelical: The History of a Movement in Crisis.* New Haven, CT: Yale University Press, 2019.

Moore, Russell. *Losing Our Religion: An Altar Call for Evangelical America.* New York: Sentinel, 2023.

Seiple, Chris, and Dennis R. Hoover, eds. *The Routledge Handbook of Religious Literacy, Pluralism, and Global Engagement.* Routledge International Handbooks. Oxford: Routledge, 2022.

Skinner, Tom. "The U.S. Racial Crisis and World Evangelicalism." Urbana, 1970. https://urbana.org/video/us-racial-crisis-and-world-evangelism.

Tisby, Jemar. *The Color of Compromise: The Truth about the American Church's Complicity in Racism.* Grand Rapids: Zondervan, 2019.

Wellman, James K., Jr. *Evangelical vs. Liberal: The Clash of Christian Cultures in the Pacific Northwest.* New York: Oxford University Press, 2008.

———, et al. *High on God: How Megachurches Won the Heart of America.* New York: Oxford University Press, 2020.

Time Line: North America

Brett Knowles

American church historian Martin Marty has aptly commented that (in religion as elsewhere) "both hurricanes and glacial forces leave altered landscapes."[1] The "hurricane" represents sudden, drastic change, the product of clearly identifiable catalytic events such as, for example, the Second Vatican Council from 1962 to 1965. By contrast, the "glacier" represents a process of gradual, subtle change, which may not be attributable to any specific causative event or series of events. These "glacial" forces therefore symbolize slow, cumulative progressions of attitudes and orientations, which cannot always be placed within a time line of dates in the same way as catalytic "hurricane" events.

Nevertheless, events are significant markers of historical process, and this time line contains entries from North America covering the period from 1539 (i.e., the baptism of the first Indigenous converts) to the present day. Country locations are placed in bold type at the end of each entry and are derived from the United Nations, Department of Economic and Social Affairs, Statistics Division (UNSD) website.[2]

---

1. Marty, "Religion in America 1935–1985," 1.
2. See http://unstats.un.org/unsd/methodology/m49/.

Year and Event

1539 Three unnamed Iroquois, kidnapped along with their chief Donnaconna by French explorer Jacques Cartier during his second expedition to Canada in 1536, receive baptism in France, the first Canadian Natives to do so; Donnaconna himself dies in France the same year, reputedly a Christian. [**Canada**]

1604–5 French colonists establish a settlement at Île-Saint Croix in Passamaquoddy Bay; after almost perishing due to the lack of resources during the winter months, the settlement relocates across the Bay of Fundy to Port Royal in Nova Scotia, where British invasion forces finally destroy it in 1613. [**Canada**]

1607 English Anglicans under the leadership of Captain Edward Maria Wingfield set up the first settler colonies at Jamestown in Virginia with the intention of reproducing the Church of England across the Atlantic. [**United States of America**]

1608 French explorer Samuel de Champlain founds the Catholic settler city of Québec near the mouth of the St. Lawrence River and begins to consolidate the colonies of "New France" in continental North America; the Jesuits begin missionary work here three years later. [**Canada**]

1613 A British invasion force destroys the Jesuit colony at Penobscot Bay in the French colony of Acadia (Nova Scotia and Maine) and drives out the Jesuit missionaries, who return to Québec to resume missionary work in 1625. [**United States of America, Canada**]

1620 The *Mayflower* Pilgrim fathers (led by a party of Independent Separatists, who had previously sought freedom from religious persecution in Leyden in the Netherlands) land at Plymouth Rock, thereby beginning the settlement of Puritan and Separatist colonies in New England. [**United States of America**]

1626 The Dutch East India Company founds a colony on Manhattan Island on the Hudson River, naming it New Amsterdam; the appointment of a Dutch Reformed minister to the colony two years later introduces Presbyterian models of church polity to the American colonies. [**United States of America**]

1629 King Charles I grants the Massachusetts Bay Company a charter empowering it to trade and colonize in New England, and to "win and invite" the Natives to Christianity. [**United States of America**]

1630 Puritan settlers, driven from England by the repressive measures of King Charles I because of their attempts to reform the Church of England from within, establish the first Puritan colonies in Massachusetts Bay, settled under the Massachusetts Bay Company charter of the previous year. [**United States of America**]

1634 Cecilius Calvert, the second Lord Baltimore, inherits a grant of American land that had been made to his father by the British Crown in 1632 and sets it up as the Catholic settlement of Maryland, a colony where Catholics could live in peace. [**United States of America**]

1636 After being expelled from the colony of Massachusetts for spreading "new and dangerous ideas," radical Independent Roger Williams sets up the colony of Providence Plantation (later Rhode Island) as a refuge for religious minorities; he later founds the First Baptist Church of Providence, the first Baptist church in America. [**United States of America**]

1639 A small party of Ursuline nuns, led by Marie de l'Incarnation, enters New France, establishing a convent in Québec and founding the first school for girls in North America. [**Canada**]

1649 The English "Rump Parliament" enacts the founding of the Society for the Propagation of the Gospel in New England. [**United States of America**]

1649 As part of a campaign of genocide, Iroquois raiding parties attack the Hurons at St. Ignace in New France, destroying the Jesuit mission there, and savagely torturing missionaries Jean de Brébeuf, Gabriel Lalemant, Antoine Daniel, Charles Garnier, and Noel Charbanel to death. [**Canada**]

1662 The introduction of the "Halfway Covenant" (whereby baptized children of godly parents are recognized as being part of the church, even though they themselves had not professed faith) in Massachusetts indicates that the Puritan ideal of a godly society had not been fully realized in the colony. [**United States of America**]

1674 François de Laval, the vicar-apostolic of New France since 1659, becomes the bishop of Québec; the creation of this fully independent archdiocese (the first in North America) marks the transition of the Canadian Catholic Church from a missionary body focused on the evangelization of Indigenous peoples to a church serving the settler community. [**Canada**]

1680s–1760s Large numbers of German migrants arrive; these immigrants (chiefly Lutheran and Reformed, but also including Amish, Baptist Dunkers, Moravians, Schwenkfelders, Swiss Mennonites, and Waldensians) add distinctive strands to the fabric of American Protestantism. [**United States of America**]

1681–82 Quaker land entrepreneur William Penn founds the Province of Pennsylvania on a basis of toleration, renouncing the use of coercion and granting free exercise of religion to all; this religious tolerance draws many persecuted minorities to settle there and is later incorporated into the Pennsylvania Charter of Privileges in 1701. [**United States of America**]

1687 Following a short-lived mission in Baja California in 1683, Jesuit missionary-explorer Eusebio Francisco Kino establishes his first mission (Nuestra Señora de los Dolores) among rural Native Americans in the Pimería Alta (Northern Sonora in Mexico and Southern Arizona in the United States). [**United States of America**]

1692 An outbreak of mass hysteria in colonial Massachusetts culminates in the Salem witch trials and in the execution of about twenty people, almost all of whom are women, for witchcraft. [**United States of America**]

1701 The newly founded Anglican Society for the Propagation of the Gospel in Foreign Parts begins its activities in America, particularly in the lower South, the mid-Atlantic colonies, and New England, as well as in those colonies that would later become part of Canada. [**Canada, United States of America**]

1734–43 The "Great Awakening" begins under Theodore Frelinghuysen, Gilbert Tennent, and (especially) Jonathan Edwards; the preaching of George Whitefield and others reinforces its impact after 1740. [**United States of America**]

1749 Enlightenment thinker and moderate Deist Benjamin Franklin urges the development of a "Publick Religion," which, although rejecting organized forms of religion, would nevertheless foster moral virtue along the lines of Christianity. [**United States of America**]

1763 The British conquest of "New France" (1756–60) forces France to cede all of Canada at the Treaty of Paris; however, Roman Catholics are guaranteed the free exercise of their religion, enabling old-school French churchmen to maintain the national Catholic culture, especially in Québec. [**Canada**]

1765–83 The American Revolution begins, in which the American colonies reject British taxation and authority; this revolution leads to the War of Independence (1775–83), the ratifying of the Declaration of Independence (1776), and the foundation of the United States of America. [**United States of America**]

1786 The General Assembly of Virginia passes Thomas Jefferson's bill guaranteeing religious liberty for all; this forms the basis of the First Amendment to the American Constitution in 1791: "Congress shall make no law respecting an establishment of religion, or prohibiting the free exercise thereof." [**United States of America**]

[1789] Pope Pius VII elevates the Diocese of Baltimore to a metropolitan archdiocese (the first such in the United States), giving it archepiscopal authority over the entire country; it remains the sole archdiocese until the elevation of the Diocese of St. Louis to a similar status in 1847. [**United States of America**]

1801 After beginning in the late 1790s, the revival known as the "Second Great Awakening" gains momentum and spreads in all directions from a series of camp meetings at Cane Ridge, Kentucky, especially among Baptist and Methodist frontier communities. [**United States of America**]

1801 Congregationalists in New England and Presbyterians in the United States adopt a "Plan of Union," uniting the two churches; however, controversy over the Congregationalist "New England theology" leads to the "Old School" Presbyterian Church ending cooperation with them in 1837 and the union with the remaining "New School" Presbyterians breaking up fifteen years later. [**United States of America**]

1810 Recent graduates of Williams College (where the famous 1806 "Haystack Prayer Meeting" had taken place, birthing the American Foreign Mission movement) establish the American Board of Commissioners for Foreign Missions to facilitate missionary work. [**United States of America**]

1815 The Unitarian controversy emerges in the United States, resulting in a rationally minded church movement, organized as a split off from American Congregationalism; this Unitarianism minimizes the supernatural, instead emphasizing the benevolence of the one God and the moral goodness of humans. [**United States of America**]

1824 The American Presbyterian revivalist (and lawyer by training) Charles Grandison Finney introduces his "new measures" revivalism in upstate New York; his writings in the 1830s widely disseminate his views on the promotion of revivals by human agency. [**United States of America**]

1830 Joseph Smith founds the Church of Jesus Christ of Latter-day Saints (also unofficially known as the Mormons, due to their appeal to the Book of Mormon as a source of doctrine) in western New York State. [**United States of America**]

1830 *The Protestant*, a magazine begun by several Protestant ministers, starts a nativist (i.e., anti-foreign) crusade against Catholic immigrants, seeing them as diluting America's Anglo-Saxon Protestant base and increasing its religious diversity; this antagonism culminates in brutal sectarian street confrontations, with hundreds of injuries, in Philadelphia in 1844. [**United States of America**]

1843–44 Adventist groups in America and England, under the influence of William Miller, predict the second coming, but after the "Great Disappointment" when this did not happen, carry on with modified expectations, becoming the Seventh-day Adventists in 1863. [**United States of America**]

1845 Editor John O'Sullivan coins the phrase "manifest destiny" in the July–August 1845 issue of the *Democratic Review*; this becomes an influential (although contested) idea that the United States would dominate its continent as a Christian republic. [**United States of America**]

1845 The Baptists and Methodists in the southern states split off from their northern counterparts over the issue of slavery, leading to the formation of the Southern Baptist Convention in Atlanta, Georgia; this becomes the dominant church in the South and eventually the largest Protestant denomination in the United States in the second half of the twentieth century. [**United States of America**]

1847 Following the assassination in 1844 of Joseph Smith, the founder of the Church of Jesus Christ of Latter-day Saints (Mormons) and ongoing conflict with its neighbors, Brigham Young leads a migration of the Church from Nauvoo, Illinois, to Salt Lake City, Utah. [**United States of America**]

1861–65 The American Civil War breaks out between the eleven slave-owning Confederate states in the South and the twenty loyalist Union states in the North; despite their differing perspectives on slavery, each side claims a strong religious base for its ideology. [**United States of America**]

1863 President Abraham Lincoln issues the Emancipation Proclamation, abolishing slavery in the southern Confederate-controlled states; abolition extends nationwide with the Thirteenth Amendment to the Constitution, ratified in 1865. [**United States of America**]

1881 Charles Taze Russell founds the Zion's Watch Tower Tract Society (later renamed Jehovah's Witnesses) for the purpose of distributing religious tracts; in the twentieth century, this grows to become a worldwide body, known for its aggressive evangelism. [**United States of America**]

1886 Archbishop James Gibbons of Baltimore becomes the first American cardinal and, as such, a vocal supporter of American democracy and a widely influential public figure. [**United States of America**]

1893 The World's Parliament of Religions meets in Chicago, marking the first formal gathering of representatives of Eastern and Western traditions, and launching worldwide interreligious dialogue. [**United States of America**]

1901 Pentecostalism emerges at Charles Fox Parham's Bible School in Topeka, Kansas, becoming a global movement through revival meetings at "Azusa Street" in Los Angeles five years later. [**United States of America**]

1908 The Vatican redefines American Catholicism as being no longer under the Congregation for the Propagation of the Faith and hence no longer a "mission," but now a mature church in its own right; thirty-two Protestant denominations unite to form the Federal Council of Churches (the forerunner of the National Council of Churches) in the same year. [**United States of America**]

1910–15 *The Fundamentals* (a set of ninety essays challenging theological liberalism and biblical criticism, published quarterly over a period of five years) defines the characteristic doctrines of what comes to be known as Fundamentalism; the gathering of six thousand conservative Christians for the first Conference of the World's Christian Fundamentals Association in Chicago in 1919 reinforces the impact of this series. [**United States of America**]

1914 A gathering of about three hundred preachers and laymen convenes in Hot Springs, Arkansas, to discuss the formation of a cooperative Pentecostal fellowship; this results in the incorporation of the Assemblies of God in the United States. [**United States of America**]

1915 White Protestant nativists in the state of Georgia revive and extend the anti-Black Ku Klux Klan to become an anti-Catholic, anti-Jewish, and anti-trade union organization. [**United States of America**]

1917 Walter Rauschenbusch's *A Theology for the Social Gospel* provides a systematic basis for the diversified social gospel movement that had emerged in the second half of the nineteenth century; this movement emphasizes the kingdom of God, applying Christian theology and ethics to the resolution of issues of social justice. [**United States of America**]

1925 Canadian Protestantism attempts to form a "national church" with the merger of the Methodist, Presbyterian, and Congregational churches into the United Church of Canada; although the Anglican Church did not take part and nearly 30 percent of Presbyterian congregations also refused to join, this was the first time that an ecumenical union of churches had been created anywhere in the world, crossing historical denominational boundaries. [**Canada**]

1925 The "Monkey Trial" begins in Dayton, Tennessee, with John Scopes, a young science teacher, being accused of teaching evolution in violation of Tennessee state law; although the court finds him guilty, the fundamentalist case against him becomes a focus for public ridicule. [**United States of America**]

1926 The Federal Council of Churches supports the Eighteenth Amendment of the Constitution (passed in 1919, banning the production, transport, and sale of alcohol in the United States), with two of its officers testifying of the churches' support for prohibition before the Committee of the Judiciary of the United States Senate. [**United States of America**]

1928 New York governor Alfred E. Smith stands in the 1928 election as the first Catholic candidate for the presidency of the United States but suffers a landslide defeat against Herbert Hoover. [**United States of America**]

1947 Pentecostal evangelists William Branham and Oral Roberts both begin healing crusades, reaching a wide public audience previously not receptive to Pentecostalism. [**United States of America**]

1948 A Pentecostal awakening at the Sharon Orphanage and Schools in North Battleford, Saskatchewan, results in a radically independent "Latter Rain" movement that spreads worldwide, helping to lay the foundations for an expansion of independent Pentecostal groups in the 1950s and the emergence of the charismatic movement in the 1960s. [**Canada**]

1949 Billy Graham gains national media coverage for his Los Angeles crusade after the media magnate William Randolph Hearst orders his editors to "puff Graham" (i.e., to make him front page news). [**United States of America**]

1952 President Dwight D. Eisenhower articulates the civic role of religion as part of "the American way" vis-à-vis "atheistic Communism": "Our form of government has no sense unless it is founded in a deeply felt religious faith, and I don't care what it is. With us of course it is the Judeo-Christian concept but it must be a religion that all men are created equal."[3] [**United States of America**]

1955 Rosa Park's arrest in Montgomery, Alabama, for refusing to give up her seat in the Colored section of the bus to a White passenger ignites the American civil rights movement. [**United States of America**]

---

3. Henry, "I Don't Care," 41.

1960 Democratic nominee John F. Kennedy defeats Richard Nixon in the 1960 presidential election to become the first Catholic president of the United States. [**United States of America**]

1960 Episcopal priest Dennis Bennett announces his experience of the baptism in the Spirit to his congregation at St. Mark's Episcopal Church in Van Nuys, California, thus launching the Protestant charismatic movement. [**United States of America**]

1962 The United States Supreme Court rules in Engel v. Vitale (370 U.S. 421) that it is unconstitutional for state officials to compose and require the recitation of a set prayer in public schools; this creates a firestorm of controversy. [**United States of America**]

1967 The Catholic charismatic movement emerges at Duquesne University in Pittsburgh, later spreading to Notre Dame University in Indiana, and disseminating worldwide from these two locations. [**United States of America**]

1968 American fugitive and felon James Earl Ray assassinates Martin Luther King Jr., American Baptist minister and Nobel Prize–winning civil rights campaigner, on the balcony outside King's room at the Lorraine Motel in Memphis, Tennessee. [**United States of America**]

1969 American astronaut Buzz Aldrin, an elder of Webster Presbyterian Church in Texas, celebrates communion on the moon, using the elements of bread and wine from his church that he had brought with him on the Apollo 11 moon landing; although NASA covers up this "secret communion" due to legal pressure from militant atheist Madalyn Murray O'Hair, Aldrin's church still celebrates a "Lunar Communion Sunday" every July, using the chalice that he brought back with him from the moon. [**United States of America**]

1976 "Born-again" Baptist Jimmy Carter is elected as the thirty-ninth President of the United States and is instrumental in moving Evangelicalism closer to the American mainstream. [**United States of America**]

1979 American televangelist Jerry Falwell forms the Moral Majority (a religiously conservative pressure group), marking the emergence of the "new

Christian right" as a significant religiopolitical force in the United States. **[United States of America]**

1983 President Ronald Reagan's "Evil Empire" speech, delivered to the National Association of Evangelicals, describes the Soviet Union as "the focus of evil in the modern world,"[4] insisting that the nuclear arms race between America and Russia is a battle between good and evil, and that evangelical leaders are crucial in "keeping America great by keeping her good."[5] **[United States of America]**

1984 Pope John Paul II, the most-traveled pope in history, becomes the first (and thus far the only) pope to visit Canada, making three visits in 1984, 1987, and 2002. **[Canada]**

1987–88 The exposure of financial and sexual scandals in the television evangelism industry (often dubbed "televangelism") demonstrates the wide public dissemination of this form of evangelical media and highlights the lack of regulation within the industry. **[United States of America]**

1989 Barbara Harris becomes suffragan (or subordinate) bishop of the Episcopal Diocese of Massachusetts and, as such, the first ordained woman bishop in the Anglican Communion. **[United States of America]**

1994 The controversial "Toronto Blessing" phenomenon emerges at the Toronto Airport Vineyard Christian Fellowship and rapidly spreads, creating a global Pentecostal pilgrimage industry. **[Canada]**

2001 Al-Qaeda hijackers carry out the September 11 attacks (known as "9/11") on the World Trade Center in New York and the Pentagon in Washington, DC; these terrorist attacks, the deadliest in history with almost three thousand deaths, lead to President George W. Bush's declaration of a "War on Terror" and the subsequent American-led invasions of Afghanistan and Iraq. **[United States of America]**

2002 Bernard Law, the senior Catholic cardinal in the United States, resigns as the archbishop of Boston over allegations of his concealment of numerous incidents of pedophilia among the priesthood, the first high-level church official to be so accused. **[United States of America]**

---

4. Reagan, "Evil Empire Speech," para. 45.
5. Reagan, "Evil Empire Speech," para. 11.

2003 Gene Robinson becomes the Episcopalian bishop coadjutor of New Hampshire, despite deep controversy over his active homosexuality; after his election, many American and Canadian theological conservatives secede from the Episcopalian Church, forming a new body (the Anglican Church in North America) emphasizing traditional Episcopalian orthodoxy and discipline. [**United States of America**]

2016 Donald Trump wins the 2016 presidential election, with massive support from Evangelicals, 81 percent of whom had supported him over Hilary Clinton, despite his notoriously hedonistic lifestyle and abrasive persona. [**United States of America**]

2018–19 A national survey by the Pew Research Center shows that Christianity is declining at a rapid rate in the United States (from 77 percent adherence in 2007 to 65 percent in 2018–19); this drop is most pronounced in young adults.[6] [**United States of America**]

2021 The uncritical support of American Evangelicals for President Donald Trump's false claims of a fraudulent 2020 election process contributes to militant Christian nationalist participation (along with other right-wing groups) in the violent invasion of the United States Senate on January 6, a "Jesus Saves" banner being prominent among the rioters on the steps of the Capitol. [**United States of America**]

Bibliography

Henry, Patrick. "'And I Don't Care What It Is': The Tradition-History of a Civil Religion Proof-Text." *JAAR* 49 (Mar. 1981) 35–47.
Hill, Jonathan, ed. *Zondervan Handbook to the History of Christianity*. Oxford: Lion, 2006.
Jenkins, Philip. *The Next Christendom: The Coming of Global Christianity*. 3rd ed. Oxford: Oxford University Press, 2011.
Johnson, Todd M. "Christianity in Global Context: Trends and Statistics." Pew Research, May 2005. https://www.pewresearch.org/wp-content/uploads/sites/7/2005/05/051805-global-christianity.pdf.
Lamport, Mark A., ed. *Encyclopedia of Christianity in the Global South*. 2 vols. Blue Ridge Summit, PA: Rowman and Littlefield, 2018.
Marty, Martin. *The Christian World: A Global History*. New York: Modern Library, 2009.
———. "Religion in America 1935–1985." Introduction to *Altered Landscapes: Christianity in America 1935–1985*, edited by David W. Lotz et al., 1–16. Grand Rapids: Eerdmans, 1989.

---

6. Pew Research Center, "In U.S."

McManners, John, ed. *The Oxford Illustrated History of Christianity*. Oxford: Oxford University Press, 1995.

Neill, Stephen. *A History of Christian Missions*. Pelican History of the Church 6. 2nd ed. Edited by Owen Chadwick. Harmondsworth, UK: Penguin, 1986.

Pew Research Center. "In U.S., Decline of Christianity Continues at Rapid Pace." Pew Research Center, Oct. 17, 2019. https://www.pewresearch.org/religion/2019/10/17/in-u-s-decline-of-christianity-continues-at-rapid-pace/.

Reagan, Ronald. "Evil Empire Speech." Voices of Democracy, Mar. 8, 1983. Speech presented to the National Association of Evangelicals, Orlando. http://voicesofdemocracy.umd.edu/reagan-evil-empire-speech-text/.

Roberts, J. M. *The Penguin History of the World*. Rev. ed. Harmondsworth, UK: Penguin, 1995.

Index of Names and Subjects

1976 Call to Action conference, 62
Abbott, Lyman, 143-44, 146, 147-48
Abrams, Minnie, 112
Acadia Divinity College, 16
Act of Religious Toleration, 55
Acts 15, 3-4
Affordable Care Act, 63
African American Church of God in Christ, 114
African Methodist Episcopal Church (AME), 44, 48, 133
African Methodist Episcopal Zion (AMEZ) Church, 44, 49
Airhart, Phyllis, 153
Aldersgate experience, 104
Aldred, Ray, 8, 15
Allen, Ethan, 73
Allen, Richard, 41-43, 156, 160
Alpha Suffrage Club, 132
American Association of Women Preachers (AAWP), 123
American Bible Society, 82
American Board of Commissioners for Foreign Missions, 10
American Colonization Society (ACS), 46
American Home Missionary Society, 82
American Revolution, 55
American Sunday School Union, 82
American Tract Society, 82
Ames, Jessie Daniel, 133
Angelus Temple, 122-23, 125, 132

Anglican Council of Indigenous People, 13
Anne, Princess, 31
Anthony, Susan B., 132
Apocalypse, 96
Apocalypticism (Jewish), 89-90
Apostolic Church of Pentecost, 114
Apostolic Faith Mission, 109
Apostolic Faith, 112
Argue, A. H., 111
Armageddon, 89, 95
Asbury Revival, 117
Assemblies of God (AG), 15, 16, 114, 115
Association of Southern Women for the Prevention of Lynching, 134
Atwood, Margaret, 29
Augustine, 32
Austin, Stephen F., 192
Azusa Street (Los Angeles) Revival of 1906-8, 109, 178

Babylon, 31-33
"Baptism of the Holy Ghost and Fire, The," 112
Bartelman, Frank, 109
Barth, Karl, 128
Baxter, Elizabeth, 109
Beaver, Henry, 174
Bebbington, David, 100
Beckwith, Josephine, 134
Beecher, Lyman, 74-75, 81
Benedict XVI, Pope, 53

Benin kingdom 39
Berg, George, 112
Berntsen, B., 112
Bethel Bible School, 108
Bethel Church, 117
Bethlehem Community Center, 134
Bethshan healing home, 109
Bethune, Mary McLeod, 131
    Bethune-Cookman University, 131
Black Elk, Nicholas, 12
Black, Walter and Frances, 107
Blackstone, William, 96, 97, 99, 100–110
Blanchet, Francis Norbert, 175, 177
Bland, Salem, 158
Boardman, William, 105–6
Boer, Gregory, 6
Book of Mormon, 78
Boston Missionary Training School (Gordon-Conwell), 127
Boston University School of Theology, 132
Branham, William, 116
British North America Act, 27, 29
Bryan Street African Baptist Church, 45
Bryan, Andrew, 45
Budd, Henry Budd *see* Sakacewescam
Burroughs, Nannie Helen, 131
Bushnell, Horace, 140
Bushnell, Katherine, 126
Butler, Anthea, 223

Cagle, Mary Lee, 133
Calvert family, 55
Campbell, Alexander and Thomas, 78
Canada, and Catholicism, xxxvii; and Christianity, xxxvii, xli
"Canadian Azusa," 110
Canadian Radio and Television Commission, 27
Cane Ridge (KY) Revival of 1801, 76, 78
Carbajal de Valenzuela, Genaro and Romanita, 111
Carmelite community of Port Tobacco, 56
Carroll, Charles, 55
Carroll, John, 55, 56
Carter, President Jimmy, 24, 206
Cartier, George-Étienne, 27–28

Cary, Lott, 46
Cashwell, Gaston B., 110
Catch the Fire, 117
Catechism of the Catholic Church, 1994, 63
Catholic Students' Mission Crusade, 59
Catholic Worker Movement, 59–60
Catholicism in North America, xxiii
    African American, 57
    Catholics, German, 57
    Catholics, Polish, 57
Celebration of Culture, 16
Chalmers, Thomas, 153
Charles I, King, 55
Chawner, Charles, 112
Chicago Training School, 122
Chown, Samuel Dwight, 158
Christian Aboriginal Fellowship of Canada, 115
Christian and Missionary Alliance (CMA), 14–15
"Christian Association," 78
Christian Democratic Party, 164
Christian, William, 105
Christian's Secret to a Happy Life, The, 106
Christianity and the Social Crisis, 87, 157–58
Christianity, as share of US population; xxiv
    and immigrants of other world faiths, 176
    in global south, xliii
    in the United States in relation to world Christianity, xxi
Christie, Nancy 161
Church of England, 13
Church of God (Cleveland), 114
Church of God in Christ (COGIC), 44, 105, 111, 115
Church of Jesus Christ of Latter-day Saints, 79
Church of the Living God, 105
Church of the Nazarene, 133
Church with the Soul of a Nation, The, 153
Church, Nation, and World Order, 160
"City on a Hill" sermon, 22–23, 91
Civil War (1861–65), 29

Coffin, Jr., William Sloan, 136–37, 150
Colored Women's League, 131
Commonsense philosophy, 139
Confederation, Canadian, 26–28, 33
Constitution of the United States, 23–24
    First Amendment, 71
    Eighteenth Amendment to Constitution, 130
    Nineteenth Amendment to Constitution, 132, 133
Continental Congress, 55
Co-operative Commonwealth Federation (CCF), 158, 162, 164
Cope, Jean Baptiste, 13
Corrigan, Michael A., Bishop, 58
Counter-Reformation, 54
Crawford, Florence, 111
Crosby, Bing, 60
Cugoano, Ottobah, 37–38

Dallas Theological Seminary, 98
Darby, John Nelson, 92–96, 99, 100–101, 106
    Darbyism, 95, 106
Darwin, Charles, 139, 142
Day, Dorothy, 59–60
de Tocqueville, Alexis, 71
Deaconess movement, 122
Dean, John Marvin, 128
Declaration of Independence, 23
Deism, Enlightenment, 23, 138
DeLille, Henriette, 57
Demers, Modeste, 175
Denver Revival Tabernacle, 123
Disciples of Christ, 78
"disinterested benevolence," 80
Dolan, Jay, 57
Doubt/uncertainty, 147–50
Douglass, Frederick, 48–49
Doukhobors, 27
Dowie, Alexander, 106–7
Dubois, W. E. B., 48
Durham, William, 110–11, 114
Dvornik, 5
Dwight, Timothy, 75

East End Mission (Toronto), 109–10, 112
Economic Justice for All (1986), 63

Edinburgh Mission Conference of 1910, 8, 18
Edwards, Henrietta Muir, 159
Edwards, Jonathan, 74, 91, 138
Elaw, Zilpha, 43–44
Encyclical *Longinqua Oceani*, 51
English Civil War (1642–51), 55
Enron, 18
Episcopal Church, 13
Epworth Evangelistic Institute, 121
Equiano, Olaudah, 39–40
Ernst, Eldon, 172
Ethiopian Baptist Church of Jamaica, 46
Evangelical Fellowship of Canada, 116
evangelicals, a call to repentance, 221, 234
    as convental pluralists, 221, 231
    defined, 100
    and megachurches, 220
    and politics, 227
    and racism, 223
    and systems of domination, 220ff.
    and wealth gap, 225
Evarts, Jeremiah, 10
evolutionary theory, 139–42
Ewart, Frank, 114

"Famous Five," 159
Fanning, 6
Farrow, Lucy, 108, 109, 112
Federal Council of Churches, 87, 148–49
Finished Work theology, 114
Finney, Charles Grandison, 74–77, 79–82, 92, 105
Fiorenza, Elisabeth Schüssler, 127
First African Baptist Church, 45
Flores, Mayra, 199
Foote, Julia, 44–45
Fosdick, Harry Emerson, 148
Fourfold Gospel, 107
Francescon, Luigi, 111
Francis, Mark, 9
Francis, Pope, 63–64
Franklin, Benjamin, 25
Free Speech newspaper, 133
Freedom Church, 133
Freedom of Faith, The, 141, 142

Frobisher, Martin, 13
Fugitive Slave Act, 43, 47
Full Gospel Tabernacle, St. Louis, 107
Fundamentalist, 98, 144–47

Gaebelein, Arno, 101
Garr, Alfred and Lillian, 112
Garrett Bible Institute/Garrett Theological Seminary, 122, 128
Garrison, William Lloyd, 47, 82
Gauvreau, Michael, 161
General Conferences of the Methodist Episcopal Church, 121
George, David, 45
George, Sam, 212
Georgetown College, 55
Gibbons, James, Cardinal, 58
Gladden, Washington, 142–43, 148, 149, 153
Glassey, Jennie, 107
global Christianity, ix
   entanglement in, xiv
Global Harvest, 117
glossolalia, 113
"God's Girls," 123
God's Word to Women: One Hundred Bible Studies on Woman's Place in the Divine Economy, 126
Goen, C. C., 77
Gordon, Adoniram Judson, 96, 106
Gordon, Charles William (Ralph), 159
Gorski, Philip, 228
Goslin, Martin, 181
Gradual Civilizations Act, 6
Graham, Billy, 84
Grant, John Webster, 164
"Great Awakening," 73–75, 78
Great Revival of 1857–58, 84
Great War impact on Social Gospel, 163
Guide to Holiness, A, 104
Gulliford, Helen, 123

Haldeman, I. M., 87–88, 93, 94, 99, 100–101
Hamilton, William, 44
Hammon, Jupiter, 39
Harkness, Georgia, 128
Hastings, Selina, 40

Haywood, Garfield T., 114
Heart-to-Heart (radio program), 123
Hebden, Ellen and James, 109–10, 111, 117
Henry, Carl F., 164
Hidalgo, Miguel, xxxvi
Higher Christian Life, The, 105–6
Higher Criticism, 139–40
Hindle, Thomas and Louise, 112
Hodge, A. A., 140
Holifield, Brooks, 138
Holy Ghost and Us School, The, 107–8
Hopkins, Samuel, 80
hospitality and mutuality, 217–18
Humanae Vitae, 61–62
Hunthausen, Raymond, 182
Hutchins, Julia, 108–9

I Believe in Miracles, 123
Ignatius Sancho, 40–41
In His Steps: What Would Jesus Do?, 153
Indian Act, 6
Indian Removal Act, 10
Indigenous Pathways, 16
infilling of Holy Spirit, 106
Interdenominational Social Service Congress, 160
International Church of the Foursquare Gospel, 111, 115, 125
International House of Prayer, 117
Iris Global, 117
Irving, Edward, 107
Ivens, William, 162

Jamestown, Virginia, 13
Jefferson, Thomas, 23–24, 26
Jehovah's Witnesses, 27, 92
Jenkins, Jerry, 88
Jerusalem Council, 4
Jesuit enclaves, 12
Jesuit Relations, 54
Jesus Is Coming, 96–97
"Jesus Only" Pentecostalism, 114
Jews, 3–4
Jim Crow, 33
Jocahim of Fiore, 90
Johnston, Barbara, 112
Jones, Charles Price, 105, 111

Joseph, 38
Juan Ponce de León, 53

Kennedy, John F., 22–23, 26
Keswick, 103, 105–6
Kidd, Thomas, 224, 226
  and color-blind gospel, 225
kingdom of Kongo (Angola), 36–37
Knights of Columbus, 58
Kuhlman, Kathryn, 116, 122, 123

"labor churches," 162
LaHaye, Tim, 88, 99, 100–101
Lakeland Revival, 117
Langford, Sarah, 104
Late Great Planet Earth, The, 99, 100
Latino Apostolic Assembly of the Faith in Jesus Christ, 114
Latter Rain movement, 116
Lawler, H. L., 112
Lay, Ken, 18
League of Nations, 163
Leake, Albert, 120
Lectures on Revivals of Religion, 77
Lee, Edward, 109
Lee, Jarena, 43
Lee, Jason, 175
Lee, Luther, 82
Left Behind novels, 88, 99
Leo XIII, Pope, 51, 59, 64, 153
Lescarbot, Marc, 10
Letters to a Young Doubter, 136
Levine, Rabbi Raphael, 181
Liele, George, 45–46
"Lifting as They Climb," 131
Lighthouse of International Foursquare Evangelism, (LIFE), 125
Lindsey, Hal, 99, 100–101
Lockwood, Walter Thomas, 146–47, 148
Lombardi, Giacomo, 111
Lopez, Abundio and Rosa, 111
Luce Clare, Booth, 60

Macdonald, John A., 27–28
MacDonald, the Most Rev. Mark, 13
Machen, J. Gresham, 145
MacLennan, Hugh, 153
Mahan, Asa, 79

Maritime Baptist statement, 160
Maroons, 47
Marsden, George, 144–45
Marshall Plan, 33
Marx, Karl, 26
Mason, Charles Harrison, 44, 105, 111
Massachusetts, Joint Convention of the General Court of the Commonwealth of, 22
Mather, Cotton, 91
Mathews, Donald G., 74
Mathews, Shailor, 145–46, 153
Maurice John Frederick Denison, 153
Mbemba, Nzinga, 37
McAlister, R. E., 114
McClung, Nellie, 159
McConnell, Francis J., 148
McCready, James, 76
McKinney, Louise, 159
McPherson, Aimee Semple, 84, 111, 115, 122–23, 125, 179
Membertou, Saqamaw, 12
Methodist Department of Evangelism and Social Service, 160
Mexico, and Catholicism, xxxvi
  and Christianity, xxxv, xl
Mi'kmaq, 12–13
migration and Christian expansion, 211
Millennial Harbinger, 78
Miller, William, 92, 93, 95
Missionary Alliance, 112
"Model of Christian Charity" sermon, 22–23
Modernist(s), 145, 157–58, 164
Mohawk, 12, 14
Montgomery, Helen Barratt, 129
Moody, D. L., 84, 106, 107
  Moody Bible Institute, 127
Moomau, Antoinette, 112
Moore, Joanna Patterson, 104
Moore, Russell, 232–33
Mormon, *see*, Church of Jesus Christ of Latter-day Saints
Morris, Charles, 64
Moss, Thomas, 132
Mother Bethel African Methodist Episcopal Church, 42–43, 83

Mount Sinai Holy Church of America, 125
mujerista, 129
Mukti Mission in India, 112
Munger, Theodore T., 141–44
Murphy, Emily, 159
My Neighbor, 158

NAACP, 133
National American Women Suffrage Association (NAWSA), 132
National Association for Colored Women (NACW), 131
National Association of Evangelicals, 116
National Camp Meeting Association, 104
National Catholic War Council (NCWC), 59
National Catholic Welfare Conference, 59
National College for Christian Workers, 134
National Council of Negro Women (NCNW), 131
National Council of Women in Canada, 159
National Federation of Afro-American Women, 131
Native American District of the CMA, 14, 15
Natural Theology, 138
Navajo, 17
negro spirituals, 35–36
Nettleton, Asahel, 75
New Brunswick, 27
New Christianity: or The Religion of the New Age, The, 158
New Haven theology, 75
New Theology, 140–48, 164
Niagara Bible Conference, 106
North America, and future of Christianity in, xv
  trends in religion and nonreligion, xxii
  and unaffiliated, xlii
North American Christian Reformed Church (CRC), 16–17
North Battleford, Saskatchewan, 116
Northern Baptist Seminary, 128, 129
Northfield Conference, 106
Nova Scotia, 27
Nyack College, 111

Obama, Barack. 63
Oberlin College, 77, 79–80, 82
  Oberlin perfectionism, 105
Oklahoma Indian Missionary Conference (OIMC), 14
Osteen, Joel, 210
Osterberg, Arthur, 109
Osterberg, Cenna and Louis, 109
Ottolini, Pietro, 111
Outlook, The, 143, 148
Ozman, Agnes, 108

Pacific edge of North America and Christianity, 169ff.
  anti-Asian sentiment, 175–76
  and Arab Christianity, 176
  and Pentecostalism, 178ff.
Paine, Thomas, 73, 148
Paley, William, 139, 142
Palmer, Phoebe, 79, 82, 104, 105
Palmer, Walter, 104
Parham, Charles Fox and Sarah, 108
Parks, Rosa, 133
Parlby, Irene, 159
Paul John II, Pope, 62
Paul VI, Pope, 61
Pentecostal Assemblies of Canada (PAOC), 15, 16, 114
Pentecostal Assemblies of the World, 114
Pentecostal Holiness Church, 114, 115
Perry, Samuel, 228
Phan, Peter C., 211
Pierson, A. J., 96
Pillar of Fire Church, 108, 124
Pius IX, Pope, 58
Pius VI, Pope, 55
Plymouth Brethren, 93 95, 106, *see* Christian (or Plymouth) Brethren
Plymouth Church, Brooklyn, 143
Poor Claires of Georgetown, 56
Portuguese, 36–37
Presbyterian Board of Social Service and Evangelism, 160

Presbyterian General Assembly, 73
primitivism ecclesiastical, 78
Prince, Nancy, 47
Prince, Nero, 47
Princeton Theological Seminary, 140
Progressive revelation, 143–47
Prohibition, 130
Propagation of the Faith, 58
Protestant Orangemen, 28
Protestant Reformation, 53
Protocols of the Elders of Zion, The, 97
Providence Baptist Church in Monrovia, 46

"Race Women," 131
Ramabai, Pandita, 112
Randall, Herbert, 112
Rapture (of believers), 94–95
Rauschenbusch, Walter, 87–88, 94, 100, 153, 157
Reagan, Ronald, 24, 62–63
"reductions," 11–12
Refugee Act, 206
Refugee Convention, 205
refugee resettlement in the United States, 204ff.
    Bhutanese Nepali refuges, 208–9
    challenges and opportunities, 212ff.
    its influence on the church, 205
    growth of, 207
    Muslim arrivals, 207
    unintended consequences of, 218ff.
Rehoboth Christian School, 17
"republican Catholicism," 55–57
Rerum Novarum, 153
Rerum Novarum, 59
Riel, Louis, 27
Riverside Church, 136, 148
Roberts, Oral, 116
Robinson, Ida Bell, 124–25
Ruether, Rosemary Radford, 130
Ryan, John A., Father, 59

Saint Mary's Seminary, 56
Saiving, Valerie, 130
Sakacewescam, 13
Salvation Army, 16
Sandy-Saulteaux Spiritual Centre, 14

Sanford, Frank, 107–8
Sangamento, 37
Scofield, Cyrus (and Reference Bible), 97, 99, 100–101
Scott, Orange, 82
Scott, Walter, 78
Scripture Doctrine of Christian Perfection, 79
Second Blessing/Second Work of Grace, 105
Second Coming, 95
Second Great Awakening, 192
Second Vatican Council (1962–65), 52, 60–62
Seiple, Chris, 230
Semple, Robert 111
Serra, Fr. Junípero, 53
Seventh-day Adventists, 92
Sewell, Samuel, 91
Seymour, William, J., 108, 109–10, 112, 117
Sharon Bible College, 116
Shaw, Anna Howard, 132
Sheen, Fulton J., Bishop, 60
Sheldon, Charles M., 153
Silver Bluff Baptist Church, 45
Simpson, A. B., 106, 107, 111
Sinclair, Upton, 123
Skinner, Tom, 220, 222; and Urbana sermon, 222
Sky Pilot, The, 150
Small, Franklin, 114
Smith, Alfred E., 59
Smith, Amanda Berry, 44, 104–5
Smith, Craig, 14, 15
Smith, Hannah Whitall, 105
Smith, Joseph Jr., 78
Smith, R. Pearsall, 105
Snyder, Susanna, 211
Social Creed of the Churches, The, 158
social gospel movement, 87, 153–64
    social gospel in Canada, 153–64
Society of Saint Sulpice, 56
Southard, Madeline, 123, 130
Southern Baptist Church, 134
speaking in tongues, 107–13
St. George's Episcopal Church, 42
St. Kateri, 12

256   INDEX OF NAMES AND SUBJECTS

St. Paul Bible College, 127
Stanley, George, 12
Stanton, Elizabeth Cady, 125, 126
State of Israel establishment, 98
"Statement of Dissent," 62
Stockton, Amy Lee, 128
Stone, Barton W., 78
Stono Rebellion of 1739, 36–37
storytelling components, ix, xiv
    history, contexts, and communities, x
    migration and global diaspora, xv
    movement, xv
    public theologies, xv
    translation, xv;
Strangers within Our Gates, 158
Sulpicians, 56
Sumner, Senator Charles, 29
Sunday, Billy, 84
Sunshine Hour, The, 123
Survival, 29

Tappan, Arthur and Lewis, 81
Taylor, Nathaniel William, 74–75
Tennent, Gilbert, 74
Terrell, Mary Church, 131
Terry, Neely, 108
Testem Benevolentiae Nostrae, 58
Texas Council of the Commission on Interracial Cooperation (CIC), 133–34
Texas-styled Christianity, 187ff.
    and Catholicism, 190
    and conservative Republicans, 187
    effect on Houston, 210
    and immigrant influence, 188ff., 190ff, 193
    independence and individualism, 193
    and Latin American immigration, 196, 199
    and Latino Protestants, 199ff.
    and Mexican Catholic communities, 191
    and political affiliation, 197
    and religious identity, 188
    as counter-story to narratives of typical American Christianity, 189
    religious change in the twenty-first century, 193
    three forms of, 193ff.
    and Vietnamese adaptation, 195
The Challenge of Peace (1983), 63
The City of God, 32
The Song of Bernadette, 60
The Tao of Enron, 18
The Way of Holiness, 79
theologies for political power, especially in Africa and the Americas, xvi
    influence of evangelicalism, liberation theologies, and Pentecostal practices for, xvi
Thompson, Donald, 99
Tisby, Jemar, 225
Tongues of Fire, 107
Treacy, Fr. William, 181
Treaty for Peace and Friendship, 13
Trinitarian Assemblies of God in the US, 114
Trump, Donald, 229ff., 232
Tuskegee Institute, 48
"Two Solicitudes," 153

Underground Railroad, 44, 49
Uneasy Conscience of Modern Fundamentalism, The, 164
Union Theological Seminary, 136
United Church Board of Evangelism and Social Service, 160
United Church of Canada (UCC), 14, 154
United Church of Christ, 136
United Church's Commission on Church, Nation and World Order, 160
United Holy Church of America, 124
United Methodist Church (UMC), 14
United Nations Charter, 131
United Nations High Commissioner for Refugees (UNHCR), 205, 206
United Negro College Fund, 131
United States, and Christianity, xxxviii
    distinctive formula, xxxix
    and First Great Revival, xxxix
    spirit of experimentation, xxxix
University of Chicago, 145

Urban Indigenous Ministries, 17
Ursuline Sisters, 54
US insurrection of 1777, 45

Vancouver Native Pentecostal church, 15
Vennard, Iva Durham, 120, 134
Villa-Valdez, Susie, 111
Vineyard movement; Association of Vineyard Churches, 116
Virgin of Guadalupe, 53
Vocational Education of Girls and Women, The, 121
Wacker, Grant, 80
Warfield, Benjamin, 140
Warren, Joseph, 109
Washington, Booker T., 47–48
Washington, George, 23–24, 26, 42–43
Way of Holiness, The, 104
Weld, Timothy Dwight, 82
Wells-Barnett, Ida B., 131, 132
Wesley, John, 79, 104
West coast religious environment, 170ff.
    challenges of, 172
    and economic change, 177
    ecumenical and interfaith collaboration, 180ff.
    features of Christianity in, 173ff.
    and Indian and First Nations, 175
    influence of Asia on, 174
    newer forms of evangelicalism, 179
    and "nones", 171
    and unchurched, 171
Western Women in Eastern Lands, 129
Wheatley, Phillis, 38–39
White Christian nationalism, 183, 221, 228ff.
    and civic nationalism, 230
    and ethno-nationalism, 230
    faithful patriotism, 230ff.

White House, 29
White United Pentecostal Church International, 114
White, Alma and Kent, 108, 124, 126
Whitefield, George, 74
Whitman, Marcus, 175
Willard, Frances, 130
Williams, Richard, 43
Williams, Roger, 228
Winnipeg General Strike (1919), 162
Winthrop, John, 22–23, 25–26, 90–91
Woman's Bible, The, 125, 126
womanism, 129
Women's Chains, 126
Women's Christian Temperance Union (WCTU), 126, 129–30, 159
Women's Missionary Jubilee, 129
Wood, Alice, 112
Woods, Lizzie, 105
Woodsworth, James Shaver, 158, 162
world Christianity versus global Christianity, xi
World Council of Churches, 128
Worldwide Apostolic Camp Meeting, 114
Wounded Knee Creek, 12
Wright, Robert A., 162–63

Xavier Labor School, 59
xenolalia, 107

Yale College, 75
    Yale University, 140
Yellow Fever epidemic in 1783, 42
Young, Brigham, 79

Zacharias, Danny, 16
Zionist movement, 97
Zuni, 17